P9-CKU-241

FYODOR DOSTOYEVSKY
A Writer's Life

"With an abundance of intimate detail, [Kjetsaa] introduces the reader to a very human Dostoyevsky: egotistic, vain, masochistic, neurotic, chauvinistic and obsessed, but also intensely spiritual, loving and capable of tremendous self-sacrifice. . . . catches the vital rhythms of Dostoyevsky's life."

The New York Times Book Review

"His biography reads much like one of his books—unlikely, dramatic, inspiring."

Dallas Morning News

"Clears away many misconceptions and gives much insight into the tangled emotional life of this tormented artist."

The Cleveland Plain Dealer

"Full of original re-evaluations of the novelist's personality and the unconscious drives that propelled it."

National Review

"This compact, highly readable biography offers fresh, controversial perspectives on many aspects of Dostoyevsky's life and work."

Publishers Weekly

"A splendid and well-researched biography that eschews easy formula and instead honors the turbulent contradictions that powered Dostoyevsky's life and art."

Kirkus Reviews

FYODOR DOSTOYEVSKY

A Writer's Life

Geir Kjetsaa

Translated from the Norwegian
by Siri Hustvedt and David McDuff

Fawcett Columbine • New York

A Fawcett Columbine Book
Published by Ballantine Books

English translation copyright © Viking Penguin Inc., 1987

Originally published in Norwegian as *Fjodor Dostojevskij—et dikterliv* by Gyldendal
Norsk Forlag. © Cyldendal Norsk Forlag A/S 1985

All rights reserved under International and Pan-American Copyright Conventions.
Without limiting the rights under copyright reserved above, no part of this publication
may be reproduced, stored in or introduced into a retrieval system, or transmitted, in
any form or by any means (electronic, mechanical, photocopying, recording or
otherwise), without the prior written permission of both the copyright owner and the
above publisher of this book. Published in the United States by Ballantine Books, a
division of Random House, Inc., New York, and simultaneously in Canada by Random
House of Canada Limited, Toronto.

Grateful acknowledgment is made for permission to reprint excerpts from the following
copyrighted works:

The Gambler by Fyodor Dostoyevsky translated by Jessie Coulson (Penguin Classics,
1966). Copyright © Jessie Coulson, 1966.
The Idiot by Fyodor Dostoyevsky, translated by David Margarsheck (Penguin Classics,
1955). Copyright © David Magarschek, 1955.
Notes from the Underground by Fyodor Dostoyevsky, translated by Jessie Coulson
(Penguin Classics, 1972). Copyright © Jessie Coulson, 1972.

Library of Congress Catalog Card Number: 88-92170

ISBN: 0-449-90334-6

This edition published by arrangement with Viking Penguin Inc.
Cover design by Richard Aquan
Cover painting of Fyodor Dostoyevsky by V.G. Perov, courtesy of Sovfoto/East Foto
Frontispiece: Portrait of Fyodor Dostoyevsky by V.G. Perov
Manufactured in the United States of America

First Ballantine Books Edition: January 1989
10 9 8 7 6 5 4 3 2 1

CONTENTS

FYODOR DOSTOYEVSKY

A Writer's Life

I

CHILDHOOD AND BOYHOOD

*"I remember my parents' love from my earliest childhood.
I look back upon my childhood with joy."*

His earliest memory came from when he was three years old. The governess had just brought him into the room and asked him to say the evening prayer in the presence of house guests. Fyodor knelt before the icon and recited his prayer: "Dear Mother of God, all my hope is in thee—give me shelter under thy wing."

Dostoyevsky never forgot this prayer. He repeated it all his life and taught it to his children. "I came from a pious Russian family," he said as an adult. "In our family we knew the Gospels almost from the cradle."

On his father's side, Dostoyevsky came from Lithuanian nobility. The family name probably comes from the Russian word for "worthy" or "deserving": *dostoynyy*. People of this noble lineage were called *dostoyniki*— or the prince's "worthy men." From the same root comes Dostoyevo, the name of a village about fifty kilometers from Pinsk in what is now White Russia. An ancestor of the writer, Danila Ivanovich Irtish, was given part of the town as a gift from the local prince in 1506, and it was his grandson who took the name Dostoyevsky. By that time, the Lithuanian Grand Duchy had already been absorbed by the Polish state, but Dostoyevsky was always meticulous in underscoring the distinction between the two places: "The Dostoyevskys are Lithuanians, not Poles. Lithuania is very different from Poland."

The geographic and religious borders between Poland and Lithuania, however, were in continual flux. At the end of the sixteenth century, members of the Dostoyevsky family could be found in Lithuania, Poland, and Russia. This was a period of great unrest: Russia and Poland were in constant strife, and a bitter and often fanatical battle was being waged between Russian Orthodoxy and Polish Catholicism. Branches of the Dostoyevsky family fought on both sides, but with varying success. The Polish side of the family attained positions of high official rank, whereas the Orthodox Dostoyevskys fared badly.

Some reasons for this decline can be found in the legal records of the period. The Dostoyevsky family had a reputation for violent behavior. Some of the stories about the family's crimes sound as if they could have been written by Dostoyevsky himself. On October 14, 1606, for example, Marina Stefanovna Dostoyevskaya lured her husband, Stanislav Karlovich, to a bathhouse on their farm. When he emerged, he was shot and wounded by one of his wife's manservants. Injured and bleeding, Stanislav cried out in pain and stumbled toward the main house, but his wife had already bolted the door. As he stood outside and begged to be let in, the servant attacked again—this time with a sword. But Marina was undaunted: "Send him to hell!" she screamed, while the dogs and pigs crowded around her husband's body and lapped up his blood. Marina hid the murderer in the barn, but a few days later he was standing next to her at her husband's funeral.

Other legal documents describe bloody ventures into neighbors' land, forged wills, and the usurpation of property belonging to the state and church. But just as there are saintly figures in the writer's novels, so there were in the Dostoyevsky family. In the eighteenth century Akindy Dostoyevsky was a monk in the venerable Cave Monastery in Kiev.

By this time, the Orthodox Dostoyevskys had settled in Volhynia, in the Ukraine, formerly the Ukrainian Grand Duchy. Due to their excesses, the family had long since lost their money and property. The future writer came from an impoverished clerical background. Both his great-grandfather and grandfather were priests in the Uniat Ukrainian Church in Bratslava, a town in the Podolia district of the Ukraine. It is here that the novelist's father was born in 1789.

Few fathers of writers have been so thoroughly analyzed or given such great significance as Mikhail Andreyevich Dostoyevsky, and none of them has inspired such controversy. There are roughly two traditions of thought concerning Dostoyevsky's father. One originates with the writer's daughter,

Lyubov; she portrays her grandfather as a despotic domestic tyrant who was stingy, drunken, violent, and depraved. The other view comes from the writer's brother Andrei; he depicts his father as a loving family man, quick-tempered, but good at heart.

Dr. Dostoyevsky was without question a complicated man with con-flicting personality traits. He was melancholy, taciturn, irritable, and sus-picious, but he was also an enterprising and energetic man who showed a tireless concern for his family and was deeply devoted to them.

Like his brother, father, and grandfather, Mikhail Andreyevich was destined to be a priest. The years he spent at seminary in Kamenets-Podolsk gave him a good education, particularly in language and literature, and he later imparted this knowledge enthusiastically to his children. But unlike his forefathers, Mikhail felt no calling to the priesthood. At the age of twenty, he left his hometown—against his father's will but with his mother's blessing. The break was dramatic, and he later failed in his efforts to renew relations with his family. None of his children ever came to know relatives on their father's side of their family.

In the autumn of 1809 (in part because of his facility in Latin) Mikhail Andreyevich was awarded a scholarship at the Imperial Medical-Surgical Academy in Moscow, which trained physicians and surgeons for the army and navy. Most of its students were young men who were neither wealthy nor of noble birth. These years were difficult ones for Mikhail Andreyevich. He, too, was without means or connections, and it was only through his indomitable will that he managed to get ahead.

Napoleon's invasion of 1812 put an end to his studies, and he was sent to the front. During the battle of Borodino, he worked in a field hospital. The following autumn he distinguished himself as a courageous worker when he participated in the evacuation of more than thirty thousand wounded from Moscow. Later he took part in a struggle against a serious typhoid epidemic that had broken out in the provinces. Dr. Dostoyevsky's grim war service—the countless amputations, the sight of ravaging disease—left its mark on his character. He was very often harsh and severe, a man who rarely smiled. His diligence and zeal, however, led to steady promotions. In 1813 he was awarded his official status as "doctor," and in 1818 he was appointed chief medical director at the Military Hospital in Moscow. Near the end of 1820, he suddenly requested a discharge from the military. His reasons were personal: a year earlier, he had married the nineteen-

year-old Maria Fyodorovna Nechayeva, and he wished to settle permanently in Moscow with her and his newborn son, Mikhail, Fyodor's older
brother.

Dostoyevsky's mother came from an old merchant family. She was a
vivacious girl who had musical talent and a feeling for the arts. Goethe's
statement about his own parents—that from his father he had been given
"die Statur, des Lebens ernstes Führen" ("his build, his neat and serious
ways") and from his mother "die Frohnatur und Lust zu fabulieren" ("Mother's cheerful spirit, her love of telling stories")—is applicable also to Dostoyevsky. Maria's father, Fyodor Nechayev, had been a wealthy manufacturer,
but he lost most of his money during the 1812 evacuation of Moscow. Her
mother's family had greater literary and artistic interests, however. Maria's
maternal grandfather, Mikhail Kotelnitsky, a cultivated and well-read man,
was a proofreader at the Ecclesiastical Press in Moscow, and her uncle
Vasily Kotelnitsky was a professor on the Medical Faculty of the University
of Moscow. When she was only thirteen years old, Maria Fyodorovna lost
her mother. A stepmother, the young Olga Yakovlevna, took her mother's
place; in the years to come, she was not to be warmly received by the
Dostoyevsky family.

Maria's marriage to Mikhail Andreyevich was an alliance more of
convenience than affection. As the daughter of a fallen merchant, Maria
was quite simply married off to a man who could take care of her. Her older
sister Alexandra was more fortunate in this respect; she married the very
rich merchant Alexander Kumanin. Alexandra was godmother to all the
Dostoyevsky children. In spite of this, relations between the two families
were strained. The proud doctor regarded the financial support given him
by his wife's family as humiliating, and his writer son had little but contempt
for these "pitiful shopkeepers." Nevertheless, the Kumanin family provided
Dostoyevsky with an important refuge when he found himself short of
money.

Maria's influential relatives may well have had a hand in Dr. Dostoyevsky's appointment to the Mariinsky Hospital for the Poor on the outskirts
of Moscow. Ivan Gilardi built this beautiful structure between 1803 and
1806 under the direct supervision of the Empress. Today the large columned
central building is headquarters for the state's Tuberculosis Institute. Two
other buildings have also been preserved. In one of these buildings, the
building on the left as seen from the street, there is now a fine Dostoyevsky
museum.

II

The young Dostoyevsky family settled in the building to the right. It is there that the future writer was born on October 30, 1821—or November 11, according to a revisionist view. At the end of his life, Dostoyevsky thought he had been born in 1822 (like many others, he was inclined to underestimate his age). The church records, however, eliminate all doubts about the year of Dostoyevsky's birth:

> On October 30, 1821, at the Hospital for the Poor, a son was born to the chief medical director Mikhail Andreyevich Dostoyevsky. Father Vasily Ilyin presided with the assistance of Deacon Gerasim Ivanov. The child was christened on November 4; the godparents were the chief medical director, Royal Councillor Grigory Pavlov Maslovich and Countess Praskovya Timofeyevich Kozlovskaya, Moscow merchant Feodor Timofeyevich Nechayev, and the merchant wife Alexandra Feodorovna Kumanina. The baptism was performed by Father Ilyin along with the other parish clergy.

A few years later, the family moved into the building on the left, where they lived on the street floor. Dostoyevsky spent his childhood years here, shut off from the rest of the world and surrounded by the hospital's poor and consumptive patients. The surrounding area was not likely to inspire cheerful thoughts in its inhabitants either. The neighborhood had once been the site of a morgue, a so-called *ubogiy dom* for vagrants and criminals, people who belonged to no parish and were therefore buried "with God" (*u boga*). Also nearby was a way station for prisoners being transported to Siberia. Just outside the family's parlor windows, prisoners trudged along Novya Bosyedomka on their way to sentences at hard labor. The dark side of life was revealed very early to Dostoyevsky. In his childhood home, he witnessed a bleak spectacle of suffering, poverty, and death. From a young age, he learned to bear this suffering deep within himself.

The family grew rapidly. Mikhail and Fyodor were born a year apart; in 1822 their sister Varvara was born, and in 1825, a brother, Andrei. Later there were three more surviving children born into the family: Vera, Nikolai, and Alexandra. Dostoyevsky was intimate with only his two elder siblings. Andrei has great significance for scholars because of the memoirs he wrote about his childhood. Besides his parents' correspondence, Andrei's memoirs are the only firsthand account that exists about the writer's earliest years.

Andrei's description of the house can be verified by visiting the Dostoyevsky museum. The first room one enters is a little vestibule divided by a low partition, the room where Mikhail and Fyodor slept on two large chests. From here one can walk into the drawing room, a rather large room with three windows overlooking the yard and two others overlooking the street. This is where Dr. Dostoyevsky gave Latin lessons to his oldest sons. For Andrei happier memories were associated with the parlor, the place where the family read out loud to one another. This room is somewhat smaller than the drawing room and also has windows on the street. Behind the parlor is a bedroom that doubled as a nursery; the two rooms are divided by a low wall. The apartment is in fact rather spacious, but it soon became too small for the Dostoyevsky family.

The Dostoyevsky children had few playmates of their own age in the hospital. A girl of nine years old, who was one of Fyodor's closest friends, was one day found raped in the hospital yard. She died shortly afterward. This terrible event made an enormous impression on Dostoyevsky, and he would return to it again and again in his writing.

The doctor tried to keep his children away from the patients, and he would not allow them to leave the hospital grounds unaccompanied by a parent or servant. But when the children did sneak off to play in the courtyard or the lovely Maria Grove, just behind the hospital, the two oldest brothers always led the mischief. Fyodor was particularly wild. His parents called him "hothead." He had a reputation for stubbornness and had a tendency to swear. "Easy now, Fedya, or you'll catch it!" his father would warn. "You'll see, you'll end up with a red cap!" The doctor, unwittingly prophetic, was referring to the red caps worn by soldiers in the Siberian penal regiments.

Dr. Dostoyevsky was hard pressed financially. His salary at the hospital was just a few hundred rubles a year, and there were times when he had to ask for an advance. This is not to say that the family was destitute, however. Besides his hospital post, the doctor had a rather lucrative private practice, but his rank carried with it certain obligations. As one of the period's etiquette manuals puts it: it is necessary to maintain a household "in accordance with one's station." Mikhail Andreyevich did as well as he could: he had his own carriage and a permanent domestic staff of seven. But he was continually haunted by fear of poverty. From morning till night he saw the misery of destitution in the hospital. Striving for social mobility and bourgeois respectability was always foremost in his mind.

With his background in the humble priestly class, the doctor had no example upon which to model his ambitions. He put all his energy into securing for himself and his family the respectable status he had long desired. The battle was hard. In those days, Russians swore by German doctors, and Mikhail Andreyevich was often pained by the feeling that he was being passed over for others. In spite of this, the archive materials show that his social status steadily improved. The doctor's days were characterized by order and routine. Decorations for "exceptional service" were awarded to him regularly, and finally he was offered the position as chief medical director at the Mariinsky Hospital. In 1837, when he was forced to resign because of his ailing health, he had earned the title of Collegiate Assessor, a title that corresponded to the rank of Colonel in the military.

In 1828 Dr. Dostoyevsky had regained for himself and his sons the noble rank that his ancestors lost when they refused to convert to Catholicism. Portrayals of Dostoyevsky as a writer from the "common people" whose origin was nearly "proletarian" are groundless. Like most nineteenth-century Russian writers, he too was a nobleman. At the same time, it is important to emphasize that the service nobility was of a significantly lower rank than the old landed aristocracy to which Tolstoy and Turgenev belonged. Awareness of such class distinctions was to be painful for Fyodor, who was no less preoccupied with rank than his father. The struggle for social status in his home certainly played a role in sharpening Dostoyevsky's empathy for human suffering—not suffering that stemmed from the pain of poverty itself, but from the humiliation of being of a lower social rank than the rich and powerful in society.

Fyodor was able to observe the distinctions of class even in his own home. It sometimes happened that servants were fired or simply ran away, but generally the relationship between the master and mistress of the house and their domestic help was one of consideration and good will. Of all the servants, Alyona Frolovna was the most important to Fyodor. She was a large, corpulent woman with a kind heart. It was not long after a fire on the doctor's country property that she came forward and offered the family her entire savings: "If it's money you need, take mine. I have no use for it. I don't need it." Dostoyevsky never forgot this incident, and later he would cite Alyona as a luminous example of the Russian people's ability to live by Christian ideals.

Old and new wet nurses paid frequent visits to the growing Dostoyevsky family. Andrei recalled, with a mixture of fear and delight, the talent these women had for telling Russian fairy tales. When the wet nurses began to tell their stories, the room fell silent. The only sound that could be heard was the scraping of the doctor's pen from the next room, where he sat writing prescriptions and death certificates. Folklore was Fyodor's first encounter with narrative art. His own artistic needs were awakened under the influence of these peasant women. "Already at three years old I was making up fairy tales," he said later. "And some of them were even quite imaginative; whether funny or frightening, I never forgot them. . . ."

Fyodor's interest in folk art was deepened by the family visits to the carnival at Shrovetide. At the carnival he saw real Russian folk theater with dancing bears, trained monkeys, delightful clowns, strong men, and giantesses. When he returned home, he always gave a lively account of all that he had seen. Dostoyevsky's admiration for this kind of comic grotesquerie appears later in his portrayal of the prisoner's love for theater in *The House of the Dead*.

Excursions from the grim environs of the hospital, however, were few and short-lived. On a single occasion, the doctor took his children along with him to the theater to see Schiller's play *The Robbers* with the great actor Mochalov in the leading role. The play was an inspiration to the future writer of *The Brothers Karamazov*: "The powerful impression this play had upon me would later have a profound effect on my spiritual development," he said near the end of his life.

Other significant events in the Dostoyevsky household included pilgrimages to St. Sergius's Trinity Monastery outside Moscow and visits to the Kremlin churches with their holy icons and beautiful ornamentation. Fyodor's religiosity developed early. Little of importance took place in the Dostoyevsky family without first holding a Mass. Even before he could read, Fyodor was deeply moved by the old Russian legends of the lives of the saints, stories that proclaimed the ascetic path to God and a selfless compassion for others. Christ was the model: to achieve purity and sacrifice, man must walk in the Savior's footsteps and suffer willingly. Dostoyevsky's creative imagination was permanently affected by this sacred image.

Dr. Dostoyevsky was a reserved man who disciplined his children without resorting to corporal punishment. When the doctor took his afternoon nap, for example, Andrei was expected to sit by the bed and keep away the flies. God help the boy should a fly interrupt his father's nap!

The children began their studies at the age of four. Their mother taught them to read and write. The Bible was, naturally, the most important text in this very religious household. But the children also studied a book translated from the German: *One Hundred and Four Sacred Stories from the Old and New Testaments Selected for Children.* This huge book, a cross between Bible stories and catechism, was supposed to be learned by heart. At the rate of one story per week, it could be mastered in two years. Older children, the reader is informed in the preface, can manage to learn it by rote in one year. Each story was provided with a list of questions meant to help prepare children for examination; three "useful moral teachings" were appended to the text as well as a concluding "pious meditation." Fedya, like Father Zosima in *The Brothers Karamazov,* read in this book about the creation of the world, Adam and Eve in the garden, the Great Flood, and the story of the resurrection of Lazarus. In these pages, Dostoyevsky first discovered the essential principles of Christianity that would later take on such great meaning in his writing. The pious meditation attached to the parable of the widow's mite is as follows:

> Never say, I don't give alms because I have so little. God sees the meaning of the heart not the size of the gift. Our Savior treasured the widow's gift even though it was small. Therefore, measure your alms with the same measurement God uses to measure you. Although your contribution may be small, God will not forget it.

But for the writer whose great themes were rebellion and suffering, the deep religious drama of the Book of Job had an enormous impact. "I am reading Job," he wrote to his wife not long before his death, "and it has moved me to a painful ecstasy. I put the book down and wander about the room for hours. I can barely restrain myself from weeping. . . . It is so strange, dear Anya, this book was one of the first that affected me deeply, and then I was only a little child."

When the children were still young, a tutor began coming to the house. The children were especially well schooled in French, and Dr. Dostoyevsky took great pride when they honored him with tributes in French on his name day. He firmly believed that book-learning was above all a means of getting ahead in the world, and he continually drilled into his children the importance of hard work and self-discipline. The doctor liked to mention the two sons of the hospital priest who had both done exceptionally well on their university exams. Imagine if his sons could do as well! "Then I will die in peace," he would tell his children. His words stayed with them forever and increased their desire for success. Dostoyevsky wrote in *A Raw Youth,* "Ever since I began to dream—that is from my very earliest childhood—I have been unable to imagine anything but that I would always, in all of life's circumstances, be first."

Unfortunately, the doctor's pedagogical skills in no way corresponded to his ambitions. It was bad enough that the children had to listen to their father lecture on geometry even on the holidays (in order not to waste any time) but worst of all were Latin lessons. During these tutorials the children had to stand at strict attention and rattle off the forms. "My brothers always dreaded these lessons," wrote Andrei. "Despite his goodness, Father was an extremely demanding and impatient man, and above all, he was quick to anger. As soon as one of them made the slightest mistake, he would start shouting." The lessons were particularly hard for Fyodor. "They laughed at me because I couldn't keep up with my brother," he wrote many years later. At such times, it was good that he could seek comfort from both his mother and Alyona Frolovna.

It is not strange that upon reading such reminiscences, most of Dostoyevsky's biographers have concluded that he had an unhappy childhood. But the author's recollections of "a happy and peaceful childhood" were not motivated solely by nostalgia. It is important to recognize that Dostoyevsky's father could also be "happy and gay" with his family—to borrow Andrei's expression.

Dostoyevsky remembered with special joy the evenings his family spent reading out loud to one another. Both parents were excellent readers, and the two oldest boys did not lag far behind them. The repertoire of readings was rich and various. Nikolai Karamzin's great patriotic work *History of the Russian State* excited Dostoyevsky's nationalism. But it was fiction that was most important to him. The family subscribed to *The Library for Reading*, a leading periodical of the day that brought them news about literary events at home and abroad. Dostoyevsky was introduced to the novel through the era's thrillers, Ann Radcliffe's horror stories, which made him "stiff with terror and rapture." The authors of the Sentimental school took on deep significance for him; and among poets, he favored the pre-Romantic Vasily Zhukovsky and the national writer Pushkin. But most of all Fyodor loved heroic works (Homer) and novels about chivalry (Cervantes, Walter Scott). When he got older, he insisted that these were the best books for young people, because the young should be given books which encourge "beautiful feelings and lofty thoughts."

For Dostoyevsky, these reading sessions served as a literary foundation for his entire life. They may also have provided the strain of sentimentality that runs throughout his work. Later, Dostoyevsky gratefully recalled his parents' enthusiasm during these evenings of reading and how they would talk with the children about what had been read. "Dearest Papa! How can I thank you for the education you have given me!" Mikhail exclaimed in a letter to his father in 1838. "It is so wonderful to meditate upon Shakespeare, Schiller, and Goethe! Such moments are invaluable."

III

Dr. Dostoyevsky's concerns about his family increased. The hospital apartment had become crowded and uncomfortable. The children had to spend their summer vacations in the dreary hospital yard, and their mother was showing the first signs of the tuberculosis that was to kill her. Mikhail Andreyevich was also unwell. His work, especially his demanding private practice, drained his strength. It was time to find a family retreat.

The restoration of their noble title had given the family the right to own property with serfs, and in the summer of 1831 Dr. Dostoyevsky bought, in his wife's name, the tiny village of Darovoye in the district of Tula, about one hundred and fifty kilometers from Moscow. The property was a little more than five hundred acres and had seventy-six "souls," or male serfs. Financially, the purchase was a disastrous one: the 1830s were a decade of almost uninterrupted crop failure; a year after the acquisition, the village was devastated by fire; and there were problems with the demarcation of the land. A former military major, Pavel Khotyaintsev, made claims to several sections of the Dostoyevsky property. When Mikhail Andreyevich brought suit, the major threatened to buy the nearby village, Cheremoshnya, so that he could surround his neighbor and "keep him in line." Dr. Dostoyevsky beat him to the purchase, but the acquisition of Cheremoshnya, a property of two hundred and fifty acres and sixty-seven "souls," was possible only by mortgaging Darovoye and thereby nearly ruining the family. Moreover, these properties were hardly auspicious holdings; the family's relatives ironically referred to them as the "miniature estates."

Nevertheless, for the Dostoyevsky children the purchase of these villages was a great event. From that time on, they were able to spend their summer vacations in the country. They were overjoyed when the carriage came to pick them up at the end of the school year and took them to Darovoye. At last they could play to their heart's content. They played "Cowboys and

Indians" and "Robinson Crusoe" with the peasant children, always with the high-spirited Fyodor in the lead role. Sometimes, however, their play went too far, as when the children helped themselves to icons from the chapel and paraded around in the field singing hymns. Maria Fyodorovna soon put an end to the blasphemous game, but the memory of this incident was probably still fresh when Dostoyevsky wrote his story about the peasant children who shoot at the Eucharist bread.

Near Darovoye was a little wood they called Brykovo, or "Fedya's Wood," where Fyodor loved to wander and gather nuts and mushrooms. But he was not always allowed to play in the wood for fear of snakes and wolves. Years later, Dostoyevsky recounted how one day when he was nine years old, he thought he heard someone call "Wolf!" and ran for comfort to a serf who was plowing in a field nearby. While he was in prison the memory of this encounter with the peasant Marey served to strengthen his love for the people. Marey became for Dostoyevsky a symbol of comfort, the embodiment of the humble and unselfish Russian people, a testimony to "the Russian people's high character."

> I could not forget the tender, motherly smile of the poor serf; I saw with new eyes how he crossed himself, shook his head, and whispered, "There, there, don't be afraid!" and how he carefully put his thick, earth-covered finger to my trembling lips. There were probably other adults who could have comforted me then, but there was something extraordinary about this meeting nevertheless. He could not have looked at me with a brighter or more loving smile had I been his own son. Who got him to do it? He was a crude serf and I the son of the man who owned him. No one would ever know about his caress, and no one rewarded him for it. Perhaps he was especially fond of children. There are such peasants. The encounter took place in a deserted field; only God was witness to the deep human feeling and fine womanly tenderness of this rough, uneducated Russian peasant, a man who had no idea that some time in the future serfdom would be abolished.

Out in the country Dostoyevsky experienced for the first time an intimacy with the Russian land. Despite the fact that most of his work is set in the city, Dostoyevsky's feeling for nature left its mark on his fiction, particularly on *Poor Folk*. Varenka says:

> I was a wild little girl who did nothing but scamper about in the woods, fields and pastures, and no one bothered me. Often I was up at dawn,

running out to the fishpond or into the woods or far down the meadow to where the mowers were. I never minded the hot sun or going astray far beyond the houses and buildings or that the bushes scratched me and tore my dress. When I finally came home, I got a scolding, but I didn't care.

Dostoyevsky returned to Darovoye in other works as well. "This small and unremarkable place came to have the deepest impact on my later life," he wrote in *The Diary of a Writer* in 1877. Stavrogin's duel in *The Possessed* takes place in Brykovo; the encounter with the "wolf" takes place in the same wood in *A Raw Youth*. In *The Brothers Karamazov*, Ivan is given the task of buying woods in Cheremoshnya, and Dmitri's dream about the burned village and weeping children is clearly inspired by the author's impressions of Darovoye after the fire. It was also in this village that Dostoyevsky met poor deranged Grushenka, who wandered around barefoot and ragged, muttering incoherently about a little child buried in the graveyard: she became Lizaveta Smerdyakova in his last novel. Finally, though, more than nature, it was the people of this rural place that had the greatest effect on Dostoyevsky. The memories of his friendship and communion with the poor peasants strengthened his conviction that serfdom should be abolished. Altogether, Dostoyevsky spent nearly two of his boyhood years in the country. These summers gave him a genuine knowledge of the Russian peasantry, a far more intimate knowledge than could be claimed by the vast majority of his fellow writers. The assertion that has sometimes been made—that Dostoyevsky had no real contact with the Russian peasant until his imprisonment in Siberia—has no foundation.

It was Maria Fyodorovna who ran the farm at Darovoye and managed all the household affairs. Every spring she went out to inspect the properties. Mikhail Andreyevich was able to get away for only a short visit in the middle of the summer. Maria's rapport with the peasants was excellent; glowing stories about her kindness were circulating in Darovoye well into this century. But her letters to her husband indicate how difficult it was to run those impoverished estates, even with her energy and willpower. Often, her letters read like an agricultural manual. She writes about poultry upkeep, pig breeding, the grain harvest, and her never-ending battle against want.

The letters she received from Mikhail Andreyevich could not have made her life any easier. As he got older, Dr. Dostoyevsky became increasingly moody and distrustful. His difficult temperament was trying for both his wife and children, and his depressing correspondence is filled with complaints and suspicions. He can't find the family silver or his wife's clothing. Perhaps the servants have stolen them, or maybe his wife has hidden them somewhere without telling him? He worries that she has stashed away money without his knowledge. And what about the child that she is carrying? How can he be sure that it is his?

Deeply offended, Maria can only swear that her current pregnancy is "the seventh and strongest bond of our mutual love." Otherwise—she does her best to comfort her downcast husband:

> Dearest love, why are you so melancholy? Why all the sad thoughts? What is it that is bothering you? I almost die when I think that you are so unhappy. I beg you, my angel, my idol, cling to my love and remember that even when I am away from you, I love and adore only you, more than my own life. The children love us, we are happy with them—what more can we ask for? Wealth? Do you think that riches will bring us happiness? No, my darling, I beseech you to forget all your gloomy thoughts. . . . Stop now, my dearest, don't be so sad at heart.

The separation from Maria was difficult for the children as well. Dostoyevsky's first extant letter is to his mother, dated August 23, 1833. He had just returned to Moscow after the summer in Darovoye.

> Dearest Mama!
>
> We have already returned safe and sound to Papa, dearest Mama. Papa and Nikolenka are also in good health. God willing, you too are healthy and well. Welcome home to us soon, darling Mama. I don't think it will take very long to harvest the rest of the barley, and you will no doubt get the wheat in little by little, too. Farewell, dearest Mama. I respectfully kiss your hands and remain your faithful son,
>
> Fyodor Dostoyevsky

The children returned to school and homework with heavy hearts after their carefree weeks in the country, but schooling called. After they had completed their education at home, Mikhail and Fyodor were enrolled in Nikolai Drazhukov's private school, and then in the fall of 1834 they were transferred to a boarding school run by Leonty Chermak, which they attended until the spring of 1837.

Chermak's boarding school for "aristocratic male children" was considered at that time to be one of Russia's finest schools. Its pupils were the sons of Moscow's most distinguished aristocrats and intellectuals, boys who were far above the Dostoyevsky brothers in social standing. In A Raw Youth, Dostoyevsky describes the pain of feeling inferior and socially insecure around these arrogant "sons of counts and senators." "You are not permitted to sit with the children of nobility; you come from a common family and are no better than a lackey!"

Keeping his sons in such a school was clearly beyond the doctor's means. Maintaining a single student for a year cost eight hundred rubles, roughly the doctor's annual salary at the hospital. But Mikhail Andreyevich was a proud man with ambitions. Rather than send his sons to a public school where thrashings were the order of the day, he chose to work himself to death and accept humiliating loans from the Kumanin family. No sacrifice was too great when it came to giving his sons a respectable education.

There were many outstanding teachers at Chermak's. Some were professors at the University of Moscow or members of the Russian Academy of Science. The school day was long and trying. It began at six in the morning and did not end until nine at night. "Particular attention" was given to subjects such as Latin and Russian, but the pupils also studied Greek, German, English, and French. They studied the "Sciences" (Bible, history, logic, rhetoric, arithmetic, geometry, history, and physics) as well as the "Arts" (fiction, drawing, and dance).

Among the teachers there was one who played a special role for the Dostoyevsky brothers: the Russian instructor Nikolai Bilevich. For him, pedagogy meant teaching his students "to think, to express their thoughts, and to reason." An author himself, he was able to pass on to his pupils the opinions and ideas of the city's literary salons. Moreover, he had been a classmate of Nikolai Gogol and was influential in exciting Dostoyevsky's admiration for this "great teacher of all Russians." On Saturdays, when the brothers returned home to the hospital, Bilevich's classes were the subject of eager discussion. "He had quite simply become their idol," Andrei reported in his memoirs.

Chermak's boarding school was known for giving its pupils a first-rate literary education. Its library was extensive, and Dostoyevsky pored greedily over its contents. His early reading was almost exclusively of Romantic works. He wept over the great Karamzin's portrait of Poor Liza, and found himself enthralled by Zhukovsky's goddess of Fantasy who capriciously lured him into a strange dream world. Then he read Pushkin with his miserly knight and shabby carriages. Dostoyevsky read foreign writers as well. Schiller shocked him with patricide in *The Robbers* but also gave him his first glimpse of the beautiful and sublime. E. T. A. Hoffmann fascinated him with his insane heroes and their doubles, and Walter Scott ushered him into an exotic world of monasteries, knights, and beautiful, proud women.

The young Dostoyevsky was already a passionate dreamer who sought solitude in order to abandon himself to the free play of his imagination. "A serious and thoughtful boy with blond hair and a pale face," one classmate wrote, describing him. The boy who had once been so wild seemed to have become "tame"; his former fire had been channeled into a passion for books. "In school I was on a first-name basis with my classmates," Dostoyevsky wrote in *A Raw Youth*, "but I cannot say that I was able to confide in any of them." "He had a tendency to lose himself in thought and withdraw," the narrator says of Alyosha in *The Brothers Karamazov*. A fellow pupil at Chermak's reinforces the autobiographical basis of these characterizations: "He wasn't very interested in our play. At recess he seldom left his books, and when he did, it was to talk with one of the oldest students."

There was in fact a great deal to talk about during this period of cultural ferment. The 1830s were a decade of reaction. Tsar Nicholas I, frightened by the liberalism of the Decembrists (who had organized a quickly suppressed revolt), clamped down on free speech. A number of liberal publications were discontinued. The philosopher Chaadayev was declared insane, and the critic Nadezhdin, who had printed his blasphemous thoughts about the hopeless backwardness of Russia, was exiled. Writers, too, suffered unhappy fates during this period: Pushkin was killed in a duel, Lermontov was banished to the Caucasus, and Gogol, broken down and disappointed, traveled abroad.

At the same time, however, the 1830s were rich and generative years in Russian literature, years that laid the groundwork for the innovations in prose fiction that would come in the following decade. Pushkin wrote masterworks such as *The Queen of Spades* and *The Captain's Daughter*. Gogol made a sensational breakthrough with his collection of unusual stories, *Evenings on a Farm Near Dikanka*, which were followed by his ruthless exposure of bureaucratic corruption in *The Inspector General* and his fantastic portrayals of the plight of the little man in his St. Petersburg stories. Many foreign writers were also translated into Russian at this time and reviewed in Russian periodicals: Honoré de Balzac, Victor Hugo, George Sand, and the Boulevard writers Paul de Kock and Frédéric de Soulié.

Fyodor read them all—an appreciable share of his knowledge of the world came from books. As a boy in boarding school, he had already begun to write; he made plans for "a novel from life in Venice." And his brother Mikhail had begun to write poems—as many as three a day!

The Dostoyevskys had encouraged this literary interest in their sons, and they could not have failed to notice that their cultivation had borne fruit. It is very possible that they had intended to give their oldest sons an academic education at the University of Moscow.

But what would happen to the children if their parents died? The melancholy Dr. Dostoyevsky was plagued by worries that his children would end up as beggars. He repeatedly told them that he was a poor man, and they must be prepared to fend for themselves in the world. He felt his strength failing him and was convinced that he would not live to be an old man. Maria Fyodorovna was seriously ill. She was exhausted from her struggles on the "miniature estates" and worn out by her husband's abnormal jealousy and brooding depressions. After her last childbirth in 1835—her eighth—the tuberculosis got the upper hand, and from early 1837 on, she could not leave her room.

In a moving account, Andrei tells how at the very end of her life, his mother insisted on keeping the door to her room open so she could listen to the family's reading sessions. Again and again, she asked her two oldest boys to read to her from the works of Pushkin and Schiller. Until the last, Maria wanted to take part in everything. Her death came at the end of February, after she had blessed her husband and children before the icon of the Savior. A life of toil and care was over. Her funeral was held at the Church of the Holy Spirit, known in Moscow for its impressive painting of the raising of Lazarus. In a poem about his mother's funeral, Mikhail described her "heavenly smile" and "luminous eyes." For Fyodor, too, his mother became a martyr figure who recurred as a character in his fiction: as Alexandra Mikhailovna in *Netochka Nezvanova*, as Arkady's mother in *A Raw Youth*, and as Alyosha's mother in *The Brothers Karamazov*.

Before Maria's death, a decision about the children's futures had been reached. The Dostoyevskys knew that their sons had pinned their hopes on the university, but a university education would provide them only with an education, not a career. This had to be taken into consideration in light of what seemed imminent—their own sickness and death. It was necessary to secure their children's futures by providing their sons with educations that would guarantee them good positions with the state. Therefore it was decided that Mikhail and Fyodor were to be taken out of Chermak's to begin schooling at the Academy of Engineers in St. Petersburg. The advantages of this were obvious: first, this military school was free, and second, it provided its students with a certain livelihood. At a time when Tsar Nicholas regarded making his country an impregnable bastion of autocracy and Orthodoxy as the primary task of his regime, Dr. Dostoyevsky reasoned that it was sensible for his sons to become military engineers. Furthermore, at the Tsar's own school they would be safe from the insidious spirit of rebellion that had become so common at the universities.

Their parents' decision was nevertheless a shock to the Dostoyevsky brothers. They were going to be writers, not officers! "My brother and I were taken to St. Petersburg to attend the Academy of Engineers and with that the future was ruined," Dostoyevsky wrote many years later. And then not long after Maria Fyodorovna's funeral, life took on an even more dismal cast when the family received news of Pushkin's death. Andrei wrote that had it not been for the family's grief about their mother, Fyodor would have asked permission to go into mourning for Pushkin. In that late winter of 1837, everything seemed lost.

Dostoyevsky's years in Moscow ended in sadness, but that does not mean that his childhood had been an unhappy one. "I will never forget the love my parents gave me as a child," he wrote near the end of his life. One must guard against drawing absolute parallels between the sad lives of children in Dostoyevsky's fiction and his own childhood in a home where his parents' chief concern was the welfare of their offspring. It is true that Dr. Dostoyevsky had a difficult temperament. He was tormented by money worries and suffered from an almost pathological suspiciousness. Yet it is difficult to say what would have become of Fyodor Dostoyevsky had it not been for his father's energy and resourcefulness. This much is certain: Dostoyevsky had much to be grateful for in his childhood. He had his mother's selfless love, his friendship with his siblings, the summers in Darovoye, the churches and monasteries that played an important role in the family's religious life, and, perhaps more than anything else, the books of his young life—the stories and poems. It was Dostoyevsky's parents who had kindled in him a profound love for literature, a love so intense and complete that not even the military discipline and harsh drilling of the Academy of Engineers would be able to crush it.

Dostoyevsky's father,
Mikhail Andreyevich
(1789–1839).

Dostoyevsky's mother,
Maria Fyodorovna
(1800–1837).

The building of the Hospital for the Poor where Dostoyevsky
spent his childhood and youth.

Moscow with a view of the Kremlin.
A lithograph from the early nineteenth century.

St. Sergius Trinity Cloister, outside Moscow.

The Dostoyevsky family's house in Darovoye.

2

ST. PETERSBURG

"Man—that is the mystery. . . .
I work with this mystery, because I want to be a man."

In early May 1837, Mikhail Andreyevich and his two oldest sons were finally ready to set out for St. Petersburg. The trip had been continually delayed because of a throat ailment that plagued Fyodor throughout the spring and gave him the deep, hoarse voice that would later make such an impression on the audiences that heard him read aloud.

Even though the brothers were depressed and disappointed about being transferred to the Academy of Engineers, a school that seemed thoroughly uninspiring, the prospect of experiencing Russia's glittering capital, the nation's "window on Europe" must have filled them with excitement and anticipation. "I don't know why, but for me St. Petersburg had always been a mystery," Dostoyevsky wrote. For the brothers, the week-long journey from Moscow to St. Petersburg meant leaving behind a city of churches and monasteries for a city of palaces and military parades. Their sheltered life within the family was over; now began a life of independence and uncertainty.

Two young romantics took their seats in the carriage. "My brother and I longed for a new life; we dreamed of something great, of everything that was beautiful and sublime. Those words were still fresh for us then and we used them without irony," Dostoyevsky recalled later.

It was not long, however, before reality gave the fledgling writers an initial shock. Along the road, Dr. Dostoyevsky stopped at a posting station so that he and his sons could refresh themselves at an inn. Suddenly, a bloated, red-faced government courier burst in the door. After a couple of glasses of vodka, he rushed out to his brand-new troika and, without a word, fell upon the peasant driver, beating him with his fists. The driver responded instantly: with all his might, he brought the whip whistling down on the horses' backs. Beside themselves with fear and pain, the animals set off at a full gallop. Violence breeds violence. This was reality, a reality that had begun to impress itself upon the two dreaming Dostoyevskys.

The scene with the government courier remained with Dostoyevsky his entire life, and it filled him with an implacable hatred for serfdom. What happened to the driver's wife that night after her husband had been beaten? Dostoyevsky speculated many years later in *The Diary of a Writer*. Should Dostoyevsky have ever wanted to found a humanitarian organization, he would no doubt have chosen the troika as its emblem and sign of warning against cruelty. "My first personal insult came from the horse and courier," Dostoyevsky wrote in his notebooks for *Crime and Punishment*. This vision of meaningless cruelty and innocent suffering is reenacted in Raskolnikov's nightmare of the old horse that is brutally whipped to death by its owner.

Further disappointments awaited the family in St. Petersburg. After they arrived, Dr. Dostoyevsky enrolled his sons in Koronad Kostomarovo's preparatory school. Captain Kostomarovo had formerly been an instructor at the Academy of Engineers, and his pupils usually did very well on the Academy's entrance exam. On September 1, the new students were presented to the school's director, Vasily Scharnhorst. The family suffered a major disappointment when Mikhail was refused on the grounds of poor health. He had to resign himself to the less fashionable Academy in Reval (present-day Tallinn). And if it weren't already enough that the brothers had to be separated, Fyodor was not awarded one of the tuition-free vacancies his father had so hoped for. It turned out that the condition for obtaining one of these openings was bringing extravagant gifts to the examiners. This episode gave Fyodor a glimpse into the Russian system of bribery that he would never forget. "What rottenness!" he wrote indignantly to his father. "We who struggle for every ruble, have to pay, while others, the sons of rich parents, are accepted without fee. Blast them!" Fortunately, the amount needed—nine hundred and fifty rubles—was provided by the Kumanin family, and Dostoyevsky was able to begin his studies in January 1838. He had placed eleventh out of twenty-three on the entrance exam.

The Academy of Engineers was one of the most beautiful schools in all of Russia, housed in a building surrounded by canals and parks that were enhanced with Roman vases and statues. Even Dostoyevsky had to admit that it was impressive. The school building was also infamous for what had occurred behind its locked gates. The cornerstone had been laid in 1798 at the beginning of the reign of Tsar Paul I. On a marble frieze in large bronze letters was written, "May the spirit of the Lord bless your house for eternity." The words contained a fatal irony: Paul I lived in this palace for only eleven days. On the twelfth day, the night of March 11, 1801, he was strangled at the behest of the heir to the throne, Alexander. The crime took place in the Tsar's bedroom, which was shortly thereafter converted into a chapel. In this chapel, surrounded by miracle-working icons, the new Tsar indulged in quasi-religious orgies with sectarian friends of both sexes. Later the school came under the direct protection of Alexander's brother and heir, Nicholas I, who was unstinting in his efforts to obtain the best possible educations for his country's future officers.

As in most military schools, discipline was strict. The rules forbade the wearing of eyeglasses or galoshes, for there were to be no "persons of weak health among the students." Instruction took place from eight in the morning until noon and then from three to six in the afternoon. From seven to eight in the evening there was an hour of independent study, and then from eight to nine the students took part in some form of physical education—fencing or dance. "If you only knew how hard they work us!" Fyodor exclaimed in a letter to his brother. "I've never seen such cramming! They're nearly draining the blood right out of us!"

The most important subjects were naturally the military ones, and these were Dostoyevsky's weakest. With his strong background in the humanities, he had to struggle with typical engineering courses such as topography, mathematics, and physics. "Mathematics is no more useful than a soap bubble," he assured his father. This attitude sometimes affected Dostoyevsky's performance on exams. "The examination was written in great haste," is a comment on one of his tests. "Despite the fact that it contains no serious errors, it would not have hurt to have had a more detailed presentation; on the whole it is clear that the writer could have taken more trouble." Fortunately, Dostoyevsky fared better at drawing and architecture. The Academy's comprehensive introduction to these fields was manifest later in Dostoyevsky's manuscripts which he illustrated throughout, and in which his drawings of Gothic cathedrals are particularly conspicuous.

It was even more difficult for Dostoyevsky to feel comfortable with the Academy's military exercises and harsh discipline. "His uniform didn't hang properly at all," commented a fellow student, who also noted that his knapsack, hat, and rifle looked rather like the scourges carried by ascetics for the mortification of the flesh. During brutal drills on sweltering summer days, the pale, thin dreamer, decked out in a black uniform with red epaulettes, was often seized by despair as the commanding officer called out his orders: "Attention! There's no such thing as sun on the front, gentlemen! Attention!"

Occasionally, Fyodor made serious blunders, such as the time he was sent as an orderly to Grand Duke Mikhail Pavlovich and in his confusion addressed him as "your Honor" rather than "your Imperial Highness." "Who is this idiot?" was the Grand Duke's irritable reply. "We generally send such people to Siberia."

The Academy attempted to give its students an education in the humanities as well. The school had acquired Vasily Plaksin as a Russian instructor. He was known for his history of Russian literature and his enthusiasm for Russian folk poetry. As a critic, he belonged to the Romantic school and was an admirer of Pushkin, Baratynsky, and Lermontov, but he was critical of Gogol, and it seems unlikely that the highly literate Dostoyevsky had much to learn from him. Joseph Cournant, the French literature instructor, however, was considerably more useful to Dostoyevsky. Cournant not only had an excellent knowledge of the classics—Racine, Corneille, and Pascal—but was well acquainted with contemporary literature and in large measure responsible for stimulating Dostoyevsky's interest in such writers as Balzac, Hugo, and George Sand.

This institutionalized literary education, however, was nothing compared to the studies Dostoyevsky undertook on his own. An officer of the watch reported that he was never without a serious book, such as Zschokke's *Family Prayer Book* or Krigge's *On Social Intercourse*. The latter was a practical book on manners and decorum, while the former was a thorough introduction to the Christian view of a number of issues Dostoyevsky would later address in his fiction: undeserved suffering, the power of a good example, man's exploitation of his neighbor, games of chance and suicide. But he read mostly fiction: Goethe, Schiller, Chateaubriand, Sand, Hugo, "nearly all of Balzac," and "all of Hoffmann in Russian and German."

While at the Academy of Engineers, Dostoyevsky had already developed his habit of working at night. Taps had scarcely been played before Dostoyevsky would sneak out to one of the palace's corner rooms. When a guard came to tell him that it was best he studied during the day, he would pack up his books and go to bed. But before long, he would return. Wrapped in a wool blanket, he would sit by a drafty window with a view of the

Fontanka Canal, and by the flickering light of a candle stump, he would give himself up to the enigmas of literature. Perhaps he had already conceived his first novel. "Man—that is the mystery," he wrote to Mikhail in 1839. "This mystery must be deciphered, and if you sacrifice your entire life to it, then you have not wasted your time. I work with this mystery, because I want to be a man."

Even in Moscow, Dostoyevsky had gained a reputation as a recluse who isolated himself from his schoolmates and buried himself in books. He must have felt even more alien among his peers at the Academy of Engineers. The 120 pupils, who were predominantly of German and Polish descent, thought only of their future careers in the military. "I can't say anything good about my comrades," he complained to his father. "What kind of people are they, anyway? They never pick up a book and don't seem to have a thought in their heads."

The Academy milieu was extremely rigorous, with merciless persecution of new pupils and poor teachers. Dostoyevsky's sense of justice was often put to the test. It is known that he defended "the fledglings" against the older students, that he took up a collection for poor peasants during drills, and that he courageously attacked the corruption rampant among the school's officers. These "rebellious tendencies" did not endear him to the school's instructors. In the spring of 1838, he failed his exams and was held back in the same class—an undisguised act of revenge on the part of a couple of teachers.

Dostoyevsky's schoolmates called him a "mystic" and an "idealist," partly because he was so interested in religion courses, but mostly because of his antisocial and hermitlike behavior. In this regard, he was very different from his lighthearted comrades. Thoughtful and grave, this "eccentric" wandered about alone without heeding his surroundings. Dostoyevsky was a gifted editor of the school newspaper and a helpful advisor to his fellows when they needed assistance with their compositions, but he made unreasonable demands on those who wanted to be his friends. For Dostoyevsky, a friend was a friend absolutely and completely, or he was relegated, along with everyone else, to the status of a stranger. It is not peculiar then that he could count his friends on the fingers of one hand: Ivan Berezhetsky, with whom he had frequent literary discussions; Konstantin Trutovsky, who drew his youthful portrait; Aleksei Beketov, who would become a leader of one of the 1840s radical circles; and Dmitri Grigorovich, who himself became a writer.

Dostoyevsky's closest friend during this time lived outside the Academy of Engineers. His name was Ivan Shidlovsky, and the writer became acquainted with him shortly after his arrival in St. Petersburg. Shidlovsky was five years older than Dostoyevsky and had just found a position in the Department of Finance after completing his university studies. But his job was not very important to him; like his friend, he was completely immersed in the world of literature, even though his own poems were no better than mediocre. The declaration Dostoyevsky made later—that Shidlovsky had been "a great person" for him—had more to do with his friend's complex and charismatic personality. Shidlovsky was a typical romantic, filled with belief in God and the high meanings of art at one moment and then seized by despair over the distance between the ideal and the real at the next. "When one looks at him, one understands immediately that he is a martyr!" Dostoyevsky exclaimed about his unhappy friend who was pining away from love. "He has faded away almost completely, his cheeks are gaunt, his glowing eyes are dry and inflamed. But with his physical decline, his spiritual beauty has become even greater."

Dostoyevsky had endless discussions with this "beautiful, exalted being" about the mysterious meaning of life and the lofty aims of poetry. "My friendship with Shidlovsky has given me moments full of a better life," he wrote to his brother. "Oh, what a pure and open soul!" Shidlovsky was soon to be torn apart by spiritual strife and the agonies of inner contradiction. He never found the harmony he sought—not as a church historian, a monk, or a pilgrim—and in the end, he gave way to drink and poverty. But for Dostoyevsky the friendship had deep significance. For two years, he studied the great works of literature under the inspired instruction of this mentor, who no doubt also gave him the encouragement he needed to pursue his dreams of becoming a writer. In Shidlovsky, Dostoyevsky was also able to observe a personality type that would recur in his novels: a divided character who wages continual war between a sincere faith in God and skeptical denial.

II

It is a tribute to Shidlovsky that even Mikhail Andreyevich was charmed by his warmth and kindness. In the period following their father's departure from St. Petersburg (Mikhail and Fyodor never saw him again), Shidlovsky became a kind of guardian for the two young men. His protection was certainly needed, because from this time on, Dr. Dostoyevsky suffered a rapid decline, never having recovered from his wife's death. He wandered about the house for hours calling her name; he carried on long conversations with her, and beat his head against the wall in despair.

His departure from the Hospital for the Poor and move to Darovoye only furthered his moral collapse. He sought comfort from the servant girl Katya, who had long been in the family's service. This "ardent" young woman bore him a son who died in infancy. From then on, only alcohol could numb the depressions of the once sober Mikhail Andreyevich. The drinking worsened his already poor health; his sight failed, and he suffered more and more frequent attacks of apoplexy.

His sons' letters brought him little pleasure. Mikhail's rejection from the Academy of Engineers, Fyodor's inability to get a scholarship and his failure in mathematics and military exercises were painful blows to the poor, proud doctor. But his greatest vexation was his sons' chronic shortage of funds. Fyodor was the worst: he had to have new boots for field exercises; he had to have a chest for his books; he had to have money for his own tea. As many as 140,000 men took part in the parades. Imagine if the Tsar noticed that he had a worn cap!

Dr. Dostoyevsky's despondent replies have been interpreted as expressions of his stinginess, but this is a misconception. In the first place, he sent all the money Fyodor requested—sometimes more—and in the second place, it is clear that his son's unremitting demands for money were primarily due to vanity, for he wanted to keep up with his wealthy classmates. Pyotr Semyonov's memoirs make this very clear: "I lived in the same camp," he wrote, "I lay in the same tent . . . and I managed just fine without any other tea than that which was handed out to us morning and night, without any other boots than the ones I was given, and without a chest for my books—even though I studied just as much as Dostoyevsky. Therefore he suffered no deprivation; he just didn't want to appear different from his comrades who kept themselves in tea, boots, and book chests."

The doctor's letters to Fyodor make pathetic reading. It is important to be frugal, he admonished. But his son was unable to understand the gravity of the situation and replied ironically, "Out of consideration for your difficult financial circumstances, I think I had better stop drinking tea."

At the end of May 1839, just a few days before his death, Mikhail Andreyevich gave a last description of the miserable conditions out on the "miniature estates":

The snow stayed until May; we had to find something to feed the cattle with. The straw roofs were taken down long ago and used for feed. There hasn't been a drop of rain since last spring, not even a little dew! The heat and the terrible wind have destroyed everything. The sown fields are black . . . there isn't a sprout to be seen anywhere. We are threatened not only with ruin but with real famine!

There is an extensive body of literature concerning the doctor's death at the beginning of June. The best-known version has it that Mikhail Andreyevich was murdered by his serfs. It is from this legend that Sigmund Freud constructed his view of Dostoyevsky, and from this legend he created another: that when the writer received the news of his father's death, he suffered his first epileptic attack. According to Freud, Dostoyevsky desired the death of his "miserly" and "brutal" father, and when he understood that his father was finally dead, he was overcome with joy and was punished by his first epileptic crisis. The outbreak of epilepsy stemmed from an Oedipal complex. His father's violent death unleashed conflicting emotions within him: feelings of satisfied revenge and feelings of intense guilt. Tormented by these "complexes," he later returned with fear and pleasure to patricide in his last novel.

Let us turn to the factual basis for this hypothesis, which must be among the boldest ever proposed about a writer. There are three main sources for the legend of Mikhail Andreyevich's murder. The first originates with the writer's daughter, Lyubov, who in 1920 wrote the following in her book about her father:

My grandfather Mikhail had always been strict with his serfs. The more he drank, the worse he became, and in the end, they murdered him. One summer day, he left Darovoye to visit his other property, Cheremoshnya, and he never returned. He was discovered later half-way between the two villages, suffocated with a pillow from the carriage. The carriage had disappeared along with the horses; a number of the villages' peasants vanished at the same time. During the trial, my grandfather's serfs confessed that it had been an act of revenge.

Another family version of the death comes from the writer's brother, the usually dependable Andrei:

His need for alcohol became markedly stronger and stronger; he was seldom sober. . . . The day it happened, a group of ten to fifteen men were working in a field near the edge of the woods at Cheremoshnya; they were, in other words, far from other people! Irritated by something the serfs did wrong, or perhaps by something that just appeared to be wrong, Father lost his temper and began to scream at them. One of the bravest in the group gave him a coarse reply, and then in fear of a reprisal, he called out to the others, "Come on, boys, we'll throttle him!" And with that cry, all fifteen let loose on Father, and naturally they killed him instantly.

Finally, there were a number of statements made about the doctor's death by peasants in Darovoye as late as the mid-1920s. According to these accounts, three peasants from Cheremoshnya planned to murder Mikhail Andreyevich. As a protest against his strictness, they refused to work, and when he came to get them, they threw themselves at him. "Naturally, they did not beat him; that would have left clues. Instead, they had made ready a bottle of liquor which they forced down their master's throat, and then they smothered him with a handkerchief."

It is initially striking about these accounts that they are all in conflict and have only one element in common, namely, the claim that Mikhail Andreyevich was murdered by his serfs. But the way in which it is supposed to have occurred is described very differently. Even the "murder weapon" is not consistent. There is reason to exercise caution in regard to these sources.

The Darovoye peasants' account is the least trustworthy. If one considers only the fact that they described conditions in a rival village where the peasants firmly denied that their relatives murdered their master, one has cause for skepticism. The confused and conflicting testimonies of these old men in Darovoye are second- or thirdhand stories. Some say that it took place in the spring, others that it was "late autumn." The entire story takes on the quality of folklore. Dostoyevsky's daughter was also writing about the past, and her story is at best thirdhand. The confusion and many mistakes that mar her book about her father give ample reason to doubt her version as well. Even Andrei, who wrote his memoirs fifty years earlier, was unable to give a firsthand account. When he was with the Kumanin family in Moscow, they directed him to the nursemaid Alyona Frolovna as a source, and she could only say that she had heard a scream.

What really happened to Dostoyevsky's father? Recent investigations into the archive materials in Tula give reason to believe the following account:

On June 6, 1839, Mikhail Andreyevich went out to inspect his peasants in Cheremoshnya. It was a very hot day; the temperature was nearly 100 degrees. The peasants were distributing manure in a vain attempt to bring life back to the scorched land. The doctor met four of these peasants and began to yell about some mistake or other that they had made. Then he suddenly collapsed, obviously gripped by one of his apoplectic attacks brought on by his anger and the heat.

The parish bailiff immediately sent word of the death to the Dostoyevsky family, and one week after the funeral, Maria Fyodorovna's stepmother, Olga Yakovlevna, came from Moscow to get the doctor's youngest children: Vera, Nicholas, and Alexandra. Before she returned home, she was summoned by the neighboring landowner, Pavel Khotyaintsev, who for several years had been filing suits against Mikhail Andreyevich. During this conversation, he told her that the doctor had not suffered a natural death; he had been killed by his serfs, but he advised Olga Yakovlevna not to take the matter any further. The children could not get their father back, and a trial would only result in the loss of their inheritance when the peasants were exiled to Siberia.

At this time the first official document about the death was submitted: the report was underwritten by the lower court in Kashira, the administrative capital of the territory where the Dostoyevsky family had its properties, and was addressed to the newly appointed governor in the district of Tula. The governor received the report on June 16, so it is inconceivable that Olga Yakovlevna would have had time to alter its contents with bribes. The report states the following:

> On the morning of June 6 of this year, the fifty-four-year-old nobleman Mikhail Andreyevich Dostoyevsky died suddenly. Mr. Dostoyevsky managed the property of his deceased wife in the village Darovoe in the *gubernia* Kashira and had been out to inspect his serfs. The investigation of this matter has given no reason to suspect that Mr. Dostoyevsky's death was brought about by violence. As will be recorded in Dr. Schönknecht's death certificate, the death occurred following an apoplectic attack caused by severe spasms which were not inhibited by the usual medicine.

The first doctor who was called, however, was a Dr. Schönrock from Saraisk, a town near Darovoye but in another *gubernia*. Why did the peasants send for a doctor from this town? Why didn't they immediately send for a doctor from Kashira, farther away but the only one who could fill out a legitimate death certificate? The answer must be that Mikhail Andreyevich was still alive and that the peasants were trying to save him. Afraid that the doctor in remote Kashira would not reach them in time, they hastened to call Dr. Schönrock. They obviously thought that their master had fallen prey to one of his usual attacks, and therefore they sent for the doctor they normally used on such occasions.

Because Dr. Schönrock belonged to another district and was therefore unable to fill out an official death certificate, the peasants also sent for Dr. Schönknecht in Kashira, even though the death had by then been confirmed. Dr. Dostoyevsky's corpse was treated in strict accordance with regulations: it lay in the field for forty-eight hours until the authorities arrived from Kashira. When Dr. Schönknecht, along with several law-enforcement officials, finally appeared at the scene on June 8, he could only confirm the conclusion that had been reached by his colleague in the neighboring district as to the cause of the death—an apoplectic attack.

The murder of landowners by their serfs was quite common in Russia during this period, particularly in villages that were beset with economic hardship and famine. On the average, twenty landowners were killed every year. Naturally the authorities were vigilant about anything that even remotely looked like peasant rebellion. When a landowner was found dead, a huge legal apparatus was set into motion to clear up any questions about peasant violence. In this instance, two doctors had confirmed that the death was from natural causes. Nevertheless, the case was brought before the governor himself, and still it was impossible to discover any confusion in the documents. If someone had attempted to falsify the case, internal contradictions would have been inevitable.

Then on July 6—a month after Dr. Dostoyevsky's death—a cavalry captain by the name of A. I. Leibrecht turned up in Kashira voicing his "suspicion that Dr. Dostoyevsky had been murdered by his peasants." The authorities promptly requested a written statement of his suspicions. Leibrecht wrote that he "had heard from V. F. Khotyaintsev [a relative of Dostoyevsky's neighbor] that one of Dr. Dostoyevsky's servant girls had heard her master scream and that her brother had forbidden her from saying anything about it, and that Dr. Dostoyevsky's peasants were so bitter that when they washed the deceased, they whipped his body and refused to carry it to church." That same day, it was decided that the case should be reopened. Soon thereafter a new statement was issued that once again concluded that Dr. Dostoyevsky had died from natural causes. And furthermore, the report went on to say, one could rest assured that there were no rebellious peasants in the district.

On July 26, a communication was sent to V. F. Khotyaintsev to substantiate Leibrecht's claim. Khotyaintsev, however, "firmly denied almost everything." Because it was one man's word against another's, a confrontation was arranged between Leibrecht and Khotyaintsev. Both men refused to appear in court, and it was not until a month later, on September 12, that a hearing was held.

At the hearing Leibrecht reiterated what he had said earlier in reference to "all of these rumors"—which were the words recorded in the hearing transcript. V. F. Khotyaintsev continued obstinately to deny his involvement and insisted that Leibrecht had brought on all of this "out of malice." Leibrecht then clarified further: he said that V. F. Khotyaintsev had asked him to go to the local administrative official and deliver the following message: "Mr. Pavel Petrovich Khotyaintsev [Dostoyevsky's neighbor] asks you [the official] to come right away so that this entire matter can be cleared up."

In an instant, the source of the rumour that Mikhail Andreyevich had been murdered was exposed. Leibrecht had been a straw man for the vengeful neighbor Pavel Khotyaintsev. Khotyaintsev's version of the doctor's shameful death left an ignominious legacy for the Dostoyevsky children and threatened the family's serfs with many years of forced labor in Siberia.

Once Khotyaintsev was exposed, he felt he could just as well play out his hand, and one month later, he came forward and demanded that the serfs be punished. The very action he had recently warned Olga Yakovlevna against he now took himself. His motives were obvious. By bringing suit against the peasants, he would not only defame his dead enemy, but would put himself in a good position to gain the two villages he had long coveted and upon which, even after the lawsuit with the Dostoyevsky family, he had maintained a number of farms. But this time the suit-happy Khotyaintsev did not have luck on his side. On November 16, yet another decision was handed down from the court: "The death must be attributed to God's judgment when it is impossible to find a party guilty of causing it."

The criminal court in Tula, however, was not satisfied with the documents that had been forwarded there, and it was decided that the matter should be thoroughly investigated yet again. The painstaking treatment of the case was due to the seriousness of the charge. During a period when famine seemed imminent, the whole interior of Russia was plagued by arson and the murder of landowners. Still, it was not possible to find the serfs guilty, no matter how hard one tried. It couldn't even be established that they had complained about their master, a very common occurrence when a landowner treated his serfs harshly. The case was resolved against Dostoyevsky's malicious neighbor in a final decision handed down at the end of October 1840. The peasants were acquitted, and Leibrecht was given a warning to be "more cautious about such matters in the future."

An appeal for caution is also in order for Dostoyevsky's biographers. Mikhail Andreyevich has been portrayed in the biographies of his son as a merciless tormenter of his serfs who was finally humbled by a violent death. It is important to note that it has been absolutely established that two doctors determined that Dr. Dostoyevsky died of natural causes, and their testimony was legally upheld in spite of considerable exertions on the part of a vindictive neighbor.

The biographers who still stand by the murder theory claim that bribes decided the outcome of the case. It is difficult to imagine, however, that a group of impoverished peasants could afford to bribe several medical and judicial authorities in two districts. Not even the wealthy Kumanin family could have managed this. Local officials would not have dared to cover up a case that smacked of peasant rebellion, and certainly not in 1838, when every civil servant was mindful of the new governor who had just ordered sweeping reforms throughout the entire province.

Some have also maintained that the question of how the doctor died is of secondary importance, that what is primary is that Dostoyevsky believed the rumor that his father had been murdered by his serfs. But there is no proof that the writer held this conviction. Both versions of his father's death must have been known to Dostoyevsky, and there is nothing to indicate that he had more faith in the murder rumors than in the official report that his father had died of his illness. On the contrary, if one looks at the impact this episode had upon his work, it seems likely that Dostoyevsky believed that the murder charge was groundless. Among the peasants who were singled out as the doctor's murderers was a man named Yefim. The name appears as Yefimov in *Netochka Nezvanova*; this fictional Yefimov is also accused through underhanded means of murder, but the entire business comes to an end when the informer is unmasked and convicted of slander. And, at the beginning of *A Raw Youth* Leibrecht (in the slightly altered spelling "Lebrecht") is negatively portrayed as a slanderer who sells family information in the form of an album of memoirs to the highest bidder.

Quite as flimsy as the murder theory is the theory that the author had his first epileptic seizure when he received news of his father's death. Fyodor had hypochondriac tendencies and generally kept his brother well informed about the state of his health. During the summer of 1839, however, he makes no mention of a seizure. At this time Dostoyevsky was sharing quarters with a hundred other pupils, and it would have been difficult to hide an epileptic seizure. Had a seizure been observed, he would have been dismissed from the Academy immediately for there were to be no epileptics among the officers of the Russian army. The very fact that Dostoyevsky remained at the Academy of Engineers excludes the possibility of an epileptic seizure at this time.

The traditional portrayal of Mikhail Andreyevich as a cruel, punishing father, of his son's hatred and relief in connection with the murder, and finally of his self-inflicted punishment in the form of an epileptic attack— all this fits perfectly within a psychoanalytic hypothesis. But the biographical foundation for this theory is more than questionable. Freud argued that if it could be shown that Dostoyevsky did not suffer from epilepsy during his imprisonment in Siberia, this would be only further evidence that his epilepsy functioned as a punishment: i.e., in exile he did not need to punish himself because he was already being sufficiently punished by the patriarchal figure of the Tsar.

Once again the facts contradict Freud's theory. The evidence suggests that Dostoyevsky's epilepsy first made its appearance in Siberia! The first time Dostoyevsky mentioned his illness—"these strange attacks that resemble epilepsy"—was in a letter to Mikhail just after his release from prison. That the illness really was epilepsy was confirmed only later, in February 1857. It is now certain that the diagnosis made at that time was correct. Freud's theory of "hysterical epilepsy" is without foundation.

The absolute parallels that have been frequently drawn between Mikhail Andreyevich and Fyodor Karamazov are also dubious. Lyubov wrote, "It continually occurs to me that Dostoyevsky thought of his father when he created old Karamazov." Freud agreed wholeheartedly, and this idea was to become almost dogma, though the writer's daughter couldn't even support her claim by referring to a family tradition. In fact, in spite of certain similarities between them such as hotheadedness and sentimentality, the two figures are very different: while Fyodor Karamazov plagues his wife to death and quite simply forgets that he has sons, Mikhail Andreyevich was a typical family man with an indefatigable concern for his wife and children. If Dostoyevsky did think of his father while he wrote *The Brothers Kara-*

mazov, it is more likely that Mikhail Andreyevich was behind the figure of the proud military captain Snegiryov, who, in spite of his drunkenness, loves his family deeply, especially his little son Ilyuskha.

Far from hating his father, Dostoyevsky clearly admired him greatly. There is no reason to believe that he did not mourn deeply upon hearing of his father's death. It is true that he rarely spoke of his father in his letters, but such reticence about a person who is truly loved seems quite appropriate. The statements that the writer made about his father do not leave us in doubt about his regard for him. "I have cried many tears over Father's death," he wrote in a letter to Mikhail in 1839. Five years later, he wrote to his brother-in-law, "Understand that I do not honor my parents less than you do." And in 1876, he said in a letter to Andrei, "Remember this, and let yourself be completely imbued with this thought, brother Andrei Mikhailovich, that it was precisely this idea—to strive to be at home with *the best people* (in its literal and highest meaning) that was fundamental to our father and mother—human aberrations notwithstanding."

In light of such statements, every attempt to identify Dostoyevsky's father with Fyodor Karamazov falls to pieces, no matter how much one occupies oneself with "human aberrations." Freud's essay on Dostoyevsky and its emphasis on patricide have given nourishment to innumerable attacks on the writer for the notion that he was a "monstrous talent," a wanton imperialist, a vile rapist. But most of all, it has been the source of the most hopelessly mistaken biographical interpretations of the author's work. When Ivan Karamazov exclaims, "Who has not wished for his father's death?" Dostoyevsky's supposed hatred of his father is immediately invoked. And when Raskolnikov kills the pawnbroker, it is naturally Dostoyevsky himself who is swinging the ax over his father's head. There must be some significance to the fact that Dostoyevsky attended school in the very building where Tsar Paul was secretly assassinated upon the orders of his own son, Alexander!

III

Even though Dostoyevsky no longer felt obligated to continue his military education after his father's death, he stayed on at the Academy of Engineers. Having no one to depend on now but himself, he worked harder at his studies and placed third in his class on the final examinations of 1841. "He does very good work," his report card stated. At this time he was also named second lieutenant and given the right to live outside the Academy building. He found a little apartment in Karavannaya Street, which he shared with a classmate, Adolph Gustav Totleben, a brother of the future Crimean War hero, Eduard Totleben.

In the years that followed, Dostoyevsky moved often. In all, twenty of his addresses in St. Petersburg are known. He apparently liked to change apartments each time he began a new work. Like his heroes, he loved corner apartments, and he always lived close to a church. For nearly four years he lived in a small three-story building near Vladimir Cathedral, not far from Nevsky Prospekt. His apartment had three rooms, but only one of them was furnished. He usually rented the other rooms to friends, although there were few who could bear to live with him for very long.

In August 1843, Dostoyevsky was finally able to celebrate having finished his last exams at the Academy of Engineers. A year earlier he had been promoted to lieutenant engineer, and everything seemed to indicate that he would have a splendid military career. But Dostoyevsky had long felt that he was "a writer, not an engineer" and couldn't imagine leaving the literary life of the capital. Instead of going off to a post as an army engineer, he accepted a modest position in the drafting office of St. Petersburg's engineering division. But he soon found this job as dull as a "frozen potato." This was no life for a writer!

In 1844 when he discovered that he was in danger of being sent on an inspection mission to a distant army camp—an assignment that would have meant great expense and a hiatus of several months in the writing of his first literary work—he took the bold step of leaving the military. It is possible that a comment from Tsar Nicholas may have influenced his decision. "What idiot drew this?" remarked the Tsar when he saw that Dostoyevsky had drawn a fortress without doors. In all events, his application for a discharge was granted on October 19, 1844.

Dostoyevsky's literary career had begun, and he looked forward to it with pleasure and confidence. "Do not worry about my future," he wrote to Mikhail. "Now that I am finally free, I will work with devilish joy!" He would find a way to make money somehow. "Pushkin managed as long as he got ten rubles a line, and Gogol was well paid—it does depend a bit on me, too," he joked. Dostoyevsky had no doubts about his calling. "On the contrary," he wrote later, "I was certain that the future belonged to me and that I was its master. . . . A flame burned in my soul, and I believed in that flame." Neither did Mikhail have any doubts. "I am convinced that he will go a long way," he wrote the family's guardians. "He is a great and original talent, and is in possession of deep learning."

Dostoyevsky's correspondence with Mikhail is the chief source of information we have about the writer's life during this period. Only the summer visits to Reval interrupted his letter writing. He had few friends, a fact which made his brother's letters particularly welcome. "You cannot imagine the shudder of joy that courses through me every time I receive a letter from you," he wrote in a New Year's greeting:

> I have discovered a new and wonderful pleasure: I keep myself on tenterhooks. I take the letter in my hand and turn it over and examine it for a while and test its weight in my hand, and when I have satisfied myself fully with looking at the envelope and seal, I put it in my pocket. . . . You cannot imagine what rapture this is for my soul, my senses and my heart! Often I wait a whole quarter of an hour, and then, finally, I throw myself greedily at the letter, tear open the seal and drink in your words, your dear words!

There are a number of descriptions of Dostoyevsky from this period. The majority of them depict a pale, introverted dreamer, a sickly, highstrung romantic with a rapid pulse. Dr. Alexander Rizenkampf, who shared an apartment with the writer for several months and attempted to instruct him in the art of German punctuality, found him "completely unequipped for the realities of life." "With his friends he always seemed to be in a good mood, garrulous, carefree, and contented with himself," Dr. Rizenkampf wrote. "But as soon as the guests were gone, he fell into deep thought; he sat in his lonely room and thought about his sad position and tried to lose himself in new literary plans, in which human suffering played a major role."

For others, the only impression of Dostoyevsky that remained with them was of an austere twenty-year-old. "He had a serious expression and it is difficult for me to imagine that he laughed or joked with his comrades," Konstantin Trutovsky wrote. His temperament was extremely sensitive and explosive. He would leave a gathering at the slightest hint of offense, and he would never forget it. In short, his friends were often put to the test, and he did little to keep them. He wanted to be "free, alone, and independent." Dostoyevsky was particularly difficult in the company of foreigners, and he did his best to avoid them. "Imagine if I married some French girl! Then I would have to take my leave of Russian literature forever!"

Nevertheless, he did not lead a monastic life. He was often seen at the theater and at concerts. In the spring of 1841, he heard with admiration the virtuoso Norwegian violinist Ole Bull, and the following year he did not miss a performance of Franz Liszt's piano concerts. On occasion, he would let himself go and invite some friends to the fashionable Hotel de France on Malaya Morskaya. Gradually, Dostoyevsky also began to make the acquaintance of women. His complaint to Mikhail that all his "Minnas, Claras, and Mariannes" were causing him "terrible confusion" suggests that his debut into this world was quite unsophisticated. One may well wonder, for that matter, whether his remark wasn't primarily an expression of a literary dandy's boastful imagination.

Along with the reflections on art and literature, money worries dominated Dostoyevsky's letters to his brother. But the young writer was not truly poor; it was just that money "ran like water" and "melted like wax" in his hands. As long as he had money, he was exceedingly generous, and others exploited him terribly. "Just let him steal," he would say. "That won't bankrupt me." But several times he came very close to it. "For God's sake, send me five rubles, or at the very least one ruble," he wrote Andrei toward the end of 1842. "I haven't had a thing to stoke the fire with for three days and don't have a single kopeck."

Some time later, according to Dr. Rizenkampf, Dostoyevsky suddenly began to behave with new confidence and pride. After a great deal of fuss and unpleasantness, he had finally managed to have an advance of five hundred rubles on his inheritance sent to him. "But already the next morning," Dr. Rizenkampf continued, "he came strolling in to me to ask for a loan of five rubles." It turned out that the future author of *The Gambler* had lost most of the money at billiards and the rest had been stolen. It was through escapades like this one that Dostoyevsky became acquainted early on with the unseemly world of usurers and pawnbrokers that he portrayed so exhaustively in his novels. There were even times when he was in danger of landing in debtors' prison. "Khlestakov declares that he is prepared to go to prison as long as it is done in a 'refined' way," Dostoyevsky wrote about the hero of *The Inspector General*. "But I—how can I go to jail in a refined way when I don't even own so much as *a pair of trousers?*"

This hopelessly impractical artist continued to be at home only in the world of books. "He had a passionate love of poetry," Dr. Rizenkampf recalled, "but he wrote only prose, because he didn't have the patience needed to write in a prescribed form. . . . Thoughts were born in his head like the spray from a whirlpool. . . . His brilliant natural gift for recitation threatened to burst the restraints of his artistic self-discipline; his hoarse voice grew to a screaming pitch, he foamed at the mouth, he gesticulated, yelled, and spat." Many have described Dostoyevsky's ability to infect his friends with his passion for literature. "It was well after midnight. We were all very tired, but Dostoyevsky stood at the door and spoke to us—nervous and excited. His low, hoarse voice was spellbinding; it was impossible to tear oneself away."

Dostoyevsky saw no reason to deny his dreamy nature. When he later looked back upon his youth, he referred to himself as "a phantast and a mystic" who was subject to the strangest experiences:

> In my youthful fantasies, I imagined myself a Pericles or a Marius, as a Christian under the Emperor Nero, or as one of the competitors in a jousting tournament, like Edward Glendinning in Walter Scott's novel *The Cloister*. What didn't I find to dream about in my youth? What didn't I live with my whole heart, my whole soul, in golden and blazing daydreams that nearly resembled opium hallucinations!

A developing writer with this temperament was naturally receptive to the metaphysically inclined Romanticism of the period. During his first years at the Academy of Engineers, Dostoyevsky's favorite writer was E. T. A. Hoffmann. He was fascinated by Hoffmann's representation of the demonic and mystical side of life and by his depiction of man's relation to a world of transcendent, supernatural powers. Earlier, Dostoyevsky had been deeply impressed by the work of Pushkin's that Hoffmann had inspired, *The Queen of Spades*. Through his encounter with Romantic poetry and its portrayal of life's grim realities, he now found himself even more enthused by the German's abilities to render fearful passions and morbid emotions. "I have a plan—to go mad," he wrote to Mikhail. "Then people can just stand there and make fools of themselves; just let them try to cure me and bring me back to reason!" Dostoyevsky was especially entranced by the figure of Alban in *Der Magnetiseur*, who through his occult activities rivals God when he gains power over nature. "It is horrible to see a man who has the incomprehensible within his power, a man who does not know what he should do, who plays with a toy that is—God!" he wrote. Already Dosto-yevsky was preoccupied with man's unholy desire to dethrone God and raise himself to the status of a man-god.

Other remarks in his letters indicate that Dostoyevsky's philosophical and aesthetic orientation was strongly influenced by F. W. J. von Schelling, Romanticism's philosopher *par excellence*. Schelling's philosophical irrationalism is evident in Dostoyevsky's violent protest against his brother's statement that "one must feel less in order to know more." "To know— what do you mean by that?" he asked irritably. "Nature, the spirit, love and God—these can only be perceived by the heart, not by the mind." The heart is the true means for reaching the highest understanding, and because of this, the distinction between poetry and philosophy is erased: "You know that the artist in the moment of inspiration comprehends God. It follows then that poetic inspiration is in reality a philosophical inspiration; and philosophy is in reality nothing but poetry, a peculiar, higher form of poetry!"

Equipped with this Romantic baggage, Dostoyevsky set out to write his first literary works: the Romantic tragedies *Boris Godunov* and *Mary Stuart*. We know that Dostoyevsky entertained his friends with readings from these plays in early 1841. Later he rejected these works of "juvenile stupidity," and nothing remains of them. He undoubtedly felt that they were influenced too much by the works of Pushkin and Schiller, from whom the titles were taken. Nevertheless, these stories are thematically characteristic of Dostoyevsky. In the tragedy of Boris Godunov—an exceptional statesman who is defeated by his moral conscience—he anticipates Raskolnikov's question about whether the strong individual has the right to take a life for the greater good. And the tragedy of Mary Stuart must have provided Dostoyevsky with the occasion to reflect upon another of his recurrent themes, the rivalry of two women who are overcome by hatred for one another.

In the 1840s, a significant change took place in Russian literature. The German metaphysical Romanticism that had been so dominant in the 1830s slowly began to lose its hold on writers. Instead, they found models in French social Romanticism, in figures like Balzac, Hugo, and George Sand. What this meant in practice was a movement toward literary realism. Following the French example, authors began to write "psychological sketches" in which specific milieus appeared with their own "local color." A critical awareness of society became more widespread. Russian writers began to concern themselves with the power of a materialistic society over people and the sad plight of the small civil servant in the official bureaucracy. Traditional Russian themes such as corruption and serfdom were formulated more acutely. In a more powerful way than before, one could sense that behind the pleas for compassion for the oppressed and victimized was a growing criticism of contemporary society, a society that did little to improve existing conditions. With his ground-breaking story of 1842, "The Overcoat," Gogol opened the way for the literature of exposé. The new writers of the period considered themselves members of the Gogol school, and one by one they emerged, each with his own idiosyncrasies and themes.

German Romanticism was not merely a passing stage in Dostoyevsky's development, however. His interest in the fantastic and the extraordinary individual remained constant throughout his career, and he maintained a conception of writing as ideal and sublime until the very end. But he was also taken with the humane appeal and the criticism of society that was so strong in the new "naturalistic school." Notably, it was just at this time that Dostoyevsky undertook the study of "the capital's proletariat" in Dr. Rizenkampf's waiting room for poor patients. Above all, he was concerned with the possibilities for representing a realistic image of humanity. Along with Gogol, Balzac had become Dostoyevsky's great idol. Inspired by the French writer's visit to St. Petersburg in 1843, he threw himself into a Russian translation of *Eugénie Grandet* during his Christmas vacation. "Balzac is great!" he exclaimed in a letter to Mikhail. "His characters are the creations of a universal spirit! Not the spirit of a time but the struggles of thousands of years have prepared for this development in the soul of man!"

Dostoyevsky's translation of *Eugénie Grandet* is hardly a masterpiece. He was very free in his rendering—shortened a bit here, added a bit there— for this was still well before the time when translations were expected to adhere closely to the original. Nevertheless, the translation was an important preparatory work for the developing writer. From Balzac he learned to penetrate human emotions, to show the power of money over people's fates. In Balzac he also discovered the meek and all-suffering woman whom he later portrayed so often in his own writing. Significantly, it was at this time that he began his first published work, *Poor Folk*. Its title is typical of the period, but it may also stand as a motto for much of Dostoyevsky's later writing.

Few writers achieve success with their first work, and even fewer alter the course of literary history with their debut. Dostoyevsky did both. From the start, critics and readers received *Poor Folk* with enthusiasm. When Dostoyevsky died, he was remembered not only as the author of the "great novels" but also as the young man who wrote *Poor Folk*.

Dmitri Grigorovich, who shared an apartment with Dostoyevsky at the time, wrote the following about the young writer's work on his novel:

Dostoyevsky could sit at his desk for days and nights at a time. He uttered not one word about what he wrote. When I questioned him, he was evasive and laconic, and once I sensed his reluctance, I stopped asking him about it. I could only see the pile of papers covered with his distinctive hand-writing: the letters fell from his pen like pearls, as if they had been etched. . . . And as soon as he stopped writing, he picked up some book or other.

This is an account of a writer who is gripped by a particular vision. Dostoyevsky himself described how he was struck by this vision. One evening when he was walking along the Neva on his way home from town, he stopped and let his gaze wander over the river and the freezing mist that had suddenly turned a violet-red as it reflected the sunset. It was nightfall, and the immense expanse of the river flashed with myriad sparks from the hoarfrost. The air was bitter cold, steam poured from the horses, and people bounced up and down to keep themselves warm. From the housetops on the opposite bank, columns of smoke rose into the sky forming strange images. It seemed as if new structures had been erected over the old ones, as if a new city was forming itself in the air. And before his eyes, life began to stir within this lofty, floating city: there, in some cramped rooms lived a young girl and a civil servant of modest means. Their lives were dull, but their noble hearts were bright, and there was something so helplessly sad about these poor people that Dostoyevsky felt his heart would break.

He had found the idea for his first novel. Before this "vision on the Neva," he had lived in a Romantic dream world of distant lands in distant times, inhabited by noble knights and Italian beauties. From this moment on, he began to dream of other things, for he had discovered that there is nothing more fantastic than reality itself. And within this fantastic reality, he had glimpsed the images of the poor scrivener Devushkin and the orphan Varenka.

"I will soon finish a novel about the size of *Eugénie Grandet,*" Dostoyevsky wrote at the end of September 1844. But his optimistic pro-nouncement was premature. He would never again have the opportunity to spend so much time on a novel as he did with his first. At the end of the year he overhauled the book completely, and he continued revising through the beginning of May 1845. "Now it is finished. This revision will have to be the last. . . . I have sworn not to touch it again."

Later, Dostoyevsky said that the book had been written "with passion, almost with tears." Grigorovich said about his first impression of *Poor Folk:*

> One morning—it was during the summer—he asked for me. When I entered his room, I saw him sitting on the divan that also served as a bed. Before him on the little desk was a voluminous notebook with large pages filled with tiny writing. "Please sit down, Grigorovich. I have just recopied my manuscript and I would like to read it to you. Sit down and don't interrupt me," he said, unusually animated.
>
> What he read to me was published soon after under the title *Poor Folk.* From the first page, I understood how much better this was than anything I had written, and my conviction was reinforced as he read on. I was beside myself with admiration and several times I wanted to throw my arms around his neck and embrace him. Only the fact that he shrank from passionate displays of emotion held me back. Nevertheless, I could not sit still and interrupted the reading several times with enthusiastic exclamations.

An arduous creation had received its first recognition. But that was only the beginning. That same night, the writer was awakened at four o'clock in the morning. Grigorovich had begun reading the manuscript to the poet Nikolai Nekrasov. They did not stop until they reached the last page, and then they burst into Dostoyevsky's room to give him hugs and congratulations.

That morning Nekrasov took the manuscript to Russia's foremost critic, the much feared Vissarion Belinsky. "We have a new Gogol!" Nekrasov said when he approached Belinsky. "With the likes of you, Gogols are springing up like mushrooms," Belinsky replied skeptically. But when Nekrasov returned that evening, all of Belinsky's doubts had vanished. "Send him to me at once!" the critic roared.

Belinsky believed that art's primary task was to portray the current problems of society, and he understood at once that *Poor Folk* was the work of a formidable talent. In Dostoyevsky's vivid descriptions of the poor and oppressed, in his portrait of the ordinary copying clerk who without even being aware of it is crushed by life, who doesn't even dare to consider himself unlucky—in this work the critic found Russian literature's "first attempt at a social novel." No Russian author had ever burst on the scene like this! At last he had discovered a fine example of a literature critical of sociey. In his battle against the false and unreal Romanticism of the era, Belinsky had long awaited such a work. "Do you know what you have written?" he demanded of Dostoyevsky when they finally met. "You have written as an artist out of spontaneous feeling, but do you know what terrible truth you have made us aware of in your work? No, at twenty, you could not possibly know. . . . This truth has clearly chosen you as an artist; it is a gift. Take good care of this gift and revere it—then you will become a great writer!"

This was beyond what even the dreamer Dostoyevsky had imagined. Intoxicated by the words of the famous critic, he stumbled out onto Nevsky Prospekt. Was he really so great? "This was the most blissful moment of my entire life," he wrote many years later. "Every time I remembered this moment when I was in prison I found new courage and strength. Still today I remember it with joy."

From a purely formal perspective, there is nothing sensational about Dostoyevsky's first work. He uses the epistolary novel to portray the relationship between the middle-aged copying clerk Devushkin and the orphan Varenka, a genre that even at the time seemed rather antiquated. Neither was the motif of the little man new. In contemporary Russian literature there were dozens of works in which the protagonist was a poor St. Petersburg clerk: the theme was beautifully realized in Gogol's "The Overcoat," a narrative about the penniless Akaky Akakavich, who makes a great sacrifice in order to get himself a new overcoat only to lose it a short time later.

There is little doubt that Dostoyevsky, like many of the period's writers, had "unfolded himself out of Gogol's overcoat." What the coat is for Akaky Akakievich, Varenka is for Devushkin. Yet it is precisely in this similarity of subject matter that a fundamental distinction between the two stories is revealed. By substituting a living human being for an inanimate object, Dostoyevsky creates something quite new. The reader witnesses the humanization of Gogol's grotesquely comic hero. While Gogol's little man is unable to acknowledge his own humanity, Devushkin realizes that he is after all a human being "in heart and mind." Gogol laughs at his hero and pities him; Dostoyevsky weeps for his hero and sympathizes with him. In his review, Belinsky focused on this point: "The author will go further than Gogol," he wrote. "Glory to the writer who loves those people who live in attics and cellars and tells their story to those who live in golden palaces: These too are human beings; they are your brothers."

Poverty is the central theme of *Poor Folk*. It is the story of Varenka's and Devushkin's miserable battle to keep themselves afloat. The clerk experiences poverty as a cruel personal tragedy, and at the same time, he analyzes its peculiar psychology. It robs people of their self-respect and turns them into "good-for-nothings" and "rats." It finally results in bitterness and suspicion. "Poor people are unpredictable," Devushkin writes to Varenka. Freethinking ideas begin to gain a foothold with him; why are some people rich and happy, while others are poor and unhappy? Devushkin is Dostoyevsky's first rebel. Trembling in fear, he mumbles ideas that Raskolnikov will later proclaim loudly and with pride.

Out of the poverty theme came another to which Dostoyevsky returned again and again in the course of his career: man's perpetual battle for self-respect. Without self-respect a man cannot be truly human; without it, his life goes to pieces.

The timid Devushkin regains his self-esteem because he meets a girl who respects him as much as she respects herself, and this convinces him that class differences are essentially meaningless. Isn't a poor person like Varenka just as worthy as a countess, he philosophizes, or is it freethinking to believe this? This same question is posed again and again in *The Brothers Karamazov*. When the drunken, suffering Maksimov says that he is no longer of any use, Grushenka answers him, "Everyone is of use, and how can we know who is more useful than anyone else?"

A central concern in Dostoyevsky's thought is that man is endowed with an essential worth that exists nowhere else in the known world. Man is a being who may easily be degraded, but to degrade him is wrong. If he is debased, man is forced either to succumb or to defend himself and fight for his own human dignity. The suffering of the Underground Man, for example, arises from the fact that he has so thoroughly lost a sense of his own worth that it has robbed him of his life.

Varenka and Devushkin are defeated in their struggle to maintain their personal dignity. The reader is witness to the tragedy of a deeply felt, unselfish love that is bruised and crushed by life's circumstances. At the end of the novel, Varenka enters an unhappy marriage with the man who has seduced her earlier, and Devushkin is doomed to live out his life in an even more wretched state than before as a tenant in the landlady's stinking kitchen corner. This hopeless ending, however, awakes in the reader a deep compassion for those who suffer, and through it one discovers the profound humanity that makes this novel such a fine beginning to Dostoyevsky's career. Posterity would confirm Belinsky's words: "This debut gives a clear indication of the place Dostoyevsky will come to hold in our literature. Even though with this work, he has not shown himself to be an equal of his predecessors, we shall have to wait a long time before we encounter another talent who comes as close to them as he has."

*Nevsky Prospekt. A lithograph from
the early nineteenth century.*

The Academy of Engineers in St. Petersburg.

Fyodor Dostoyevsky.
Portrait by K. Trutovsky, 1847.

Mikhail Dostoyevsky.
Portrait by K. Trutovsky, 1847.

Vissarion Belinsky.
K. Gorbunov, 1843.

3

DREAM AND CATASTROPHE

". . . and aren't we all more or less dreamers!"

Because of a delay at the censor, *Poor Folk* was not printed before the middle of January 1846. But by that time, the novel already had been for many months the chief topic of conversation in the city's literary salons. "Half of Petersburg is talking about it!" Dostoyevsky exclaimed three months before its publication.

The fame that had come to the young writer might well have turned anyone's head, but for the unbalanced Dostoyevsky it proved to be too much of a good thing. For years he had suffered from an inferiority complex in relation to his rich and wealthy acquaintances. Now it was they who came to visit him. Suddenly, he found himself at the top, the subject of discussion in scores of publications, and his pride and arrogance knew no limit.

> Well, dear brother, I doubt that my fame will ever be greater than it is now. Everywhere I am the object of an unbelievable esteem, the interest in me is, quite simply, tremendous. I have come to know people of high standing. Count Odoyevsky asked me to honor him with a visit, and Baron Sollogub is tearing his hair out in frustration. Everyone regards me as a prodigy. I can't even open my mouth without it being repeated that Dostoyevsky said this or Dostoyevsky plans to do that. . . . Really, dear brother, if I began to recount all my triumphs, I would soon run out of paper.

It wasn't only the visits from barons and counts that incited Dostoyevsky's vanity. Most important was the fact that he was finally an *insider*.

Through Nekrasov and Grigorovich, he was introduced to one of St. Petersburg's foremost literary circles. The gatherings were held at Ivan Panayev's house at the corner of Fontanka and Nevsky Prospekt. Dostoyevsky attended the circle in elegant attire—tie and tails with a top hat—to read from his sensational first novel. "At the time, he was a shy man," a listener recalled, "but the reading made an overwhelming impression on all of us."

In the beginning, the members of the Panayev circle worshiped Dostoyevsky. The great Belinsky showed him "tremendous favor" and treated him like "his own son," and the promising Turgenev—"a truly gifted writer, an aristocrat, who is also beautiful, rich, wise, and refined"—was plainly "in love" with him. Every day he was besieged with more flattering invitations to participate in various literary projects.

Intoxicated by all these expressions of respect and friendship, Dostoyevsky promptly fell in love with Panayev's wife, the beautiful Avdotya Yakovlevna. His immersion in books and manuscripts had given him little time to cultivate his emotional life, and his love for Avdotya stands as the single passion of his youth. In her, he finally encountered a woman whose cultural background was equaled by her outer beauty. The fact that her husband continually deceived her with other women only inflamed the young Dostoyevsky's passion. She was, for that matter, known for responding to her husband's adultery with affairs of her own. His acquaintance with Avdotya was for the writer an introduction to a kind of woman who would occupy a significant place in his life and art: the *femme fatale*.

Madame Panayeva gave the following portrait of Dostoyevsky's Socrates-like entrance into the fashionable company:

> It was evident, from a single glance at Dostoyevsky, that he was extremely nervous and impressionable. He was thin, short, fair-haired, with a sickly complexion; his small grey eyes darted from one thing to another, and his pale lips were stiff and contorted. He already knew most of the guests, but he appeared plainly confused and did not take part in the conversation. Everyone tried to involve him and help him overcome his shyness so that he would feel part of the circle.

But when Dostoyevsky did manage to overcome his uncertainty, he transformed completely. His lack of confidence gave way to the kind of unbridled vanity that he exhibited in his letters to his brother. Not without irony, but not without sympathy either, his worldly hostess further described the young Dostoyevsky:

Because of his youth and nervousness, he did not know how to conduct himself; and he would quite openly express his own conceit as an author and his high opinion of his own literary talent. Completely overcome by his unexpected and brilliant entrance into the literary world, showered with praise by qualified literary critics, he was unable to hide his pride from other young authors who had made more modest debuts in their own writing careers. These young authors were easily insulted; with his irritable and arrogant behavior, he seemed to provoke them intentionally by implying that his talent was immeasurably superior to their own.

In a circle of young, ambitious writers, all of whom were struggling to achieve literary reputations, such behavior was bound to have fatal consequences. Led by the often affectionate but extremely vain Turgenev, the members of the circle began to persecute "the new, red pimple on Literature's nose."

The final break came in the fall of 1846, when Turgenev took the ridicule too far. During one of the gatherings, he began to make fun of a man out in the provinces who went around imagining he was a genius. "Dostoyevsky turned white as a sheet, his entire body began to shake, and he ran from the room without listening to the end of Turgenev's story," Avdotya wrote. Dostoyevsky never returned to the circle after that day. "These people are scoundrels," he wrote to Mikhail in November, "envious profit-seekers." A quarter of a century later Dostoyevsky took bitter revenge by depicting Turgenev as the conceited salon radical Karmazinov in *The Possessed.*

There is no question that envy played an important part in the circle's persecution of Dostoyevsky. "The exaggerated praise that he gave to *Poor Folk,*" Turgenev wrote years later, "was among Belinsky's initial blunders that clearly demonstrated the decline of his critical powers." And now his protégé was running around from one press to another insisting that each page of this tear-jerker be printed in a specially embellished frame. As late as 1880, Dostoyevsky was forced to make public disclosures to the press in order to repudiate this rumor. On the other hand, it is quite understandable that he provoked his colleagues. "I have a terrible vice: a boundless pride and vanity," he confessed in a letter to his brother. "Even when my heart burns with love, I am completely incapable of uttering a single kind word. At such moments I have no control over my nerves. I am aware only that I am ridiculous and offensive, and I suffer terribly from the knowledge that my fellows have received an unjust impression of me. They think me callous and heartless."

The huge success of *Poor Folk* made the break with the Panayev circle particularly painful. From a pinnacle of fame, he had suddenly plummeted to become "the Knight of the Rueful Countenance," to quote one of several lampoons depicting Dostoyevsky. His ailing health threatened to collapse entirely. Working at night, smoking too much, and leading a sedentary life all contributed to growing dizziness, hallucinations, and depression. At the end of April, he reported to his brother that he had been "deathly ill in the full meaning of the words: my entire nervous system was seized violently; the sickness affected my heart and caused powerful hemorrhaging and an infection in the heart tissue that was just barely subdued with compresses and leeches."

Dr. Stepan Yanovsky, Dostoyevsky's new doctor friend, later believed that these nervous attacks, which were accompanied by depression and fears of death, were the early signs of the writer's epilepsy. Today, the illness might be called psychosomatic. In all events, it is clear that Dostoyevsky became even more sensitive than he had been before. "For me St. Petersburg is hell," he wrote after the break with the circle. "It is terribly hard to live here, so terribly hard."

Dostoyevsky's bad health may well have been a factor in his increasingly difficult relations with Belinsky. Their falling out did not take place until 1847, but by then the two men had long been on a collision course concerning both literary issues and politics.

Even in his critique of *Poor Folk*, Belinsky had had a few objections, and in his reviews of Dostoyevsky's following works, his objections became harsher. In Belinsky's view, literature's function was to present problems for debate and exert a moral influence on society. This was what Dostoyevsky had done in his first novel. But in his later works, Belinsky argued, he reverted to the romantic cultivation of what is peculiar and unhealthy. Whereas Belinsky had developed into a champion of the Natural School's critical realism, Dostoyevsky remained an idealistic romantic who insisted on the right to employ fantastic events and utopian visions in his work. He refused to allow politics to bridle his art, which is not to say that he was opposed to realistic depiction, but rather that for him realism was a tool for investigating human psychology. For Belinsky, on the other hand, realism had become the only valid literary method. Only through the depiction of current reality could the writer attain his objective: to portray and analyze the life of the people, and in so doing reveal the status quo and the way to change it for the better.

After a while it became very clear that the revolutionary critic and the utopian writer were heading in different directions. And the "raging Vissarion" did not hesitate to speak his mind about his disappointment and condemnation. "In our time, the fantastic belongs only in the madhouse, not in literature, and should be left to the charge of doctors, not writers," he wrote in his review of *The Double*. "What terrible nonsense!" he wrote about the mystical-fantastical "Landlady." "Every new work of Dostoyevsky's is a further step down. . . . I think, dear friends, we may have hit bottom with this genius."

Belinsky's scathing criticism was a big disappointment to Dostoyevsky, particularly when it was measured against the effusive reception that the critic had given *Poor Folk*. Dostoyevsky had fallen swiftly from favor. Perhaps he was only a passing literary vogue. Perhaps he would never become a Gogol. In *Netochka Nezvanova*, he portrayed his growing doubts about his own talent and his bitter disappointment over the injustice of those who had once been his friends:

> This much must be understood: talent needs sympathy. But just wait and see what kind of people flock to you as soon as you have achieved even the smallest success. They won't give a second thought to that which you have gained through hard work, self-denial, hunger and sleepless nights, all this they will look upon with contempt. They will not encourage you or comfort you, these friends; they won't point to what is good and true within you; all they will do is point out your faults with malicious glee.

There is reason to believe, however, that it was ideological differences more than anything else that led to the break between Dostoyevsky and Belinsky. When they first came to know each other in 1845, Belinsky was still under the influence of French utopian socialists—Saint-Simon, Lamennais, Charles Fourier, and Etienne Cabet. The utopian socialists were primarily preoccupied with the moral content of the Gospels. For them Christ was a divine figure who had been sent to earth to preach love and brotherhood. Their goal was to free Christ's teaching from the reactionary distortions of the church and to attempt to realize the best for the people— the enslaved and persecuted. The utopians believed in a Christian socialism which taught that God had chosen humanity to participate in the completion of creation. Man was not innately evil but "beautiful," "perfect"; the soul of man was "a ray from the Godhead." For them socialism did not mean revolution but rather a kind of modern version of the Sermon on the Mount, which called for brotherhood in a time marked by a universal struggle for money and power. "God said that all men should be brothers," Saint-Simon wrote. "Within this high command lies all that is holy in the Christian religion."

This humanitarian perspective informed *Poor Folk* and all of Dostoyevsky's work in the 1840s. But Belinsky went further; by the mid-1840s, he began to liberate himself from the Christian socialism of the utopians. He found himself increasingly sympathetic to the critique of religion and the materialistic view of divinity that was expressed by such Left Hegelians as David Friedrich Strauss and Ludwig Andreas Feuerbach. The repudiation of Christ's divinity was followed by the repudiation of his moral teachings.

The result was that Belinsky's ideas, which once had been bound to Christianity, were now linked to atheism. In contrast to the utopian's "socialism without hate," Belinsky's revolutionary socialism was actively opposed to Christianity, the religion that had created the moral principles of a society that now was to be destroyed so that a new communistic world could be built. In 1845, even before Belinsky's friendship with Dostoyevsky, he wrote to Alexander Herzen that for him the words "God" and "religion" evoked only "darkness, gloom, chains, and whips."

In his memoirs, Dostoyevsky wrote that "the passionate socialist" Belinsky brought up atheism in their very first conversation, and that he (Dostoyevsky) "received his instruction passionately." But these words must be seen in light of the trauma that his later "revolutionary" activity brought about, when his guilt feelings disposed Dostoyevsky to exaggerate his ideological agreement with Belinsky. His strong belief in free will and the immortality of the soul made it difficult for him to follow his mentor in the direction of atheism and communism. Even though Christianity is seldom alluded to directly in Dostoyevsky's early work, there is nothing to indicate that he had lost the faith of his childhood. On the contrary, he attended church diligently, fasted regularly, and often spoke to his friends about Christian love and mercy. "Dostoyevsky's surest medicine against spiritual ailments was always prayer," Yanovsky wrote, "and he prayed not only for the innocent, but for flagrant sinners." There are a number of accounts that tell how Dostoyevsky winced each time Belinsky attacked Christian teaching. The critic even had the gall to call Christ a "scoundrel"!

Although Dostoyevsky's Christian socialism contained a revolutionary message, its ideological distance from Belinsky's subversive atheism was clear from the very beginning. Especially repugnant to him must have been Belinsky's belief that human beings are not responsible for their evil desires but are simply forced to do evil by an unjust society. In "The Grand Inquisitor" Dostoyevsky returns to this idea—that there is no crime and no sin, only hunger and the hungry.

There are generally striking parallels between the ideas of Ivan Karamazov and Belinsky. Ivan's refusal to accept a future world harmony if it was to be achieved through meaningless suffering echoes Belinsky's rebellion in the early 1840s against Hegel's theory of synthesis. "What good does it do me to know that reason will conquer, that all will be well in the future, if fate has destined me to experience chance, the irrational, and the triumph of brute force?" Belinsky asked in 1841. "I don't even want my happiness to be free, if I cannot feel at peace about my fellow men. . . . It is said that discord is the condition for harmony; this is perhaps advantageous and beneficial for music lovers, but not for those who are fated to be the expressions of this disharmony."

Dostoyevsky's discussions with Belinsky were of central importance to his development. The doubts Belinsky raised about the fundamental premises of Christianity had a fruitful effect on Dostoyevsky's inquiry into existential problems. The man who suddenly loses his faith, who chooses to "return his entrance ticket," would be a frequent theme in his writing. In Belinsky, Dostoyevsky had the opportunity to observe a human being who hungered for revenge on the past. "And I have burned everything that I once worshiped."

His break with the Belinsky circle led Dostoyevsky to seek new soulmates. He found them in the so-called Beketov circle, which he began visiting in September 1846, shortly after Belinsky's highly critical review of *The Double*. The power behind this group was Aleksei Beketov, a former classmate of Dostoyevsky's at the Academy of Engineers, along with his younger brothers, Andrei and Nikolai, who studied the sciences and later became professors of botany and chemistry. Like Dostoyevsky, they were ardent supporters of utopian socialism, and they all came "to rail against oppression and injustice"—to borrow the expression of one of the circle's members. The circle even attempted to put Fourier's ideas into practice by forming a commune. Apparently, it was the penniless Dostoyevsky who proposed the idea. For thirty-five rubles a month, Dostoyevsky was provided with his own room as well as dinner and tea. To judge from letters to his brother, the commune functioned very well, at least for Dostoyevsky, who probably made good use of the collective savings. "These are active, intelligent people with good hearts, fine people with strong characters. They have made me well with their company," he reported at the end of November.

Among the writers in the Beketov circle, Dostoyevsky became especially fond of the poet Aleksei Pleshcheyev and the Maikov brothers—Valerian the literary critic and Apollon the poet. He was impressed with Pleshcheyev's passionate proclamation of the principles of Christian socialism, and comforted and pleased when Valerian Maikov defended him against Belinsky in a way that must have reflected very closely the writer's own view of his work: "Whereas both Gogol and Dostoyevsky portray the real world, Gogol is primarily a social writer, and Dostoyevsky is primarily a psychological writer. For the former, the individual is significant as a representative of a particular society, for the latter society is important because of its impact on an individual personality." Maikov focuses on a characteristic feature of Dostoyevsky's novels: society portrayed through the consciousness of his characters. For Belinsky, this represented a deviation from the principles of the Natural School, but Maikov believed that this internalization of the portrayal of society was desirable, because it invigorated the school, and he condemned Belinsky as dictatorial and inflexible for not allowing the writer to develop according to his own lights.

The sympathy of this "intelligent and promising" critic helped Dostoyevsky to find himself during a period of crisis. When Maikov was killed in an accident in the summer of 1847, his death was a painful loss, for he was perhaps the one critic who understood the originality of Dostoyevsky's early work.

When the Beketov circle was disbanded with the brothers' move to Kazan in early 1847, Dostoyevsky had already been introduced to a new circle which met at the home of the Maikov brothers' father, Nikolai, a distinguished member of the Academy of Art. The host had decorated his beautiful apartment on Morskaya Street himself, and his neoclassical portraits of women were famous all over St. Petersburg.

In this cultivated circle, Dostoyevsky acquired an excellent understanding of classical art and philosophy. It may have also been here, where the spirit of antiquity seemed so alive, that he first glimpsed his vision of the Golden Age—a time of innocence and happiness, peace and tolerance, a time before men knew war, sin, or evil. Inebriated by utopian socialist ideas,

Dostoyevsky believed in the realization of this vision. "The time of trial is over, the Golden Age lies before us!" Dostoyevsky read in the writings of Pierre Joseph Proudhon. It is against this ideological background that Dostoyevsky's "revolutionary" beliefs of the 1840s must be seen.

And yet, it seemed that the peace and tolerance of the Golden Age were still far away. Even in the Maikov family's refined temple of the intellect, Dostoyevsky was subject to violent outbursts which made painful apologies to his hostess necessary afterward. "I beg for your forgiveness," he wrote in May 1848. "Yesterday I left your house in such a volatile state that the whole situation became improper. . . . I fled purely from instinct, because I sensed that weakness in my character which can flare up in certain 'extreme moments' with such *hyberbolic* excess."

Dostoyevsky's increasing distance from the Belinsky circle was also due to financial circumstances. In 1846, Nekrasov bought the ailing periodical *The Contemporary*, which, with Belinsky as its head, soon became Russia's leading radical organ. But unlike his colleagues, Dostoyevsky had not been able to free himself from *The Contemporary*'s competitor, *Notes of the Fatherland*. He had come to depend upon the advances he received for unfinished works and had become a slave to the journal's demanding editor, Andrei Krayevsky.

After a period of relative good fortune owing to his inheritance and royalties from his work, the writer once again began to fill his letters with references to economic worries. "When will I ever get out of this debt?" he complained in December 1846. "Krayevsky's system keeps me enslaved and dependent. Everything is ruined, talent and youth, hope and creative desire." At the end of his life, Dostoyevsky gave this characteristic advice to a young writer: "Remember that you must never sell your soul. . . . Never accept payment in advance. All my life I have suffered from this. . . . Never give a work to the printer before it is finished. This is the worst thing you can do . . . it constitutes the murder of your own ideas." In spite of this, one cannot but wonder if the pressures and deadlines were not in the end beneficial to Dostoyevsky, in that they kept him in a state of tension necessary for the swift expression of the ideas that continually welled up within him.

Dostoyevsky's habit of giving away money to those who were just a bit poorer than himself could hardly have helped his finances. In the summer of 1847, he organized a collection for a drunk who wandered about St. Petersburg's suburbs offering to "whip himself" for money from the area's summer visitors.

These circumstances made it difficult for Dostoyevsky to concentrate on a big new project. In order to keep his creditors somewhat at bay, he had to accept job offers of proofreading and newspaper work. In the summer of 1847 he published four feuilletons in the *St. Petersburg Times*, articles that demonstrate that even as a young man, Dostoyevsky had a great gift for journalism. Both informal and intimate, Dostoyevsky's reflections gave his readers insight into the daily life of the capital.

The elements of greatest interest in the feuilletons, however, are the satirical portraits of contemporary literary circles. Dostoyevsky, who was later to have such strong Slavophile leanings, presented himself in these articles as a "Westernizer": in order to overcome its backwardness, Russia must model itself upon the West, he argued. He opposed the Slavophile inclination to view the Kremlin as the ideal monument to Russian nationality, and instead hailed the city on the Neva, the incarnation of Peter's "great idea," as the symbol of Russia's desire to attain Western enlightenment.

Even though Dostoyevsky had long been an enthusiastic supporter of emancipation for the serfs, there is little in these articles that betrays his later belief that the Russian people were in possession of special virtues and moral qualities. "What are the people?" he asks in one of the feuilletons. "The people are ignorant; they lack education and look for their leaders among those in the learned class." This position is in diametric opposition to the stand Dostoyevsky took after his imprisonment. His view of the intelligentsia as the leaders of the people is typical of the impatient "Westernizer" of the 1840s. And it was precisely this perception of the intelligentsia's vanguard role that brought Dostoyevsky into contact with the radical Petrashevsky circle.

II

Mikhail Butashevich-Petrashevsky, six months older than Dostoyevsky, was by 1846 notorious in St. Petersburg for his outrageous and rebellious behavior. He was rumored to have appeared one day at Mass in a woman's dress and to have begun to pray with the women. People were scandalized (not the least because the lady had a beard) and the police were called. "My dear lady," asked the officer, "apparently you are a disguised man?" "And you, my good sir, are apparently a disguised woman," Petrashevsky is said to have answered pertly before he disappeared into the crowd. Most people found it difficult to take this eccentric seriously as he wandered about in his enormous cape and sombrero. There were those who commented that he had more "intellect than wisdom." In all events, he attracted a great deal of attention to himself with his singular style.

Petrashevsky had received his early education at the famous Alexander Lyceum in Tsarskoye Selo, and there he had gained a reputation as a rebel. Later he had studied law at the University of St. Petersburg, which had landed him a position as a translator in the Ministry of Foreign Affairs. Like Dostoyevsky, Petrashevsky had early become enamored of the utopian socialism of Fourier. The two became superficially acquainted in the spring of 1846, when Petrashevsky accosted Dostoyevsky on the street and wanted to know the idea for his next book. But it was not until a year later that the writer began to attend Petrashevsky's Friday night gatherings.

To call the Petrashevsky circle "revolutionary" in the word's current meaning would be an exaggeration. In a letter to Alexander Herzen, Mikhail Bakunin reported that it was made up of the "most innocent and harmless company" and that its members were "systematic opponents of all revolutionary goals and means." This was hardly a unified organization. "They had only one thing in common," an observer of the group wrote in his memoirs, "their youth—still untouched by the experience of life."

On these Friday evenings, ten to twenty people of highly varied backgrounds gathered in Petrashevsky's ramshackle apartment to discuss incendiary questions. It was exciting to play at liberalism, particularly over a glass of wine, and the host always had plenty of wine, even if it was of variable quality. When the debate became too heated, the assembly was called to order with the aid of a little bronze bell. As aging men, the participants remembered this bell as a "terrible revolutionary weapon."

Gradually the discussions began to take on a more radical character as the number of guests increased. Dangerous topics such as emancipation of the serfs, reform of the judicial system, and the struggle against censorship were taken up, generally under the leadership of some "specialist."

A common theme of discussion was the great disparity between social classes in the country. "What are we witness to in Russia?" the temperamental Nikolai Mombelli asked in his memoirs: "Millions of people live in conditions of the most terrible suffering, without the most fundamental human rights, either because of their heritage or because they lack the means of existence, while at the same time a tiny caste of the privileged wallow in luxury and vanity." The Tsar should see for himself the joys of subsisting on the pitiful bread mixed with straw that made up the everyday diet of ordinary peasants in the Vitebsk district, Mombelli suggested.

Among the guests some were determined to describe the paradise that would come into being after the collapse of the "rotten, centuries-old structure," at which time people would live in "prosperity, abundance, and joy." Few, however, were willing to discuss practical measures for making this vision a reality. The circle's host was himself opposed to any struggle that was not certain of victory and even declared himself prepared to kill the man who dared set himself up as the "revolution's dictator."

Luckily, there were many rooms in Petrashevsky's apartment. Its greatest attraction was a large book collection which he had assembled through his connections in the Ministry of Foreign Affairs. At a time when one in four books was forbidden by the censor, Petrashevsky's guests had access to all that Europe had to offer in the way of politically subversive writing. Books by radical authors such as Strauss, Blanc, and Proudhon now took up an appreciable share of Dostoyevsky's reading.

Dostoyevsky and Petrashevsky never developed a close relationship; between them there was only mutual respect and sympathy. Like Belinsky, Petrashevsky quickly developed from a utopian Fourierist to a material socialist. A few years earlier, he had created an uproar by publishing a *Pocket Dictionary of Foreign Words That Have Entered the Russian Language*. The book was in fact a kind of socialist encyclopedia that included definitions of such words as "materialism," "natural rights," and "mysticism," definitions that served as diatribes against Russian society. The remaining copies of a second edition were later confiscated and burned by the authorities, who found in this "poison book" a mixture of "socialism, communism, and other forms of current madness."

By this time, Petrashevsky had long since abandoned his Christian faith. In his view Christ was little more than a "well-known demagogue whose career met with a very unhappy end," and during debates he condemned religion as a hindrance to progress. Even though Dostoyevsky shared Petrashevsky's view of the intelligentsia's instructive role among the people, he found it difficult to tolerate Petrashevsky's blasphemous remarks about religion and could not accept his friend's view that legal reform should take precedence over the liberation of the serfs. The writer never really felt at home in this atheistic circle of salon radicals, and often months would go by between his visits.

The revolutionary activity in Western Europe in the winter and spring of 1848, however, quickened Dostoyevsky's political commitment. News of the February revolution created an atmosphere of panic at the Winter Palace. Rumors circulated that the Tsar himself had come running into the ballroom and ordered his dancing officers to their mounts: "Saddle your horses, gentlemen! A republic has been proclaimed in France!" Every day brought further announcements of greater freedom for people in the West, and the hunger for freedom was infectious. The secret police had estimated that the number of peasant rebellions had quadrupled. When the cannon sounded its warning during the St. Petersburg flood in the autumn of 1848, many were already aware that the revolution had begun. The result was that the Tsar's regime became more oppressive. Plans to emancipate the serfs were tabled; the censor became even more prohibitive. Even the word "progress" was stricken from the official lexicon.

There was tremendous ferment in intellectual circles. The numbers in attendance at Petrashevsky's grew continually, and by the fall of 1848, Dostoyevsky had become a regular guest. Information about his involvement with the Petrashevsky circle is scanty. A deep-rooted suspiciousness prevented him from writing letters at this time, and furthermore, his most significant correspondent, his brother Mikhail, had just moved to St. Petersburg. After his arrest, Dostoyevsky quite understandably trivialized his involvement with the circle. "Everybody who knows me is well aware that I am not a prattler," he wrote. "I do not like to speak loudly or at length even with my few friends, and even less so in society where I am known to be taciturn, reserved and unsociable." To the investigating commission, Dostoyevsky admitted speaking only three times on the subject of personality and egoism.

But to judge from the accounts of others, Dostoyevsky was considerably more active during the meetings. Among other things, he read subversive poems by Derzhavin and Pushkin as well as passages from his own works. If Dostoyevsky never became a wholehearted supporter of the group, his reasons were the same as they had been in his dispute with Belinsky: his differing view of the role of art. The writer did not like Petrashevsky's criticism of him for refusing to employ literature as a propaganda tool in the service of social change. Dostoyevsky replied to these accusations by saying that art was an end in itself and that the tendency to put art in the service of politics constrained the writer's freedom and weakened artistic quality.

Dostoyevsky must also have reacted to the general inclination of the

Petrashevsky circle to seek their models for Russian society in the socialist doctrines of the West. The highly regimented, barracklike existence in Fourier's "phalanxes" were in Dostoyevsky's mind "worse than slave labor." Hadn't Petrashevsky himself built a "collective" for his peasants only to watch them set fire to it the day before they were to move in? There were already plenty of socialist-like institutions in Russia. Why not develop the cooperative and communal institutions that had been a reality on Russian soil for centuries? Here existed the foundation for a new, Russian form of communal ownership. There was no need to import Western socialism that would lead sooner or later to an unfree anthill society.

Rather than importing foreign institutions, one should concentrate on getting rid of serfdom, an indigenous and evil institution. For Dostoyevsky, serfdom was morally reprehensible, a blight upon society, and he never tired of railing against the violence and misuse of power that were the result of man's right to own other men. For many of those in attendance at Petrashevsky's circle, the passionate writer must have appeared to be an ideal political agitator. "To this day, I can see Fyodor Mikhailovich before me at one of Petrashevsky's evenings," Ippolit Debu wrote many years later. "I can still hear his words about how a sergeant in the Finnish regiment was made to run the gauntlet because he had taken revenge on the squad commander for his barbarous treatment of his men, or his words about how landowners abused their serfs." Pyotr Semyonov gave a similar picture of Dostoyevsky at this time:

> Dostoyevsky was never and could never be a *revolutionary*, but as a man of feeling he was easily moved to indignation and hatred at the sight of violence perpetrated against the oppressed and victimized. This is what happened when he heard about a sergeant in the Finnish regiment who had to run the gauntlet. It was only under such circumstances that Dostoyevsky felt ready to run into the street with a red flag, but there were not many in the Petrashevsky circle who could have imagined doing so.

Such sentiments are understandable in the young Dostoyevsky who had witnessed the brutal blows of the government courier and who was well aware of his own father's harshness toward his serfs. There were very few among the theorizing salon radicals in the Petrashevsky circle who would have dared take an active part in the struggle against serfdom. Among those few was the silent, proud Nikolai Speshnev, who was soon to give Dostoyevsky his first lessons in the art of conspiracy.

Speshnev had begun to frequent the Petrashevsky circle in December 1847, after having spent five years abroad. This wealthy, cosmopolitan aristocrat was from the first a mythic figure. The romantic conquests of his European wanderings were as innumerable as his revolutionary contacts. In addition to utopian socialism, he had studied secret societies and the *Communist Manifesto*, and it was rumored that he had even been a volunteer in the so-called Sonderbund War in Switzerland.

Like Stavrogin in *The Possessed*, Speshnev, with his imperturbable mien and enigmatic superiority, did nothing to suppress these rumors. "He was tall with chiseled features," a female admirer wrote, "and his dark brown curls fell over his shoulders in waves, and his eyes were filled with a quiet melancholy." Others commented that his "astonishing manly beauty" might have been a model for the Savior himself. Even the anarchist Bakunin was impressed by this "cold" and "calm" man, "a gentleman from head to foot." "He had great power over others," Bakunin noted. "Everyone looks up to him and expects something special from him." "This man has a singular destiny," Dostoyevsky exclaimed several years later. "Wherever he goes, he is surrounded by awe and respect paid to him by those of open and reserved natures alike."

The "first Russian Communist" had little but contempt for the verbose armchair radicalism of the Petrashevsky circle. Beauty and ugliness, good and evil, nobility and baseness—all this was merely "a matter of taste." What Russia needed was not endless discussions about changes made from the top, but a socialist upheaval from the bottom, and a subsequent erection of a strong state that would guarantee "food for all." In one of his speeches, he declared that only verbal propaganda was possible in Russia. "And therefore, gentlemen, since we are left only with the spoken word, I intend to use it, without the slightest shame or conscience, to propagandize for socialism, atheism, terrorism, and all that is good. And I advise you to do the same."

Despite his authority and prestige, Speshnev received little support, and in December 1848, he broke all ties to Petrashevsky. During that revolutionary year, he nevertheless managed to recruit a handful of converts, and with these he attempted to establish a "Russian Society." Among its members was Dostoyevsky.

It is not easy to understand what the deeply religious Dostoyevsky saw in this "secretive guest." But Speshnev's powerful personality, which appeared even more pronounced when compared to the "prattlers" of the

Petrashevsky circle, must have made a tremendous impression on the young idealist and blinded him to reality. At last he had found a man of action! And in reference to the most urgent question, the emancipation of the serfs, he and Speshnev were of one mind. Dostoyevsky probably nurtured a hope that this reform would come from above, from the Tsar, but what if this did not occur? "Then let it happen through rebellion!" he is said to have exclaimed.

The goal of Speshnev's Russian Society was to lay the groundwork for political revolution. Its members were to spread discontent in the government and to set up contacts within those groups who were already dissatisfied: students, dissidents, peasants, and soldiers. Its members were also required to swear a loyalty oath that obliged them to take part in armed struggle as soon as the "executive committee" gave the signal for revolution. And finally they were required to recruit new members for the organization. This arrangement, including the threat of execution for betraying the cause, is recapitulated in *The Possessed*, which was written under the influence of the trial against Sergei Nechayev. Dostoyevsky later admitted that he could himself have been a "Nechayevist" in his youth. "I would have abandoned all reason had it not been for the catastrophe that changed my life," he wrote. "I was seized by an idea, and compared to it, both my health and my troubles seemed trivial."

One January evening in 1849, Dostoyevsky paid an unexpected visit to his friend Apollon Maikov, who had also frequented the Petrashevsky circle. He had come on an "important errand." Would Maikov join the secret society? "Petrashevsky," Dostoyevsky said, "is nothing but a fool, a charlatan and a chatterbox—nothing serious ever comes out of him." Therefore a group of "serious people" had formed a secret plan of action. "With what goal?" Maikov asked, frightened. "With the goal of creating a revolution in Russia, of course," Dostoyevsky answered. "We have already set into motion a plan to get a printing press . . . everything is ready."

"Dostoyevsky sat there like the dying Socrates before his friends," Maikov wrote. "He wore only his nightshirt, which was unbuttoned at the collar, and was so eloquent in his description of the sanctity of the cause and our duty to save the fatherland that I finally began to laugh and joke." Didn't he realize how serious this was, Maikov continued, that the entire enterprise was doomed to failure, and that he must get out of it as fast as he could? "No, that's my business," Dostoyevsky answered darkly. "But understand

that there are only seven people who know about this. You are the eighth—
there must not be a ninth."

The writer must have known that he was gambling with his future.
But it was too late. He had succumbed to Speshnev's powerful personality
and had begun to feel less and less free. Dr. Yanovsky reported that at this
time Dostoyevsky became more and more depressed, irritable, and touchy.
He would quarrel over a trifle and often complained of dizziness. When
Dr. Yanovsky certified that there was no organic reason for these symptoms
and that they would soon pass, Dostoyevsky protested: "No, they will not
pass; they will torment me for a long time, because I have accepted money
from Speshnev (he named a sum of around five hundred rubles) and now
I am *with him*, I am *his*. I will never be able to pay back such a sum, and
he will never take back the money, that is the kind of person he is. . . . Don't
you understand that I have a Mephistopheles of my own around my neck!"

The heaviest burden of all was the knowledge that he had accepted
money. Accepting payment is used as a determining argument in *The Possessed* by Peter Verkhovensky when he reminds Kirilov of his promise to
commit suicide. "You have bound yourself to it. You have given your word.
You have taken money. All this you must admit."

III

One would think that the many disappointments and pressures that Dostoyevsky endured at this time would have made him unfit for creative work.
But his youthful writing is, at least in terms of genre, the most varied of his
career. Most of this fiction is admittedly short, and none of it can compare
with *Poor Folk*, but together these works are testimony to the young Dostoyevsky's artistic range and his desire to assert his originality.

In *Poor Folk*, Dostoyevsky had portrayed his characters with sympathy
and compassion. In *The Double*, published only a few weeks later, he
abandoned his role as humanitarian and turned psychologist. He had begun
to investigate the depths of the human psyche, and what he discovered was
not necessarily intended to inspire compassion in the reader.

The Double is a study in persecution madness. The author traces a
man's inevitable path toward psychological disintegration, but he chooses
a difficult form in which to carry this out. The outside world is depicted

through the eyes of a madman, and it is not always easy to determine the author's view of his character. As a result, *The Double* has become one of Dostoyevsky's most controversial works. "The idea is excellent," Dostoyevsky wrote thirty years later, "and I have never contributed anything more significant to literature than this idea. But I was very unlucky with the form of the story."

The relationship of *The Double* to Dostoyevsky's first work is obvious. When Devushkin is called in for a hearing with the General, he gives the following account of his fear: "My heart began to shudder within me; I don't know why I was so frightened; I only know that I was panic-stricken as I had never been before in my whole life. I sat rooted to my chair—and I pretended there was nothing the matter—as though it were not I." In this passage, Dostoyevsky described the terror that in his subsequent work would lead to the protagonist's division and the appearance of the double. Golyadkin is also an oppressed civil servant, a man warped by the state bureaucracy and terrified of losing favor with his superior. But in him all that he has repressed is unleashed in insanity. It is doubtful, however, that Golyadkin's madness is purely the result of environmental factors. Unlike his colleague in *Poor Folk*, Golyadkin is rather well off. He suffers not from poverty but from vanity, the base ambitions of a social climber. He has already come up in the world a bit. He is a titular councillor, a title that corresponds to captain in the military. In spite of this, he remains an underling and has fallen in love with the chief's daughter. Doesn't he after all deserve further promotion?

One of the central themes of *Poor Folk*, the struggle for self-respect, is transformed in the *The Double* into the struggle for self-promotion; while self-respect is a condition for being human, self-promotion may lead to pride and "pride goeth before a fall." Golyadkin has pretensions of significance in a society that teaches that everyone must know his place. He imagines himself a hero, but at the same time he is aware that he is merely playing a role that does not suit him. In his struggle for promotion, Golyadkin is outstripped by the chief's nephew, who also beats him in the contest for the chief's daughter. He is locked out of the milieu to which he pretends to belong. When his stifled attempts at self-assertion show themselves to be bankrupt, Golyadkin's double appears. Some have claimed that the double is a person of flesh and blood, while others—probably correctly—maintain that he is only a phantom, the product of Golyadkin's vanishing hold on reality. In any case, for Golyadkin Sr. Golyadkin Jr. is quite real. He is simultaneously a creature of a wish-fulfillment dream and nightmare.

In the beginning, Golyadkin Jr. is polite and humble, just as Golyadkin Sr. had once been. But as soon as the double has won Golyadkin's confidence and discovered his secrets, he begins to exploit him shamelessly. In his victorious superiority, the double is the image of Golyadkin's repressed, unconscious desires and at the same time an expression of the guilt that accompanies them.

Ruin is inevitable. Golyadkin cannot assert himself without violating the ethics that keep him subservient. And his primitive ambitions and vain desires deprive him of the sympathy that Dostoyevsky had so generously bestowed on Devushkin in *Poor Folk*. In Dostoyevsky's satirical portrait, Golyadkin is an instance of pathology, a man who is himself largely responsible for his problems. Though the writer's original intention may have been to show how Russian society creates damaging pressures on its members, the novella reads today as the story of a sick man's nervous breakdown. It lacks both the critical exposure of society and the human sympathy Belinsky had hoped to find in a work by the author of *Poor Folk*.

In "A Faint Heart" (1848) Dostoyevsky returns to the miserable world of the civil servant, and again it is the psychology of the little bureaucrat rather than his environment that preoccupies the author. Once again Dostoyevsky tells the story of a civil servant who goes mad, but this time the main character is more sympathetic and the fable more original: the protagonist goes insane from gratitude. Is it possible for a human being to lose his mind from feelings of gratitude? It is possible if he has no capacity for its expression, if he feels that he is undeserving of his good fortune, and if beneath his happiness he hides feelings of servile obedience and inferiority.

As is often the case in Dostoyevsky's fiction, the story is rooted in real events. The model for Vasya Shumkov, "the weak heart" who feels undeserving of his good luck, was a young author named Yakov Butkov. Dostoyevsky knew him well. They worked together at *Notes of the Fatherland*. Butkov grew up in impoverished circumstances in a small provincial town. Early in the 1840s, this self-taught young man came on foot to St. Petersburg to make his living as a writer. In his first story, he described the lot of poor writers battling hunger in filthy garrets and how they trembled in fear before their "betters" in the city's bureaucratic offices. The story appealed to current tastes, and the periodical's omnipotent editor, Andrei Krayevsky, expected great things from this industrious if somewhat absentminded contributor.

Then one day misfortune struck. Butkov was drafted. Conscription was a serious matter in Russia: the term of service was twenty-five years. Fortunately Krayevsky had a connection in the right place and was able to buy the young man's freedom. Butkov was beside himself with joy; the editor had saved his life! But Krayevsky demanded ample payment for his beneficence: very soon Butkov found himself wretchedly dependent on his benefactor, for Krayevsky overwhelmed him with crushingly hard, poorly paid work and, in the end, let Butkov die in a hospital for the poor.

"A faint heart" is a name Dostoyevsky gave to a number of characters in his early work. The expression is always connected with the tyranny of the poor and the defenseless. These faint hearts allow themselves to be so completely oppressed by their fates that even happiness strikes them as a deviation from the natural order of things. They feel that happiness is only on loan to them and that they will have to pay for their moment of joy a hundred times over. So for the oppressed, even happiness is poisoned by feelings of guilt and inferiority.

How then can a man be in a position to bear his own happiness? All human beings must be happy. Vasya is among Dostoyevsky's many dreamers, those who believe that the human right to happiness will only be realized when enemies embrace. Joy cannot exist for a single individual. Only a universal brotherly love will bring joy and harmony to all people. "A Weak Heart" is a testimony to the utopian Christian influences on Dostoyevsky. In these early works, Dostoyevsky dreamed of a utopia that existed beyond the cold morass of St. Petersburg, and this is the final vision of the story—in the blood-violet colors of the sunset, Vasya's friend sees the dawning of a new city, a millennium in which even the weak hearts would find happiness.

In this story, one encounters a combination of two character-types who inhabit Dostoyevsky's early work: the little bureaucrat and the dreamer. "Do you know what a dreamer is, gentlemen?" Dostoyevsky asked in one of his 1847 feuilletons. He gave the following description of this "neuter being":

The dreamer is a St. Petersburg nightmare; he is the incarnation of sin, a tragedy—silent, secretive, gloomy, wild, full of fears, catastrophes, peripeteia, intrigues and resolutions, and I do not say this in jest. You perhaps have yourself encountered such an abstracted being, with his vague, cloudy eyes, his often pale and anguished face, continually consumed by some superhuman task and seemingly exhausted by great exertions, but in reality he accomplishes absolutely nothing.

That Dostoyevsky feels akin to this dreamer is made clear at the end of the description: "And are we not all more or less dreamers?" There is little doubt that the author was familiar with this type of person from his own experience.

In "White Nights" (1848) Dostoyevsky tells the story of a dreamer as he is depicted in all Romantic writing—which is not to say that the ambitious and introverted Dostoyevsky can be absolutely identified with this kind and openhearted character. The hero in the story has wasted his life on daydreams, whereas the young writer was well known for his industriousness. The dreamer has accomplished nothing, and Dostoyevsky was already famous. And whereas the dreamer lives alone without friends or acquaintances, the writer was at that time living in a collective.

Yet he suffered from the same weakness. His condemnation of the dreamer is considerably toned down from his feuilleton sketch of the previous year; the political commitment has disappeared—there are neither starving clerks nor terrorizing superiors—and the entire story is imbued with an atmosphere of music, love, and romantic fantasy. The material world plays a minor role in this most lyrical of all his stories.

The events unfold during several "white" nights in June, nights of an enchanted, almost otherworldly beauty. The nameless dreamer meets the young Nastenka down on one of the river's piers. She is standing there waiting for a lover who does not come. The dreamer falls in love and feels that the bliss of romantic fantasy is about to come true. He who once regarded real life as impoverished and undesirable is suddenly willing to sacrifice all his "years of fantasy" for a single day of that pitiful reality. But the dream of reality is also uncertain and short-lived. Nastenka's lover returns, and the dreamer withdraws once again into loneliness and isolation. He had been given only a brief time of nearness to her heart. He expresses his sorrow indirectly, not with high-sounding complaints about unhappy fate; rather he is happy to have received the gift that just one moment of bliss represents. "Oh Lord! One moment of bliss! Isn't such a moment enough, even for the whole of a man's life?" With this, the writer ends his story.

The pathos of resignation, of a broken heart, informs this passage. And these words are expressed fifteen years later by the reflective Underground Man, who, with Nietzsche, believes that man may dream as long as he is conscious of what he does. The misery over losing reality threatens to become the self-hatred of a bruised ego, and the story becomes a message about the dangers of fantasy nourished in isolation.

Dostoyevsky knew well the danger of dreaming a life away, but he also knew that dreams are necessary. He liked people who were full of longing, who were not satisfied with what could be easily obtained. From his earliest years, he was plagued by the pain of loneliness and isolation, and it haunted him for his entire life. Out of this pain came his longing for the unity of all people, his longing for universal oneness, and within this longing there was always hope. One can always hope for that which has not yet come to pass, that which one wants to believe in, and wants to hope for.

But the distance between the dream and reality was too great. The dreamer of "White Nights" had experienced this, and now it was the dreamer Dostoyevsky's turn. A dream had driven him to rebellion and now it pushed him to the brink of catastrophe.

During the winter of 1848–49, the Petrashevsky circle spawned a number of offshoots. The participants in these new groups belonged to the original circle's left wing. By forming smaller splinter groups, they hoped to be able to concentrate on their special interests and at the same time create a surer defense against infiltration. Petrashevsky was known for inviting all kinds of people to his gatherings, and suspicions within the group that there might be informants among them had grown steadily stronger.

The most radical of these splinter groups met at the apartment of Sergei Durov and Alexander Palm. Pleshcheyev and Dostoyevsky were the initiators of this new circle, and Speshnev also frequented the group after Dostoyevsky invited him. The Durov circle began as an artistically oriented club whose members gathered for literary readings and to listen to music. But before long Speshnev had managed to incite a revolutionary fervor. Outrage against censorship and serfdom were expressed with increasing boldness. Wasn't it time to take some action? "There are three ways to achieve political goals," Speshnev directed. "Intrigue, propaganda, and violence. If I were to take action I would choose the last, and the means would be a peasant uprising."

In his campaign to radicalize the Durov circle, Speshnev was aided by his disciples. His officers, Nikolai Mombelli and Nikolai Grigoryev, eagerly began to write articles against the government, and Pavel Filippov suggested that the group begin the illegal distribution of pamphlets and brochures. Speshnev had good connections with radical periodicals abroad and was ready to help writers who felt constrained by the censors. It was at Speshnev's, in earshot of Dostoyevsky, that Grigoryev read his "A Soldier's Conversation," a subversive propaganda piece in which the Tsar himself is mocked and ridiculed. There is some evidence to suggest that Dostoyevsky, like his less radical brother, found himself in opposition to the conspiracy that now began to take shape. But we also know that he was eventually sentenced for "participation in plans to write articles against the government and to distribute them by means of a printing press."

The gatherings at Petrashevsky's continued, however, and they functioned something like plenary sessions. Here, too, the discussion became more daring. "No, Tsar Nicholas is not a human being," Mombelli said, "he is a monster, a beast—he is the equivalent of the Antichrist of the Apocalypse." Petrashevsky's views were not significantly milder. "We have already sentenced the existing social order to death," he declared at the celebration of Fourier's birthday on April 7. "Now we have only to carry out the execution."

The authorities were thinking along the same lines—but in reference to the Petrashevsky circle. As early as March 1848, the Minister of Internal Affairs, Lev Perovsky, had become suspicious of its incautious agitations during St. Petersburg's elections of nobility. Ivan Liprandi, one of Perovsky's leading officials, was asked to keep the gatherings under surveillance. In early 1849, he managed to place an informant inside the Petrashevsky circle, one of his relatives by the name of Pyotr Antonelli, who regularly turned in detailed reports of the discussions. From Antonelli's reports, we know that Dostoyevsky was present at two of the circle's last meetings, on April 1 and 15, and that at the last of these meetings, he read Belinsky's forbidden *Letter to Gogol* that had just been sent to him by Pleshcheyev. He had read the letter twice before this at Palm's and Durov's apartment.

Belinsky's letter is a scathing attack on Gogol's defense of serfdom in *Selected Passages from My Correspondence with Friends*. "That you ground your teaching in the Orthodox Church," wrote Belinsky, "I can understand; it has always been behind the whip and the servant of despotism, but why have you dragged Christ into this? What does he have in common with the Church, particularly the Orthodox Church?" No, what Russia needs, Belinsky continued, "is not sermons (it has enough of them) or prayers (it has more than enough of them)—what Russia needs is for its people to be awakened to their own human dignity." These words went right to the heart of the young Dostoyevsky. Serfdom was and would always be incompatible with true Christianity.

The reading created a sensation among those present. "The entire group was spellbound," Antonelli wrote in his report. Dostoyevsky, however, said nothing about his success as the declaimer of Belinsky's opinions. On the contrary, he maintained that he had read the *entire* correspondence between Gogol and Belinsky without taking either side. Nonetheless, we know that immediately after the reading he allowed the letter to leave his possession so that it could be copied, a letter which according to the prosecuting officials was "filled with rash proclamations against the highest authorities and the Orthodox Church."

Liprandi kept Perovsky fully informed about the activities of the Petrashevsky circle. At the same time, Perovsky attempted to keep the matter hidden from the secret police or the Third Department of His Majesty's Imperial Chancellery, for he wanted to be the one to shine as the savior of his fatherland. In addition, he was eager to give his rivals in the Third Department a lesson in administrative efficiency. This was a matter of the utmost gravity, he assured the Tsar. There were even rumors of a proposed attack on His Majesty's life! Within a short time everything would be ready for the disclosure.

Understandably enough, the Tsar became impatient. He contacted Count Aleksei Orlov, chief of the secret police and in reality the country's prime minister. On April 20, Liprandi was given orders to cease his investigation and produce his findings. He went immediately to a top official in the Third Department, General Leonty Dubelt, and handed over three folders containing the names and addresses of the participants in the Petrashevsky circle, along with an exhaustive description of each person's activities. Like Count Orlov, Dubelt was annoyed that the investigation had been carried out without the knowledge of the secret police. He was not pleased that the Department of Internal Affairs had trespassed on his territory. This rivalry was not without significance in the ongoing investigation.

The very next day, Count Orlov sent a detailed report to the Tsar. The report on the Petrashevsky circle—these "champions of communism and new ideas"—had inspired "Europe's gendarme" to swift and secret action. Not even General Ivan Nabokov, commandant of the Peter-Paul Fortress (and relative of the future celebrated author of *Lolita*), would know about the forthcoming events. In response to the police report, the Tsar wrote to Count Orlov:

> I have read all of it. It is a serious matter, even if it were all only idle talk, it would still be criminal and intolerable in the highest degree.

Go ahead with all the arrests you deem necessary, but try to avoid the publicity that could result from the large number of troops that may be needed.

Nabokov must not be notified in advance. It is best that he gets the message directly from me. Make sure that this happens.

God be with you. God's will be done.

That same day, April 22, Count Orlov gave the following secret orders for the arrest:

To Major Chudinov, St. Petersburg police division:

On the orders of the Tsar, I hereby command you to arrest the former Engineer Lieutenant Fyodor Mikhailovich Dostoyevsky who lives in Scheil's house at the corner of Malaya Morskaya and Vosnesensky Prospekt in Bremer's apartment on the third floor. The arrest shall take place early tomorrow morning at four o'clock. All papers and books must be sealed and brought with Dostoyevsky to the Third Department of His Majesty's Imperial Chancellery.

During the arrest, you must be careful that no papers are hidden. It is possible that at Dostoyevsky's you will find such large numbers of papers and books that it will be impossible to bring them to the Third Department right away. If this is the case, you must protect these in one of the rooms and seal them.

If, during the impounding of the papers and books, Dostoyevsky should maintain that certain papers belong to someone else, you should disregard this entirely, and also seal them.

During the discharge of this mission that is given you, you must demonstrate the utmost vigilance and care for your personal safety.

The chief of the secret police, General-Lieutenant Dubelt, will ensure that you are assigned an officer from the St. Petersburg police as well as the necessary number of gendarmes.

General Adjutant Count Orlov

"May God bring you luck in everything," Orlov wrote in a follow-up letter to Dubelt. Dostoyevsky was, according to the report, "one of the most important" of those to be arrested. But the arrest itself took place without dramatic incident.

Early in the morning of April 23, 1849, Dostoyevsky returned home to his apartment near Isaac Cathedral after a visit with Grigoryev. Indeed, the two had discussed the press that was now ready to be installed at Nikolai Mordvinov's. Not long after Dostoyevsky's return home, he was awakened by the rattling of swords. "Former Engineer Lieutenant Dostoyevsky? His Royal Highness has given the order for your arrest!" The apartment was ransacked; books and papers were confiscated. On the table lay an old coin that the police seemed particularly interested in. "It isn't counterfeit, is it?" asked Dostoyevsky, who had just put on his clothes. "Hmmm. . . . we had better look at it a bit more closely," muttered the policeman. Together they walked out to the carriage that was soon on its way to the headquarters of the secret police on the Fontanka canal. A short time later, the writer was under lock and key in the Peter-Paul Fortress along with twenty-three other prisoners.

White Nights. *M. Dobushinsky, 1922.*

M. V. Butashevich-Petrashevsky.

N. A. Speshnev.

*Excerpt from the report written
by secret agent Antonelli.*

S. F. Durov.

*The beginning of the order
for Dostoyevsky's arrest.*

4

AT THE SCAFFOLD

"I was guilty; I recognize this fully.
I was convicted for my intention (but nothing more)
to act against the government. I was judged
in a legal and just way."

In the Peter-Paul Fortress, a few hundred meters from the Winter Palace, Dostoyevsky was placed in the Alekseyevsky Ravelin in cell number nine. In this ravelin Peter the Great's son Alexsei had been tortured to death on the order of his father. Later it housed several of the Decembrists, five of whom were hanged. It was one of them who called the fortress an "abominable monument to autocracy with the Tsar's palace in the background."

Now the Petrashevsky group were to suffer for their disloyalty to the Tsar. Even to think of escape was futile. No one had ever escaped from the Peter-Paul Fortress, and the Alekseyevsky Ravelin was the most strictly secured. This dismal jail was reserved for the nation's most dangerous political criminals—exclusively for those imprisoned on orders from the Tsar. Even the men who worked at the fortress were not privy to what went on in this "secret building." Corpses of dead "numbers" were removed under the cover of night and were swiftly taken away by the police. Here the Fortress Commandant could do as he wished without the slightest restraint from outside authorities. Not even the Minister of Internal Affairs had access to the Alekseyevsky Ravelin.

The damp, dirty cells were cold and dark. Only a thin line of sky could be glimpsed on a clear day. Conditions were hard, especially during the first three months, when the prisoners were totally isolated from the outside world and were not even allowed into the prison yard. The air in the cells was clammy and thick, the food bad, and the drinking water had a "strange taste." Nearly all the prisoners suffered from serious stomach disorders. It was worst for Petrashevsky, who began to spit up blood and had to ask that he "be fed the same food the soldiers prepared for themselves." The cells swarmed with fleas, lice, cockroaches; rats ran freely across the floors. The prisoners were not able to wash themselves properly; as the months went by, they became covered with a "black and filthy layer like fishscales." And the cells were noisy; groans and sighs could be heard at all hours of the day or night, as well as knocking on the walls—the prisoners' only form of communication. But above all, the loneliness and monotony created a terrible psychic burden. Everything was designed to break down the prisoners, and one by one they broke down. Two died.

Dostoyevsky's health had already deteriorated before his imprisonment. He had been ailing the entire month of March and was for part of the time confined to his bed. It was almost miraculous that he managed to survive the following months. He suffered from hemorrhoids, constriction in his throat, scrofula, nightmares, and increasing sleeplessness. "I sleep on the average five hours, and every night I wake up three or four times," he wrote to Mikhail. "It is worst at dusk—by nine o'clock it is already pitch black in the cell. . . . It is astonishing how much toughness and vitality there is in man . . . never thought it was possible, but now I know from my own experience."

By the middle of July, conditions began to improve. New linens were brought for the hard bunks, and the prisoners were allowed to write letters and accept books and money. Dostoyevsky could once again enjoy tea and a pipe, and he could even take a daily walk in the prison yard where there were "almost seventeen trees."

But, most important, he was now permitted to have a little light in his cell. And as usual he did not waste his time. He threw himself into the reading of Shakespeare, was delighted by a translation of Charlotte Brontë's *Jane Eyre*, and read with pleasure his own masterful study of childhood psychology, *"Netochka Nezvanova,"* which had been newly published in *Notes of the Fatherland* without mention of the author's name. Within a short time, he had made plans for three stories and two novels. It is a tribute to Dostoyevsky's indomitable spirit that he wrote "A Little Hero" at this time, one of his most cheerful works, about a young boy's first love. "The mechanism is not broken; it still works," he wrote with grim humor to his brother, "but this eternal brooding, without any stimulation from the outside to revive my thoughts and give them new life, must in the end impoverish the spirit. It is like living inside a vacuum from which the air is little by little being pumped out."

That the air had not gone out of Dostoyevsky was evident in his courageous conduct during the four-month investigation that now began.

II

Shortly after the arrests, the Tsar appointed a Commission of Inquiry to "uncover all the participants in this criminal case." They were to set an example for what was in store for the revolutionary offspring of Holy Russia.

The Commission of Inquiry was formally headed by General Nabokov. As commandant of the Peter-Paul Fortress, Nabokov could most easily alter the treatment of the prisoners according to the commission's collective will. But he was not a man of great intelligence. From his perspective, every person who ended up in his fortress automatically deserved the nation's severest punishment. For all practical purposes, therefore, the commission was headed by Prince Pavel Gagarin, one of the country's leading officials. The other members were Count Vasily Dolgorukov, who had earlier played a role in exposing the Decembrists and was a favorite of the Tsar; General Yakov Rostovtsev, chief of the nation's military academies; and finally General Leonty Dubelt, the man feared by all of St. Petersburg, the local chief of the secret police. Above all of these "inquisitors," as they were called, was the Tsar himself—it was he who was the "Grand Inquisitor."

According to Liprandi, there was no doubt that the activities of the Petrashevsky circle could easily have led to revolution in Russia—the authorities were faced with a conspiracy that threatened them with "a fundamental subversion of the entire social and political order." But in his eagerness to expose "the revolutionaries," Liprandi had gone too far. The Tsar's top men found it difficult to admit that the country they had a part in governing had been so close to revolution. The secret police were also less than eager to make a big fuss about a case in which they had not been involved. The result was that Liprandi was kept out of the Commission of Inquiry, which did not demonstrate the zeal and fervor expected of it. On the contrary, its members seemed eager to make the number of guilty parties as small as possible. In Holy Russia, there could only exist a "handful of

insignificant young men" who dreamed of "overthrowing the sacred institutions of religion, law and property."

Nevertheless a comprehensive investigation took place that lasted for
several months and involved nearly three hundred people. A mountain of
paper was used—more than nine thousand pages—and the most important
documents in the case were published in three enormous volumes. "Bring
in half the capital if you must, as long as the conspiracy is uncovered,"
the Tsar wrote to the Commission of Inquiry. But many were soon shown
to be innocent, among them Dostoyevsky's two brothers, Mikhail and Andrei. In the end fewer than two dozen had to face a military court. The
fact that they all managed to escape with their lives can be attributed to
their stubbornness and perseverance. While the Decembrists had humbled
themselves and begged for mercy, the Petrashevsky group appeared before
the awesome commission with courage and solidarity.

Petrashevsky served as a good example to his fellows. He wrote words
of advice and encouragement to his comrades on pieces of stucco, and
during the interrogations his tactic of taking the offensive sometimes resulted
in transforming him from the accused into the accuser. When he was asked
how he thought the case should be investigated, he bravely replied:

> There are two means of legal procedure. The first is that which is inscribed
> in our law and which Catherine the Great described with these words: "It
> is better to forgive the guilty than to condemn one person who is innocent."
> The other means was devised by Cardinal Richelieu who said the following:
> "Give me ten words written by the accused and I will find him guilty of
> an offense that merits the death penalty." Naturally, I desire the first means
> of procedure, but it is clear that here the second means is under way. In
> his charge, Dubelt presumed to say, "We know that you have burned a
> series of documents; I have seen the ashes myself." If the Cardinal were
> resurrected, he would undoubtedly regard himself as a pupil of Dubelt.
> He at least grounded his accusations on some fact or another; Dubelt, on
> the other hand, grounds his accusation on the little pile of ashes that was
> left after I had smoked my pipe.

Reports of this kind of impudent behavior were said to have prompted
the Tsar himself to become involved in the interrogations of Petrashevsky.
Cables were extended from the telegraph machine in the Winter Palace to
the Peter-Paul Fortress, but the electric shocks that were administered
to the prisoner only made his answers bolder. Furious, the Tsar was said

to have brought his prisoner a poisoned drink. But Petrashevsky was suspicious; when he put his fingers into the glass, he felt a stinging pain like a burn. One should be extremely cautious about believing this story, but it was recorded in a letter written by Natalya Fonvizina, who met Petrashevsky shortly afterward in Tobolsk and was apparently shown the burns.

Dostoyevsky displayed similar courage. He did not in any way seek to save himself by shifting the blame onto his friends. On the contrary, he tried to protect them by accepting blame for actions that may well have sent him to the scaffold. Even when General Rostovtsev tried to flatter him by saying that the author of *Poor Folk* could not possibly be involved in such a sordid affair, and sought to tempt him with release should he cooperate, the writer remained loyal to his fellow prisoners and was silent. And his words for the circle's leader were also unflinching: "I have always respected Petrashevsky for his honesty and noble heart."

In his detailed fifty-page report to the Commission of Inquiry, Dostoyevsky did not hide his participation in the Petrashevsky gatherings, but he denied that this circle of many voices had any united revolutionary goal. The circle was composed of dreamers, the writer maintained, of young people who were enchanted by the "beauty" and "love of mankind" presented in Fourier's "peaceful system." "All of my liberalism has consisted of a desire for the best for my Fatherland, of a desire that everything should move forward to perfection," he assured the commission. Only so far as it was forbidden to desire "something better" could he be called a "freethinker."

He was certainly interested in social questions, but he had never become a socialist. "Socialism," he wrote, "is chaos—alchemy before chemistry, astrology before astronomy—and yet I believe that the present chaos can develop into something harmonious, sensible, and beneficial, just as chemistry has developed from alchemy and astronomy from astrology."

Even though he had been a part of discussions about the latest political events in France (who had not?), this was hardly tantamount to being an opponent of autocracy in his homeland. "Impossible. Nothing could be more nonsensical than a republican government in Russia."

Yes, he had also discussed the censor, he confessed. He had complained about the censor's "unreasonable strictness" in a time that no longer even had room for a national poet like Pushkin. He had attacked the authorities' tendency to regard all new works with suspicion, their condemnation of even the smallest suggestion of a negative portrayal of Russian reality:

Is it possible to paint only with light colors? How can the light side of a picture be visible without the dark side? Can there be a picture without both light and shadow? We can only perceive the light because there is shadow. We are told that we must write only about the hero's virtues. But it is impossible to know virtue without vice; the very concepts good and evil are rooted in this—that good and evil have always existed side by side.

In his testimony, Dostoyevsky not only came forward and acknowledged his opinions, but also openly criticized the system his judges represented. Yet despite his boldness in this and other testimony, it was apparent that Dostoyevsky was doing his best to minimize his role in the Petrashevsky circle. There is no falsehood in his report, but it is not the whole truth. Dostoyevsky said nothing about the Durov circle until he was pressed by the commission, and even then he attempted to explain it away as a harmless group of people interested in the arts. He responded similarly when interrogated about the printing press. He had only heard talk about a *lithograph*, he insisted—no one had talked about *printing*. In general it was difficult to find an opening with Dostoyevsky. General Rostovtsev judged him "a clever, independent, cunning, and slippery character."

Because of the prisoners' lack of cooperation and its own halfhearted effort, the Commission of Inquiry did not succeed in uncovering the full extent of the Petrashevsky circle's activities. Speshnev's secret society was not discovered, despite the fact that a copy of the oath its members were to sign was found. Nor did the police ever locate the printing press: Mordvinov's relatives managed to lift a locked door off its hinges and get rid of the entire press. "The whole conspiracy evaporated," Dostoyevsky commented many years later when an account of the case was published in Leipzig.

How serious was Dostoyevsky's involvement with the Petrashevsky circle? It is difficult to find a reliable answer to this question in his own work. In later reminiscences, he was inclined to exaggerate his revolutionary past. He liked to point out that he had ended up in Siberia as a political criminal and did not deny that he could have become a terrorist. On the other hand, in his report to the Commission of Inquiry, he understandably tried to trivialize his participation in the circle, blaming French revolutionary literature as an influence that had impressed itself upon his brain and gripped his heart, but at the same time assuring the commission that the infatuation was not serious. He had gone astray on a path from which he now wished to depart as quickly as possible. Consequently, there are those who have

argued that Dostoyevsky's activities in the Petrashevsky circle were inciden-
tal, that he already hated socialism in his youth and in some sense had
sought out the circle as an opportunity to suffer. Apollon Maikov's description of the "dying Socrates" who declared that everything was "ready" for
the "upheaval" gives little support to this view. There is no question that
the writer took part in a plan to acquire a secret lithograph for the distribution
of anti-government propaganda. Though he may have suffered from doubts
and anxiety, he had been a participant in a serious crime that a military
court would be forced to regard as bordering on revolutionary. Dostoyevsky
knew why he had landed in the Peter-Paul Fortress, and he did not betray
the cause either during the interrogations or at the scaffold.

On the other hand, it is an exaggeration to view Dostoyevsky as a
forerunner of the October revolutionaries or to maintain that his involvement
was consciously grounded in a "class struggle." In the heat of debate, the
writer was quite capable of calling for revolution—he was a passionate man.
But most sources indicate that he hoped for reforms from above, and that
he did not in fact believe in any other means of change. Indeed, he later
maintained that he never had been an adherent of the Petrashevsky circle's
extreme idea that a constitution should be imposed through violent means.
Politically, the writer was at this time a typical follower of Fourier's ideas,
of a socialism "without hate or struggle"—a far cry from plots against the
government and property. Nevertheless, for the military court his "desire
for something better" was in itself a crime, a crime that came very close to
revolutionary action.

After five months of work, the Commission of Inquiry handed in its
report to the Tsar on September 17. They had not succeeded in uncovering
a secret plot or any organized group of propagandists, but called the whole
case a "conspiracy of ideas" and made no recommendations for sentencing.
The case was then passed on to a mixed military-civil court made up of
three general adjutants and three legislators. The court's judge was Adjutant
General Vasily Perovsky, a brother of the Minister of Internal Affairs. Because of the commission's flimsy findings, the Tsar feared that the sentencing
would be too lenient. He desired a severe sentence, so that his forthcoming
"pardon" would have the greatest possible effect. He therefore gave the court
the status of a military court and demanded that the sentencing be carried
out according to military criminal law. Because a majority of those accused
had no connection to the military, this constituted a breach of Russian law,
but in this instance, the Tsar believed that the end justified the means. The

most important thing was that the "miscreants" be punished, and as harshly as possible. Nobody could carry this out better than a military court. The intent of the "conspiracy of ideas" had been the overthrow of the fatherland's existing laws and national order, and for a military court evil intent was almost as bad as evil action. After deliberations in this vein, fifteen of the twenty-three accused were sentenced to death, six were released under surveillance, and two were allowed to go free. One of the latter had gone mad during his incarceration. When the court had completed its task on November 16, Dostoyevsky received the following sentence:

> The military court finds the accused Dostoyevsky guilty in that he, after March of this year, accepted a copy of a subversive letter written by Belinsky from the accused Pleshcheyev and read this at various gatherings—first at the home of the accused Durov and then at the home of the accused Petrashevsky, and thereafter gave the letter to the accused Mombelli for further copying. Dostoyevsky was furthermore present at the accused Speshnev's during the reading of the rebellious work, "A Soldier's Conversation," written by Lieutenant Grigoryev. Therefore the military court has, according to the criminal code Part V, Book I, articles 142, 144, 169, 170, 172, 174, 176, 177, and 178, condemned the former Engineer Lieutenant Dostoyevsky—for failing to report Belinsky's criminal letter about religion and government and· Lieutenant Grigoryev's vicious work—to forfeit his civil rights and to death by firing squad.

The case was then handed over to a highest court, the General-Auditoriat, which was composed of people of a considerably lower station. It was therefore easier for the Tsar to manipulate this group of men, and he consequently got what he wanted: all twenty-one were now condemned to death. The court ruled that even though no secret society had been uncovered, such a society would undoubtedly have been formed had not the criminals been arrested so soon. At the same time, however, the court cited a number of mitigating circumstances: several of the participants had been repentant, they were all young and impressionable, and thanks to the timely intervention of the authorities, their actions had not had injurious consequences. In light of this, the General-Auditoriat took the liberty of suggesting milder sentences to the Tsar. It was recommended that Dostoyevsky be given four years at hard labor and forfeit his civil rights. Tsar Nicholas accepted the recommendation and reduced the sentence. "To four years at hard labor and thereafter service as an ordinary soldier" read Dostoyevsky's sentencing papers written in the Tsar's own hand on December 19.

Some have called the Tsar's punishment "extremely harsh." In reality, it was surprisingly mild. In Russia it was a fast rule that a person condemned to hard labor automatically lost his civil rights. By giving Dostoyevsky a term as a soldier after his imprisonment, the Tsar made an exception to this practice, and the writer was probably correct when he commented later that the Tsar had with this act taken his "youth and talent" into consideration. This much is certain: comparable accusations of revolutionary or counterrevolutionary activity in Russia today would be met with much stiffer punishment.

However, the comedy that the Tsar now directed was gruesome indeed, in part to give his subjects the shock of their lives, in part to demonstrate his gracious clemency. "We have already condemned the present social order to death," Petrashevsky had said. "Now all that remains is to carry out the death sentence." Instead, the death penalty was now pronounced on the members of the Petrashevsky circle. The Tsar added his own twist to the execution.

Until the announcement of the pardon, one and all were to be regarded as condemned to death. Not until the last moment—just before the final command—would the Tsar's forgiveness be proclaimed to the sinners. The Tsar took part eagerly in the formulation of the procedural directives for this demonic human experiment. His instructions included a precise account of expenses: the transportation of the prisoners, seven swords to be broken over the heads of the young nobles as a symbol of their loss of civil rights, eight ankle fetters, and shrouds for them all. The Tsar thought it reasonable that the wealthiest of the prisoners should cover these expenses. Petrashevsky and Speshnev had to produce three thousand rubles for the props of this tragicomedy. Only the peasant who raised the scaffold was graciously paid by the Tsar.

Even the Tsar's advisors were repelled by this monarchic display of vengeance. A request from the heir to the throne for a day's reprieve was curtly rejected. Others suggested that perhaps it was unnecessary to dress the prisoners in shrouds and command the soldiers to take aim—this too was rejected. On one point only did the Tsar allow himself to be persuaded— they were to dispense with digging graves at the execution site. Even had the death sentences been carried out, it was unfeasible to bury the corpses under one of the capital's military drill grounds. "Graves shall not be dug," read the Tsar's final order.

III

Early in the morning on December 22, the inmates were wakened by shouts and the noise of tramping feet in the corridors. At last they would hear their sentences. It could hardly be more than a few months of exile.

Dostoyevsky was brought his own clothes and put in a carriage. Escorted by mounted policemen with sabers, the carriage along with twenty others drove out of the Peter-Paul Fortress.

It was a cold, overcast morning; snow fell intermittently. The windows were covered with frost. The prisoners had no idea where they were being taken. When Speshnev tried to make a peephole in the window's thick layer of ice, he was brusquely reprimanded by a prison guard. The Tsar's detailed plan outlined the route: first across the Neva River, not far from where Dostoyevsky had had his great vision a few years earlier, then along the riverbank to the Arsenal, and then finally along Liteynaya and Vladimirskaya to Semyonovsky Square—the regiment's drilling grounds.

When the prisoners emerged from the carriages, they were met by a priest in full burial vestments carrying a Bible and cross. "Today you shall hear the just decision in your case," he said. "Follow me." They stumbled forward in the snow beside the lines of soldiers to the sound of a drumroll. The troops had been painstakingly selected from those regiments that had officers among the condemned. This was a particularly nasty notion of the Tsar's: the officers were to be executed by their own men.

There were three thousand silent witnesses to the macabre spectacle, for the most part people on their way to work. The atmosphere was tense; people pitied the "unfortunate ones" and had no idea why they were being executed. Only a few officers were aware of the pardon. Not until later in the day did the regime announce "the Tsar's display of mercy." But for the Petrashevsky group everything indicated momentary execution. A scaffold covered with a black cloth had been raised in the middle of the square; it was four by four meters wide and two meters high. Three stakes had been placed in the frozen ground, and behind the scaffold was a line of carts— apparently laden with empty coffins.

It was simply unbelievable. Did they really only have a few minutes left among the living? "It's not possible that they mean to execute us," Dostoyevsky whispered in a faltering voice to Durov. But Durov only pointed in silence to the waiting carts.

There are conflicting accounts about how the writer went to the scaffold. Some claim that he walked with swift, energetic steps, others that he was gripped by a "mystical terror" and seemed barely to understand what was happening. He later declared that he attached no faith to the contention that it was possible to go to one's own execution with a peaceful heart.

The prisoners were placed in two lines on the scaffold facing the troops. On the left were the nine who were to be sent to prison; on the right stood the other twelve; Alexander Palm, who in the end had escaped with only a loss of rank, was placed behind the others.

Just before the first three, with Petrashevsky in the lead, were to be taken to the stakes, a memory of Victor Hugo's "The Last Day of a Condemned Man" flitted through Dostoyevsky's mind. Even as he faced his death, literature pursued him. He is even said to have confided a few words about his most recent story to his neighbor in line.

"Present arms!" Again the drumroll sounded ominously across Semyonovsky Square. An officer came forward onto the scaffold and began to read the sentences in a great hurry to the prisoners who stood in their summer clothes in the freezing weather. "It was cold," Dostoyevsky recalled, "terribly cold."

"After the careful consideration of the Military Court, the General-Auditoriat has reached the conclusion that all of the accused are guilty as charged, whether to a greater or lesser degree, of intending to overthrow the Fatherland's existing laws and national order, and are therefore condemned to death before a firing squad."

One after another, the guilty were called. It was not long before Dostoyevsky heard his name: "The former Engineer Lieutenant Dostoyevsky—age twenty-seven—for participation in criminal plans, for the circulation of a private letter containing rash statements against the Orthodox Church and the highest authorities, and for the attempt to distribute subversive works with the aid of a lithograph—condemned to death before a firing squad."

The golden spire of a church nearby gleamed in the clear sunlight. He remembered later that he had stared intently at this spire and at the rays emanating from it. He could not take his eyes away from these rays of light. It was as if they were his new spirit, and in three minutes he would become a part of them. He was frightened by the unknown and the terror of what was to come. But he said that the worst thing during these minutes was the constant, nagging thought, "Think if I don't die. Imagine that I am turned back to life, imagine how endless it will seem. A whole eternity! And this eternity will belong to me! Then I will live each minute as a century, without losing any of it, and I will keep an account of each minute and not waste a moment!" He said that in the end this thought had become so unbearable that he wished that they would shoot him at once.

Finally, all the sentences had been read. The officer folded up the papers, stuck them in his side pocket, and descended from the scaffold. The condemned men were given white shirts with hoods and long sleeves. Petrashevsky could appreciate eccentric clothing, but this was a bit much. "Gentlemen," he cried and waved his long shirt sleeves. "How ridiculous we are in these clown suits!"

The priest mounted the scaffold and faced the prisoners, quoting from the Bible: "The wages of sin are death." And yet, he assured them, physical death was not the end. Through faith and the recognition of their sins, they could still inherit eternal life. Only one of the condemned men went forward to confess, but they all kissed the cross.

"I understood nothing before I saw the cross," Dostoyevsky recalled years later at Semyonovsky Square. "They could not bring themselves to trifle with the cross! . . . Then they couldn't play such a tragicomedy. . . . I understood it well. . . . Death was not to be avoided. If only it would come as quickly as possible. . . . And then I was seized by a profound indifference. Yes! Yes! Yes! Indifference. I cared not for life or for those around me. Everything seemed meaningless beside that terrible moment when I would pass into the unknown, into darkness. . . ."

"Now you've done your job, priest!" one of the generals called out. "You have nothing more to do." The priest slunk away.

Dostoyevsky said goodbye to Durov and Pleshcheyev. "We will be with Christ," he whispered to Speshnev. "A handful of dust," answered the other with a scornful smile. Incarceration had radically altered Speshnev—his former beauty had vanished.

With their hoods over their faces, Petrashevsky, Mombelli, and Grigoryev, the first three, were led down from the scaffold. Petrashevsky's gallows humor was vibrant till the end. "Mombelli, lift your feet. You don't want to enter the kingdom of Heaven with a cold." Before he was tied to the stake, Petrashevsky managed to push back his hood. He was determined to look death in the eyes.

Three platoons, each with sixteen men, were lined up fifteen steps from those who were to be executed. With loaded rifles, the soldiers took aim. Half a minute of excruciating, terrible suspense passed. Where were the shots? Suddenly someone appeared waving a white cloth and the soldiers lowered their rifles. A carriage sped into the square. A sealed envelope for Adjutant General Sumarokov—the Tsar's pardon. By the time the three who were to be shot had been untied from their stakes, Grigoryev had lost his mind.

General Adjutant Sumarokov stepped forward and announced the Tsar's decree of mercy. At first there was no joy over the pardon. "Who asked for this?" Durov said irritably. "They could just as well have shot us," commented Debu. All of them were gripped by indifference. Only Palm cried, "Long live Tsar Nicholas!" But shortly afterward, he was weeping because he was not to follow his comrades. Petrashevsky was the insurrectionist to the last. When blacksmiths came to put him in chains, he protested loudly. They had no right to touch a nobleman. He wanted the whole thing to be undone. Then he grabbed the hammer himself and put on his own foot-irons. Weighted down by the shackles, he tottered around and bade goodbye to his friends. After that he was put in a troika and sent directly from the execution site to a lifetime of exile. Many of the spectators wept.

A Danish historian wrote, "Had he [Dostoyevsky] been executed, it would have been an expression of the system's capriciousness—and yet there was only one caprice in the system, that he survived and became one of the giants in world literature."

It is certain anyway that after a doctor's examination in the Peter-Paul Fortress, Dostoyevsky felt a joy in life rush through him once again. "I cannot remember a happier day. As I walked back and forth in my cell in the Alekseyevsky Ravelin singing the whole time, singing loudly, I was so glad for the life that had been given back to me."

At this time he wrote his farewell letter to Mikhail. The letter is a moving confession, a hymn to the joy that is found only through suffering:

Peter-Paul Fortress, December 22

Dear brother, beloved friend! Now everything is decided! I have been sentenced to four years in prison (probably at Orenburg) and will thereafter serve as an ordinary soldier. Today, December 22, we were driven to Semenovsky Square, where our death sentences were announced. We kissed the cross, swords were broken over our heads, and we were given shrouds to wear. After that, three of us were lined up against stakes for execution. Three by three we were called forth. I was in the second group and had no more than a minute to live. Then I thought of you, dear brother, of you and yours. At the end, only you were in my thoughts, and only then did I know how much I love you, dear brother! I managed to say goodbye to Pleshcheyev and Durov, who stood beside me. At that moment, the drumroll sounded. Those who stood bound to the posts were brought back, and we heard the news that His Majesty had granted us our lives. Then the actual sentences were read. . . .

Dear brother! I am not despairing. I have not lost courage. Life is life everywhere, life is within us—not without. And even there I will be surrounded by people. To be a man among men, to be a man always, not to allow oneself to be broken, to fall—this is life's goal and meaning. I have understood this. This thought has become a part of my flesh and blood. Yes, truly! That head that created, that lived for the highest life of art, that has become accustomed to the highest life of the spirit, that head has already been severed from my shoulders. What remain are only memories and images, the ones I have created and those to which I have not yet given form. Oh, these will surely cause me great suffering! Yet I still have my heart, the same flesh and blood. I can still love, suffer, feel pity, and remember, and this too is life. One sees the sun!

There are also sad thoughts in the letter. He is filled with fear at the thought that he may never be able to give life and form to the images within him. Better a lifetime in prison with a pen in hand! But his will to live triumphed over reality. The sham execution on Semyonovsky regiment's drilling ground had given him new insight into life's meaning:

When I look back at the past and think of all the time I squandered in error and idleness, lacking the knowledge needed to live, when I think of how often I sinned against my heart and my soul, then my heart bleeds. Life is a gift, life is happiness, every minute could have been an eternity of happiness! If youth only knew! Now my life will change; now I will be reborn. Dear brother, I swear that I shall not lose hope. I will keep my soul pure and my heart open. I will be reborn for the better. That is my whole hope, my whole consolation.

That same day, Dostoyevsky heard that he would be among the first group to leave for Siberia. He asked for a farewell meeting with his brother but was refused. Nevertheless, a request from Mikhail was granted, and on Christmas Eve, 1849, the brothers took leave of each other. Their mutual friend Alexander Milyukov was present, and he later gave a moving account of the parting. Dostoyevsky arrived with Durov. Both were dressed in prisoners' garb—sheepskin jackets and felt boots.

> There were tears in the eyes of the eldest brother; his lips trembled, but Fyodor Mikhailovich was calm and tried to console him.
>
> "Don't cry, dear brother," he said. "This is not a funeral. I am not to be laid in my coffin. They aren't beasts in prison. They are men, perhaps better than I am, perhaps worthier than I am. . . . Yes, we will see each other again, I do not doubt this. . . . And you can write to me and send me books; I am permitted to read. . . . And as soon as I am out, I will write. I have experienced much in these last months; I have been through a lot and will see and experience even more—you shall see how much I will have to write about.

Not long after, Dostoyevsky was taken to a blacksmith who put iron chains on his legs. The shackles weighed ten pounds and made it painful and difficult to move. For more than four years he wore these irons. In these he worked and slept. Finally he was placed in an open sledge with a gendarme. Two of his comrades, Durov and Yastrzhembsky, sat in other sledges. Led by a government courier, the procession set out on the long journey to Siberia.

The Peter-Paul Fortress.

The Peter-Paul Fortress. The Alekseyevsky Ravelin.

The list of names of those "criminals who have been condemned to death."

The mock execution at Semenovsky Square.

The beginning of Dostoyevsky's letter to his brother,
December 22, 1849.

5

SIBERIA

───────────⌣───────────

"I waited for my freedom.
I wanted my freedom back as soon as possible. I wanted
to test my powers again in a new battle."

All his life, Dostoyevsky had been a confirmed city dweller. He has, in fact, been called "the voice of the modern city." The journey to Siberia was his first long trip through his native country, and, with the exception of the return journey, it would be his last.

The three-thousand-kilometer trip by sledge over endless snow flats was unlikely to inspire a desire for more. The arduous stretches without pause or exercise were almost unbearable. And it was painful, too, when people came "in whole towns" to stare at the train of prisoners. But the cold was the worst of all. "It was as if my heart had stiffened from the cold; even later, in a warm room, it was impossible to warm up my body." When they passed over the Urals, the temperature sank to forty degrees below freezing. "There we stood on the border between Europe and Asia, a blizzard raging and howling around us. Before us lay Siberia and an unknown fate, behind us was our past—it was so sad, tears filled my eyes."

On January 9, after more than two weeks of strenuous traveling, they approached Tobolsk, the threshold of "the house of the dead." Prisoners from the entire nation were sent from this gathering place on to many different prisons in Siberia. The new arrivals were ushered into a large room where they were prepared for their ongoing journeys. Nearly three hundred people were packed together—men, women, and children of different ages and races. Some were put in chains, others had their heads branded. With dread, Dostoyevsky looked upon these marked convicts destined to long confinements. They sat, lethargic, chained to the wall in clammy, suffocating cells. On the face of one of the most infamous criminals, he detected a "fearful spiritual apathy, an appalling combination of bloodthirstiness and insatiable sensuality."

The Petrashevsky circle were not treated much better than hardened criminals. When Yastrzhembsky saw the narrow, filthy cells and heard the drunken howls from the card-playing inmates in the next room, he thought of suicide. But in Dostoyevsky there were still hidden reserves of strength. "Dostoyevsky was small, weak, and he looked so very young," one of the town's doctors reported. "He was remarkably calm, even though he wore heavy irons on both his arms and legs."

The writer's calm and gift for summoning courage in times of crisis brought comfort and encouragement to his fellow prisoners. He managed to get tea and candles brought to them and then produced a box of cigars he had received from his brother as a farewell gift. "We spent the night in friendly conversation," Yastrzhembsky recalled. "Dostoyevsky's sympathetic voice and great amiability, even his capricious outbursts, just like a woman, had a soothing effect on me. I gave up my extreme decision."

A true consolation for the Petrashevsky group was the sympathy they received from the Decembrists and their relatives. For nearly a quarter of a century, these rebels had languished in Siberia's jails, but they were not alone. In many cases, their wives had sacrificed everything to follow their husbands into exile. And now they came out to show their solidarity and greeted the newly banished men with food and clothing: Natalya Fonvizina, Iosefina Muravyova, and Praskovya Annenkova with her daughter Olga (who would later marry Konstantin Ivanov, one of Dostoyevsky's schoolmates at the Academy of Engineers).

Through her friend Maria Frantseva, the daughter of a government prosecutor in Tobolsk, Natalya Fonvizina was able to arrange a meeting with the Petrashevsky men, held in the quarters of a prison official; the inmates were each given a New Testament, the only book they were allowed to take with them to prison. A ten-ruble note was tucked inside the binding of each copy: Dostoyevsky would soon discover that money was of greater worth in prison than freedom. "We met with the great martyrs who had voluntarily followed their husbands to Siberia," he wrote gratefully. "For twenty-five years, they, who were completely innocent, had suffered the same deprivation as their condemned husbands. Our meeting lasted one hour. They gave us their blessing for our continued journey."

On January 20, Durov and Dostoyevsky were sent to Omsk. "They are to remain in irons and are not to be given any privileges," read the orders from the Governor-General in West Siberia. Nevertheless, through the enterprising Olga, they were able to obtain a coach. Walking those final six hundred kilometers might well have broken the "small, weak" writer.

Just outside of Tobolsk, near the banks of the Irtysh River, where Raskolnikov was to atone for his crime, Dostoyevsky and Durov bid a final goodbye to the wives of the Decembrists and the free world. Maria and Natalya stood alongside the road in the thirty-below-zero weather. The sledge stopped, and the prisoners jumped out. Dostoyevsky was "emaciated, small, and not particularly handsome," Maria recalled. The heavy chains clanked and rattled. "We said a hasty goodbye to them in fear that some other travelers would see us with them, and we were only able to tell them not to lose courage and that even where they were going, there would be kind people to take care of them."

On January 23, when Dostoyevsky and Durov first set eyes on the prison, or *ostrog*, they must have thought of these words. It lay outside the fortress in Omsk, constructed in the early eighteenth century as a defense against steppe nomads, but soon after converted to a military prison. From the outside, the *ostrog* resembled a large courtyard, two hundred feet long and one hundred fifty feet wide—an uneven hexagon surrounded by high stockades. A favorite pastime of the inmates was counting the fifteen hundred stakes in the yard. Each stake represented one day, and when they had at last finished counting one side of the hexagon, they were overcome with a childish delight. Only a small piece of sky and a high embankment over-grown with scrubs were visible through the cracks when the prisoners peered out at freedom. "Inside was a world in itself that resembled no other. It had its own laws, its own apparel, codes, and customs; it was a house of the living dead, and life here resembled no other place on earth, and its people too were different." Yes, here in the *ostrog*, it was essential to keep up one's courage.

There was little that indicated that they would be taken in hand by "good people." The commandant of the fortress, Colonel Aleksei de Grave, was in fact quite humane, and a letter of recommendation to him from Natalya Fonvizina clearly had an effect, but the prison inspector, Major Krivtsov, was even more sinister than they had feared: a drunken tyrant who would suddenly explode with insults and threats of flogging at the slightest offense. Unfortunate was the man who slept on his left side or talked in his sleep! "His red, cruel face had the most depressing effect on us," Dostoyevsky wrote. "It was as if a poisonous spider struck out at a fly that was already caught in the web." Krivtsov was removed from his post a few years later and spent his last days as a vagrant in Omsk.

In the guardroom, Dostoyevsky was shaved on one side of his head. He was also given a gray convict's suit with a yellow check on the back. He was then taken to one of the single-story buildings that served as the prisoners' barracks. His impression of it was dismal and it did not improve with the years.

> I remember how I came to the ostrog one January evening. It was dusk; the prisoners had just returned from work and were lining up for roll call. A petty officer with long mustaches opened the door for me, and I stepped inside that extraordinary building, where I would spend so many years and experience so much—of which I would not have the slightest knowledge had I not lived through it myself. For example, I would never have been able to imagine how unpleasant and painful it was that not once during my entire imprisonment was I able to be alone for even a minute. During my work, I was always watched; in the ostrog I was with my two hundred comrades and never, never alone. Of course, one was likely to find oneself in much worse straits than this.

The barracks was a large, dilapidated building with rotten floors and a leaky roof. Dirt lay in thick layers on the floor, it was cold in winter and stifling in summer. The hard, uncovered bunks were designed for thirty men—the prisoners were squeezed together like sardines. In the evenings, there was racket and uproar, the clanking and clanging of chains, swearing and crude laughter, smoke and stench. The feeble glare from the tallow candles exposed shaven heads, branded faces, ragged clothes—degradation and misery. Fleas, lice, and cockroaches swarmed everywhere. A huge bucket in one corner gave off a heavy suffocating stink throughout the room—the "defecation pail" that Alexander Solzhenitsyn would describe one hundred years later.

We should be cautious, however, about taking the parallel too far. In spite of many similarities—the loss of freedom, forced labor, and the prisoners' incessant counting—Dostoyevsky's depiction of the Tsar's prison in *The House of the Dead* is considerably less terrible than Solzhenitsyn's depiction of Stalin's concentration camp in *One Day in the Life of Ivan Denisovich*. And the censor was not entirely to blame. Censorship was no stricter in the 1860s than in the 1960s. But changes in conditions of the death house are seldom for the better. While Solzhenitsyn, alias Zhukov, experienced each day as a battle for survival, Dostoyevsky as Goryanchikov could eat as much as he wished. And when he tired of the prison food, he could always get himself something better: meat in the *ostrog* cost only a few kopecks per pound. The "good day" described by Solzhenitsyn's hero in his prison camp would undoubtedly have been a bad day for Dostoyevsky's hero.

Of course, Dostoyevsky's rendering is frightening enough, and it is biographical down to the smallest detail. The artistry does not in any way weaken the realistic picture that is drawn of the House of the Dead. Recent investigations of the prison records in Omsk have revealed that, with the exception of his own, Dostoyevsky didn't even change the prisoners' names. Still, censorship considerations made the book's descriptions milder than reality. *The House of the Dead* is an artistic rendering in which the writer's personality nearly disappears behind the narrative of a fictional character. "Sometimes I still dream of that time and no dream is worse," Dostoyevsky remarked in *The Diary of a Writer*. "It may have been noticed that up to this time I have not written about my life in prison. I wrote *The House of the Dead* fifteen years ago using a presumed name—a criminal who is supposed to have killed his wife. I might add that there are still people who believe that I was exiled for the murder of my wife."

In the book, one becomes acquainted with a great variety of people from the Russian empire: soldiers, peasants, noblemen, sectarians, Tartars, gypsies, Jews, and Poles. All types of criminals are represented, from smugglers, counterfeiters, and highway robbers to rapists and murderers—a number of them men with ten to twenty homicides on their consciences, bestial and dangerous. Dostoyevsky divided the prison population into categories: the talkers and the silent ones. The latter category held particular interest for him. There were three types: the good and happy, the evil and dark, and the despairing.

There were not many who were good and happy, but among them, Dostoyevsky found his few friends. One of them was a Muslim, Ali, whom Dostoyevsky taught to read from his New Testament. The writer was delighted when Ali admitted that "Isa" was a "holy prophet." "And what was it you liked best?" his tutor inquired. "When he says to forgive, love, not hurt others, love even your enemies. Oh, how beautifully he says it!" The young Tartar had indeed defied the law that environment is the determining influence on human behavior.

The "dark and evil" and "despairing" prisoners were, however, the most exciting, men like the Tartar Gazin, the "giant spider," who had specialized in the slow murder of children; or the informer Aristov, "a lump of flesh with teeth and a stomach and an insatiable desire for the rawest and most brutish pleasures"; and the fearless Petrov, the born revolutionary leader who would joyfully have led his devoted followers to their ruin at the barricades. Petrov stole Dostoyevsky's Bible on the writer's first day of imprisonment. The sinner confessed his crime that evening but without displaying the least regret or chagrin. Pangs of conscience were not common in the *ostrog*. "It is just this kind of person who could murder someone for twenty-five kopecks and for these kopecks buy a bottle of liquor, when on some other occasion he would leave one hundred thousand rubles untouched," Dostoyevsky commented. In this house of the dead, his earlier belief in the innate goodness of man was shaken. He saw that what in reality inhabited this "godlike" being stank of sin. Evil was not purely the result of an unlucky position in society; its origin was above all internal.

The daily, forced life with these stunted human beings gave Dostoyevsky a unique opportunity to study the psyche of the great sinner. This knowledge was to become a principal source for his novels. Raskolnikov recalls the proud and power-hungry type of prisoner who refuses to bow before "bloodshed in accordance with conscience." The sensualist Svidrigailov has characteristics of Aristov, the depraved aristocrat who lets nothing interfere with the satisfaction of his corrupt desires. Petrov, the man of great strength with no outlet, brings to mind Stavrogin, the revolutionaries' uncrowned king in *The Possessed*. And features of the patricide Ilinsky appear in the character of Dmitri in *The Brothers Karamazov*.

But the prisoner who had the greatest impact upon Dostoyevsky was unquestionably Orlov—"the great murderer," who was sent to the hospital nearly unconscious after being made to run the gauntlet but who revived completely by the next day. "One could see immediately that his powers of self-control were unlimited, that he despised all punishment and torture and feared nothing in the world. One saw in him only an unbounded energy and a thirst for revenge, an absolute decision to attain the goals he had set for himself." This man, "the incarnation of the mind's triumph over the flesh," was truly a person of dimension! "I can say with assurance that I have never in all my life met a person with a stronger, steelier character." Dostoyevsky observed him closely for a week and then began to question him about his "accomplishments":

He was not particularly pleased with my cross-examination, even though he answered quite openly. But as soon as he understood that I wished to pry into his conscience to discover if he didn't feel the slightest bit of remorse, he gave me a scornful and superior look, as if I had suddenly become a stupid little boy with whom it was impossible to discuss anything. Yes, in his face there was even something that resembled pity. . . . But down deep, it was impossible for him to feel anything but disdain for me, and there was no doubt that he regarded me as a weak and submissive creature who was in every way inferior to him.

Dostoyevsky's ability to see greatness not only in the "pious" prisoners but also in the most terrible criminals led him to reevaluate his entire view of mankind, and crime became one of the most significant psychological motifs in his work. When he wrote his great novels, crime was a central preoccupation of each new work; and most important of all, he not only pitied the martyr but identified with the criminal.

Shortly after his arrival, Dostoyevsky was assigned to daily labor with penal group 55. The prison records show the following question under the heading "Fyodor Dostoyevsky, age twenty-eight"—"What manual skills does he have, and can he read and write?" The answer: "Unskilled labor. He can read and write." The records also note that he has "a small scar over his left eyebrow" and "behaves well."

This is not to say that the prison authorities were pleased with him. Once when "eight-eyes" (Major Krivtsov) discovered that Dostoyevsky had not gone to work, he was just barely saved from corporal punishment. Dostoyevsky was often threatened and harassed when he directed a play put on by the prisoners in the winter of 1852. On another occasion when he had just returned from the prison clinic, he made a retort to an order, and the Major is said to have implemented a punishment that triggered his first epileptic seizure. This story originates with Alexander Rizenkampf, Dostoyevsky's childhood friend, who at that time was practicing at the hospital in Omsk. It is supported by one of the writer's barracks-mates, who claimed that after complaining about the food, Dostoyevsky was given fifty lashes and was in the hospital for two weeks. Shortly afterward he began to suffer from epilepsy, and his comrades would bind him with their prison garb as he lay and convulsed on the bunk.

The reliability of these accounts is difficult to judge. A number of them have a secondhand quality and are refuted in other sources. At the least, it is certain that Dostoyevsky was often a witness to the punishment of others. Up to twelve thousand blows could be administered as punishment when someone was running the gauntlet, but most collapsed after half that number. After every two thousand blows, they were dragged into the hospital for "treatment"—with sheets drenched in urine. At such times, Dostoyevsky would open the door to the sickroom and say to the surgeons: "Child, dear child! Take good care of him . . . take good care of the unfortunate."

Dostoyevsky's pity for all the *ostrog*'s unfortunates grew with the years. "I wonder where they are now, all those who were prisoners there?" he mused in 1876 when an acquaintance told him about a visit to the prison.

Nevertheless, he was far from popular among his fellow prisoners. He was taciturn, contemplative, and he rarely smiled; one memoirist described his demeanor as that of a "wolf in a trap." His hat was worn far down on his forehead, he looked gloomy and repressed, he walked with his head down and his eyes on the ground, and his face was wasted and marked by serious illness. "The prisoners didn't like him, but they had respect for his moral authority. Glumly, and not without hatred for his superiority, they watched him but stayed away from him. When he understood this, he too kept his distance from them. Only on the rare occasion when he was in difficulty or was very depressed would he make conversation with his fellow inmates." The fact that from time to time he tried to put a damper on the conviviality by calling the prison guard—that he refused to obey the unwritten laws of the barracks—only increased his unpopularity. "What are you thinking of? Have you come to introduce new rules to the prison?"

His relationship with the political prisoners was particularly strained. Indeed, he had always been suspicious of foreigners, but in the *ostrog*, as his nationalism grew, his dislike turned to hatred. "The French," he maintained, "cannot be said to resemble human beings at all, and the English and the Spanish are mere caricatures." In the eyes of the Poles, Dostoyevsky was condescending and contemptuous of everything that was not Russian. His malevolence for the Poles indeed knew no bounds: "If I discovered even a single drop of Polish blood in my veins, I would instantly demand bloodletting," he snarled.

And yet his instincts for self-preservation made him cautious. From the other prisoners he learned how to hide his belongings and how to protect his feet from the chafing fetters. He learned to eat *tyura*, a kind of porridge made from bread crusts and mixed with vodka; and he learned to get women by bribing the guards—the whole thing went on with shackles, under the watchful eyes of a superior.

In the sauna baths, there was little difference between murderers and political prisoners. Dostoyevsky's apocalyptic vision of the naked truth is famous:

> When we closed the door to the bath itself, I thought I had entered hell. Imagine a room twelve paces long and the same width which was to hold a hundred men, at any rate not less than eighty at one time. The prisoners were divided into two groups; all together there were nearly two hundred men who were going to bathe. The room was so filled with steam that one could not see a thing; it was dirty and disgusting and so crowded one didn't know where to stand. . . . Up on the shelf fifty birch switches rose and fell in unison. Everybody whipped himself lustily. More steam was being made all the time. It wasn't just hot; it was like a red-hot oven. Everyone shouted, howled, and shrieked, and a hundred chains clinked and clattered as they were dragged accross the floor. . . . Some men got entangled in the chains of others when they wanted to get through, then got caught on the heads of those who sat underneath them, and fell, swearing and dragging along the others with them. Filthy water poured all around. . . . It was as if everyone was in an intoxicated, excited state, yowling and scream-ing. . . . The shaven heads, the red scalded carcasses seemed even more hideous than before. Scars from earlier whippings and blows stood out vividly. It looked as if these men's backs were covered with fresh welts. What horrible scars! I shuddered when I looked at them. Then they released more steam—the whole bath was filled with a thick, burning cloud. Every-one screamed and yelled. Through the cloud of steam I could see the battered backs, shaven heads, crooked hands and legs. . . . I thought that if ever we should arrive in hell, it would be strongly reminiscent of this place.

Whereas the Petrashevsky members in other prisons had quickly gained a number of privileges, there was no chance of easing conditions in the fortress where Durov and Dostoyevsky had landed. In response to the ini-tiative taken by the Decembrists, an inquiry was sent to the Governor-General in West Siberia about how the new prisoners were to be treated. The answer was brief and to the point: "according to the law." Nothing else could have been expected, either. The Tsar had himself decreed that better treatment would occur only through the prisoners' good behavior or royal benevolence "and absolutely not through the indulgence of local authorities; reliable officials shall be appointed to maintain strict and relentless surveillance over the prisoners." The Tsar saw no reason to hurry with a display of his benevolence. In 1852 when the fortress commandant sought to get Dostoyevsky and Durov transferred to a lighter work detail and released from their ankle shackles, the petition was rejected out of hand. Assurances of the two men's "good behavior, obedience, and diligence" were to no avail.

The result was that Dostoyevsky was treated just as harshly as murderers and rapists, at least for his first two years in Siberia. Everything was run by military command. The awareness that the labor was forced and that it took place under the surveillance of armed guards was almost worse than the work itself, even though it was difficult. Carrying bricks and firing and pounding alabaster were common tasks. Standing knee-deep in the ice-cold water of the Irtysh River and unloading cargo from barges was especially miserable. Dostoyevsky's rheumatic pains were almost intolerable, and once he nearly died from a severe case of pneumonia. Worse than the forced labor were the chains. Shoveling snow in Omsk's busiest street with those shackles on was humiliating. And it was terrible to lie locked between murderers at night, he complained to Prince Mikhail Volkonsky during a visit. When he was young, Dostoyevsky had always feared falling into a deathlike sleep; here in the *ostrog* he felt as if he were buried alive. His survival was due only to his ability to meet crises and his stubborn struggle to stay alive.

Ivan Troitsky, the head of the military hospital in Omsk, became a refuge for Dostoyevsky in his difficult life. The sickly writer was often brought here, and Troitsky sought to make his stays as comfortable as possible. Among other things, he gave him newspapers and books, especially the works of Dickens. Otherwise, on those rare occasions when he was permitted to do so, he would go to visit his former schoolmate Konstantin Ivanov, who had become the adjutant to the General of the Engineering Corps in the fortress. This was a useful connection: Ivanov loaned him money and arranged for specific improvements in his work detail. His acquaintance with Colonel Ivan Zhdan-Pushkin, inspector for the cadet school in Omsk, where Dostoyevsky would later send his stepson, was also advantageous. In general, he became a master at gaining entry to the homes of "powerful people," who were to help him in his upcoming struggle for rehabilitation.

And yet, the city of Omsk itself, center of the military and civil administrations in West Siberia, had a depressing effect on him. "During the summer, one suffers from the heat and dust storms. I haven't seen anything of nature at all. The city is unbelievably dirty, crammed full of military personnel and an utterly depraved population." Those who called this God-forsaken out-of-the-way place the Athens of Siberia must certainly have had active imaginations!

The fact that the four years in the *ostrog* were worse for Dostoyevsky than for most others was due not only to his poor health but also to his feelings of total isolation. He did not receive a single letter from his terrified brother, and he himself had few opportunities to write. Only rarely was he met with compassion—such as the time he was given alms by a peasant girl: "Unfortunate man, take this kopeck for Christ's sake." Often the only one who could comfort him was the prison dog, Sharik. His separation from the other prisoners was painful to him; he felt keenly the people's bitter hatred of the intelligentsia and nobility. "You noblemen have hacked us to death," was a common refrain. "Once you were our masters and you used to torment the people. Now that you have been reduced to the lowest of the low, you want to be our brothers."

The unyielding strain that rose from the consciousness of being caught in an untenable position, condemned by the authorities and hated by his fellow prisoners, was seen clearly in the uncensored letter Dostoyevsky sent to his brother upon his release. "Their hatred of the gentry knows no bounds. They received us with hositility and took pleasure in our misfortune. They would have eaten us alive had they been given the chance."

Dostoyevsky had plenty of time to ponder these reproaches and consider the claim that "nothing is more difficult than winning the confidence of the people." He concluded that the people's age-old hatred of the aristocracy was fully justified. This insight filled him with feelings of guilt and initiated the profound reexamination of all the values that he had laid out in his letter to Mikhail from the Peter-Paul Fortress. He was in the process of "being born in a new form."

In my absolute spiritual solitude, I reexamined the whole of my former life. I scrutinized every minute detail. I thought very carefully about my past. Alone as I was, I judged myself harshly, without mercy. Sometimes I even thanked my fate because it had sent me into solitude, for without it, this new judgement of myself would never have happened.

This reexamination led the former rebel to gain a new respect for the authority of the Tsar and a faith in the sacred mission of the Church for the Russian people. By taking upon himself the great suffering of atonement for what he now considered a youthful error, Dostoyevsky experienced the cathartic power of his own suffering. And he became convinced that it was precisely this suffering that was the deepest need of the Russian people.

Just as important was his hard-earned conviction that the upper cultural stratum of Russian society must unite itself with the people. It was essential to build a bridge over the cleft that Peter the Great's forced Westernization had created between the people and the elite. As a member of the Petrashevsky circle, Dostoyevsky had regarded himself as an enlightener of the people, but what right did the intelligentsia really have to lead the people? Even the dregs of the masses had retained qualities that the intelligentsia's self-appointed "leaders" had long since lost: a belief in God and a consciousness of sin. In reality, the intelligentsia had nothing to teach the people. On the other hand, the people had a great deal to teach the intelligentsia. Whereas others might have become misanthropic while living with thieves and killers, Dostoyevsky was filled with love. "What a wonderful people! No, this time has not been wasted! If I have not seen anything of Russia, I have surely come to know the Russian people—and few or perhaps no others have a knowledge as intimate as mine."

With pride and happiness, Dostoyevsky rediscovered the people's great talent for music and theater and, above all, their remarkable meekness and humility in the face of oppression. In a stalwart Old Believer who protested the regime's attacks against the mission by setting fire to a church, he witnessed an admirable ability to "suffer for the faith," to "carry his cross for the faith." "He cried softly, and every once in a while, I heard him say, 'Do not forsake me, dear God, give me strength. My little children, my dear children, we will never see one another again!'"

The awareness that they had been condemned by the state made the prisoners cling all the more to God. During the regular church services, Dostoyevsky saw his fellow inmates humbled in prayer, fully conscious of their own unworthiness:

The prisoners prayed devoutly, and every time they brought with them a poor kopeck to buy candles or to make an offering. "I too am a man," the convict may have thought as he threw his small coin into the collection box, "in God's eyes we are all equal." After morning Mass, we took Communion. When the priest, wafer in hand, spoke the words "Receive me Lord, even as a thief," nearly everyone kneeled immediately and the chains clanked, for each man understood the words to be directed specifically at him.

And Belinsky had maintained that Russians were a "profoundly atheistic people"!

Even in these murderers and miscreants, Dostoyevsky found a spark of humanity and a glimmer of the divine. For them, too, the distinction between good and evil was the fundamental human category. And out of this observation sprang his belief that the people in their besmirched lowliness hid a promise of mercy and a dream of Christ. The Russian people must not be judged for what they are, but for what they wish to be!

If these representatives of the people were capable of demonstrating such piety in "the house of the dead," imagine the greatness of their moral superiority beyond the stockade—in the Russian *muzhik*, who regarded all criminals as "unfortunates" and forgave them because of the punishment they had to endure; in peasants like Marey, who had comforted him once as a child. Who knew? Perhaps also the peasant convict with the shaven head and branded forehead, who stood there bawling out his crude ditties in a hoarse, drunken voice, was also a Marey. Yes, it was essential to go back to the people, to love all that was the people's. And the path to the people was to be found only through the acceptance of "the people's truth"— embracing the teaching of the Orthodox Church in which they believed. He had set foot upon the soil of the Russian nation and he would never leave it.

While it is true that Dostoyevsky fought his way toward an unshakable belief in the Russian people and the Russian soil, it is difficult to argue that his years in prison led to a decisive change in his religious life. In a letter to Natalya Fonvizina just after his release, he gave the following description of his credo:

I believe that nothing is more beautiful, profound, sympathetic, reasonable, brave, and perfect than Christ. With a jealous love, I say to myself, not only that his equal cannot be found, but that it does not exist. And more, if someone should bring me proof that Christ is outside the truth, then I should prefer to remain with Christ than with the truth.

For many this credo is a sign of Dostoyevsky's ultimate conversion. But if that were the case, he would not have been open to the problematic assertion "if someone should bring me proof that Christ is outside the truth . . ." For someone who believes Christ's words, "I am the way, the truth and the life," this dilemma is incomprehensible. Dostoyevsky's credo is more a "testament to doubt": Christ is an aesthetic ideal, but he himself remains "a child of skepticism and doubt." Still, his desire to believe had been strengthened by the time he spent with corrupted human beings of every possible description; if he believed it was because these people believed.

In January 1854, the four-year prison term was finally over. Early in the morning in mid-February, Dostoyevsky made the rounds in the barracks and took leave of his fellow prisoners. Some took his hand as friends. For others he remained a "master," not a comrade; and there were those who turned away from him and refused to answer his farewell.

Durov, with whom he had had almost no contact during their internment, was released at the same time. Prison had nearly made an invalid of him—"he had been snuffed out in the *ostrog* like a candle." With tremendous effort, he managed to hobble to the smithy to be released from his shackles. Then it was Dostoyevsky's turn. His fetters fell to the ground. "Freedom, a new life, resurrection. What a glorious moment!"

The first half of his sentence had been served. In early November, the Governor-General had sent an inquiry to the Department of Defense about what should be done with Dostoyevsky. The reply was not encouraging. The letter was received by the Chief of the Third Department, and Count Orlov had not forgotten the obstinate writer. After a long while, orders were given that Dostoyevsky was to be conscripted as a private in the Siberian Seventh Line Battalion. The division was quartered in Semipalatinsk, not far from the Chinese border. Whereas his prison term had been restricted to four years, no limit was set for his military service.

II

After a revivifying stay with the hospitable Ivanov family, Dostoyevsky traveled to Semipalatinsk. The journey took him over the Kirghiz steppe, a dreary landscape without trees or grass. Every once in a while the monotony was broken by a caravan of camels or a group of nomad tents. And yet, for the freed prisoner, the trip was a great experience. At the end of his life, he would tell friends that he had never felt as happy as when he drove along the Irtysh River "with the clean air around me and freedom in my heart."

Semipalatinsk, founded under Peter the Great, lay on the right bank of the Irtysh. With its low, fenced-in wooden houses, the place resembled a little village. A single church was the town's only stone structure. More than half of the five to six thousand residents were Muslims. There were seven mosques, and minarets were a dominant feature—but not a particularly inspiring one for an Orthodox writer. There were few stores, no bookstore, and only a few people who subscribed to newspapers "from Russia." When the mail came on Monday, residents were sure to ask for news about the Crimean War, but their interest was not great. The town was comfortingly situated far from Sevastopol. There was no cultural life to speak of—the city apparently had only one piano. When the clerk for the battalion, with Dostoyevsky's help, attempted to put on a play, the occasion ended in scandal when the performers began singing obscene ditties during the intermission. The ladies fled; only the battalion's commanding officer remained, and he sat there half-drunk, chortling away with his men. In this dusty, tired provincial outpost, people were mainly interested in gossip, cards, and vodka.

The Seventh Line Battalion was composed chiefly of released prisoners, exiled peasants, and people who had been paid as surrogate conscripts. Morale was low, dissatisfaction was high; it was for all practical purposes a punishment division, not the least for Dostoyevsky. The form of punishment had been changed, but he remained a political prisoner to be kept "under the strictest surveillance." "When will we be free at last, or at least as free as other people?" he asked Natalya Fonvizina. "Maybe it won't happen until we have no need for freedom any longer. In my soldier's cap, I am the same prisoner as before."

Nevertheless, after his arrival in Semipalatinsk on March, 2, 1854, Dostoyevsky's life became easier. During the first period of his service, he continued to live in barracks, but at least these bunks were covered with felt mattresses, and no one held a rifle over him day and night.

His term in prison had left scars, but on the outside, he remained unchanged—laconic and pensive. "He was of medium height and flat-chested," remarked one of his roommates in Company 1.

With his shaven, emaciated cheeks, his face looked ill and made him appear old. He had gray eyes and a serious, morose expression. In the barracks, none of us soldiers ever saw him smile. . . . He told us nothing of his past and he was not talkative. As for books, he had only a New Testament, but he took very good care of it. It was obvious that it meant a great deal to him. He never wrote in the barracks, but then soldiers didn't have much free time anyway. He rarely went out; mostly he sat there lost in thought.

Still, a number of soldiers liked the despondent newcomer. "With my whole soul I felt that Private Dostoyevsky, always sad and depressed, was an infinitely good person, whom one could not but like," recalled the seventeen-year-old son of a soldier. There were few among these soldiers, if any, who knew that their battalion had been graced by a well-known author.

The work could be very draining. There was continual unrest among the local Kirghiz population, and the Russians had to be vigilant. Dostoyevsky marched, drilled, and took part in numerous parades and inspections. On a single occasion, he participated in running the gauntlet, and on that same day, he suffered a seizure. He was himself never formally punished; only once he received a blow on the neck from a petty officer, though that blow was humiliating enough. When he later spoke of it, he trembled with bitterness. Otherwise he was a model soldier who never shirked his duties. "He was always correct and punctual in his duty," the company commander remembered. "One could never find fault with him."

It was not long before Dostoyevsky—the former nobleman and famous author—gained a number of privileges. Among other things, he was released from his unpleasant guard duty and received permission to live alone. In the spring of 1854, he moved to the Russian section of town and rented a room from a military widow for five rubles a month. The room was small and dark and a host of cockroaches and fleas gave him little peace for work. On the other hand, the widow's two light-footed daughters who cooked and cleaned for him were a great pleasure. The mother clearly exploited their youth and beauty. "Working for a nobleman is a great honor for them. Not all young women are lucky enough to bed down with a serviceman."

The battalion commander was responsible for Dostoyevsky while he lived in this house. There was also a sergeant who was supposed to keep an eye on him, but he allowed himself to be easily lost. After having been watched constantly for five years, Dostoyevsky was finally able to relish the joys of solitude.

But the greatest change in his life after imprisonment was the opportunity once again to read and write. For four years, the New Testament had been practically his only text. He had read only a few works of fiction and had much to make up for.

His first letters to his brother were filled with requests for books. "Buy cheap, densely printed volumes." He needed works of history, economics, physics, and philosophy. He wanted to study the Church Fathers, Kant, and Hegel. His desires were impressively broad—prison certainly had not stifled his intellectual interests. "Books—they are my whole life, my sustenance, my future!" Jealous and competitive, Dostoyevsky pored over the recent works of his literary colleagues: a play by Ostrovsky, novels by Turgenev and Pisemsky. And who was this "L.T," who had just published *Childhood, Boyhood and Youth*? He liked the work but wondered if it wasn't just another passing literary fad. "I believe that he will write very little, but perhaps I am mistaken." That he certainly was—Tolstoy was to leave ninety volumes to posterity. Otherwise, he was not greatly impressed by his contemporaries. Turgenev lacked self-control, Ostrovsky lacked ideals, and Pisemsky wrote too quickly. Dostoyevsky was confident that he would manage to make his way.

Even in the *ostrog* Dostoyevsky had begun to prepare for his comeback with several hundred little sketches and notes about the prisoners' lives, language, and temperaments. The work he was planning, *The House of the Dead*, was to be his trump card. But first he had to behave himself and gain the right to publish. "I will probably get permission at the very latest in six years, perhaps earlier," he wrote to Mikhail right after his release. "Much can change, but I'm not exactly writing nonsense now. You will hear about me." This steadfast belief in his own talent would be expressed again a few years later: "Nobody yet knows the extent of my powers or the scope of my talent."

A stifled attempt to return to the world of literature may be seen in a highly patriotic ode Dostoyevsky wrote several months after he had arrived in Semipalatinsk, "On European Events in 1854." With the aid of his military superiors, he managed to get the poem sent to General Dubelt in the Third Department. But even though the poem fulminates with the bombast of official wrath over the declaration of war by the Western powers and pays tribute to the notion of the restoration of an Eastern Empire under Russian rule, it never got any further than the Third Department's vast archives.

Unhappy and depressed, Dostoyevsky continued his life in the wilderness. Perhaps the worst of it was that the mail was so unbelievably slow; because all his correspondence had to be investigated and censored by the Third Department, a letter took up to two months to arrive. Only once in a rare while did Dostoyevsky get a chance to send an uncensored letter back to European Russia along with an acquaintance. His poverty, too, made him extremely miserable. When he was out with friends, he never dared to take off his soldier's coat because his pants were so dirty and ragged. In order to improve his finances, he went around from house to house giving private lessons. He was a strict and inflexible teacher, but when his students got the answers right, they were often rewarded with a bag of sweets. He had a sweet tooth himself, as a matter of fact, but tried to keep himself away from the constant flow of liquor. "He who drinks immoderately lacks respect for human dignity—both in himself and in others." Gambling, however, was a greater temptation, and only his poverty kept him from it. "Oh, the way they played yesterday. The excitement was tremendous! If only I had had some money. . . . This devilish gaming is a real downfall. . . . I can see very clearly that is an abominable passion, but my desire is nearly irresistible."

Once in a while, Dostoyevsky was treated with visits from old acquaintances: the geographer Pyotr Semyonov who would become famous as the result of his exploration of the Tien Shan mountain terrain, and the ethnographer Chokan Valikhanov, the first Kirghiz scientist. Dostoyevsky had great expectations for Valikhanov's studies of his homeland and his work for cultural and economic relations between "the steppes" and Russia.

A new friend, Baron Alexander Wrangel, was to have great significance for Dostoyevsky. In November 1854 he came to Semipalatinsk as the public prosecutor. The twenty-one-year-old lawyer was a great admirer of Dostoyevsky and had witnessed the mock execution on Semenovsky Square. And after that, he had come to know the writer's brother. Mikhail took the opportunity presented by Wrangel's departure to send along gifts and books to his brother. As soon as Wrangel arrived, he sent word to Dostoyevsky. He described their meeting as follows:

Dostoyevsky did not know who had invited him or the reason for the invitation and therefore was at a loss for words when he first arrived. He was wearing a gray soldier's coat with a high collar and red epaulettes. He looked morose. His sickly, pale face was covered with freckles and his blond hair was cut short. He was a little over average height and looked at me intensely with his sharp, gray-blue eyes. It was as if he were trying to look into my soul and discover what kind of man I was. Later he admitted to me that he had been very worried when he heard the "public prosecutor" wanted to meet him. But when I offered my apologies for not having visited him first, when I brought out the letters, packages, and greetings and spoke to him in a friendly way, he changed at once and began to trust me.

This meeting marked the beginning of a long and devoted friendship. There were many who wondered how the new public prosecutor—a typical gentleman who was conscious of his high noble rank—could keep company with a common soldier, and they warned him against the bad influences of associating with a former revolutionary prisoner. Wrangel, however, was eager for the town's leading citizens to get to know Dostoyevsky. After delaying for a long time, the military governor himself, Peter Spiridonov, consented to a meeting. "All right, bring him, but it has to be kept simple. Tell him to wear his soldier's coat." It was not long after that meeting that the doors of the city's homes were opened to Dostoyevsky. He was well liked by everyone, especially women, who were drawn to his fate. To one of them, an ordinary peasant woman, from whom he used to buy bread, he wrote a long love letter, which was later lost.

The summers in Semipalatinsk were so hot that one could boil an egg in the sand. The city had been dubbed "the Devil's sandbox" for a reason. So the two friends thought it would be wise to rent a small summer house outside the city. Here in "Cossack Garden," they gardened enthusiastically, growing flowers and vegetables. Dostoyevsky loved to water the dahlias and carnations because the task reminded him of childhood days in Darovoye. And Wrangel persuaded him to go on short riding excursions. But in spite of the distinctive natural beauty of the steppe, Dostoyevsky had little enthusiasm for the landscape, which didn't make an impression on him, Wrangel recalled. He was too "absorbed" in the study of humanity. Only the splendid night sky lit with stars brought him peace and comfort, just as it would Alyosha in *The Brothers Karamazov*.

What Dostoyevsky liked best was to pace back and forth in his room, lost in thought and talking to himself, with his frock coat buttoned up and his pipe in his mouth. "Something new was always being conceived in that head of his," commented Wrangel. The Baron was himself interested in the natural sciences and studied erudite monographs on geography and archaeology, but that was not to Dostoyevsky's taste. "Aargh, put away those professor books!" he told his friend, and suggested that they begin a translation of Hegel's *History of Philosophy* and Carus's *Psyche.*

Politics were a frequent topic of discussion. Dostoyevsky, whose views had now become conservative, maintained that at the moment it was absurd to think of introducing a constitutional government in Russia. Recent political events, however, were a source of unrest and worry. The Crimean War was going poorly for Russia. The "colossus with clay feet" had begun to totter from thirty years of reactionary misrule. On February 18, 1855, the Tsar died. Many believed that he had taken his own life. The announcement of his death reached Semipalatinsk on March 12, and Dostoyevsky and Wrangel attended the funeral Mass that same day in the city's cathedral.

Tsar Nicholas's death and the outcome of the war in the Crimea were bitter news for a patriot like Dostoyevsky. But at the same time, the Tsar's death spawned new hope for all the intellectuals who had been languishing in Siberia since Nicholas's accession. Now perhaps they would be given amnesty. Baron Wrangel immediately took action to try to help his friend. Wouldn't it be possible to put in a good word for Dostoyevsky to General Dubelt or Count Orlov? he asked his sister in a letter. It would be terrible should this extraordinary man die as a soldier in Siberia!

Dostoyevsky followed the endeavors on his behalf with suspense and expectation, for even though he was better off as a soldier than he had been as a prisoner, he remained isolated from the literary world. In a new ode, he comforted the widowed Empress in her grief, "He never could have been great without you!" The writer showed his work to the Governor-General, Gustaf Gasfort, who noted the poem's "warm, patriotic feelings" and forwarded it to the proper authorities. "Dostoyevsky," Gasfort wrote in his letter, "is a good worker and is deeply repentant of his crime." Might it be possible, in consideration of his good behavior, for Dostoyevsky to procure from the new Tsar a promotion to the rank of *unter-ofitser?*

Dostoyevsky's "warm, patriotic feelings" were soon rewarded. An acquaintance of the Wrangel family, Prince Peter of Oldenburg, brought the poem to the Empress, and on November 20, 1855, the writer was promoted to *unter-ofitser* in light of his good behavior and eagerness to serve. But despite the fact that Dostoyevsky was the first of the Petrashevsky circle to be promoted, he still did not have the right to publish, and he did not have his freedom. And now he needed his freedom more than ever, because he was making plans to get married.

III

Shortly after his arrival in Semipalatinsk, Dostoyevsky had become acquainted with Alexander Isayev, a drunken former customs officer. "He was careless as a gypsy, vain and proud, and had no self-discipline whatsoever," Dostoyevsky wrote of this man, who with his cloying sentimentality became a prototype for the character of Marmeladov in *Crime and Punishment*. Still, Dostoyevsky was not without respect for Isayev. He had great sympathy for "noble" and "ambitious" people who had fallen to a state of complete degeneracy. "Fyodor Mikhailovich's lenience with other people knew no bounds," Wrangel wrote. "He excused all their shortcomings with arguments about insufficient education and bad environmental influences. He would also often find explanations in their nature and temperament. 'That's just the way God made them,' he used to say."

Isayev's wife was the primary object of the writer's interest and sympathy, however. Maria Dimitrievna Isayeva was the daughter of a high school director in Astrakhan. Her maiden name was Constant; her grandfather had fled France during the Revolution. In all events, her marriage to the poor civil servant was an unhappy one, both for her and for her seven-year-old son, Pasha. After a number of scandalous scenes, the city's better families had closed their doors to the Isayevs. Only Dostoyevsky held out. Day after day, he would admonish the unemployed sot, give lessons to his son, and console his consumptive wife. He tried to get Wrangel to come along with him, but his friend was above socializing with the dubious company that frequented the Isayev household.

Dostoyevsky pitied Maria and wanted to help her. Like the narrator's mother in *A Raw Youth*, she was a "helpless being" with whom one didn't exactly fall in love but whom, for some reason, one suddenly pitied. "You feel sorry for them and then attracted," Versilov explains," and then you cannot tear yourself away from them."

Maria's suffering in her life with Isayev served only to increase the writer's desire. For him love meant self-sacrifice. If the price to be paid was agony and misery, then the intensity of his passion only grew. Within a brief time, his sympathy had become a passion that brought him both joy and sorrow. "At the least, I have lived. Even though I have suffered, I have still lived," he wrote later.

Maria Dimitrievna was a thin, pale, sickly blonde, a woman who was a dangerous combination of Katerina Ivanovna and Natasya Filippovna—

passionate, intense, fickle, and hysterical. "This woman is still young, twenty-eight years old; she is beautiful, educated, very wise, good, sweet, gracious, and has a fine and noble heart," he assured his brother half a year after their first meeting. Dostoyevsky had immense admiration for this persevering woman, for her valiant ability to endure her hopeless fate. She was a "knight in woman's clothing" who sometimes reminded him of his mother.

Wrangel, who had the dubious pleasure of observing the relationship close up, wrote:

> She was kind to him, not because she cared deeply for him, but rather because she felt sorry for this unhappy man who had been treated so harshly by fate. It is possible that she was even attached to him, but she was never really in love with him. She knew that he suffered from a nervous illness and had no money. He was a "man without a future," she said. But Fyodor Mikhailovich misconstrued her sympathy for reciprocated love, and he loved her with all the ardor that a young man can show.

But the relationship was from the first founded on misunderstanding. Mutual pity was to show itself a poor substitute for mutual love: they probably sensed that their attraction was founded on pity and began to hate each other for that reason. Was Maria merely flattered by the attentions of a once famous writer, or was she on the lookout for a new provider for herself and her son? Dostoyevsky's doubts intensified when Isayev got a post as the caretaker of an inn in 1855 and took his family with him to Kuznetsk, a backwater town about six hundred kilometers from Semipalatinsk. Dostoyevsky went around half-crazed after he heard about the move. And she who had just "shown" him that she loved him! "The worst is that she consented to the move," he complained to Wrangel, "she didn't even offer any protest!"

Near the end of May, the Isayev family left Semipalatinsk. Dostoyevsky and Wrangel accompanied them part of the way. Wrangel got the future caretaker drunk on champagne so that Maria and Dostoyevsky could sit and enjoy the moonlight. "I will never forget their parting," Wrangel wrote. "Dostoyevsky stood there and sobbed like a small child."

But that was only the end of Act One in this romantic drama. Its continuation is difficult to describe in detail. Of Dostoyevsky's letters— whole notebooks long, according to Wrangel—only the first remains, and Maria's letters have been lost. Dostoyevsky also described the relationship in his correspondence with others, but in these letters, whole passages have been carefully crossed out by Dostoyevsky's second wife. A look at that first letter from Dostoyevsky to Maria shows us why. It is an inflamed piece of prose, written by a man consumed by and grateful for his blinding passion. "You are an admirable woman with a singular heart of almost childlike goodness," he wrote. "Simply the fact that a woman reached out to me was a great event in my life. A man, even the best of men, often shows himself to be nothing but a blockhead! A woman's heart, a woman's sympathy and concern, of which we men have no conception and which we in our stupidity often do not even notice, is irreplaceable. And all this I have found in you!"

Dostoyevsky responded to Maria's complaints with the greatest understanding. If only he could help her! About her burden of a sick old grandmother, he was furious. His usual compassion for the weak and helpless was drowned in his contempt:

I can vividly imagine that grandmother of yours, and the way she goes about annoying and bothering you, the abominable old crone! She should have kept herself going to the end of her days with her lapdogs! I do hope that Alexander Ivanovich will be able to get a will out of her without having to take her under your roof. She must be made to see that this is the best solution. Otherwise, she must agree in writing to die within three months (and to pay three thousand rubles per month). On the other hand, you must not give her a room. Imagine being forced to take care of her lapdogs, you with your frail health! Oh, such old ladies are absolutely unbearable!

All in all, the letters that came from Kuznetsk brought him more pain than joy. Maria's complaints about sickness and poverty grew more shrill. The writer despaired; he became suddenly superstitious and went to visit fortune-tellers. "He became even thinner than before," Wrangel wrote. "He was morose, irritable; he wandered around like a shadow and even had to suspend his work on *The House of the Dead.*"

What if Wrangel arranged a meeting of the lovers halfway between Semipalatinsk and Kuznetsk? Dostoyevsky was thrilled with the idea, but he could not obtain permission to take such a long trip. With the help of the military doctor, Wrangel spread the rumor that the writer was seriously ill and must not be disturbed for several days. In great haste, they set off for the scheduled meeting. All for naught! Dostoyevsky's despair was indescribable when, upon their arrival, he found only a message that Maria was unable to come because of her husband's illness.

Then, in the middle of 1855, news arrived that Isayev had died. Pasha was beside himself with grief, and Maria was tormented by loneliness and insomnia, but worst of all was their penury. She had even had to borrow for her husband's funeral. "Want tugged at my sleeve, and I put out my hand and had to accept . . . charity," she wrote. Didn't he pity her?

Dostoyevsky certainly did. He borrowed money and sent it to her; he tried to get Pasha into the cadet school in Omsk. But he could not win her love, and every day his fears that she would choose another increased. Undoubtedly suitors were lining up to propose to the lovely widow—this "heavenly angel." And then, just as he had feared, she wrote and timidly asked for his advice. What should she do if "an older man of good character, a well-situated government official" asked for her hand?

Dostoyevsky suddenly found himself in the same position as Devushkin in *Poor Folk*, who had had to watch his beloved Varenka go off and marry the old and wealthy Bykov. And just like Devushkin, he was degraded to the position of an errand boy while his beloved made wedding plans. He had to hurry up and help her get her widow's pension before she married again. He had almost predicted his own future! He, the only one who had a right to her! "Oh, God preserve us from this terrible, frightening emotion," he wrote to Wrangel on March 23, 1856. "The joys of love are great, but the suffering is so horrible that it is better never to have loved at all."

The same despair informs his letters to his brother. The fact that this woman had become the whole world for him made him deaf to all objections. "I live and breathe only for her . . . she has promised to become my wife. She loves me and has shown me that she does. But she is so alone and helpless. . . . Oh, I am so unhappy, so unhappy! I am tortured, killed! My soul quakes. I have suffered for so long; for seven years, I have endured the most unimaginable tortures, but there must be some bounds! I am not made of stone!" At the same time he asked his brother not to disclose his love to his sisters. What he feared most of all was "sound advice."

Vain in her power over Dostoyevsky, Maria continued to play on his *"jalousie incomparable."* Tenderly, comfortingly, she assured him that the wealthy official did not really exist. She had only wanted to test his devotion! This seems rather to have been a way of breaking off their relationship without hurting Dostoyevsky too badly. Soon after that, she began to describe her encounters with a "young, sympathetic teacher with a noble soul." Dostoyevsky had left *Poor Folk* only to land in the pages of "White Nights": a younger rival had come on the scene. "Dostoyevsky languished with jealousy," Wrangel noted. "It was awful to watch his dark mood and how it affected his health." To express his misery the writer resorted to Latin: "Eheu!"—alas—is an expression that recurs in his journal from this period.

Now it was time for all uncertainty to end. During an official trip to Barnaul in the summer of 1856, Dostoyevsky risked an unpermitted excursion to Kuznetsk. "I have seen her again," he exclaimed in a letter to Wrangel. "What a noble, angelic soul!" But the joy of reunion was soon overshadowed by bitterness. Maria could only reiterate her love for the schoolmaster, a dull youth named Nikolai Vergunov. "She wept and kissed my hands, but she loves another," Dostoyevsky acknowledged miserably. And yet she did not want to send him away without hope. "At the same time, she said, 'Don't cry, don't be sad, all is not over yet; it is you and I and no one else.' Those were her actual words. Oh those days I spent with her—the bliss, the unbearable agony! At the end of the second day, I left her *filled* with *hope*."

Not long after, he received a letter saying that she loved the schoolteacher after all. Oh, what did she want with that fellow anyway? He was five years younger than she and earned only three hundred rubles a year. What kind of a man was a coarse schoolteacher from Siberia for a refined, cultivated woman like her? Wouldn't she merely ruin herself all over again? And wouldn't this teacher begin to reproach her before long for taking advantage of his youth simply to satisfy her sensual needs? Perhaps this pure and heavenly angel shouldn't have to listen to such insults! "My heart nearly bursts at the thought of it! Her happiness is more important than my own. I have spoken to her about all of this. . . . She listened to me and was afraid, but with women emotions always win, even over the soundest reason."

A meeting between Dostoyevsky and Vergunov understandably did not result in any clarification of the dilemma. "I have met him," Dostoyevsky wrote to Wrangel. "He stood there beside me and cried. I guess that is all he is capable of—crying." Didn't this schoolteacher understand that he was in the process of ruining a woman's life for his own happiness? He had no money and was much, much younger than she! But Vergunov was only offended by these attacks, and Maria defended him warmly.

Reluctantly, the writer admitted that he had lost another round. But at least she should not be subject to want and poverty. Couldn't Wrangel do something for this teacher? "Praise him to high heaven. . . . He is apparently not without talent. . . . I do all this for *her* and for her *alone*," is how Dostoyevsky ended his unhappy plea.

Maria tortured her suitors and then tortured herself because of them. Within this sadomasochistic game, she discovered a pleasure that was very close to Dostoyevsky's own feelings. He suffered, too, but his suffering was also a source of arousal. Suspense, tears, passion, insults, and longing united to create a single burning sensation that confirmed the power of existence. Sometimes he felt that he loved her even more than before, simply because she had tortured and betrayed him.

In Maria's eyes, Dostoyevsky continued to be a man without a future. If only he could raise his status by being promoted to an officer. "Naturally, I would then come before all others," he wrote to Wrangel. It really was asking too much for such a woman to marry a worthless *unter-ofitser*.

When Wrangel received no reply to his inquiries in St. Petersburg, Dostoyevsky took a bold step to help his own cause. At the Academy of Engineers, he had become acquainted with Eduard Totleben, whose supervision of the fortification of Sevastopol during the Crimean War had earned him a reputation throughout Europe, and who now had become a darling of the Tsar. On March 24, 1856, Dostoyevsky wrote a long letter to the Adjutant General in which he explained his "sorrowful past."

"I was guilty. I recognize this fully. I was convicted for my intention (but nothing more) to act against the government. I was judged in a legal and just way." But since that time his views had changed dramatically, and it was difficult for him to continue to pay for that which he had abandoned long ago—"for that which has now been transformed within me to its opposite." Therefore the military could not possibly fulfill his life's goals. Besides, he could demonstrate significant success as a writer. If only he could regain his right to publish! "I have always regarded the vocation of a writer as noble and good, and I am convinced that only in this field will I be of any real use."

Wrangel immediately contacted Totleben, who was deeply touched by Dostoyevsky's letter and promised to use his influence with Tsar Alexander II. When the Tsar also received an ode for his coronation in which Christ himself is depicted as the model for royal love and forgiveness, the matter of Dostoyevsky's promotion was finally taken up. By late autumn, the Tsar had come to the following resolution:

It pleases his Majesty to recommend that the Minister of War give his written consent to the promotion of Fyodor Dostoyevsky to Second Lieutenant in one of the 2nd Army's regiments. And if this should be unfeasible, then he is to be discharged at the rank of 14th class and given a civil post. In both events, he should be allowed to occupy himself with literature in the possibility that he may publish his work according to the law.

Dostoyevsky was promoted to officer status on October 26, 1856. It was a happy day, but his joy was tempered by the fact that the authorities had decided to keep him under secret surveillance. Only when his behavior had been judged "blameless" in every respect would he be allowed to publish.

In April 1857 Dostoyevsky was given the green light to publish his new works. "A Little Hero," the story he had worked on in the Peter-Paul Fortress, was printed in August. By this time he was already well under way with his short novels *Uncle's Dream* and *The Village of Stepanchikovo*, which were both printed in 1859.

These works were of lesser quality than what he had written earlier and far below what he would write in the future. In fact, they are so weak that later in life he preferred not to be reminded of them. "The more cuts the better," he wrote in 1873 to a colleague who wanted to write a theatrical version of *Uncle's Dream*. And Dostoyevsky's name was not to appear on any posters.

The best that can be said for these works is that they offer an impressive testimony to the scope of Dostoyevsky's talent. By demonstrating the fertile ground in which his imagination worked, they speak of his artistic ability. No sooner had he been released from his trials in prison than he began work on humorous sketches about life in the provinces. *Uncle's Dream*, the tale of the attempt to marry off a young girl to a mournful old prince, is a farce; while *The Village of Stepanchikovo*, which depicts a freeloader as a tyrant, is a comedy that makes satirical jibes against a literary master—Gogol.

The books do, however, point to the future of Dostoyevsky's work, the former in its introduction of the proud woman who decides to sacrifice herself, and the latter in its portrait of a downtrodden person who takes revenge for his earlier oppression. Still, this comic genre was not for Dostoyevsky. With the exception of the scandal scenes, the humor is heavy-handed, and his understandable fear of the censor kept the work remote from the realities of Russian life. At a time dominated by thoughts of political reform, he was writing about senile old princes and noble landowners without a word about the country's problems.

The result was that Dostoyevsky had real difficulty getting the novels published, despite the supportive sentiments of editors at several journals. Nikolai Nekrasov at *The Contemporary* and Mikhail Katkov at *The Russian Messenger* only shook their heads when they read these *passé* works. "Dostoyevsky is finished as a writer" was Nekrasov's sad comment. "He won't write anything more." When these manuscripts were finally printed in less influential journals for very modest fees, there was not a single review—a disappointing resumption of a promising career. This was not the kind of work to offer at a time when Turgenev had just published *A Nest of Gentlefolk* and Goncharov had become famous for *Oblomov*. And it did not help matters either that St. Petersburg's literary circles were ridiculing the former radical for his "laudatory odes" to the power of the Tsar and autocracy. Dostoyevsky's struggle to return to literature was difficult. The feelings and thoughts that had been conceived in the darkness of imprisonment needed more years before they could bear fruit.

But at least he had become an officer and therefore had a better chance with Maria. "I think of nothing else," he wrote to Wrangel in November 1856. "If only I could see her, hear her. I have become an unhappy madman. This kind of love is an illness; I am sure of that." And in a letter to Mikhail, "How this will end, I do not know. I will go out of my mind or even worse if I can't see her again. . . . She is one of God's angels whom I have met on my way and our suffering has bound us together."

A woman caught between two men—this theme runs through all of Dostoyevsky's early work from *Poor Folk* to *The Landlady* to "White Nights." He understood this configuration as well as anyone both from literature and from life. In a letter to Wrangel, who was then suffering in an unhappy liaison with the wife of General Gerngros, Dostoyevsky emphatically confirmed the hopelessness of an alliance that was not founded on mutual love. This woman was unworthy of him, Dostoyevsky wrote; he must have mistaken her character. Couldn't he see that she was only toying with him? And didn't he see how naïve her games were? "You will make her happy by leaving her alone. That is what she wants, too; I am sure of it."

Giving advice to others, however, was easier than taking his own advice, and Dostoyevsky continued to misinterpret Maria's pity for love. He could understand that she had a hard time making a decision, that she wished to remain "friends" with both him and the schoolteacher, but now he had to have an answer, and it had better be positive!

At the end of November, he made yet another trip to Kuznetsk, this time in the full uniform of an officer. We do not know what made the greatest impression on her—his promotion or his vow to give Pasha a good education. In all events, she gave her consent. "She loves me now; of this I am absolutely sure," he wrote to Wrangel. At the same time, he felt a new concern for his poor rival. Couldn't Wrangel put in a good word for him with the Governor-General, so that he could at least get himself a teaching degree? This he truly deserved, this excellent young man who had now become for him "dearer than a brother."

The battle for Maria's favor had been draining, and now that he had finally triumphed, Dostoyevsky felt little but exhaustion and indifference. The excitement was in the past, victory had come too late, and the price had been too high. Now both his stepson and his rival had to be educated. The letters Dostoyevsky wrote after he returned to Semipalatinsk show no sign of pleasure for the upcoming wedding. Instead, they are filled with dry calculations for necessary expenditures and imaginative speculations on how to obtain loans. He had only one mattress and one pillow. And Maria needed new attire, he explained to his brother: lovely blue dress material, a mantilla, half a dozen Dutch handkerchiefs, and two bonnets "preferably with blue ribbons, not expensive but pretty."

The Kumanin family, which had always been a guardian angel for Dostoyevsky when he needed money, was initially opposed to the marriage. As soon as he had managed to escape one misfortune, he wanted to drag another person along with him into another. Nevertheless, after a delay, they sent him six hundred rubles. He got another few hundred from his brothers and sisters, and he borrowed the rest from acquaintances in Kuznetsk.

On February 6, 1857, the marriage papers were signed in Kuznetsk. "Both are of legal age to marry," it says in the church records. "The groom is thirty-four years old, the bride twenty-nine, and both are in command of their full faculties."

Only a few people were present at the church during the nuptials, which took place on February 15. Among the witnesses was Vergunov. The atmosphere must have been tense: the bride standing before the altar with her groom and her lover on either side. Dostoyevsky was uneasy and harassed by doubts. What if she changed her mind at the last minute and fled the church with his rival in close pursuit? Or what if his rival murdered her in a fit of jealousy, or if he himself should lose his mind? In these agonizing minutes, the writer may have experienced what he later portrayed in *The Idiot*, when Nastasya Filippovna runs off with Rogozhin just before her wedding to Prince Myshkin.

But the epilogue to the romance between Dostoyevsky and Maria Dimitrievna was not so dramatic as the one in the novel, though it was just as sad. Already on their "honeymoon," as they traveled back to Semipalatinsk, their unhappiness began. The nervous tension of recent days became intolerable for Dostoyevsky, and he suffered a reaction to them. During their stay in Barnaul, he was stricken with a fierce attack that was immediately diagnosed as "real epilepsy." Since his imprisonment, Dostoyevsky had been haunted by the suspicion that he might have epilepsy. The initial catalyst for the disease, he believed, was his grueling experience on Semenovsky Square. When he looked back, he realized that he had had several attacks in Siberia, some quite clearly brought on by the drinking his fellow soldiers pressured him into. But the doctors refused to believe him, and the illness had remained undiagnosed until now. If he wasn't careful, the doctor now advised, he could suffocate from the throat spasms; he should seek the help of a specialist as soon as possible.

In a way, the doctor's advice helped to decide matters. His illness was a good reason to seek a discharge from the military. As an epileptic, he could not continue to serve as an officer. And as for his marriage, a seizure occurring practically on the wedding night was a bad omen. A notion of the dread that Maria must have felt when she watched her convulsing and unconscious husband is seen in Dostoyevsky's description of Prince Myshkin's seizure in *The Idiot*, when even Rogozhin loses his composure:

It is a well-known fact that epileptic fits, the *epilepsy* itself, come on instantaneously. At that instant the face suddenly becomes horribly distorted, especially the eyes. Spasms and convulsions seize the whole body and the features of the face. A terrible, quite incredible scream, which is unlike anything else, breaks from the chest; in that scream everything human seems suddenly to be obliterated, and it is quite impossible, at least very difficult, for an observer to imagine and to admit that it is the man himself who is screaming. One gets the impression that it is someone inside the man who is screaming. This, at any rate, is how many people describe their impression; the sight of a man in an epileptic fit fills many others with absolute and unbearable horror, which has something mystical about it. It must be assumed that it was this impression of sudden horror, accompanied by all the other terrible impressions of the moment, that paralyzed Rogozhin, and so saved the prince from the inevitable blow of the knife with which he had been attacked. Then, before he had time to realize that it was a fit, seeing that the prince had recoiled from him and suddenly fallen backwards down the stairs, knocking the back of his head violently against the stone step, Rogozhin rushed headlong downstairs and, avoiding the prostrate figure and scarcely knowing what he was doing, ran out of the hotel.

Maria regretted her decision almost immediately, and she did not keep it to herself. Why hadn't she chosen the young teacher over an ageing epileptic? How could a woman with any self-respect love a jailbird, a man who had spent four years in prison with thieves and assassins? "A woman who lets herself be wed always takes revenge on her husband afterward" are Peter Verkhovensky's cynical words in *The Possessed*, and they are not without foundation in Dostoyevsky's own unhappy experience in his marriage to Maria. "My life is hard and bitter," he wrote at the end of 1858. Dostoyevsky suffered from a growing presentiment of an early death—his "heavenly angel" vanished from his letters.

A harrowing home life with the fickle, jealous Maria caused a swift deterioration in Dostoyevsky's health. The seizures came with ever greater frequency, and each time the aftermath was worse; he suffered from complete exhaustion, lasting amnesia, and deep depression. In December 1858, he received the following recommendation from the battalion physician in Semipalatinsk:

The patient is thirty-five years old and of a rather weak constitution. In 1850 he suffered his first epileptic seizure, which manifested itself in screams, a loss of consciousness, spasms, foaming at the mouth, and respiratory difficulties with a weak and quickened pulse. In 1853 he was stricken with another attack, and lately they have been coming at the end of every month.

At the moment, Mr. Dostoyevsky feels extremely enervated and suffers from frequent nervous pains that are the result of an organic disease in the brain.

Although Mr. Dostoyevsky has suffered from epilepsy nearly without pause for four years, the condition has not improved, and therefore he is unable to continue in his Majesty's service.

On April 17, 1857, Dostoyevsky's hereditary nobility was restored, a show of favor that he interpreted as "total forgiveness" for his crime. Equipped with his doctor's report, he sent in his petition for a discharge on January 16, 1858, accompanied by a plea to be allowed to live in Moscow. However, he was then informed that as a former political prisoner he could not count on access to the capital. The writer chose Tver (the present Kalinin) as his residence. This city had strong connections to both Moscow and St. Petersburg. Dostoyevsky did not receive his discharge until one year later on March 18, 1859, when he left the military with the rank of lieutenant. The Tsar decided, nevertheless, that Dostoyevsky should continue to be kept under secret surveillance.

On July 2, 1859, the couple was finally able to leave Semipalatinsk. On their way, they passed through Omsk to pick up Pasha, whom Dostoyevsky had managed to place in the cadet school there. His stepson was already well on the way to becoming a disagreeable young man who would later bring his stepfather much pain. They continued through Chumen, Yekaterinburg (the present Sverdlovsk), Nizhni Novgorod (the present Gorky), and Vladimir. Seeing Europe again was exhilarating:

One fine day near evening, at about five o'clock in the afternoon as we came to the foot of the Ural mountains, we reached the boundary between Europe and Asia. . . . We stepped out of the open carriage and I crossed myself as I thanked God for at last bringing me to the promised land. Then we took out our bottle of orange liqueur and raised our glasses in a farewell toast to Asia and went into the woods and picked heaps of wild strawberries.

An entire decade of suffering was in the past. Dostoyevsky's resurrection as an artist and a prophet was imminent.

The place where he began his new life was auspicious. The meaning of his exile cannot be given too much importance. His suffering—the fact that he spent four years in prison; that he lived and worked with the nation's worst criminals; that he suffered the same fate as the Decembrists, those heroes of Russian youth—all this was to give him great strength and authority. When he was asked later what right he had to speak for the people, he had only to lift his trouser legs and point to the scars left by his chains: "Here is my right!" Then there was silence. Dostoyevsky was to become not only a great writer but also a great martyr, who, like Christ, had been tortured and punished as an enemy of the state.

But most important, his suffering caused a transformation of his ideas and values, his rebirth in a new form. "At the time, fate came to my rescue," he said near the end of his life. "Prison saved me. . . . I became a completely new person. . . . Yes, Siberia and imprisonment became a great joy for me. . . . Only there was I able to lead a pure and happy life; it was there that I came to see myself clearly and there that I learned to understand Christ." He gave a similar reply to a lady who expressed dismay at all the unnecessary suffering he had had to endure. "You are mistaken. I have no complaint at all. It was a good school. It strengthened my faith and awakened my love for those who bear all their suffering with patience. It also strengthened my love for Russia and opened my eyes to the great qualities of the Russian people."

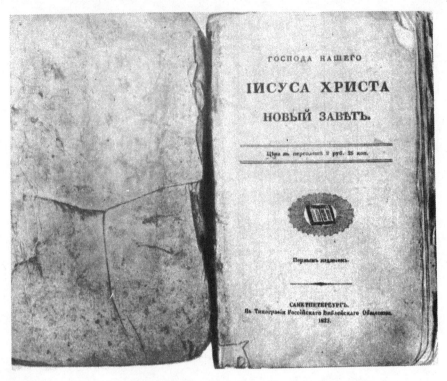

The title page of the New Testament Dostoyevsky was given as a gift in January 1850.

The stockade surrounding the prison in Omsk. From an 1897 photograph.

Prisoners. N. *Karasin, the 1890s.*

Semipalatinsk. Photograph from the late 1850s.

Maria Dmitrievna,
Dostoyevsky's first wife.

Dostoyevsky. Photograph, 1859.

6

HOMECOMING

"The word, the word is a great thing!"

"I have taken on the burdens of family life and bear them," Dostoyevsky wrote when he finally arrived in Tver after a month and a half of traveling. "But I have no feeling that life is over and no desire to die."

His optimistic outlook was valuable, because aside from a moving reunion with his brother Mikhail at the end of August, there was little to be cheerful about in this "incredibly boring city." "Cloudy, cold, stone buildings, no traffic, nothing of interest—not even a decent library. A real jail!" The prices were sky-high, the people selfish; he was miserable from the first day.

For a writer who dreamed of making a brilliant comeback, this was not the place to be. Well aware that a number of the Petrashevsky circle had been given back their full freedom, Dostoyevsky found a place near the post office and began working to have the injunction lifted against his living in the capitals. Old and new contacts with "powerful persons" were exploited to the utmost. Through Baron Wrangel, he sent another letter to Adjutant General Totleben. He had to live in St. Petersburg, he argued, partly in order to seek medical help for his illness, partly to put his stepson into one of the city's schools, but more than anything else so that he could return to literature. "Eduard Ivanovich! Save me once again! Use your influence as you did three years ago. . . . All my hope is in you. I know that I am a great burden to you, but please forgive a sick and unhappy man. Yes, I am still unhappy." A similar letter was sent to the chief of the secret police, Prince Dolgorukov.

Before long, the writer also ingratiated himself with the Governor-General in Tver, Count Pavel Baranov, who advised him to send a plea directly to Tsar Alexander II. He would deliver the letter himself through his nephew, Count Vladimir Adlerberg, currently the Court Royal Councillor. The Governor-General, who regularly received police reports on Dostoyevsky, could confirm that he was behaving himself "exceedingly well."

"I, a former political criminal, venture herewith to offer my humble plea before your exalted throne," began Dostoyevsky's letter to the Tsar. "Bring me back to life; give me the chance to be useful to my family and perhaps also to my Fatherland. . . . I know that I am unworthy of Your Majesty's beneficence, that I am the last who should dare hope for Your Majesty's mercy. But I am unhappy, and you, our ruler, are infinitely merciful. Forgive me for this letter and do not punish with your wrath an unhappy man who is in need of mercy."

Weeks passed. The wheels of bureaucracy turned slowly, and the fact that he had used several channels only delayed the matter further. "The situation is sad and difficult," he complained to his brother in the beginning of October. "I wonder if there will ever be an end to my misfortunes, if God will give me the opportunity to embrace all of you and begin a new and better life!"

Finally, at the end of November, news came that the "all-merciful" Tsar had given permission for the move, "yet the already implemented secret surveillance of Dostoyevsky shall continue in St. Petersburg."

Dostoyevsky was back in St. Petersburg around the middle of December 1859. Almost exactly ten years had passed since he had departed from that city in ankle chains. Much had happened in his life and in his thinking since that time, and a great deal had happened in the development of Russian society. Russia, too, was soon to free itself from its chains. The 1860s have been called "the Russian spring." The new Tsar had begun comprehensive reforms. More than a hundred newspapers and periodicals were founded; the censor was more lenient; women were admitted to universities. For the first time the curse of serfdom could be discussed in Russian publications. People waited with great excitement for a manifesto that would announce the abolition of serfdom.

In the United States it took a civil war to bring about similar reform; the Tsar ended the problem with a single stroke of his pen. Through a manifesto of February 19, 1861, nearly 40 percent of the population, or 20 to 25 million peasants, were freed from serfdom. Russia was jubilant. "There has never been anything higher or more holy in all of Russia's thousand-year history" was Dostoyevsky's comment. No longer were the peasant masses so much cattle to be bought and sold by landowners.

Nevertheless, when it became clear that the impoverished peasant masses had to *buy* their land, the disappointment was great. It is true that they were able to get long-term loans from the state, but this did not prevent the peasantry from sinking into ever-greater poverty. The fact that the land became the joint property of the peasant commune and not the private property of each individual peasant was tantamount to another form of enslavement. The radical émigré Alexander Herzen had originally welcomed the reform with the words "You are victorious, Galilean!" But now he wrote in his periodical *The Bell* that this "was a liberation to hunger and home-lessness." In a short time, hundreds of peasant uprisings broke out all across Russia. The nation found itself in a period of restless ferment; there were even those who spoke of "revolutionary conditions."

Dostoyevsky experienced these dramatic reversals with joy and fear, but it was not long before he chimed in with his opinion and threw all his energy and eloquence into the political controversy. He expected "a great renewal" in Russia. This period of reform was for him "not less significant than the time of Peter the Great." The essential questions involved the Russian peasant and the future of the nation. He struggled to arrive at independent and original views on both issues.

At the end of 1858, Mikhail had been granted permission to publish a political and literary weekly called *Time*. But it was not until his energetic brother arrived on the scene that the plans came alive. As an old hand at journalism, Dostoyevsky had long hoped for a forum where he could appear before the larger Russian public. He felt a need to express all the thoughts that had built up in him during his time in Siberia. To participate in forming opinion during "the time of the Great Reformer" seemed to him a challenging mission.

Inspired by the growing political interest among the public, the brothers decided in 1860 to expand their plans for the journal. *Time* became a "thick" monthly that entertained a long list of topics from foreign policy and economics to philosophy and literature. As a former convict, the writer could not be the editor of the journal, but even though Mikhail became the editor and official publisher, it was Fyodor who was the driving force behind the venture. In September 1860, it was he who gave account of the journal's ideological foundations.

This ideology has been called *pochvennichestvo*, a name that comes from the Russian word for "soil" or "ground": *pochva*. The name was intended to emphasize the belief that the "civilized" members of Russian society must recover their national and popular roots. Peter the Great's reforms had been costly for Russians. They had created a schism between the great peasant mass and the "educated" class. But now Russians could begin to recognize their own character as a people:

> We know now that we cannot become Europeans, and that we are not in a position to be pushed into any Western forms of life that Europe has created out of its national foundation but which are foreign to us and to which we are opposed—just as it would be impossible for us to wear a foreign suit that was not tailored to our measurements. We have finally understood that we have our own, highly original nationality and that our task consists in creating a new form, our own form, that has grown up from our domestic land, and which was conceived by the spirit of the people.

This new understanding, however, was not intended to bring about the repudiation of Peter the Great's reforms. On the contrary, it was time for Russians to understand their momentous international task:

> We know that we can no longer hide ourselves from the rest of humanity behind a Chinese wall. We foresee, we foresee with awe that the character of our future activity will be to the highest degree universal, that the Russian idea is perhaps the synthesis of all the ideas that Europe has developed with such great tenacity and courage in each of its nations; and that all the antagonisms within these ideas will be reconciled and developed further in the Russian people.

Within the context of the history of ideas, Dostoyevsky's program constituted a development of Slavophile ideas from the 1840s, but without their glorification of the aristocracy or their isolationism. Unlike the Slavophiles, Dostoyevsky did not oppose borrowing from Europe as long as these loans did not conflict with Russia's national foundation and he had no desire to glorify pre-Petrine conditions. If Russians had never come into conflict with Western Europe, they would not have been made aware of the cleft between the people and the intelligentsia. On the other hand, he attacked the Westernizers for their indifference to Russian culture and their materialistic social views. His own program was highly idealistic and repudiated any notion of class struggle. "The foundation for our future development," wrote Dostoyevsky, "cannot be, as everywhere in Europe, the enmity between classes or between the conquerors and the conquered. We are not Europe; among us there are not and shall not be conquerors and conquered."

The Russian peasant was not rebellious or revolutionary, but humble and pious, the bearer of ideals that were lost to the radical, Westernized intelligentsia. In a time of division and irreconcilable conflicts, it was necessary to return to the Russian national source, and this would have significance for Europe as well. Dostoyevsky energetically maintained Russia's role as the *reconciliator* of the antagonistic ideas that characterized European culture, but not to the extent that he nursed illusions about combining European civilization and the spirit of the Russian people. No, it was the Russian spirit, with its primal ideals of "universality" and "reconciliation" that would influence European civilization. With their peculiar ability to enter other cultures imaginatively and understand other peoples, Russians were in a position to reconcile the conflicts in Europe and bring them together into a sublime synthesis. It was this "Russian idea" that from now on became the determining factor in Dostoyevsky's political thought. Behind this idea was his need to unite his great respect for Western culture with his recently discovered love for the Russian people.

The Dostoyevsky brothers' magazine was subject to attacks from both the left and the right. Still, within a short time they had accumulated more than four thousand subscriptions. This success was due chiefly to Dostoyevsky's considerable talent as an editor and his ability to give the journal a modern, liberal profile. Within a few months, several of the country's leading writers had published in *Time*: the playwright Ostrovsky, the satirist Saltykov-Shchedrin, the novelist Pomyalovsky, and poets such as Nekrasov, Maikov, and Polonsky.

The magazine's greatest asset, however, was Dostoyevsky, who in addition to *The House of the Dead* (1860–62, also called *Notes from the House of the Dead*) and *The Insulted and the Injured* (1860–61) wrote many articles. Most of these articles were anonymous, and investigations of the prose with the aid of computer analysis have shown that scholars are prone to give the writer credit for more contributions than he actually made. Still, more than twenty articles bear the unmistakable stamp of his journalistic mastery.

Dostoyevsky's attempt at a thematic "reorientation" in *Uncle's Dream* and *The Village of Stepanchikovo* had been a failure. In his "second debut" he wisely returned to the "humane" direction he had been following when

Poor Folk was published fifteen years earlier. His renewed interest in this direction can be seen in his choice of translations for the journal. "The founding idea of nineteenth-century art is the rehabilitation of the socially oppressed pariah," he wrote in an editorial comment on a translation of Hugo's *Notre Dame de Paris*. The first translation he chose for *Time* was accordingly Elizabeth Gaskell's *Mary Barton: A Tale of Manchester*, a book that had created a sensation in Europe with its exposé of the poverty and misery in the modern industrial city. The book's exhortation to protect the poor and orphaned and help those in need is also typical of Dostoyevsky's own works in *Time*.

But *The House of the Dead* was the work that had the greatest success—the story of the country's most heinous criminals written by a newly released prisoner. The work had direct relevance to the current debate on necessary reforms in the Russian legal and penal systems, and its message that there was no greater agony for man than to be deprived of his freedom could not but attract attention in a period of liberalization. But what guaranteed the work immortality was the extraordinary artistry in the writing. "One saw in the author a new Dante who had descended into the inferno," one contemporary critic recalled, "and this inferno was made all the worse by the fact that it existed not only in the writer's imagination but also in reality."

The Insulted and the Injured was also a great popular success. Even its title was a stroke of genius. To this day it has stood as a kind of trademark for Dostoyevsky. The plot, too, was clearly designed to attract a large popular audience. Readers followed with breathless excitement the story of Natasha's selfless love, the proud young Nellie and her demonic father, Prince Volkovsky, and finally Ivan Petrovich, the sympathetic dreamer-writer who nobly advances his rival's cause—according to the best Dostoyevskian model.

The critics, however, were more preoccupied with the book's melodramatic effects. This divergence of opinion between critics and the mass of readers was common in the judgment of Dostoyevsky's works. In his own time, Dostoyevsky was primarily a popular writer, and he was proud of it. Not until after his death did critics begin to acknowledge that the readers had been correct in their high evaluation of his work. This applies also to *The Insulted and the Injured*. Even though Dostoyevsky confessed that he had written "a feuilleton-novel" and "a very wild piece of writing," there is much in this work that anticipates the great future novels. It is enough to mention that Prince Volkovsky is clearly an early version of Dostoyevsky's "great sinner."

Just before his new novels came out, Dostoyevsky published a two-volume edition of his early works, and a number of critics seized this opportunity to make an overall evaluation of his work. The article "Downtrodden People" by Nikolai Dobrolyubov, the revolutionary student of Belinsky, became particularly well known. For this critic, the central theme in Dostoyevsky's work was respect for the humanity of others, his "compassion for the person who does not even believe that he has the right to be an autonomous human being." This appraisal is strongly reminiscent of Belinsky's review of *Poor Folk* half a generation earlier. But this time, just as before, radicals found fault with much of Dostoyevsky's social philosophy. Disappointed, they had to admit that because the characters were themselves largely responsible for their own degradation, this latest novel's social message was greatly weakened.

But what truly separated Dostoyevsky from the radical critics was his deviant view of the nature of art. In Siberia, Dostoyevsky worked on a literary-philosophical treatise (it has unfortunately been lost), and during lively discussions with his fellow workers at *Time*, he renewed his interest in the topic. Idealist critics such as Nikolai Strakhov and Apollon Grigoryev were particularly important in stimulating his views, for in both of them he found support for his understanding of the artist as prophet and for his belief in the significance of the artist's intuition and creative freedom. He developed these ideas in a series of articles directed against Dobrolyubov.

During this period there were two significant and opposing directions in Russian literary criticism. One position maintained that art stood high above the present and the everyday, while the other maintained that art had a right to exist only if it found its sources in concrete reality, and if, through the exposure of want and injustice, it contributed to the creation of a new society. Above all, literature should be *useful*.

Dostoyevsky took a third position. As a realist, he never doubted that reality was literature's crucial source. But his understanding of reality went deeper than the one prevailing among materialist critics, since for Dostoyevsky, there was no distinction in principle between fantasy and reality, and reality was far more than the merely tangible.

I have my own particular opinions about the real. What most call fantastic and impossible is often for me real in its actual and deepest meaning—the true reality. A record of everyday events is for me far from realism, rather it is the opposite. In every single newspaper, you can find stories about absolutely real yet absolutely strange facts that our writers would reject and call fantastic—these things hold no interest for them. And yet these stories are the deep and living reality, because they are facts. They happen every day, every moment; they are in no way exceptional.

The radical critics' demand that reality be depicted "as it is" was meaningless for Dostoyevsky; reality was necessarily shaped by the person who experienced it: what may not be reality for *you* may be reality for *me*. The task of the writer was to explode the boundaries of the so-called real world. Within perceptible "reality" exists another sphere, the fantastic, which is not in any way superfluous to a writer's concerns. "The fantastic must be so intimately bound up with the real that one almost believes in it."

Dostoyevsky's own authorship may well be characterized by two words that he used in his notes—"fantastic realism." This expression not only connotes a realistic depiction with powerful fantastic elements but also indicates Dostoyevsky's suspicion of naturalism or "factualism," as he called it in his notes. Indifferent, factual reports of reality are worthless and meaningless. Rather, a writer must be inspired by a message, preferably of a moral character. "In poetry, passion is essential, an idea, a passionate direction."

The radical critics' insistence that art must serve a particular political view was for Dostoyevsky the equivalent of assigning to art "a shameful destiny." A literary work must stand or fall on its "artistic merit," he explained to Dobrolyubov. The utilitarian claim that the formal aspects of a work were of secondary importance so long as its goal was good and its purpose clear struck Dostoyevsky as a contradiction in terms. Only fully realized artistic works could fulfill their goals.

But what does it mean to say that a work is "artistic"? Dostoyevsky defined it thus: "To say that a novelist is 'artistic' means that he possesses a talent to express his thoughts in characters and images so that when the reader has finished the novel, he has fully understood the author's thoughts. . . . Therefore, artistry is quite simply the ability to write well." A writer without talent is in no position to serve a cause. Dostoyevsky compares such a writer to a lame soldier who is given orders to invade a fortress.

The radical critics' requirement that art must at all costs be "useful" to people and society seemed to Dostoyevsky ambiguous and unsatisfactory. How can we know what will show itself to be useful? Can we say with assurance how useful *The Iliad* has been to mankind? No, Dostoyevsky believed, when it comes to this we encounter breadths that cannot be measured with any precision. Sometimes a work of art may appear to deviate from reality and serve no useful purpose, because we cannot see clearly what paths it may take to become useful. Beauty is an ideal, and because man will never be able fully to comprehend that ideal, it cannot determine either the path or the goal of art.

The consequence of such a perspective is the belief that art must be free. Dostoyevsky noted, "The freer art is to develop, the faster it will find its real and useful path. And when the aims of art are indistinguishable from the aims of mankind, the more useful it will be to mankind if it is allowed to develop freely. In other words, art will always serve humanity as long as one does not try to circumscribe its freedom."

In and of itself, Dostoyevsky was not opposed to Dobrolyubov's wish that literature portray society's problems, but when this wish became a requirement, it was time to sound a warning. Such a requirement betrayed a lack of understanding for art's fundamental laws and the freedom of inspiration. "It means quite simply that one refuses to acknowledge art as an organic whole," he wrote.

The mandate that art serve the common good exposed the failure of the materialists to comprehend humanity's innate longing for beauty. The great meaning that Dostoyevsky attributed to beauty shows the influence of Schiller's study of the aesthetic principle in mankind and his profound belief in the unity of goodness and beauty. "We believe that art has its own integral and organic life," wrote Dostoyevsky. "Art is just as much a human need as food and drink. . . . Human beings hunger for beauty and accept it unconditionally because it is beautiful."

This view of beauty's significance in human life is also present in Dostoyevsky's novels. "Man can live without bread and science," says Stepan Trofimovich in *The Possessed*. "But he cannot live without beauty." And elsewhere, "Beauty is useful, because it is beautiful, and because man will always need beauty and its ideal. If a people have protected the ideal of beauty and the need for beauty, this guarantees that people's highest evolution."

In this way beauty becomes a means for making human life fuller and better. Like Schiller, Dostoyevsky was prepared to identify beauty with goodness and the morally perfect. For him the aesthetic is a religious category.

He spoke of beauty "saving the world." Christ carried the beautiful within him and gave humanity a share in this ideal through his words—man does not live by bread alone.

II

Through his two new novels and extensive journalistic activity, Dostoyevsky soon recaptured his position as one of Russia's foremost authors. He settled in a place near the journal's editorial offices, where he would arrive every day at about three o'clock in the afternoon more or less rested after a night's work. He wrote as he never had before. "When I am in the middle of writing something, I think only of it; I think of it when I am eating and sleeping and yes, even when I am talking to others." It is not strange that the other journalists found him tense and weary. "He was a bit above average height and looked older than his forty years as he hurried about, fatigued and stooped," one of them wrote. "His eyes darted quickly from one person to another; between his heavy eyebrows was a deep, dark furrow and his searching penetrating expression made a highly unpleasant impression."

Within a short time, Dostoyevsky had found a new place for himself among the capital's literary circles. The most important of these circles held its gatherings at the home of one of his friends from his youth, Alexander Milyukov. "Fyodor Mikhailovich occupied quite naturally a prominent place in this circle," wrote Nikolai Strakhov. "Everyone regarded him as a great writer not only because he was so well known, but because he had so many ideas and was so passionate in his defense of them." During heated debate, he would raise his voice to a single fervent shriek. At such times he kept everyone spellbound with his beautiful eyes, high forehead, and wide homely face.

In this early period, Dostoyevsky sailed with a favoring wind. "My name is worth millions," he burst out in joy and self-importance. His notebooks filled with plans for new works, and the good will of the public was an inspiration to him. He did not complain about his former life as a convict: his extraordinary experience had given him insights into the souls of the Russian people, insights only he could express. "When I look at you, I can see the hardships you have had to endure," commented a lady. "Hardships, what hardships?" replied Dostoyevsky and changed the subject.

No, Dostoyevsky had not been broken. "There, you see, we didn't go under after all!" he whispered with a smile to Alexander Palm during an evening of readings. Old friends found him happier and more energetic than ever before. He wasn't the least bitter, and rejected the view that the Petrashevsky circle had been treated unjustly—"the people would have convicted us," he said.

Dostoyevsky partook eagerly in St. Petersburg's cultural life from the moment of his arrival. He was especially active in the Literary Fund and the Society for Aid to Needy Writers. As the Society's secretary, he was made aware of the want that plagued Russian writers and did his very best to help. Many letters have survived that attest to the gratitude of Dostoyevsky's colleagues for his support of their cause.

Because of his fame, Dostoyevsky was often called upon to take part in philanthropic and educational events. In April 1860 he debuted as an actor in *The Inspector General*. Dostoyevsky chose the role of the curious postmaster, "one of the funniest roles not only in Gogol but in all of the Russian theatrical repertoire." The audience saw a fine comic actor "who knew how to evoke a real Gogolian laughter," to quote the theater director.

This kind of success inspired Dostoyevsky to take up his old plans to write for the theater, plans that were never realized but preoccupied him until his death. Alexandra Schubert, who was married to his friend Stepan Yanovsky and was considered to be among St. Petersburg's finest actresses, was a further inspiration for his theatrical ambitions. The study of female character had become "a hobby" for the man who no longer had conjugal relations with his sick wife and so found himself captivated by the vivacious brunette. A short time later, when Alexandra Schubert left her husband and continued her acting career in Moscow, Dostoyevsky was tempted to follow her. His letters indicate that theirs was an intense friendship but that the relationship was hopeless. "I am so glad that I now am absolutely sure that I am not in love with you," he concluded his last letter to her. "This means that I can be all the more devoted to you without fearing for my heart." This time Dostoyevsky was spared an all-consuming passion.

The writer also found himself charmed by Yelena Stakenschneider, who would be a loyal admirer until his death. She was an almost crippled woman who used crutches, but this made her appeal all the more to Dostoyevsky's compassion—a feeling that was just as powerful for him as sexual passion. For Yelena, Dostoyevsky was foremost a teacher of life. She described him reading at a benefit for Sunday schools early in the 1860s along with other prominent authors such as Benediktov, Shevchenko, Maikov, and Polonsky. He read from *The House of the Dead* with a "weak, monotonous voice," she said—as a reader he still had much to learn before he would attain his later mastery—but the returned martyr was met with several ovations.

At Stakenschneider's salon on Znamenskaya, Dostoyevsky had an opportunity to meet the new young nihilists. Immediately attracted to these young people who refused to bow before any authority, he felt for them a peculiar combination of respect and revulsion. Their extreme materialism, their insistence that all spiritual values should be transformed into socially useful acts were in fundamental opposition to his beliefs, but their idea that "all is permissible" and their will to go beyond all thresholds nevertheless appealed to his rebellious spirit.

In May 1862, the nihilists gave Dostoyevsky a real cause for alarm when he found outside his door a proclamation in the form of a leaflet entitled *Young Russia* that was signed by "The Central Revolutionary Committee." Russians were to be the first to "realize socialism," the proclamation stated, and the revolution was just around the corner. "Soon, very soon, the day shall come when we will unfurl our great red flag—the flag of the future—the red flag. With resounding shouts, 'Long live the Russian Socialist Democratic Republic!' we will march on the Winter Palace and crush those who live there." The desire for freedom among young people had degenerated into subversion. And this was the flower of Russian youth!

At nearly the same time, a series of fires broke out in St. Petersburg. The city's famous "white nights" turned red and bloody for more than a fortnight; large sections of the city fell to ruin; the streets were filled with thousands of homeless people. Both within the country and without, people were gripped with fear. A few hinted at government provocation, but most blamed the nihilists. Alarmed, Dostoyevsky hurried off to see his radical writer colleague Nikolai Chernyshevsky, who denied any responsibility for either the proclamation or the fires. The government soon took a number of counterinitiatives—universities and publications were shut down and several writers were arrested, among them Chernyshevsky.

Things looked bad for *Time* as well, because the magazine had bravely defended the students against the accusations of arson. The article was forbidden by the censor and Mikhail was called before a hearing. Fyodor, too, must have felt the ground giving way beneath his feet.

As soon as the fires had been put out, he was off on his first trip abroad. He wanted to see Europe while he still had "vigor, enthusiasm, and poetry."

Actually, the trip was a "health tour" that had been approved by the secret police as long ago as May on the grounds that Dostoyevsky needed to consult foreign doctors. To judge from his letters and travel stories, however, there was little time for medical consultations. Everything seems to indicate that the reasons he cited in his visa application were a pretext. The three hectic months he spent outside Russia's borders were more than anything else a period of observation during which Dostoyevsky was forced to come to terms with Europe.

Many years had passed since Dostoyevsky wandered about the Hospital for the Poor dreaming of traveling abroad. In the meantime his enthusiasm for Europe had chilled considerably. Even during his early years in St. Petersburg, he had developed a barely suppressed xenophobia, and this hatred for all things foreign had been inflamed by his exile in Siberia. He retained a respect for Western philosophy, but its people and society were anathema to him. As he took his seat on the train leaving for Europe on June 7, 1862, little of his boyish enthusiasm for "life in Venice" had survived.

His travels took him to Berlin, Dresden, Wiesbaden, Baden-Baden, Cologne, Paris, London, Lucerne, Geneva, Genoa, Florence, Milan, Venice, and Vienna, and he visited a number of these cities twice. One would think that Dostoyevsky would have gotten *something* positive out of this trip, but no, he found simply what he sought: his *Winter Notes on Summer Impressions*, published in the first issue of *Time* in 1863, is truly the most damning account of the West ever written by a Russian.

Even before he had crossed the border, the cutting attacks began. In his train compartment Dostoyevsky was seated by a "full-blooded Englishman" who perfectly coincided with his expectations of a cheerless, phlegmatic people:

He uttered not one syllable to us throughout the entire trip. During the day, he read a book with minuscule English print that only Englishmen can tolerate and which even they find unpleasant. In the evening, as soon as the clock struck ten, he removed his boots and put on a pair of soft slippers. He had obviously acquired this habit once and for all and was not about to give it up while traveling.

Russians, too, were taken to task in *Winter Notes*, or rather those Russians who let themselves be impressed by the West. Dostoyevsky caustically ridiculed those of his countrymen who settled abroad, people who "forget their mother tongue and listen to Catholic Fathers." He made acrimonious fun of Russians who swoon over imagined "attractions": "Indefatigable, they stand there and ogle a Rubens nude, taking it for the Three Graces because their guide book recommends it." But he would not be fooled. Even the Cologne Cathedral did not appeal to him: "I thought it looked like a chivalric object, a vast piece of bric-a-brac all squeezed together, of the sort used as a paper weight on a writing desk, but of course well over a hundred feet tall."

Otherwise, Dostoyevsky was chiefly preoccupied with people and social conditions, not with nature or museums, and what he saw filled him with disappointment. On the French border, four silent men suddenly appeared in his train compartment—obviously "spies" from the secret police. As if he didn't have enough of them at home! In Paris the hotel manager subjected him to further grilling—height, eye and hair color, scars or other distinctive markings? At last he had arrived in the land of freedom! "Paris is the most virtuous city in the world," he noted. He was just as ironic in his description of the virtuous words uttered by the French bourgeoisie as a scintillating accompaniment to the sound of splashing fountains in the Palais-Royal. Beneath the cultivation of virtue was only avarice. To save a small fortune, to own as many things as possible—this was the Parisian's "moral" cornerstone.

The fact that this greed was veiled in good manners and eloquence only made it more repugnant. "All the French have a wonderfully noble air. Even the most miserable little Frenchman, who will gladly sell you his own father for a franc and throw something else into the bargain, even he possesses at that moment such a sure and natural nobility that one just has to stand there gaping in wonder." The same malicious tone permeated his letters from Paris. "The Frenchman is calm, decent, and polite, but false, and money is everything to him. He has no ideals. Don't expect a Frenchman to have convictions or even considerations. The general level of education is frighteningly low."

Dostoyevsky shrewdly analyzed the proud French slogan "Liberty, Equality, Fraternity." These words do not belong in this society of greed; one can be free here only if one has millions. Equality before the law is an illusion, as is fraternity. When everyone is exclusively obsessed by his own needs, there is no concern left for others. "One must instinctively feel drawn to brotherhood and communion," wrote Dostoyevsky, but this is not possible in egotistical, materialistic France, and he did not anticipate any change. The need to own was rooted just as deeply among workers and peasants as among the bourgeoisie. Nor would socialism succeed in undermining this need to possess. No one would be willing to sacrifice as much as one iota of his freedom "to be sufficient unto himself." In other words, wherever socialism might become reality, it certainly wouldn't be in France.

Haut-bourgeois Paris was at least characterized by calm and order, but industrial London stood out in glaring contrast. On the streets he saw people wearing beautiful clothes in expensive carriages, side by side others in filth and rags. The Thames was poisoned, the air polluted; the city seemed marked by joyless drinking and wife abuse. The writer was particularly horrified by child prostitution:

Here in the Haymarket, I saw mothers who brought along their young daughters and taught them their occupation. And these twelve-year-old girls took you by the hand and asked to be accompanied. One evening, in the swarm of people I saw a little girl dressed in rags, dirty, barefoot, emaciated and battered. Through her rags I could see that her body was covered with bloody stripes. She wandered senseless in the crowd . . . perhaps she was hungry. No one paid her any attention. But what struck me most was her sad expression and the hopelessness of her misery. It was rather unreal and terribly painful to look at the despair and cursed existence of this small creature.

When he visited the London World's Fair with "civilization's shining triumphs," Dostoyevsky again found himself possessed by feelings of fear and dejection. Appalled, he recoiled from the hubris that had created the Crystal Palace's "colossal decorations." Here was something taken to its absolute limit, he maintained, here man's prideful spirit had erected a temple to an idol of technology:

This is a Biblical illustration, this speaks of Babylon, in this a prophet of the Apocalypse is come to life. You feel that it would take unbelievable spiritual strength not to succumb to this impression, not to bow before this consummate fact, not to acknowledge this reality as our ideal and mistake Baal for God.

As many other Russian travelers in London had done before him, Dostoyevsky seized this opportunity to call upon Herzen, who was known all over Europe for his critique of the Tsar's autocracy. They had met once before, in the fall of 1846, but at that time Herzen's impression had not been "particularly pleasant." This time the encounter went better; they were both skeptical about the ability of the liberal bourgeoisie to create a just society in Europe. Despite their differing views on Tsarist rule, they shared a faith in the Russian peasants who were not yet affected by the destructive egoism of civilization and who continued to live together in the peasant commune. "Yesterday Dostoyevsky came to visit," Herzen remarked laconically. "He is very naïve, and not too clear-headed, but he is extremely amiable. He has an enthusiastic belief in the Russian people." Otherwise little is known about their meeting. Herzen's name was forbidden in Russia, and Dostoyevsky could not discuss the visit in his letters.

Even less is known about the meeting that, according to police reports, Dostoyevsky had with Bakunin, the man who had been sentenced to death several times for his revolutionary activity in Europe. He had just escaped from Siberia and was now ready for new assignments. "A destructive passion is a creative passion," Bakunin had declared, and with this slogan, he had become the leading anarchist of the period. Dostoyevsky had always felt a kind of horrified fascination for such agitators, and his conversation with Bakunin was surely significant for the later reckoning with nihilists that he composed in *The Possessed*.

The final part of Dostoyevsky's travels abroad—his trip down the Rhine and his stay in Switzerland and Italy—was apparently more pleasant. In Geneva, he met Strakhov and together they crossed the Alps by the way of the Mont-Cenis pass. Their tour took them through Turin, Genoa, and Livorno; by mid-August they had arrived in Florence, where they stayed in the Hotel Pension Suisse in the Via Tornabuoni. From here it was not far to the Gabinetto Scientifico-Letterario of G. P. Vieusseux, where Dostoyevsky managed to read several books in a week, among them Hugo's *Les Misérables*.

During their stay in Florence, they also found time for museum visits, but aside from Raphael's *Madonna della Sedia*, little impressed Dostoyevsky. He had barely entered the Uffizi before he ran out again. His enthusiasm was also restrained when it came to the layout of cities and to rivers. The straight streets of Turin only reminded him of St. Petersburg, and Florence's Arno was by no means more beautiful than the Fontanka at home. His xenophobia smoldered continually. During one dinner, he alarmed Strakhov by cruelly attacking a waiter. "Don't you realize that I'm a human being, too?" the waiter muttered to the great champion of brotherhood and community.

Strakhov had better memories of their many conversations. Among other things, he recalled the writer's skeptical reaction to those people who asserted that 2 plus 2 equals 4. Such people did not understand that there exists a stage of suffering in which 2 plus 2 *does not* equal 4, Dostoyevsky said. He had greater sympathy with those who claimed that 2 plus 2 equals 5. These conversations generally took place over an evening glass of wine. "In this respect, however, Fyodor Mikhailovich was extremely moderate," wrote Strakhov. "In twenty years, I cannot once remember seeing him drunk." Epilepsy and alcohol were an unhappy combination, as Dostoyevsky had discovered through bitter experience in Siberia.

In early September 1862, Dostoyevsky once again set foot on Russian ground. With renewed energy he entered the political debate. "The salvation of Russia lies with her people and in her native soil," he wrote in *Time*'s programmatic statement at the end of the year. In the course of a few months, the journal had taken on a decidedly more nationalistic profile. It therefore came as a shock when the magazine was suddenly banned by the authorities at the end of May 1863 on the grounds that it had published an article that was contrary to "all patriotic sentiments."

The reason for the suppression was the journal's hesitant response to the Polish rebellion. In January 1863, Poland rose in armed revolt against Russian hegemony. The Poles wanted national independence and the restoration of their earlier borders. But help from the West failed to materialize and the uprising was quickly suppressed. Herzen was one of the few who supported the Polish cause. "We desire independence for Poland because we desire freedom for Russia," he wrote in *The Bell*. But in Russia, opinion was split. Revolutionaries supported Herzen, while reactionaries applauded the brutal response of the regime. The liberals were uncertain—many dreamed of a compromise.

One might suppose that this would have been a clear-cut issue for Dostoyevsky. His hatred for the Poles ran deep, and his belief in the "Russian idea" prevented him from sympathizing with rebellion against the Tsar. Nevertheless, the question was extremely delicate: on the one hand, supporting the official policy would destroy the journal's reputation among its readers; on the other, a declaration of sympathy for the Poles would result in the banning of the magazine. At the same time, it was necessary to speak out on an issue that concerned so many Russians.

After much discussion, Strakhov was assigned the task of expressing the journal's position: he was instructed to avoid political aspects of the question and instead give a philosophical treatment. Strakhov's article, printed in the April issue as being by "a Russian" and entitled "A Momentous Question," took the position that the Polish-Russian dispute was essentially a battle between two civilizations—a false European one and the true Russian one—and that a resolution would not come until the Russians had won a "spiritual victory" over the Poles. Therefore it was necessary for Russians to come to understand their own singular nationality in order to develop their own culture.

The overheated political climate of the time, in which everyone was coming forth to bless Russian arms, did not allow for such obscurantist speculations. Moreover, a couple of unlucky formulations were misinterpreted as meaning that Poles were culturally superior. It did not help matters when *Time* tried to clarify its patriotic position by pointing to the passage about "illustrious Polish civilization bearing death in its heart." In Moscow, the uproar over the article was so great that the Tsar did not hesitate to outlaw the publication.

The closing of *Time* was a terrible blow for Mikhail Dostoyevsky. He had just sold his tobacco factory and was now without means to support his family. Fyodor, too, took it hard. His epileptic seizures increased in both frequency and intensity. Now they sometimes occurred just a few days apart.

Strakhov wrote about one incident during Easter, 1863. Dostoyevsky sought out his friend late one evening and quickly fell into an intense discussion of a topic that was preoccupying him:

> He expressed a lofty and joyous thought, and when I acknowledged his words with some remark, he turned to me with enthusiasm—it was obvious that his inspiration had reached a climax. He paused for a moment, as if he were searching for a word and had already opened his mouth. I looked at him with expectant attention. I felt that he was about to say something important, that I would be privy to some revelation. But just then he let out a strange, drawn-out, meaningless sound and fell unconscious to the floor.

Dostoyevsky had reported a similar visitation of this "holy disease," also at Easter, during his exile in Siberia. An old friend had come to visit him and they were conversing. Dostoyevsky was upset by his friend's atheism. "God exists! God exists!" he shouted, quite beside himself with excitement.

At that same moment the church bells tolled for the morning service, and the room echoed with their sound. "And then it was truly as if heaven had come down to earth and overwhelmed me. I truly felt God and was filled with Him. 'Yes, God exists!' I screamed, and more I cannot remember." These ecstatic experiences convinced Dostoyevsky that Muhammad had spoken the truth when he told of his visit to Paradise. "Surely he went to Paradise during an attack of the same form of epilepsy from which I suffer."

There is an extensive literature on Dostoyevsky's epilepsy. Most experts believe that it was the result of a lesion in the temporal lobe, and they characterize his seizures as psychomotor epilepsy. It is extremely rare, however, that a person with this kind of epilepsy experiences ecstatic auras, so rare, in fact, that such cases are referred to in medical texts as "Dostoyevsky epilepsy." "In certain moments," he told Strakhov, "I experience a joy that is unthinkable under ordinary circumstances, and of which most people have no comprehension. Then I feel that I am in complete harmony with myself and the whole world, and this feeling is so bright and strong that you could give up ten years for a few seconds of that ecstasy—yes, even your whole life."

Dostoyevsky experienced the "moments of eternal harmony" that Kirilov describes in *The Possessed*. The frightening thing was the terrible clarity and then the furor. "If it lasted for more than five seconds, it would be more than the soul could bear. In those five seconds, I relive my whole life, and for them, I would gladly give my life—because they are worth it." In his portrait of Prince Myshkin, Dostoyevsky also philosophizes about these ecstatic moments:

> He was thinking, incidentally, that there was a moment or two in his epileptic condition almost before the fit itself (if it occurred during his waking hours) when suddenly amid the sadness, spiritual darkness and depression, his brain seemed to catch fire at brief moments, and with an extraordinary momentum his vital forces were strained to the utmost all at once. His sensation of being alive and his awareness increased tenfold at those moments which flashed by like lightning. His mind and heart were flooded by a dazzling light. All his agitation, all his doubts and worries, seemed composed in a twinkling, culminating in a great calm, full of serene and harmonious joy and hope, full of understanding and the knowledge of the final cause. But those moments, those flashes of intuition, were merely the presentiment of the last second (never more than a second) which preceded the actual fit. This second was, of course, unendurable.

Reflecting about that moment afterwards, when he was well again, he often said to himself that all those gleams and flashes of the highest awareness and, hence, also of "the highest mode of existence," were nothing but a disease, a departure from the normal condition, and, if so, it was not at all the highest mode of existence, but, on the contrary, must be considered to be the lowest. And yet he arrived at last at the paradoxical conclusion: "What if it is a disease?" he decided at last. "What does it matter that it is an abnormal tension, if the result, if the moment of sensation, remembered and analyzed in a state of health, turns out to be harmony and beauty brought to their highest point of perfection, and gives a feeling, undivined and undreamt of till then, of completeness, proportion, reconciliation, and an ecstatic and prayerful fusion in the highest synthesis of life?" These vague expressions seemed to him very comprehensible, though rather weak. But that it really was "beauty and prayer," that it really was "the highest synthesis of life," he could not doubt, nor even admit the possibility of doubt.

The writer Dmitri Merezhkovsky raised the question whether these seizures didn't give Dostoyevsky a physical sensitivity more acute than others, enabling him to see what others do not see. "Who knows?" he asked. "Perhaps we have touched upon what is deepest and most original in Dostoyevsky's nature, on the very enigma of his physical and spiritual makeup." Medical experts have also linked the writer's religious experiences with his illness. His auras had to leave their mark—they became a deciding factor in his world view. Behind his apparently realistic pyschology lies a metaphysical, *mystical* understanding of man and existence.

But the everyday experience of epilepsy, with its often serious head injuries and humiliating incontinence, stood in sharp contrast to the experience of auras. Dostoyevsky rarely had any warning of an oncoming attack. Often he would only feel that everything had begun to thicken into darkness before he collapsed and was racked and tortured. His loss of memory was serious—he would forget how his friends looked or the names of his characters in the novel he was writing. One of his correspondents remains unknown, because Dostoyevsky simply forgot his name. His detailed rough drafts were not only a sign of his commitment, but essential to a man who might begin his workday without remembering what he was writing about.

He suffered most from the depressions that followed his seizures. He felt like a criminal, that he was guilty of some terrible offense, perhaps even something as serious as that which he has Stavrogin confess to in *The*

Possessed. In a letter to Turgenev, Dostoyevsky wrote, "If you only knew how depressed I can be for weeks after such an attack."

After his trip in Europe, Dostoyevsky noticed a definite improvement in his health, so a year later, he made plans to take another trip and consult with doctors in Berlin and Paris. "Here at home there are no specialists in this illness, and the doctors give me so much conflicting advice that I have lost all confidence in them." The military governor of St. Petersburg supported his petition with a long letter to the Third Department:

> The epileptic seizures, from which he has long suffered, have never been so frequent as they are now, particularly in the last month. With each attack, his memory grows weaker. He can no longer recognize his friends; he can't remember the books he reads; in the course of a couple of days he can completely forget what they were about. Moreover, after each seizure, he feels so intolerably depressed that he could easily be driven to madness or despair. Therefore, Dostoyevsky now plans to visit famous European epilepsy specialists, in particular Dr. Trousseau, Dr. Herpin, and Dr. Romberg, and to possibly undergo treatment for several months.

But the most important reason for his trip abroad was love—the great love of his life.

III

Apollinaria, or Polina, Suslova was the daughter of a peasant who had bought his freedom from serfdom and later managed the estate of the very rich Count Sheremetyev. His children inherited their father's energy and ambition, especially the youngest daughter, Nadezhda, who obtained a medical degree in Zurich and became Russia's first woman doctor. Polina, too, attended lectures, and had literary ambitions besides. Like many students at that time, she was sympathetic to the emancipation of serfs and women. Once again, Dostoyevsky met a *femme fatale*: "Passionate, hot-headed, and crazy" was the way her later spouse, the young philosopher and Dostoyevsky scholar Vasily Rozanov, described her.

During this time, Dostoyevsky was very popular among students, particularly women, and he was often invited to their gatherings and lectures. One evening, probably in early autumn 1861, Polina was present when he read from *The House of the Dead*, and the twenty-year-old girl was enthralled. He wasn't handsome as he stood there—pale, sickly, and melancholy—but he was a true martyr for the cause against oppression, a cause that she herself had championed in the radical student movement.

Dostoyevsky's love for Polina came about for different reasons than his love for Maria. Polina was not a nervous, suffering woman with forbidding red splotches on her cheeks; she was not a woman who inspired his compassion. Quite the contrary, she was a picture of health—dazzlingly beautiful, a hot-blooded beauty with great feline eyes and a proud head held high and framed by thick red braids.

Polina's nature was even more complex than Maria's. She was domineering, fanatical, and prone to divide the world into villains and saints. At the same time, she was childlike, a dreamer filled with naïve enthusiasms, and a girl with an "open heart." It isn't strange that the middle-aged writer was taken with this charming, exciting young woman with roots in the Russian peasantry. Dostoyevsky's cheerfulness and optimism upon his return to St. Petersburg can be explained to a large degree by his relationship with Polina. She flattered his masculine pride and returned to him his faith in love.

From the evidence, it seems that their relationship did not become intimate until after Dostoyevsky returned from his first European trip in autumn 1862. Undoubtedly, Polina was flattered by his passion. It gave her increased prestige among her fellow students, and this was important to her. In her vain head, she could concoct bold plans—she even speculated about assassinating the Tsar. "One sleight of hand, and then suddenly you belong among the famous, the geniuses, the great people, the saviors of humanity" was the way she justified her plan.

Sexually the relationship was a disaster. Dostoyevsky did not fulfill Polina's expectations. Even during their first encounter, she experienced the distance between Dostoyevsky the lover and Dostoyevsky the martyr. The result was a spiritual sore that never healed. "At that time, free love was the vogue," Lyubov Dostoyevsky wrote in her book about her father. "Young and beautiful, Polina was carried along by the spirit of the times and threw herself into the service of Venus, going from one student to another, and by this means intending to promote the progress of European civilization."

There is little evidence to support this portrait of Polina as a simple tart. The daughter's characterization was apparently inspired by her mother's quite understandable jealousy. In spite of all their talk about "free love," the students of the period could be very puritanical. The highly principled Polina had vowed not to submit to a man before she was twenty-two, and there is no reason to doubt her word that Dostoyevsky was her first lover.

The reason why this tryst was traumatic can be plainly seen in Dostoyevsky's conception of love as inseparable from suffering and pain. It was difficult for him to love without also suffering. For him, love was hurting and being hurt. In his encounter with Polina, love must have been swiftly transformed into the cruelty of lust. As a proud person, Polina rebelled against male domination of women and the masculine need to own and master. She had expected something "lofty" from this man. Their meeting became for her a humbling memory that had perhaps characteristics of the narrator's cynical treatment of Liza in *Notes from the Underground*.

However, I overcame my reluctance and lifted my head slightly; after all, I had to raise it some time. . . . And then, purely because, as I am convinced to this day, I was ashamed to look at her, a different feeling was kindled in my heart and flared up all at once . . . a feeling of mastery and ownership. My eyes glittered with passion and I squeezed her hands hard. How I hated her and how strongly I was attracted to her at that moment! One feeling reinforced the other. It was almost like revenge . . . ! At first her face expressed what might have been perplexity, or perhaps even fear, but only for one instant. Rapturously, ardently, she embraced me.

A quarter of an hour later I was scurrying round the room in frantic impatience, at every other moment rushing up to the screens and peering through the crack between them at Liza. She was sitting on the floor, leaning her head against the bed and probably crying. But she was not going, and that was what annoyed me. This time she knew everything. I had insulted her finally, but . . . with me to love meant to tyrannize and hold the upper hand morally. All my life I have been unable to conceive of any other love, and I have reached the stage when I sometimes think now that the whole of love consists in the right, freely given to the lover, to tyrannize over the beloved.

Though one must not draw absolute parallels between Dostoyevsky and the Underground Man, there is much to indicate that Polina was in Liza's position, and that Dostoyevsky shared his protagonist's contention that there is no equality in love. "In the relationship between man and woman, one of the parties will inevitably be the inferior and feel humbled," he said later. And this party was generally the woman. "Marriage is always slavery for a woman. The very fact that she has surrendered herself is already slavery, and after that she will always be dependent on the man."

In his implementation of such thoughts, Dostoyevsky met with resistance from Polina. She came from a proud and ambitious family and found the role of slave humiliating. This was the main reason for their later conflicts and very likely the source of her hatred of men and desire for revenge. "If you should ever marry, you will hate your husband and leave him after the third day," he later told Polina. "You cannot forgive me for the fact that you once gave yourself to me and you must take revenge for it; that is a truly feminine trait."

Many bitter confessions in Polina's diary tell of her humbling relations with Dostoyevsky. He would not allow her to take part in his literary plans; she never had access to his creative laboratory. For him, she was simply a lover whom he could dominate at will. But she refused to accept his view of her as only a mistress. A draft of a letter she must have written to Dostoyevsky during summer 1863 has survived:

> You are angry and ask me not to write that I am ashamed of my love for you. I would not write such a thing. . . . I have never been ashamed of my love: for me it is beautiful, even great. But I could have written that our earlier relations made me blush. This can hardly come as a surprise to you, because I have never concealed it. Many times before I traveled abroad I wanted to break off. On the other hand, for you the relationship was decent. You behaved like a man preoccupied with large, serious matters but who nevertheless does not forget to enjoy life. A famous doctor or philosopher once said that a man must have permission to get drunk once a month. Please do not be angry at me for speaking so openly. You know that I don't usually bother with the forms.

There are a number of such criticisms, and they can be traced back to the couple's initial sexual encounter. "He was the first one to kill my faith," she noted in her diary. "I hate him. He made me suffer when there was absolutely no reason to suffer." And she summarized her unhappy experience thus: "I see clearly that I will never again be able to love, that I will never find happiness in love, because every caress will inevitably remind me of this humiliation and pain."

Polina was disappointed by the greedy, cruel passion of a man who had just shed so many tears of pathos over the ideal love he depicted in *The*

Insulted and the Injured. He had proved himself to be the same kind of male chauvinist as all the others. He would not even divorce his tubercular wife. She wanted to leave her middle-aged lover; as a first step she broke off all relations with Dostoyevsky's other female friends. "I am amazed by A's silence," Yekaterina Korsini wrote to Dostoyevsky from Düsseldorf in December 1862. "What is going on with her? And where is she?"

They continued to see each other anyway, and in the summer of 1863 they planned to go abroad together. But the closing of *Time* and the attempts to get the journal back on its feet forced Dostoyevsky to delay his departure. Polina did not want to wait: she left St. Petersburg early in the summer and headed for Paris.

In August, Dostoyevsky finally got under way, having obtained a considerable loan from the Literary Fund, offering his works as a guarantee. This money was to come in handy, for soon he felt an overwhelming desire to gamble. Dostoyevsky had become acquainted with roulette in Germany during his first trip abroad, when he had beginner's luck and added several hundred francs to his travel fund. This time, as he entered the splendid Cursaal in Wiesbaden, he was determined to continue his success, no matter how much he longed for Polina. Suddenly love was secondary. Or perhaps painful premonitions of what awaited him in Paris kept him in "Roulettenburg."

Methodically, Dostoyevsky went to work. For four days, he studied the game and the players, and very quickly he came to the conclusion that only *he* could master this game. It was really so pathetically simple—all that was required was that one play *systematically* and keep a cool head. "That's all it is," he wrote to his sister-in-law. "If one does that, then one cannot lose— one has to win. That's not the problem. But how can the person who knows this secret find the strength and understanding to use it well?"

Dostoyevsky's lack of self-control made him a typical "system-player." If one could only discover a "tendency" in the roulette wheel—if, for example, ten times in a row, the wheel ended its wild dance by landing on red, then all one had to do was to bet on black. The fact that roulette has no system, that each round is independent of all the other rounds before and after, that in the long run the bank must win—all this was for Dostoyevsky the empty talk of anxious souls with no head for numbers. Nor did he listen to the warnings of fellow gamblers. "Woe to him who cannot hear that beyond the seductive ringing of the casino's gold is the triumphant laughter of the devil." Instead, he put his faith in all kinds of gambling handbooks that called the casinos the "German California" and instructed players on how to "ruin the banks" through "fail-proof systems."

"The best way to avoid losing at roulette is to stop playing the game," an American gambling expert has written. But as a gambler Dostoyevsky must have felt that he had signed a contract with fate that said that sooner or later perseverance would pay off. Against every reasonable theory, he insisted that one had to be able to make a profit from roulette. He was to suffer terrible indignities because of this error, and yet he held to the belief until the very end. As late as in A *Raw Youth*, he expressed the conviction that "One must win at gambling if one can only remain calm and calculating."

In earlier biographies, Dostoyevsky's gambling affliction has been explained as a result of his poverty and his desire to win a large fortune. But actually the desire to win was secondary. "It is the battle that they love, not the victory," Pascal wrote. Dostoyevsky's behavior confirms the accuracy of this statement. "The main thing is the game itself," he later wrote to Maikov. "If you only knew how it carries one away!" And once he had become swept up in the game for the game's sake, only *losing* could satisfy him. Like many gamblers, Dostoyevsky was possessed by an unconscious desire to lose and punish himself by losing. This he achieved to an extraordinary degree each time he played himself "to the skin," as he was wont to call it.

This time, too, it went rather well at first. When he sat at the table on the fifth day, he won, by his own account, more than ten thousand francs. He took the money home and packed it in a suitcase, determined to go on to Paris the next day, when the desire to play again became intolerable. On the morrow, he lost half of it.

"He who is lucky at gambling is unlucky at love," teased a Frenchman as Dostoyevsky went to cash in his chips. And it was true enough: the hot-blooded Polina was no Penelope who wasted her time waiting for an ageing lover. As Dostoyevsky sat pondering his system in Wiesbaden, she lay in the arms of a Spanish medical student named Salvador, enjoying the pleasures of a great passion. With his uncomplicated nature and ardor, the young man had completely swept her away. This had nothing in common with her former humbling relations with a lascivious male chauvinist. "You are too late," she told Dostoyevsky when he finally arrived in rainy Paris.

Polina recorded Dostoyevsky's reaction to the news in detail in her diary: "He dropped his head. 'Polya,' he said. 'Let's go somewhere and tell me what has happened or I will die.' " As soon as they were in his hotel room, he fell at her feet, embraced her knees, and said, "I have lost you; I knew it would be this way. Have you given yourself to him completely? Are you happy? Are you prepared to go with him to the ends of the earth?" "No," Polina answered, "he doesn't love me anymore." "Oh, Polina, do not be so unhappy. I was prepared for your falling in love with another man. You fell in love with me by mistake, because you have such a generous heart. You waited until you were twenty-three years old. You are the only woman who makes no demands, but what use is it? A man and a woman are very different—he takes, she gives."

Dostoyevsky took his defeat hard. This time he had lost everything. He had been betrayed in love and once again had met with a younger, victorious rival. If he could only arrange a meeting with him—but this time he was not granted that painful pleasure. As soon as Salvador had had his way with Polina, he retreated and sent one of his friends with a message saying he had been stricken with typhus. But the very next day Polina saw him large as life. He had betrayed her in a most shameful fashion. "When I came back to my room, I had an hysterical attack!" she wrote. "I screamed that I would kill him."

Dostoyevsky's daughter gave a dramatic description of just how this act of revenge was to be carried out:

> At seven in the morning she turned up in my father's room, woke him and produced a giant knife she had just bought. She declared her lover an accursed wretch and said that she would take her revenge by stabbing him in the neck with the knife. She was on her way to him now, but wanted to come by my father's just to tell him about her intended crime. I don't know whether my father was fooled by this vulgar comedy, but at any rate, he advised Polina to put down the knife and go with him to Germany.

Dostoyevsky once again found himself in his usual role as the comforting, sympathetic friend of the woman he had lost to a younger rival. Oozing compassion for Polina, sincerely sorry for her unhappy affair, he assured her that this Spanish heartbreaker could not be a "real man" and it was silly for her to "destroy herself for his sake." At the same time, he suggested that they should travel to Italy together and he would be just like "a brother" to her.

An incident at the Papal Nuncio's in Paris indicates that behind this mask of calm Dostoyevsky hid tremendous rage. Twice before he had visited the Monsignor to get a visa to Rome—in vain. When the abbot informed Dostoyevsky for the third time that the Monsignor was taking his coffee and could not be disturbed, Dostoyevsky leaped from his chair and said, "Tell that Monsignor of yours that I spit in his coffee! If he doesn't sign my passport at once, I'll force my way in to him and make a scene!" "I guess I was a bit hot," Dostoyevsky confessed with a bewildered smile as he told Baron Wrangel about the incident later. As with so many other events in his life, this one found its way into his work—in this case, in *The Gambler*.

Polina's agreement to a "brotherly" arrangement with Dostoyevsky did not mean she had forgotten the faithless Spaniard. "I am still very much in love with him and would give half my life to get him to show his regret." Nor did it mean that she felt any closer to Dostoyevsky. If she was unable to take revenge on Salvador for her wounded pride, she could always avenge herself on Dostoyevsky. *He* would be the one to pay for Salvador's crime. "En route he told me that he was hopeful," she wrote contemptuously after they had arrived in Baden-Baden in early September. "I did not say anything, but I knew that nothing was going to happen. He was apparently glad that I was not against leaving Paris, but that is nothing on which to build hope— quite the contrary."

Tortured by the unattainable Polina, Dostoyevsky once again was driven to the casinos, and once again was sacrificed to what he called "the agitation of passion." He hoped to find in roulette all the satisfaction Polina had denied him, and more. He had discovered a certain means of nursing his psychic masochism. Like all gamblers he tried to rationalize his deeper motives—he needed money so badly! But in reality it was the game itself, its excitement, and most of all the unconscious need to lose, to hurt and punish himself that moved him to make ever bolder wagers. And Polina did not oppose his gambling. She learned quickly that his losses only gave her greater power over her companion.

"The gambling tables draw hither much disreputable society and must be considered as a very serious disadvantage to the place," an English tour guide wrote of Baden-Baden's Conversationshaus. But such bourgeois warnings were hardly enough to dampen Dostoyevsky's pathological obsession. After the harrowing experiences in Paris, it was harder than ever to stick to his "fail-proof system." Just when he had managed to net a profit of six hundred francs, he began to lose, and when he left the casino, he was three thousand francs poorer than when he arrived. He was shabbily attired and took every loss very hard, according to Prince Pavel Vyazemsky, who had the dubious pleasure of running into him among the rough and brazen crowd of gamblers.

In desperate letters, Dostoyevsky now tried to retrieve the money he had sent to his brother and sister-in-law in a moment of overconfidence from Paris. Finally, he brought his very last coins to the casino. "With four twenty-franc pieces, I won thirty-five within a half hour," he said. "This remarkable luck fired me up once again. I put the entire thirty-five down on one round and lost all of it. After we had paid the hotel manager, we had only twenty francs left for the trip. In Geneva, I pawned my watch." Surely it was scenes like this one that made him compare the hell of the casino with the bath scene in *The House of the Dead*. And yet he comforted himself in a letter to his sister-in-law: "So many things happen in our lives, and were it not for these experiences, very simply—life would be dull."

His relations with Polina had become extremely difficult. She played the coquette and teased him with constant reminders of their agreement. After her disappointment in Paris, this childlike woman had metamorphosed into a heartless *femme fatale*, who relished greatly the power she had over her love-starved companion and the vengeance she nurtured against her faithless lover. The colder she was to Dostoyevsky, the more impassioned he felt about her. Their trip to Italy was soon to develop into a fateful duel.

In St. Petersburg, it had been Dostoyevsky who was the master of the situation. There he had hurt and dominated her, but now master and slave had exchanged places; the conqueror had become the conquered. The fact that she had betrayed him with Salvador had only strengthened his love for her. His suffering had become his pleasure. "The one who loves is never rational," he said many years later to one of his friends. "Do you know how one loves? If your love is pure and you love this purity in your woman and then suddenly discover that she is really frivolous and immoral, then you will come to love this immorality in her, this ugliness and filth that you abhor—such is love."

Dostoyevsky's agonizing position between hope and hopelessness is recorded in Polina's diary. Late one evening in Baden-Baden they had just had tea together. She had taken off her shoes and was lying on the bed. She asked him to sit a bit closer, took his hand and held it tightly for a long while.

I said that I had been unfair and unkind to him in Paris, that it must have seemed as though I had been thinking only of myself. But I had thought also of him; I didn't want to say it so as not to hurt him. Suddenly he stood up as if he were leaving, but he stumbled over my shoes that lay near the bed and turned around just as quickly and sat down.

"Did you want to leave?" I asked.

"I just wanted to shut the window."

"Well, just shut it then."

"No, it doesn't matter. You have no idea what just happened to me," he said with a peculiar expression.

"What was it?" I looked at him, his face was very agitated.

"Just now I wanted to kiss your foot."

"What for?" I asked confused, almost afraid, and pulled my foot up underneath me.

"Yes, I suddenly had the desire and decided to kiss it."

Afterward, he asked me if I wanted to go to sleep, but I said I would rather sit awhile with him. When I got tired and wanted to get undressed, I asked if the chambermaid wouldn't come and clear away the tea service. He said she wouldn't come. Then he looked at me in a way that made me embarrassed, and I told him so. "I, too, am embarrassed." he said with a strange smile. I hid my face in my pillow. Then I asked yet another time if the chambermaid wouldn't come and he assured me again that she would not.

"Now, go into your own room. I want to sleep," I said.

"Right away," he said, but he stood there a bit longer anyway. Then he gave me a passionate kiss and started lighting a candle. My candle was almost burned down.

"You will have to lie in the dark," he said.

"No, I have a whole candle there."

"But this is mine."

"I have another one."

"You always have an answer," he said, smiling, and went out. He did not close the door and returned shortly afterward under the pretext that he wanted to shut the window. He came over to me and suggested that I get undressed.

"Yes, I will get undressed," I said, but let him understand that I was just waiting for him to leave.

He left once more, but was back yet another time under another pretext. Finally he left for good and closed the door.

Scenes of smoldering desire such as this one show the degree to which Dostoyevsky was pining during his travels with Polina. "Pleasure is something we all want," the hero of *The Gambler* says, "and heedless, unbounded power, even over a fly, is a kind of pleasure." Dostoyevsky found it humiliating to leave Polina more or less in a state of deshabille at one o'clock in the morning: didn't she know the saying "Russians never retreat"? But when he felt very depressed, she would try to cheer him up. Suddenly she would become warm and loving, would embrace him and—cry. He really was so sweet and good, and he had done so much for her!

One day when they were eating dinner in Turin, Dostoyevsky saw a little girl who was getting a lesson from her teacher. "Imagine such a girl with an old man," he told Polina, "and then suddenly some Napoleon appears and gives the order: 'The entire city must be annihilated!' That's the way the world has always been."

Dostoyevsky's time with Polina afforded him rich opportunity to confirm how little compassion there is in humanity. "I am not happy," he complained to her as they finally arrived in Rome. "I look at everything dutifully, as if I were doing my homework . . . but you will discover that in the long run it is impossible to torture a man in this way. One day he will become tired of making further efforts." But that his passion still had not dampened can be seen in Polina's description of their encounter with the Herzen family during their passage to Naples. When Dostoyevsky introduced her as a "distant relative," she took her revenge by flirting with Herzen's young son and making her companion wild with jealousy.

During his restless travels with Polina, always afraid of being thrown out of hotels for lack of funds, Dostoyevsky had the idea for *The Gambler*. Insolvent as he was, he immediately tried to sell the unwritten book to a publisher in St. Petersburg. "I have never yet sold a work (with the exception of *Poor Folk*) without getting an advance," he wrote to Strakhov from Rome. "I am a literary proletarian, and he who wants my work has to be prepared to pay in advance. I myself curse this arrangement, but now that I have begun with it, I will probably never be able to do away with it."

Three years later, in *The Gambler*, a finely wrought novel about a man who "does not dare not to believe," Dostoyevsky describes not only his experience of the casino's hell, but also his destructive relationship with Polina. The narrator is gripped by feelings that must have continually plagued Dostoyevsky during his tortured coexistence with the young woman.

And now once more I asked myself the question, "Am I in love with her?" And once more I did not know how to answer it, or rather I answered once more, for the hundredth time, that I hated her. Yes, I hated her. There were moments (to wit, at the end of every one of our conversations) when I would have given half my life to strangle her! I swear if it had been possible to bury a sharp knife slowly in her breast, I think I would have seized it with pleasure. And yet I swear by all that's holy that if on the fashionable peak of the Schlangenberg she had indeed said to me, "Cast yourself down," I would have done so immediately and even enjoyed doing it. I knew that. One way or another the matter must be settled. She understands all this very well indeed, and the idea that I recognize with full certainty and clarity all her inaccessibility to me, all the impossibility of realizing my fantastic dreams—that idea, I am convinced, gives her extraordinary pleasure; otherwise could she, cautious and clever as she is, be on terms of such intimacy and frankness with me? I think that up to now her attitude to me has been like that of the empress of antiquity who would undress in front of her slave, not considering him a man.

After a month and a half of traveling, the two finally parted company in Turin. Polina went back to Paris to track down her beloved Salvador, while Dostoyevsky headed for Bad Homburg to try his luck once again at the tables, this time with the advance he had received for *The Gambler*.

Under the leadership of François Blanc, Bad Homburg had become the most important gambling city in Europe. Legendary gamblers like Thomas Garcia and the Maltese Vincento Bugeja had made the city a Mecca of chance. Here hundreds of thousands of francs changed hands in a matter of minutes, but sooner or later the bank always came out ahead. *"Mettez rouge ou mettez noir, c'est toujours Blanc qui gagne"* was a sardonic saying that circulated among Homburg's gamblers. At his death in 1877, Blanc left behind a fortune of nearly one hundred million. Dostoyevsky had a reason for giving the "greedy, grasping" female character in *The Gambler* the name "Blanche."

Of all the big gamblers, Russians were known to be the most passionate, and foremost among them was the Countess Kiselyova, who sat at the tables twelve hours a day and who every year dropped enormous sums. The impoverished Dostoyevsky must have been completely out of his element in this place. His pitiful wagers were probably scarcely noticed—the writer's name does not once appear in the casino's *livre des jeux*. Yet no one pursued the fickle roulette wheel with greater eagerness. The exhilaration Thomas De Quincey sought from his drops of opium, Dostoyevsky found in gambling. This was truly tempting fate! He could really push himself to the limit! Even though the advance diminished quickly, he clung desperately to the masochistic pleasures the game provided.

Apparently bad luck in love was not tantamount to luck in the game. His losses at the green table made it necessary for him to send out demeaning calls for help both east and west. Not until Polina had pawned her watch and necklace was he able to begin his return journey, and a new loan from Dresden, probably from the writer Aleksei Tolstoy, got him back to St. Petersburg.

When they parted in Turin both Dostoyevsky and Polina must have felt that their affair was coming to an end. They stayed in touch with each other for a long time, but their letters make it clear that passions were cooling. "Apollinaria is a great egotist," he told her sister in a letter in the spring of 1865. "I still love her, yes, I love her very much, but I wish I did not. She does *not deserve* such a love. I feel sorry for her, because I predict that she will always be unhappy. She will never find either a man or happiness. He who demands everything from another and pronounces himself free from all responsibilities will never find happiness."

This prophecy would show itself to be true. Polina's later life—first as a follower of the radical populist movement in the 1870s, then as the wife of Rozanov, who was twenty years younger than she, and finally as a reactionary nationalist with anti-Semitic sympathies—was a long continuing tragedy. She retained her explosive temperament to the very end, however. When Rozanov wrote to her at her family home to arrange a divorce, Polina's father gave the following description of his daughter: "A human devil has come to live in my house, and now I cannot bear to be in it."

Nevertheless, the relationship between Dostoyevsky and Polina was considerably more than an "episode." He felt more than merely sexual passion and she more than hate and vengeance. A spiritual closeness developed between the two—they shared a love for the Russian peasant and a contempt for the West. And most of all, they had enormous sympathy for one another. Polina's importance for Dostoyevsky may be seen in nearly a dozen female characters that inhabit his work—from Polina in *The Gambler* to Grushenka and Katerina Ivanovna in *The Brothers Karamazov*. In his last letter, he referred to her as "my eternal friend."

Dostoyevsky.
Photograph, 1861.

The Insulted and the Injured.
V. Knyasev, 1884.

The title page of the first issue
of the Dostoyevsky brothers'
journal Time.

Apollinaria Suslova.

Fire in St. Petersburg. A lithograph from the 1860s.

Dostoyevsky. Photograph, 1861.

7

YEARS
OF CRISIS

"Everything around me has become so cold and empty . . ."

Only a catastrophe could tear Dostoyevsky away from the gaming tables in Bad Homburg. He was called home to his dying wife.

Little is known about Maria Dimitrievna after the couple moved from Siberia. There are several dubious stories that all have the quality of legends. Dostoyevsky's daughter is once again guilty of distortion— she reports that Nikolai Vergunov, Maria's young lover from Siberia, followed the couple back to Russia and soon afterward resumed his relationship with the writer's wife.

More reliable is the story that during their early period in St. Petersburg, Dostoyevsky and Maria remained close. Nikolai Strakhov recalled the woman's "pallor and delicate facial expression." But the move brought Maria great unhappiness. Especially difficult was her relationship with her brother-in-law Mikhail, who had always regarded his brother's marriage to a sick woman as a serious mistake.

Maria felt ostracized and became suspicious and introverted. Dramatic breakup scenes occurred more and more often between husband and wife, and in the end they separated. The humid climate of St. Petersburg aggravated her symptoms, and she took up residence in the provincial city of Vladimir.

After she moved, Maria grew worse. Hour after hour she would sit lethargically in her rocking chair. Then she would suddenly jump up and wander restlessly about the room and stop to shake her fist furiously at the picture of her husband. "You convict!" she would shout. "You miserable convict!"

When Dostoyevsky finally arrived in Vladimir at the end of October 1863, he found Maria worse than he had ever seen her. In November they moved to Moscow where she was kept under the constant care of the writer's brother-in-law Dr. Alexander Ivanov. But her condition grew more critical, and her physical deterioration was accompanied by a series of psychological problems. Among other things, she experienced strange hallucinations— "The demons, look at the demons!" she would cry out. Not until the doctor had opened the window and driven them out with his handkerchief would she grow calm, at least for a little while.

"Maria Dimitrievna thinks of death constantly. She is very sad and often in despair," Dostoyevsky wrote in January. "These moments are very trying for her. Her nerves are at their breaking point. She has pain in her chest and has become as thin as a matchstick. Horrible! It is painful to look at her."

She didn't want to hear about her son. When Pasha finally arrived, she waved him away from her. He had become a wastrel, a young man who indulged frequently in the excesses of the good life. Dostoyevsky was burdened by the consciousness that he had not been a good father to Pasha. He continued to feel responsible for him and warned him against his indolence. "He who refuses to do anything in this world can only become a scoundrel and an idler," he admonished. "Try to get as much done as possible in the shortest time."

Dostoyevsky lived by this adage himself. Feeling miserable and unwell, he listened to the coughing and wheezing of his dying wife as he sat up at night writing the darkest of all his works, *Notes from the Underground*. The optimism and joy he had felt in the years after his return from Siberia had disappeared. Heavy in spirit, he wrote the cynical manifesto in which he made a break with his past.

In this work, Dostoyevsky gave up all the dreams of his youth. Those visions had proven to be lies, torn loose from the muck and misery of reality. The dreamer of "White Nights" becomes a mad anti-hero who throws himself headlong into proud and lonely vanity. The work is a protest against those who wish to transform man into a useful individual for the common good, and a scathing rejection of the contention that man can be manipulated through his environment into correct behavior.

The catalyst for Dostoyevsky's reckoning with his past was Chernyshevsky's recently published novel *What Is to Be Done?* This book presented a materialist view of the world and promised a future utopia of good people living in perfect harmony. If only people would question what is useful and seek to satisfy their "rational egoism," society would be changed into a paradise. According to Chernyshevsky, human beings are "rational egotists" who must see that their own interests are best served by serving others. Love yourself and then you will love others. Almost immediately, the book became a Bible for the era's radicals, but Dostoyevsky rejected this naïve view of the future with its happy people in crystal palaces. Self-righteous cynics had found themselves a real weapon—that there is no distinction between utility and goodness. Dostoyevsky believed that people are only minimally able to organize themselves according to a preconceived rational plan. Human nature is irrational and whimsical. Life cannot be governed by reason alone; the human will to freedom must be considered. Thus, the Underground Man refuses to accept a social system that its supporters claim will be of benefit to all. What is most valued in life is neither pleasure nor happiness, but freedom. Freely chosen pain is preferable to forced happiness. The good life means prosperity and security, say the utilitarians. Not for me, replies the Underground Man. I want to follow my own stupid impulses. I abhor the anthill society in which each person is supposed to help every other with useful labor. To hell with well-organized civilization!

Nevertheless, Dostoyevsky found it difficult to rid himself of his earlier faith in socialist utopias. The Underground Man's passionate defense of eccentric ideas, the sarcastic tone he uses when he defends himself indicate that he is dissatisfied with his own ideology. With reason, Dostoyevsky was afraid that the tone of the work would be "too severe and savage," and the censor confirmed his fear. "What is one to do with these idiots at the censor?" he complained in exasperation to his brother. "Those places where I have scorned everything *for the sake of appearance* and even indulged in blasphemy, they have left untouched. But the places where I have demonstrated that it is necessary to put faith in God, they have censored everything. One would almost think that these censors were conspiring against the government."

Dostoyevsky recorded his understanding of the Underground Man in his notebook:

I am proud that I was the first to describe a true representative of the Russian majority, the first to show the ugly and tragic side of his nature. The tragedy exists precisely in the recognition of ugliness. . . . I am the only one who has portrayed the tragedy of the underground, a tragedy that comes from suffering, from the recognition that there exists something better that cannot be reached, and not the least from the conviction of these people that all human beings are alike so that it does not pay to get on an even keel.

With its exposure of human instincts and its fusion of idea and character, *Notes from the Underground* may be seen as a prologue to Dostoyevsky's later novels of ideas. "You should continue writing in this genre," advised Apollon Grigoryev. In Dostoyevsky's next work, the arrogance of the Underground Man is taken further, from an inability to act to crime, from theory to practice. Raskolnikov's idea had escaped the notebooks and armed itself with an ax.

Maria grew worse. In early April 1864, Dostoyevsky wrote, "My wife is near death—literally. Every day we wait for her to die. Her suffering is so terrible and affects me, too, because . . ."

He did not finish the sentence; he was obviously haunted by guilt. In the last years, he and his wife had had little in common, but still he suffered from pangs of conscience. Not long afterward, she began to hemorrhage; this was what finally killed her. On the evening of April 15, after it was all over, Dostoyevsky wrote to his brother: "Promise me that you will remember her with a good word. She has suffered so much that I cannot imagine why everyone should not reconcile himself with her."

He described his own reconciliation with Maria in a letter to Baron Wrangel:

> Oh, dear friend, she loved me boundlessly and I loved her infinitely, and still we were unable to live happily together. . . . We could not stop loving each other; the more unhappy we were, the more tied we felt to each other. It may seem strange, but that was the case. She was the most honest, noble, and magnanimous woman I have ever known. Even though I suffered terrible agonies as I watched her slow death, even though I fully appreciated her worth and knew what I took to the grave, I still had not imagined how empty and painful it would be when the grave was covered with earth. And now it has been a year, and I still have this feeling; it has not diminished in the least.

Dostoyevsky's despair over Maria's death can also be seen in his enigmatic reflections on the meaning of love the day after she died. He refers to the moral strength that helped him find the necessary "earthly equilib-rium" in a crisis:

April 16. Masha is lying before me on the table. Will I ever see Masha again?

To love another as oneself according to Christ's commandment is im-possible. Man is bound on earth by the law of personality. The Ego holds him back. Only Christ was able to do this, but Christ is a perpetual and eternal ideal towards which man strives and according to the law of nature must strive against. . . .

And therefore on earth man strives towards an ideal that is opposed to his nature. When man sees that he has not lived up to the commandment to strive for the ideal, that he has not sacrificed his Ego to other people or to another person (Masha and I), he suffers and calls this state sin. Man must suffer unceasingly, but this suffering is compensated for by the heav-enly joy of striving to fulfill the commandment through sacrifice. This is the "earthly equilibrium"; without it, life would be meaningless.

For Dostoyevsky, the year 1864 was a long series of misfortunes. *Time* had been shut down because of a misunderstanding, and the Dostoyevsky brothers hoped somehow to salvage the journal, at least under a new name. Fyodor suggested that it be rechristened *Truth (Pravda)*, and that the editors could save face with their former subscribers by printing the following slogan on the cover—"Time demands Truth." It soon became clear, however, that there were no grounds for such optimism. The authorities had long been suspicious of the Dostoyevsky brothers and were not prepared to permit the existence of a new journal with *Time*'s "damaging tendencies." The liberal spirit of Tsar Alexander's early rule was over. When Mikhail finally got permission to publish a magazine in January 1864 with the rather igno-minious and non-Russian title *Epoch*, it was only because he had indicated that the new magazine would be ideologically to the right of *Time*.

The program for the new journal guaranteed an approach friendly to the government. Social criticism and political satire were banned, and for-eign policy had to be filtered through the official view. "The treatment of foreign policy will be founded on Russian interests and the good of our society," stated the journal's declaration of purpose. "The events of last year, the country's patriotic sentiments, and the strength of our people will be the basis of the editor's elucidation of all foreign-policy issues."

After the success of *Time*, it was uninspiring to begin work on a journal that had to a large degree committed itself to functioning as a mouthpiece for the government. From the beginning the editors had the feeling that they had taken a wrong turn. The delay in receiving permission to publish and Mikhail's lack of practical ability only made a bad situation worse. When the first issue finally came out toward the end of March, it was too late to find new subscribers. Immediately, *Epoch* was burdened with a huge deficit. And the journal's primitive equipment nearly drove Dostoyevsky into despair.

But when he returned to St. Petersburg at the end of April, Dostoyevsky nonetheless tried to realize his goal of making *Epoch* Russia's leading journal. However, the letters he wrote beseeching big names such as Turgenev and Ostrovsky for contributions got no results, and the magazine became steadily duller. *The Contemporary* ridiculed the "idiots" and "moon men" at *Epoch*, who after tremendous delays published "collected works" but no current pieces. Dostoyevsky replied to the accusation with "The Crocodile," a satirical piece that many interpreted as a malicious attack on the imprisoned Chernyshevsky. A man who has been eaten by a crocodile continues to spout his socialist rubbish from inside the belly of the crocodile—the Peter-Paul Fortress. "It was painful to look at Dostoyevsky at the time," an acquaintance wrote in his memoirs. "He looked like a poisoned beast who still went about showing his teeth."

Mikhail was not able to endure the hardship—his continual battle with creditors, the constant threats of being thrown into debtors' prison. On July 10, he died of a liver infection. Losing his brother was terrible for Dostoyevsky. "Now I am suddenly alone and fear has overcome me," he wrote in a letter to Baron Wrangel. "My whole life has gone to pieces; it doesn't seem to have meaning any longer . . . everything around me has become so cold and empty." The same gloom informed his letters to his brother Andrei after Mikhail's death: "That man loved me more than anything in the whole world—even more than his wife and children, whom he adored . . . now what lies ahead of me is epilepsy and cold, lonely old age."

To make matters worse, Mikhail left behind a large family and a debt of twenty-five thousand rubles. The family let Dostoyevsky know that they held him responsible for Mikhail's misfortunes. Wasn't he the one who had persuaded his brother to sell his tobacco factory and start that stupid journal? These accusations as well as his desire to keep his brother's name unblemished prompted Dostoyevsky generously to take on Mikhail's debts and the care of his family. "Naturally I am now in their service," he wrote to Andrei.

"But for such a brother I am ready to sacrifice both my head and my health."

He received from his aunt Alexandra Kumanin two notes worth ten thousand rubles, and with what was left of this money (most of it disappeared into creditors' pockets) he tried to continue managing *Epoch*, putting his faith in the acquisition of new subscribers at the turn of the year. "At that time, everything depended upon the magazine," he wrote later. "If it was successful, all debts could be paid and the family would be saved from penury. To discontinue the magazine would have been a crime."

Dostoyevsky's fellow writers could only shake their heads over this desperate battle. If he had received permission to be the journal's editor, there might have been hope, but instead, a man with no knowledge of literature was given the job, and he proceeded to make the periodical even drearier. In September, the journal's foremost contributing editor, Apollon Grigoryev, died, broken down by drinking and debts. Three deaths in six months! Dostoyevsky did not write a single line; his time was entirely taken up with editorial work, proofreading, and dealing with contributors and the censor. Moreover, he had to worry about his alcoholic brother Nikolai, and his dissipated stepson Pasha. He barely slept three hours a day.

II

Dostoyevsky fought to keep *Epoch* alive not only for financial reasons; the journal had become an important means of getting to know people who stimulated him to new awareness and eased his loneliness. He had an eye for the women on the *Epoch* staff, and liked to cultivate women writers as protégées. He had little luck as a talent scout, however, probably because the erotic intention took precedence over the artistic one. After Maria's death and his break with Polina, Dostoyevsky began to entertain the possibility of remarriage. One of the women who made her interest in the writer known was a young girl named Martha Brown.

Driven both by poverty and a desire for adventure, Martha had left Russia for Europe at the age of sixteen. "I have always believed that life exists in order to have exciting experiences," she told Dostoyevsky. Her travels in Europe, however, were a series of aimless ramblings from country to country and man to man, during which she married a sailor from Baltimore. After several years she returned to Russia where she sought support from the writer who had "such great prestige with intelligent people."

Dostoyevsky was flattered by Martha's letters and helped her when she turned up in *Epoch's* editorial offices looking for work late in the autumn of 1864. Dostoyevsky had a penchant for adventurers who chose to gamble recklessly with their lives. He certainly sympathized with the Bohemian Martha. We know that near the turn of the year he visited her in the hospital, and there is also evidence to suggest that he asked her to live with him. Even though Martha was not sure she could satisfy him "in a physical way," she was clearly happy to have met a man who found beauty even in her dubious past. Their relationship seems to have been somewhat like the bond between Prince Myshkin and Nastasya Filippovna in *The Idiot*, and yet there could not have been a deep spiritual understanding between them. In her letters, Martha praises the writer for his "equanimity, tolerance, and practical judgment"—words that do not exactly attest to a penetration of Dostoyevsky's highly complex personality.

He did not fare much better when he sought female company in the highest aristocratic circles. In the autumn of 1864, he received two short stories from a small town in the Vitebsk district. The stories, one about an unhappy love affair and the other about a monk seeking the truth, were clearly written by a woman who had thought it best to conceal her identity behind a male pseudonym. Dostoyevsky was impressed, although he did have some criticisms of the new writer—"remember that an author's greatest talent lies in the ability to cut," he wrote. "He who can cut his own will go far." Still there was no doubt that the stories were publishable. "You are a poet," he concluded. "Read serious books and life will do the rest. Besides that, you must have faith. Without faith you will get no results."

The stories were written by one Anna Korvin-Krukovskaya, a beautiful twenty-one-year-old woman with sparkling eyes and long blond hair. But Anna was more than pretty; she was unquestionably the most gifted woman Dostoyevsky ever knew well.

The daughter of a wealthy landowner, Anna had received an excellent education at home. For years she dreamed of medieval knights and of personal triumphs in that distant world. Later she became involved in the radical student milieu of St. Petersburg and decided that she wanted to study medicine. (It was her sister Sofia, however, who was to achieve academic glory in the family. She became the first woman professor of mathematics— at the Högskola in Stockholm.) But Anna was not given permission to study. Her father, a domineering general, was very angry when he discovered that she had accepted money for her stories. From a girl who corresponds with a strange man without her parents' blessing and even takes money from him, one can expect anything! "Now you sell your stories, perhaps you will be selling yourself next!"

But when Anna read her stories aloud, her father softened, and in the end she was allowed to correspond with Dostoyevsky on the condition that her letters were censored before she mailed them. She was even permitted to meet with the writer the next time the family traveled to St. Petersburg. "But remember," the general said pointedly to his wife, "you must take responsibility. Dostoyevsky does not belong to our circle. What do we know about him anyway? Only that he is a journalist and a former convict. Not much of a recommendation. We had best be careful."

When Dostoyevsky finally met Anna in St. Petersburg at the beginning of March 1865, the young woman's mother had made every possible arrangement to prevent the two from being alone. This at once put Dostoyevsky in a bad mood, and he sat there tugging on his beard looking very old and sickly. The next visit, when he found Anna and Sofia at home alone, was more satisfying. The fifteen-year-old Sofia instantly fell in love with him, not only because of his genius but also "because of all that he has suffered."

Dostoyevsky became a frequent guest of the Korvin-Krukovsky family, whose home he visited three to four times a week. It is possible that he saw in them a last chance to save *Epoch*. But the general was right; Dostoyevsky did not belong in this refined circle of high society. This became obvious when he sat himself down in a corner during a large party and began, quite improperly, to flirt with Anna. The mistress of the house was finally forced to remind him that her daughter had a duty toward the other guests as well. With that, the festivity ended for Dostoyevsky. Irritable, gloomy, and pained with jealousy, he looked on as Anna "with the smile of an angel" conversed with a vain, self-satisfied colonel who had long been designated as her future husband. "The New Testament was apparently not written for aristocratic ladies. It says that a man should leave his father and mother and cling to his wife. I wonder what certain mothers would say to that, those who only think of marrying their daughters off in the most profitable way possible?"

Sofia Kovalevskaya reports several such blunders on the part of Dostoyevsky. The mistress of the house was particularly aghast when the writer began to list Stavrogin's future crimes in *The Possessed* in front of her daughters!

Dostoyevsky's attempt to hide his shyness behind a mask of aggression had, on the whole, an unpleasant effect on those around him. He always insisted on being the center of attention. Fyodor Mikhailovich could not bear it when several people conversed together, Sofia recalled. "He spoke only in monologues, and only on the condition that he liked those who were present and that they listened to him with unflagging attention."

He could also be irritable and peevish with Anna, who had revolutionary sympathies and later became a well-known member of the Commune during the siege of Paris in 1871. Their discussions went especially poorly when the topic of the nihilists' criticism of Pushkin came up. A few years earlier, Dostoyevsky had predicted that there would come a time when even Pushkin's memory would be soiled. "Today's youth will surely live to see it," he said, "for us it would be better that we did not live so long." And now the nihilists had been repudiating Russia's national poet for quite some time. Sofia wrote:

> "The young people of today are slow and stupid!" Dostoyevsky would cry out. "A pair of well brushed boots are worth more to them than all of Pushkin."
>
> "Pushkin does seem a bit antiquated for our time," replied my sister, who knew very well that nothing made him angrier than a lack of respect for Pushkin.
>
> At such times, Dostoyevsky, furious, would take his hat and declare that it was impossible to discuss anything with a nihilist and that he would never again cross the threshold of our house. But naturally, the next day he was back again as if nothing had happened.

Dostoyevsky's courtship of Anna was destined to be hopeless, and the jealous Sofia's tale of how she once discovered him and her sister on a sofa in the middle of an intimate conversation is pathetic: "Dear Anna, try to understand me," said Dostoyevsky, "I fell in love with you the moment I saw you, no, even before; when I read your letters, I had a premonition of this. And I don't love you as a friend, but with passion, with my whole being."

"Everything went black before my eyes," Sofia wrote. "I was overcome with a feeling of bitter loneliness and deep offense; it was as if my blood rushed to my heart and from there burst into my head in one burning stream." And to imagine that Anna wouldn't even have him! "He is good, wise, and brilliant," her sister told Sofia, "but I don't love him in the way he loves me. I don't love him in a way that allows me to imagine marrying him. . . . He needs a wife who can give her entire life to him, who will think only of him. I can't do that. I want my own life. Besides, he is very nervous and demanding, and he seems to grab hold of me and suck me into him. I am never myself when he is around."

Nevertheless, there was no real break between them. They continued to write to each other and met quite often during the late 1870s, by which time Anna was married to the Paris Commune member Jaclart. For Anna, there was never any question of being in love with Dostoyevsky, and one may speculate as to whether he didn't exaggerate when he later reported that she had consented to his marriage proposal. Furthermore, it was he who did not keep her to her promise. Still, his description of this proud young woman seems accurate: "Anna Vasilyevna is one of the finest women I have ever met. She is exceedingly wise, has a literary education and a true and good heart. She is a girl with high moral qualities, but her beliefs are diametrically opposed to mine, and she is much too honest to abandon them. A marriage to her would therefore have not been happy." The writer's second wife agreed with this evaluation: "Anna Vasilyevna lacked the indulgence necessary in every good marriage, especially in a marriage with a sick and sensitive man like Fyodor Mikhailovich."

But there was a great deal to preoccupy Dostoyevsky besides courtship. Russia had been hit by an economic crisis. One journal after another folded, and *Epoch* was in a state of continual decline. The subscription policy for 1865 was a failure and in March, after the thirteenth issue, the journal ended.

New debts. New worries. "Oh, dear friend," he wrote to Wrangel, "I would happily do my time in prison over again if I could pay my debts and feel like a free man. . . . And at the same time, I continually have the feeling that I have just begun to live. Ridiculous, isn't it? Many lives—like a cat."

He certainly could have used nine lives. When the magazine went under, he was left with a debt of more than fifteen thousand rubles. And so it began again, the demeaning rounds from one benefactor to another. Subscription notes had been bought by people of all kinds—merchants' wives, lawyers, even a farmer with the auspicious name of Seymon Pushkin. When the notes became worthless, the police appeared and threatened to confiscate Dostoyevsky's belongings. "You are ordered to stay in your apartment until the appointed time," stated the official request of June 5,

1865. "Otherwise the seizure will take place in your absence." In short, Dostoyevsky lived every day in the shadow of debtor's prison. It is not strange that money and the lack of money were significant themes in his work.

For a long time, he had planned to write a novel with the working title *The Drunkard*. He had recently witnessed the waste and misery of drunkenness when a group of broken-down alcoholics appeared at Apollon Grigoryev's funeral. They made a powerful impression on him. Here was material for a social narrative about depraved people. But how was he to find peace to work with the creditors closing in on him and threatening him with prison?

In order to get time to write, he decided a trip abroad would once again be necessary. He tried to acquire money for the trip by selling his idea for *The Drunkard*, but Krayevsky said no—he was obviously not excited by a novel on this sad but topical problem. Dostoyevsky asked to be relieved of his position in the Literary Society so that he could take out a loan. The loan was woefully insufficient, however, and in order to realize his flight from his creditors, Dostoyevsky was obliged to sell a new three-volume edition of his works to a crude speculator named Fyodor Stellovsky. They agreed upon three thousand rubles for the edition, a laughably tiny sum considering the writer's popularity. And the agreement was saddled with a bizarre additional clause—if Dostoyevsky did not submit a new novel before November 1 of the following year, Stellovsky would have the right to publish all his works free of charge for nine years. This was rather like playing roulette with his writing career, and the fact that Stellovsky made back most of his money after only a few days was aggravating indeed. He had acquired a number of Dostoyevsky's now worthless subscription notes and had used his strawmen to redeem them.

Finally, at the end of July 1865, Dostoyevsky left Russia with a measly hundred and seventy-five rubles for travel money. He checked into the Hotel Victoria in Wiesbaden, just a few meters from the Cursaal. He reported the results of his gambling in a letter to Turgenev:

> Two years ago in Wiesbaden I won close to twelve thousand francs in a single hour. Even though this time I was not looking to improve my finances, I still would have liked to win a thousand francs to have something to live on during these three months. But in the course of five days in Wiesbaden, I have lost everything. I am completely broke—I even gambled away my watch, and I owe money at the hotel.

He asked Turgenev for one hundred thaler but received only fifty, a debt that was not repaid until ten years later. A visit from Polina proved only embarrassing—he sent her off with a plea to find money. Baron Wrangel, now stationed at the Russian embassy in Copenhagen, did not intercept the call for help because he was on vacation in St. Petersburg. Nor did Herzen respond positively to his unstamped letter begging for money. The hotel manager denied him food and candles—"You don't deserve it!" While the other guests ate their dinner, Dostoyevsky was advised to take a long walk. But when he found that the walks only made him hungrier, he shut himself up in his dark hotel room.

A humiliating situation, but one clearly advantageous to his creativity. He never worked better than when he had lost everything and had relieved his guilt through the merciless punishment of the roulette wheel. During his stay in Wiesbaden, he began to give life to one of his greatest masterpieces, *Crime and Punishment*. Out of *The Drunkard* developed the psychological story of a crime. The hero's situation in the novel is conspicuously like the author's own at the Hotel Victoria. Raskolnikov also lives alone in a hideous little room; he, too, is refused dinner and owes rent so that he is forced to sneak past his landlady on the stairs.

When Dostoyevksy finally received money from Wrangel, it was seized by the hotel manager, who threatened to notify the police. It was time to go home. Better to be locked up in a debtor's prison in St. Petersburg than in detestable Wiesbaden. In the end, Dostoyevsky was rescued by the city's Russian priest, who paid the required amount and put him in a coach.

His trip back home took him through Copenhagen, where he celebrated a joyful reunion with his old friend from Siberia. "He had become thinner and he looked old," Wrangel recalled. He advised Dostoyevsky to take a position with the state. "A certain ruble is better than the hope of a million." Their conversation was lively; they talked of their times together and of mutual acquaintances of both sexes. When Wrangel complained of a former lover's deceit and fickleness, Dostoyevsky gave him comforting advice. "Let's always be deeply grateful for those days and hours of happiness, for the caresses a beloved woman has given us. It is impossible to ask that she should always live for you and think of you—that would be unworthy and egotistical. We must try to conquer such feelings."

His relationship with Polina was obviously over. Many years later, she would look him up in his apartment in St. Petersburg but he would not recognize her.

After his arrival in St. Petersburg in the middle of October, he sold *Crime and Punishment* to Mikhail Katkov, editor of *The Russian Messenger*. Serial publication began in January 1866. The writer was aware that this work "would perhaps be my best." If only he could get the quiet he needed to concentrate on the novel and not ruin it because he was pressed for time! "Writing a novel is a poetic activity that demands imagination and steadiness." But the creditors did not let up. The stress increased the frequency of his seizures, and he was also tormented by fevers and hemorrhoids. Even the thought of his agreement with Stellovsky brought him to the brink of despair. He complained to Anna Korvin-Krukovskaya that he was forced to write one novel during the day and the other at night. "I am sure that not a single one of our authors, living or dead, has had to write under the circumstances that I always am working under."

Adding to the strain caused by toiling over his novel, the news he received on April 4 was profoundly shocking to Dostoyevsky. A young nihilist, Dmitri Karakozov, had attempted to assassinate the Tsar, Russia's "Little Father." When the writer heard the news, he was so agitated that his entire body shook. Someone had shot at the Tsar! For him the Tsar was connected to the people "as a father is bound to his children." This was an attempt at patricide. And is not the son who strikes out against his father the image of man striking out against God? Karakozov, Karamazov. The root of both names comes from the Turkestan word *kara* for black—the sign of anarchy and spiritual darkness.

To find the calm he needed to finish *Crime and Punishment*, Dostoyevsky decided to spend the summer on the Korvin-Krukovsky estate, at a safe distance from the clamoring creditors. The general, however, was furious when he found out that this dubious man had made plans to finish his novel in such close proximity to his daughters, and he made it clear that Dostoyevsky was not welcome. Instead, the writer went to Moscow, where he could personally oversee the printing of his novel.

The summer of 1866 was extremely hot, and before long Dostoyevsky could no longer work in the city. When his brother-in-law Alexander Ivanov and his sister Vera traveled to their country house in Lyublino, he accompanied them. These two months in the country, just a few kilometers from the capital, offered welcome diversions from the aggravation and money worries. In a stone house near the Ivanov family, Dostoyevsky found a quiet workplace where he was able to write every day. At dinner time he joined his relatives, impeccably attired in a starched shirt, gray trousers, and a blue jacket. His beard was thin, but when he came alive at mealtimes, everyone acknowledged that he looked young for his age.

Lyublino was a beautiful place that offered countless opportunities for peaceful walks and exciting fishing trips. The reminiscences of others from this summer show a side of Dostoyevsky that is unlike the usual image of him as morose and irritable. He was cheerful and energetic; he danced and sang. The youthful atmosphere at the Ivanovs' was very probably the cause of his good humor. The children gathered around him and he played with them all. "I am very fond of children, you see," he said with a smile. "It is one of my weaknesses." Ivanov had several children of his own, most of them in their teens, and he also had invited a number of his students from Moscow. Dostoyevsky loved the company of these young people; he teased and flirted, wrote jocular poems, told ghost stories, and organized plays and concerts. He was reported to have been a wonderful King in *Hamlet*, his head wrapped in a sheet.

He grew especially close to his nieces, the twenty-year-old Sonya, whom he liked to call his "heart-child," and the eighteen-year-old Masha, a favorite pupil of Nikolai Rubenstein. For hours she sat at the piano and played the music of her uncle's most beloved composers, Mozart and Beethoven. The *Pathétique* sonata would inevitably submerge him in a whole world of vanished feelings. Masha did not, however, manage to interest him in Chopin. He disliked Chopin's "consumptive" music—and besides, the man was Polish.

In the sympathetic circle at Lyublino which he later depicted in *The Eternal Husband*, Dostoyevsky's winning nature came into full bloom. He loved to talk with the young people and impressed them all with his gift for conversation. N. von Vogt, who was sixteen years old when he met Dostoyevsky, gave the following account of his impressions:

Fyodor Mikhailovich spoke slowly, calmly, concentratedly—it was obvious that serious thought was going on in his head. His small, gray eyes penetrated his listeners. Usually his eyes showed good humor, but it happened too that they flashed strangely and angrily, especially when he discussed a question that preoccupied him deeply. But no matter what he talked about, there was something secretive about everything he said. It was as if he wished to speak directly, but at the same time hid his thoughts in the depths of his soul. Once in a while he would tell a completely fantastic story, something unbelievable, and he created wonderful images that were long remembered by his listeners.

But even when the play and conversation were at their most animated, Dostoyevsky could become suddenly thoughtful and withdraw from the gathering. "It was as if something were bothering him," remarked one guest. He had been struck by an idea and had to hurry back to *Crime and Punishment*. When the young people came to look for him later, he would be annoyed and angry and would drive them away. He did not like to talk about his work, and it was not very tempting to ask about it. A terrified servant reported that the writer wandered around at night muttering to himself about a murder he planned to commit.

III

Dostoyevsky had revealed the subject of his novel when he offered it to *The Russian Messenger*. His summary of the book is not just an ingenious advertisement, but also an exemplary presentation of the novel's intention:

> A young man from a bourgeois background has been expelled from the university and is living in dire poverty. Because of his rashness and instability he has become prey to certain strange, "unfinished" ideas which are in the air and has decided to free himself from his miserable position in a single stroke. He has decided to murder an old woman who lends money on interest. This old woman is stupid, deaf, sick, and greedy. . . . She takes horrific interest rates, is cruel, and torments her younger sister who works for her. She's fit for nothing. What is she living for? Is she useful to anybody? Such questions drive the young man out of his mind. He decides to murder and rob her in order to find happiness for his mother, who lives in the provinces, and to rescue his sister from a landowner. She lives on the estate as a companion and is continually harassed by the landowner's lechery. . . .
> Completely by accident, he manages to carry out his plan quickly and successfully. Nearly a month passes before the final catastrophe. There is no suspicion of him and no cause for any. In this month, the entire psychological process of the crime unfolds. The murderer is faced with insoluble problems; he is tormented by undreamed of, unexpected feelings. God's truth and earthly law triumph, and in the end, he understands that he must turn himself in.

Katkov smelled a best-seller and sent out three hundred rubles as an advance to Dostoyevsky. He was right. The public received the novel enthusiastically—if with a degree of alarm. Strakhov wrote in his memoirs:

The novel *Crime and Punishment* made an extraordinary splash. It was the only novel one read in 1866, the only book literate readers discussed. And when they discussed it, they usually complained about its overwhelming power and the fact that it made such a painful impression on readers that those with strong nerves fell ill and those with weak nerves had to give up reading it.

Among those who had to put the book down was Turgenev. The first chapter impressed him considerably, but not long after that, he began to have doubts. In his view, Dostoyevsky was far too self-absorbed. There was something cranky and spoiled about this novel, something that summoned up the atmosphere of a hospital. "The first part of *Crime and Punishment* is excellent," he wrote to the poet Afanasy Fet, "but the second part reeks of moldy self-analysis." He gave his final verdict in a letter written in late autumn 1866: "I've given up reading *Crime and Punishment*—the whole thing reminds me of an interminable stomachache. God save us from it during the cholera season!"

Many contemporary readers were shocked by Dostoyevsky's grim portrait of Russian society. "This isn't a novel; it's like the notes of an investigating judge—a gruesome photograph!" Ivan Borisov wrote in a letter to Turgenev. The author's powerful descriptions of stinking stairways, filthy courtyards, sinister pubs, and the fact that he chose as protagonists a drunkard, a murderer, and a prostitute prompted an aesthetically oriented critic like Nikolai Akhsyarumov to compare his initial impression of the novel with the sensations of "a torpid, frightening dream."

Just as powerful was Dostoyevsky's revelation of Russian nihilism and its theory that the end justifies the means. Many felt that the author had availed himself of ideas that were in the air, that this was a new exposé of the Russian nihilist—a relative of Turgenev's Bazarov, only far more fanatical and blind. Spokesmen for radical literary criticism did everything in their power to deny both that Raskolnikov's ideas were widespread in Russia and that he was in any way a typical representative of students at the time. The reviews indicate that they clearly believed that Dostoyevsky had libeled the younger generation.

The Contemporary's position on the novel was typical of this view. After the death of Dobrolyubov, Grigory Yeliseyev became the journal's leading critic, and in February 1866, not long after the publication of the novel's first chapters, he made a scathing attack on what he thought was an extremely weak book:

> You see before you a hero who is possessed by a passion. The author writes and toils, using all his power to portray the depth and breadth of this passion. The result is a book that shows no talent, that is immature, sloppy, rhetorical, a book that not only displays the author's lack of the power of observation, but also his inadequate artistry and his insufficient experience in depicting passion, a book that bores the reader to death and does not at all help to explain the character of the hero. . . . But the author is delighted with the nonsense he has written and apparently deludes himself that he is someone who knows the soul of man—someone on the order of a Shakespeare.

And not only had Dostoyevsky betrayed art, Yeliseyev wrote, even worse, he had betrayed realism and the Russian Student. For polemical purposes he had written a novel without posing for himself the necessary question of whether what he was writing could actually exist in the world. Where could one find a student who would murder a pawnbroker for a few rubles? Nowhere, of course. Therefore, Dostoyevsky's novel was "the most stupid shameful fabrication, the most abject work." Wasn't it Belinsky who once reminded Dostoyevsky that the fantastic belonged in "the madhouse, not in literature," asked the reviewer, who concluded his article with the question, "I wonder what Belinsky would have said about this new figment from the imagination of Mr. Dostoyevsky, a figment that has accused an entire group of young people of having committed a simple murder for gain."

Rarely has a review been more unfortunate in its evaluation. Dostoyevsky's novel is anything but a figment. Contemporary sources show that several young men were so impressed by the book and identified so strongly with the hero that they planned similar crimes. And when the novel was still at the printer's, a double murder was committed in Moscow which, even in its details, resembled Raskolnikov's murder of the pawnbroker and her sister. Even the criminal's appearance was similar to Raskolnikov's: "large, dark expressive eyes, long thick flowing hair."

Crime and Punishment is distinct in several ways from the period's realist novels. Dostoyevsky's book is quite realistic in its depiction of social need and poverty, but it is more difficult to call the book realistic, if one means by that a portrait completely free of fantastic elements. One must return to German Romanticism to find a work in which dreams and reality overlap as they do in this novel. Not to speak of the coincidences: again and again, people run into each other on the street or in pubs; some even conveniently live next door to each other.

Such coincidences would have been unthinkable in a book by the realist Tolstoy, but Dostoyevsky had a different conception of realism than the one that prevailed among his literary colleagues. He turned against the "imitation of reality" and wanted to penetrate the surface. What was most important was not people's behavior or appearance, but the inner, unseen motives for their actions. The writer's task was to uncover "the man in man," and in order to create this kind of realism, it was sometimes necessary to look to the absurd and fantastic.

The charge that Dostoyevsky had painted an unjust and distorted picture of radical youth appeared repeatedly in the major radical periodicals of the time. In the humor magazine *The Spark*, an attack on Dostoyevsky took the form of a satirical story called "The Double: Fyodor Strizhov's Adventure." The story is dedicated to Dostoyevsky and in a footnote the reader is informed that "the author has imitated Dostoyevsky, from whom he has borrowed significantly for his story." This long-winded story tells of one Fyodor Strizhov (Dostoyevsky), whose double goes to the publisher where *Transgression and Retribution* is being printed. He feels that the novel's bias should have been made more obvious and he suggests a number of additions. It is not enough, for example, that Raskolnikov has promised to marry the landlady's daughter even though he doesn't like her; the book must state blankly that "nihilists condemn love and recognize only the cigar." Raskolnikov is perceived as a caricature of a nihilist, and Dostoyevsky is seen as an author trying to disguise his propensity to caricature with scenes reminiscent of *The House of the Dead* and *The Insulted and the Injured*.

The reviewer in *The Week* admitted that the book provided an excellent psychological analysis of Raskolnikov's character. But what good was this when the pitch was so obtrusive? If Dostoyevsky was unhappy with the younger generation, that was his business. Several authors had preceded him in that—in this respect his book resembled Turgenev's *Fathers and Sons*. But whereas Turgenev had given a "faithful representation without resorting to filthy insinuation," Dostoyevsky is guilty of hitting below the belt, because he clearly implies that "liberal ideas and science lead young men to murder and young women to prostitution."

The reviews made it clear that *Crime and Punishment* was going to be lumped together with the period's many antinihilist novels. Critics were so indignant over what they saw as Dostoyevsky's unjust attack on the new generation that they closed their eyes to those aspects of the novel that deserved favorable attention from the political left, such as its exposé of social wretchedness and the brutal influence it has. This point, however, was at the center of Dmitri Pisarev's lengthy critique of *Crime and Punishment*.

After the deaths of Dobrolyubov and Grigoryev, Pisarev had become Russia's most influential critic. Unlike his fellow radicals, he immediately understood the importance of this novel and wrote a sixty-page review divided into two articles. Pisarev was thought of as the quintessential nihilist—the very prototype for Bazarov in *Fathers and Sons*. One would think that he especially would have been offended by Dostoyevsky's "libel," and he does emphatically disassociate himself from the notion that Raskolnikov's theory is in any way related to the ideas that preoccupy young radicals. What he stressed was the portrait of Raskolnikov as a person who loses in his battle for existence. Oppressed by his environment, he loses all hope for a better future and becomes apathetic. In this desperate situation he falls prey to his peculiar theory—the right of a superior individual to put himself above the law.

For Pisarev, then, the superman theory is a product of the terrible circumstances Raskolnikov is forced to struggle against, a struggle that leaves him enervated. The only real cause of the murder is the student's miserable living conditions, his hopeless poverty. Raskolnikov does not commit the crime because after philosophical rumination he becomes convinced that is is permissible and necessary. On the contrary, he allows himself to be swayed by his philosophizing because outside circumstances push him into the crime. His theory is really just a pretext. Raskolnikov made the theory to order, wrote Pisarev. He further opposed the idea that the hero is a monomaniacal madman, as had been claimed by others. If he were mad, how could one follow his thoughts and all their subtle ramifications? Every one of his thoughts and actions is satisfactorily motivated, wrote Pisarev: no, "the cause of his illness is hidden not in his brain but in his pocket."

Pisarev gave a penetrating view of Raskolnikov's poverty and showed that the student never could have managed to subsist on the paltry wages he earned for occasional tutoring. Under his grim living conditions, the hero is doomed to ruin. The materialist critic was quite concrete in his description of Raskolnikov's situation:

> Neither diligence nor conscientiousness in the discharge of his work, nor any application of his powers or energies would have brought him a meal to satisfy the needs of his youthful organism, or given him clothes to protect him sufficiently from the cold, damp, and filth, or provided him with a place to live where he could breathe into his lungs an adequate supply of fresh air.

According to Pisarev, Raskolnikov had been right in the sense that he had understood that he could never save his sister with honest work. But could he really have done it through dishonest means—by killing the pawnbroker? In his despair and exhaustion, Raskolnikov forgets to ask himself this question and commits a murder that is not only morally reprehensible but completely pointless.

> Let us suppose that he had succeeded in murdering the pawnbroker and had found a whole California in her chest. Let us suppose that he had managed to cover all his tracks and that the entire matter was enacted according to plan down to the last detail. But what then? How would he have made use of that stolen money?. . . By showing extreme caution and patience, Raskolnikov might perhaps have been able to avoid police suspicion, but under no circumstances would he have been able to keep from the limelight those people who would have gained from his crime.

Pisarev's review not only functioned as a critique of the society Raskolnikov lived in, but also had a certain revolutionary appeal. If man is to survive, a new society must be created, he suggested. Within the established society, man is doomed to ruin, whether he lives inside or outside its laws. Pisarev rejected as illusion the notion that Sonya's Christian message can offer Raskolnikov salvation. When in the end the hero puts his trust in the good-natured but limited and thoroughly unenlightened Sonya Marmeladov, who like the nymph Egeria offers him "wise and freeing advice," it is due to a character weakness born of his suffering, his fear of punishment, and his terror of hurting his mother and sister.

Everything seemed perfectly lucid to Pisarev, with one exception. Where in the world did Raskolnikov find the "peculiar," "demented" theory that a superior individual has the right to murder? Pisarev disdainfully rejected the idea that this monstrous theory was the product of current socialist ideas circulating among young people, and insisted that in any case it was completely untenable. When Raskolnikov maintains that men like Kepler and Newton had the right, the duty to kill a person standing in the way of their discoveries, he is doing these pioneers a disservice. Science belongs to a realm in which bloodshed is not an issue. A scientist who uses violence to rid himself of opposition ceases to be a scientist and becomes a scoundrel. And a stupid scoundrel at that, because it is not human beings who stand in the way of his work, but environmental circumstances that enable men to oppose scientific truth. These circumstances cannot be altered through force; they can be changed only through the proclamation and achievement of that very same scientific truth. Out of love for the truth, wrote Pisarev, unusual men like Kepler and Newton have sometimes been martyrs, but love of an idea never turned them into executioners, for torture persuades no one and cannot serve the idea in whose name it takes place.

Pisarev unquestionably shed light on essential aspects of Dostoyevsky's novel, clearly revealing its profound humanism and exposing Raskolnikov's theory as evidence of the novel's point of departure—human suffering. Nevertheless, his criticism is lacking in some respects. He had no understanding of the spiritual search that Dostoyevsky depicted as coming out of suffering or of the aspects of the book that one might describe with the words sin, penance, and purification. He undervalued the hubris that is so pronounced in Raskolnikov's character.

Other reviewers made much of the relationship between Dostoyevsky and Raskolnikov. According to Akhsyarumov, the author, having established Raskolnikov as a hardened criminal who doesn't feel the slightest compunction about innocent people suffering from the crime he committed, forgets this and gives him a number of positive traits that seem highly unlikely in such a criminal. This false coloring casts a kind of pale halo of the fallen angel around Raskolnikov's head," he wrote, "which does not suit him at all."

Strakhov, too, considered Dostoyevsky's relationship to his hero. In his view, there could be no question that Dostoyevsky had portrayed a real nihilist. He had shown nihilism at its most extreme development, when it can go no further. The book's merit lay in his keen eye for the time's spiritual malaise and his acute diagnosis of it. Strakhov wrote. "The instability of our moral foundation—that is the theme."

Even though Dostoyevsky gave a frightening account of the consequences of nihilist thought, it does not mean that he wrote an ordinary antinihilist novel. The writer's attitude toward Raskolnikov, according to Strakhov, differed from those that other writers took toward their protagonists. Up until then, nihilists had been depicted as caricatures, people with "empty minds and empty hearts," and writers had been content to ridicule their strivings for liberation, whether it was a young girl chopping off her braids or a young man ceasing to greet ladies with a kiss on the hand. Even Turgenev's Bazarov was, because of his pride, more repellent than attractive, and with each passing year, the nihilists increasingly bore the brunt of satire and ridicule. Raskolnikov, however, is a gifted man of real character who is ruined by a dangerous idea. Dostoyevsky had not given himself the cheap task of creating a caricature of nihilism, but the far more important one of showing the tragedy of nihilism as a soul's disfigurement after terrible suffering. Dostoyevsky achieves this not only by choosing a hero who has great intellectual and emotional capacity, but also by making him sympathetic. It is clear, wrote Strakhov, "that the author portrays his hero compassionately. He does not laugh at the younger generation, he weeps for it."

The novel's purpose, as Strakhov saw it, was to show how theory battles against life in the soul of man, but life wins. He would have liked Dostoyevsky to give a more definitive victory to life, however, and regretted that he had not offered a more explicit portrayal of Raskolnikov's conversion. Here he touched on the question of whether one can say that within the frame of the novel Raskolnikov actually undergoes a full-fledged redemption. There are still scholars who believe that in his generosity toward Raskolnikov Dostoyevsky gave him such powerful arguments against the status quo that Sonya's answer is inadequate, just as Zosima's answer seems unconvincing next to Ivan's indictments in *The Brothers Karamazov*.

On the whole, however, Strakhov praised the novel. The writer had given a real, living portrait of a typical Russian man who does not hesitate to take to its very end the path on which his errant reason has brought him. Strakhov viewed this ability to abandon oneself without compromise, without stopping halfway, as a worthy Russian trait, and he concluded his review by expressing the hope that it would soon show itself in noble actions rather than ruinous ones—as in the novel.

Notably, Dostoyevsky was enthusiastic about Strakhov's review. "You are the only one who has really understood me," he said.

Anna Korvin-Krukovskaya.

Notes for Crime and Punishment.

The marketplace in St. Petersburg
where Raskolnikov kisses the ground. A lithograph from the 1850s.

Woodcuts by Torsten Billman: At the Marketplace.

Crime and Punishment.   Raskolnikov and Sonya.

8

MARRIAGE AND
FLIGHT

*"The difference in our ages is an atrocious one—
she is twenty and I am forty-four. But I am becoming more
and more convinced that we shall be happy together.
She has a kind heart and the ability to love."*

When, at the end of September 1866, Dostoyevsky returned to St. Petersburg, he had not yet finished *Crime and Punishment*. What worried him more, however, was his agreement with Stellovsky. The deadline—November 1—drew steadily closer, yet he had still not written a line of the new novel. In desperation he attempted to procure a few months' grace, even declaring himself willing to pay a large forfeit. Stellovsky's refusal was categorical. In his view it was now impossible for Dostoyevsky to fulfill his obligation; at last he had the writer where he wanted him. For the next ten years he would have a writing slave at his side.

Not even Dostoyevsky's friends had much faith that he could succeed in writing a two-hundred-page novel in four weeks. They suggested that he should sketch out the plot and allow them to proceed with the writing, finally sewing the whole thing together himself. Dostoyevsky rejected this proposal; he could not sign a work that had been written by others. Finally, Milyukov came up with the bright idea that he should hire a secretary. Through a colleague he got in touch with Pavel Olkhin, one of the city's leading stenographers, who passed the buck to his most proficient pupil, the twenty-year-old Anna Grigoryevna Snitkina, asking her if she would be willing to work as secretary to the writer Dostoyevsky.

Snitkina agreed. Dostoyevsky had been the favorite author of her recently deceased father, and she herself had read his *The House of the Dead* with tears in her eyes. Indeed, so captivated had she been by his books that at school she had been known as "Netochka," after one of his heroines. The prospect of now meeting the writer and possibly helping him in his onerous mission filled her with joyful anticipation. The pay was not so bad, either—thirty rubles: she appreciated that.

At shortly before eleven-thirty on October 4, 1866, she stood on the corner of Malaya Meshchanskaya Street and Stolyarny Lane looking up at Dostoyevsky's apartment in an ugly tenement building inhabited by poor tradesmen and craftsmen—and found herself thinking of Raskolnikov's dismal lodgings in *Crime and Punishment*. Nor was her first encounter with the writer a particularly promising one:

> When I set eyes on Dostoyevsky, I thought he looked rather old. But as soon as he began to speak, he at once became much younger—his age could hardly be more than between thirty-five and thirty-seven. He was of average height and held himself unusually upright. His light-brown, slightly reddish hair was pomaded and carefully combed. But what struck me first and foremost were his eyes: one of them was brown, while the other was completely filled by its pupil—one could not see the iris. This discrepancy lent his gaze an enigmatic expression. His pale, wan features were immediately familiar to me, probably because I had seen so many portraits of him. He was wearing a dark blue coat which was slightly worn, but his shirt was brilliantly white and clean.

The writer made Anna sit at a little table in his study and proceeded to stroll about while he smoked one cigarette after another. Not even the strong tea was capable of getting the conversation going. Dostoyevsky seemed tired and preoccupied, and told her he had recently had an attack of epilepsy. He said he did not have much faith in stenography, but supposed they ought to give it a try. "Yes, let's get on with it right away," Anna replied. "But if you find you can't work with my assistance, you must please tell me at once. I won't take it at all amiss if it doesn't work out."

Dostoyevsky picked up a journal and began to dictate at a furious speed. Anna had to interrupt him and ask him to continue at a normal tempo. Oh, it was going so horribly slowly! And she had even managed to leave out a sentence. How could it possibly work? No, he was really far too tired to dictate now. She would have to come back at eight o'clock. Then they would begin on the novel.

As Anna was on her way out, he began to reflect that perhaps he had been a bit severe, and he made an attempt at a parting compliment. But not even that was particularly successful:

"I was really glad when Olkhin recommended me a female secretary, and not a male one. Do you know why?"

"No."

"Because a man would quite certainly have taken to drink immediately. But you won't, I hope?"

I felt like laughing, but managed to suppress my smile.

"No, you may rely on me," I answered. "I shan't take to drink."

When Anna showed up the following afternoon, she had with her a handsome clear copy of the beginning of "Roulettenburg." Such was the provisional title of *The Gambler*. But she was still in doubt as to whether anything would come of this collaboration. It might not make any difference, anyway. Why should she sit in this unpleasant apartment taking dictation from this peevish man? "She would certainly have been terrified if anyone had said that for the next fourteen years she would spend her time taking down Dostoyevsky's works in shorthand," her daughter later observed.

Little by little, however, the collaboration began to go better. The writer's skepticism about the art of stenography gradually diminished as the manuscript pile grew. Every day they stuck at it for four hours, and never before had his work gone so quickly. This *Gambler* novel wasn't going to be so bad after all! True, Anna found it hard to forgive the central character's moral weakness and uncontrollable passion for gambling. But Dostoyevsky assured her that it was perfectly possible to be possessed of an iron will and yet lack the strength to resist the lure of roulette. In this respect the novel was rather a prediction of the future than a farewell to the past.

He also came closer to his secretary in human terms. She looked rather appealing as she sat there, young and smiling, with her oval face, high forehead, and sparkling gray eyes. He believed she was religious—a few years ago she had even planned to enter a nunnery. And what an interest she took in the characters of his novels! More and more often she began to share in his memories from the past. The mock execution on Semyonovsky Square received proper treatment—he had observed that it made an impression on young girls. But what about the future—what advice did she have to give him? Should he go and settle down in Constantinople, give himself up to roulette, or should he instead remarry and start a family? Anna said she thought it would be better for him to get married and seek his happiness in family life.

> "You really think I ought to remarry? Do you think there is any woman who would have me? And what sort of wife should I choose? One who is intelligent, or one who is good?"
> "You must take one who is intelligent, of course."
> "Oh no, if I am to choose, then I should rather take a good wife, one who loves me and who cares about me."

He asked her why she had not found a husband. Anna replied that she was then being courted by two men, but omitted to mention that she was engaged to one of them. She said she had respectful feelings for both, but that if she were to marry it would have to be for love.

"Yes, love is absolutely essential," the writer eagerly agreed. "If a marriage is to be happy, it isn't enough for a couple to feel mutual respect."

Attired in a lilac dress that made Dostoyevsky blush, Anna arrived with the conclusion of the novel on October 30, his birthday. When on the following day he went to Stellovsky's, he discovered that the bird had flown. In an attempt to prevent the manuscript being delivered on time, Stellovsky had left St. Petersburg. No one at the editorial office was willing to accept the manuscript, either. It was only late in the evening, just before the deadline was up, that Dostoyevsky succeeded in obtaining a receipt for the package from a district police official. With Anna's help, he had written an entire novel in the space of twenty-six days. And the speed had actually improved the work, given it more suspense, and heightened the tempo of its plot. No wonder, then, that a few days later he called on Anna in order to extend their contract.

Anna Grigoryevna lived in Peski, which in those days lay on the outskirts of St. Petersburg, not far from the Smolny Monastery. Her father, Grigory Snitkin, was of Ukrainian descent and had served as an administrator of the Tsar's palaces. Her mother, Maria Anna, came from the gifted Finnish-Swedish Miltopæus family and spoke Swedish better than she did Russian. In the seventeenth century her great-great-grandfather had been professor of rhetoric and rector of Åbo Academy. Her father was a surveyor in the Finnish province of St. Michel, where as a child Anna Grigoryevna had been a frequent guest.

Out in Peski the Snitkin family had bought a few pieces of land and had built some tenant farms. The houses were mortgaged, it was true, but Anna was nonetheless regarded as a "pretty girl with a fortune." One of the farms belonged to her, and the experience of running it had given her a good insight into financial matters. She was generally known for her practical flair and her sensible view of the problems of everyday life. She had finished school with excellent grades, and in order not to be a burden on her parents had recently started to learn shorthand.

Dostoyevsky was well received in Peski. The house soon succumbed to his magic influence. To be sure, he was poorly dressed; he had false teeth and a sickly appearance. But all this merely increased Anna's compassion for him. He might not be handsome, but he was at least charming when he unrestrainedly threw himself into a rendering of *La donna è mobile* to the accompaniment of a street singer. "He was still young!" Anna replied laughingly when later on her daughter asked her how a young girl could fall in love with a man who was twenty-five years older than herself. "If only you knew how young your father was in those days! He laughed and joked and enjoyed everything, just like a young man. Indeed, he was a good deal more lively and charming than the young people of those days, for they always wore glasses and looked like old zoology professors." How empty and insignificant her young suitors looked when compared with this deep, confused man whom it had taken three weeks just to find out what her name was. But she did not like him to play the senile old man when he was together with her. The twenty-five years that separated them were quite enough for her to cope with.

When on November 8 Anna arrived in order to start work on the conclusion of *Crime and Punishment*, she found Dostoyevsky in a strangely exalted mood. His features were unusually animated, almost inspired; it was as if he had become much younger. And then he began to tell her about a dream he had just had. He had been sitting in front of a chest putting his manuscripts in order. Suddenly, he had caught sight of something glinting among the papers. It was a tiny but wonderfully brilliant diamond! And now he could not for the life of him remember what had become of it. But it had been a good dream!

Anna didn't know much about dreams. She herself dreamed only about cats and teachers. So she was more interested when the writer began to talk about the new novel he had been working on during the last day or two. The main plot was complete, only the conclusion was still causing problems. Here the temperament of a young girl played a decisive role. Perhaps Anna could help him?

"Who is the hero of your novel?"

"An artist who is no longer really young—about my age."

"Oh, tell me, tell me about him, please."

And, like an answer to my prayer, there followed a dazzling improvisation. Never, either before or since, have I heard him deliver such an animated and inspired narration. The longer he kept it up, the more clearly I realized that it was his own life he was telling me about, with a few changes here and there concerning people and background. As he spoke, everything he had told me earlier in fragments was here gathered into a whole. Only now did I receive a detailed, uninterrupted account of his relationship with his deceased wife and his relatives.

"And then what happens is that this artist, at this decisive moment in his life, meets a young girl who crosses his path, a girl of about your age, or perhaps a couple of years older. Yes, let's call her Anya, so as not to have to use the word 'heroine' all the time. Anya's a pretty name. . . . But is it really possible that this young girl, so distant from him in age and temperament, could ever come to love this artist of mine? Wouldn't that be a psychological impossibility? Yes, it's that that I'd like to hear your opinion about, Anna Grigoryevna."

"Why should it be so impossible? If this Anna is, as you say, not a frivolous coquette but a girl with a good and sensitive heart, why should she not fall in love with your artist? What does it matter that he's sick and poor? It's not wealth or outer lustre that count! And she wouldn't be making any sacrifice either. If she loves him, she'll be happy too, she doesn't need to feel the slightest remorse about it."

I spoke with great warmth. Fyodor Mikhailovich looked at me, moved.

"You really think she could love him all her life?" He said nothing for a while, just stood there, seeming to hesitate.

"Put yourself in her place," he said at last, in a trembling voice. "Imagine that it is I who am this artist, that it is I who have entrusted my love to you and asked you to be my wife. What would you say to that?"

Fyodor Mikhailovich was in a state of such confusion and anguish that I finally understood that all this was not simply a question of literary entertainment, and that I would deal his pride and self-esteem a terrible blow if I were to give him an evasive answer. Then I looked into his dear, anxious face and said:

"I would say that I love you, that I will love you all my life!"

Anna described this proposal forty years after the event, at a time when she called her husband "my life's sun." The end of the description comes across as true and authentic. As Dostoyevsky was saying goodbye to his betrothed, he smilingly observed that now he had finally discovered his "little diamond." "No, you're wrong there, Fyodor Mikhailovich!" Anna laughed. "You certainly haven't found a diamond—just a very ordinary little stone." But it was just such a "very ordinary little stone" that Dostoyevsky needed most of all.

At the outset, there was scarcely any question of a deeper kind of love, either on his side or hers. Anna had neither the looks of a Polina Suslova nor the intellect of an Anna Korvin-Krukovskaya. In this respect she was a substitute, no more nor less. The writer had now begun to find his solitude oppressive and, what was more, he wished to be a father. Earlier in the year he had made proposals to two other women, each time without success. Now at last he had found a woman who could give him both a child and the care he needed. Through her work on *The Gambler* she had, moreover, demonstrated that she could be extremely valuable to his creative activity. The most important thing, however, was that unlike Maria and Polina, she was evidently prepared to be submissive to him.

For Anna the passions played an even lesser role. Hers was an "intellectual love" created out of sympathy for a gifted man. Her choice was also significantly determined by the prospect of being able to help one of Russia's most important authors. She had a strong need to help others, and here was someone who really needed her attention. The fact that she could at the same time satisfy his personal pride only served as a plus. She was well aware that she was now on the way to becoming a part of the history of Russian literature.

Unfortunately, she lacked the spiritual dimensions for such fame. She had little feeling for the depths in her husband's writing. Unlike most of the other women in his life, she found no place in his novels, apart from the dedication to *The Brothers Karamazov*. Her memoirs and diary entries clearly show how remote she was from the giant who lived by her side. For the most part she relates only trivia: family quarrels and scenes of jealousy, the price of neckties and ice cream. Maxim Gorky speaks in this connection of her "astonishingly limited intellect and spiritual poverty." Dostoyevsky was compelled to discuss his literary plans with other women, particularly his niece Sonya Ivanova, who was the same age as Anna.

Several commentators have, nevertheless, viewed this marriage as one of the most important in Russian literary history. This much is certain: Anna came to play a major and advantageous role in Dostoyevsky's life. Over the years her persevering endurance and pragmatism enabled her to cope with the problems of everyday life in such a way that he was able to devote himself exclusively to his literary work. Leo Tolstoy was right when he said that "life would have been quite different for Russian writers if they had had wives like Anna Grigoryevna." Dostoyevsky's writing might well have been much the poorer if he had not had Anna.

As might have been expected, the engagement aroused strong misgivings among Dostoyevsky's numerous relatives. How could he take it into his head to make such a decision without first obtaining their consent? His sister-in-law Emilia Fyodorovna thought it his duty first and foremost to help Mikhail's family. What would happen to the payments now? Pasha was already dreaming of taking over the publishing rights after his stepfather's demise. And then this slip of a girl came along and ruined everything! It was bound to go wrong—an old man and a pure young girl!

Anna was universally ostracized and regarded with suspicion. To a proud and independent girl like her this was humiliating. Soon the constant intrigues also became a burden to Dostoyevsky. During one particularly bad patch he turned up in Peski without his winter overcoat. A recently convened family council had determined that he should pawn it until he got another advance on his novel.

Indignantly Anna writes in her memoirs:

I was deeply shocked that Fyodor Mikhailovich's family could be so heartless. That he wanted to help his relatives I could readily understand, but he should not at the same time put his life and health at risk.

To begin with, I spoke quietly and calmly, but little by little I completely lost my self-control. I began to hold forth like a madwoman, weeping and wailing that he had obligations to his betrothed. Fyodor Mikhailovich was alarmed at this violent outburst and did all he could to calm me down. My mother heard me weeping and hurried in with a glass of sugar water. I became a little less agitated, felt ashamed of myself and asked forgiveness.

He explained that he always pawned his overcoat as many as five or six times each winter without fail.

"I was so used to this pawning of my coat that I didn't give any particular thought to it this time either. If I had known that you would be so badly affected by it, I would never have allowed Pasha to take my coat to the pawnshop."

Dostoyevsky had to promise that this would not be repeated, and that he would stay indoors until the advance arrived and the coat was redeemed. Otherwise, however, there was no doubt as to which was the more dominating of the pair. The writer watched jealously over Anna's morality and kept her away from all the French novels that lay on his writing desk. A writer must experience everything; the same did not apply to a young girl. In one of his first letters to her he writes, concerning his solicitous attitude: "You have been given to me as a gift from God so that none of the seeds of your soul and none of the riches of your heart shall perish, but may grow profusely and attain abundant flowering. I have received you as a gift, so that I may be redeemed from my great sins when I give you back to God, fully developed, fortified and preserved from everything that is base and poisonous, from everything that kills the spirit."

Even so, he was unwilling to act as Anna's guardian and thus enable her to sell her house and increase her dowry. That would merely lead to even greater demands from their creditors. On the other hand, he had no objection to her putting his financial affairs in order. The interest payments on the credit notes were a bottomless chasm, and in addition there were the relatives' demands for support. Anna set energetically about clearing up the tangles. Fortunately Katkov was obliging—he could never forget that the novel about Raskolnikov had gained him some five hundred new subscribers. Only after Dostoyevsky had been to Moscow and had collected a large advance on his next novel was it possible to fix the date for the wedding.

The ceremony took place in St. Petersburg's Trinity Cathedral on February 15, 1867. Exactly three years earlier he had married for the first time in a poor little church in Kuznetsk. This wedding had little in common with the first one. On that occasion he had been plagued by the thought that the whole thing might end in scandal. Now there was no reason to worry on that account. The church was brilliantly lit, the singing wonderful, and the bride submissive: she made sure that he was the first to go and stand on the carpet in front of the priest. During the wedding reception, held in the couple's new apartment on Voznesensky Prospekt, the writer's enthusiasm knew no bounds: "Come and look, see how lovely she is! A miraculous human child! With a heart of the purest gold!"

Anna, too, was pleased, in spite of the formidable wedding expenses. "Fyodor Mikhailovich was a hospitable soul, and there was no lack of fruit and sweetmeats and champagne," she noted. "The guests did not depart until midnight, and afterward we sat for a long time remembering the great day."

Anna found the early months of the marriage extremely trying. It was hard enough for her to adapt herself to her husband's working rhythm—in general, he slept during the day and worked at night. What was worse was that, as a consequence of the champagne-soaked nuptials, he was soon stricken by a double attack of epilepsy, which brought his wife to the point of desperation. In her memoirs she described it like this:

> Suddenly he broke off in the middle of a sentence, rose from the sofa and leaned over toward me. I surveyed his altered features with wonder, and at that very moment there came a fearful, inhuman shriek, and he began to sink farther and farther forward. . . . An hour later there came a new attack, and this time it was so violent that he cried out with pain. Horrible! For several hours I sat listening to his cries and groans; his face was distorted with pain, his eyes stared crazily, his incoherent speech failed to make any sense. I was almost certain that my beloved husband was in the process of going insane. . . . The gloomy, oppressed state of mind which always follows the attacks lasted for over a week. "It is as if I had lost the dearest being upon earth, as if I had just come back from a funeral," was how he used to describe his condition after an attack.

The greatest threat to the marriage, however, came from Dostoyevsky's relatives. The home of the newlyweds was daily besieged by visitors, and Anna had to serve them and keep them amused. The family was ill-pleased with the inexperienced housewife, and there was no lack of backbiting and rudeness—especially from Pasha, who had come to settle in with his stepfather. Dostoyevsky showed little talent for sticking up for his wife, and soon there were stormy scenes.

The relatives' constant badgering gradually became intolerable to Anna. And now they were even beginning to harp on about how they all ought to spend the summer together in Pavlovsk! It became clearer and clearer that if the marriage was to be saved, they would have to get out of St. Petersburg as soon as possible and go away, preferably abroad. But where would they get the money? Pressure from the creditors was increasing; threats of foreclosure and debtors' prison were the order of the day. For a time Dostoyevsky seriously toyed with the idea of accepting a term in a debtor's prison—perhaps there he would find material for more *Notes from the House of the Dead*! But it was, of course, uncertain whether he would be able to write anything during such an incarceration. Meanwhile the creditors kept up the pressure. The seven thousand rubles he had received for the publication in book form of *Crime and Punishment* disappeared overnight and merely led to increased demands from those who had not yet had their claims met. Anna, however, knew what to do. Resolutely she went away and pawned her dowry—the furniture, the piano, and the silver—and with the money thus obtained, the couple set out on their delayed honeymoon abroad.

Their departure came as a surprise not only to the writer's crestfallen relatives, but also to the local police officer. His superiors immediately sent a secret report to the Department of Foreign Affairs which stated, "The former Lieutenant Fyodor Mikhailovich Dostoyevsky, presently under police surveillance, set off abroad on April 14:" Who had issued him a passport, and for how long? The chief of police could take it easy: four months later the message came through that the secret police had given its permission for the trip.

II

When Dostoyevsky left St. Petersburg on Good Friday, 1867, he could scarcely have had any idea of the sufferings that awaited him en route. He and his wife planned to be away for three months. Instead, their sojourn abroad was to last for four years and three months. For him, these years of travel soon became like an exile. They were to be the most difficult years of his life.

The unpleasantness began in Berlin, where they rested after the exhausting rail journey. The writer's xenophobia was swift to flare up. At the Hotel Union they were not given a samovar, and the absurd German eiderdowns were impossibly hot to sleep under. An attempt to work off his resentment with a proper Russian steam bath was only partly successful. The Germans were a constant source of irritation. Neither he nor Anna had a decent command of the language, and whenever they failed to make themselves understood it was invariably the Germans' fault.

Dostoyevsky's rage at Germans also took its toll on his life with Anna. He grew sour-tempered and peevish, and during a walk on Unter den Linden he made some critical remarks about her gloves. In anger and despair, Anna went running back to the hotel, where she fell into a state of anxiety about whether her husband was now going to send her back to Russia. Or what if he had gone and thrown himself into the river? When Dostoyevsky at long last returned, he reassured her by telling her that this was a thought impossible for a Russian: "One would have to have awfully little respect for oneself in order to throw himself into such a small and wretched river as the Spree."

This scene more or less formed the pattern for their subsequent life together, at any rate the early years of it. If the diary which Anna kept during the first months is anything to go by, hardly a day passed without the couple's quarreling, and there was always some trifle or other to set their tempers alight. Fortunately, however, not a day seems to have gone by without a reconciliation, either. "I am very, very happy," Anna wrote to a female friend. "Indeed, how could one be anything other than happy with a man such as Fyodor Mikhailovich? Such a magnificent, sincere, and infinitely good human being! If only people knew him better. It's true that he is always gloomy and irritable, but if only people knew how much human warmth and goodness are concealed beneath all that. The better one comes to know him, the more attached to him one becomes."

Dostoyevsky had high expectations of Dresden. Earlier he had had occasion to admire its parks and art gallery, and was now hoping for inspiration to help his writing. He arrived instead in a sad town that still bore the scars of Saxony's recently concluded war against the Prussians. The hospitals were full to overflowing with wounded soldiers, and the streetscape was dominated by cripples and the occupation soldiers.

The famous picture gallery containing almost two and a half thousand items was, however, intact. As soon as they had installed themselves in the handsome but expensive Stadt Berlin, they hurried out to give the gallery a closer inspection. When Dostoyevsky found himself unable to remember the way, he asked a chance passerby for assistance:

"Excuse me, my good sir, but where is the picture gallery?"

"What?"

"Where is the picture gallery?"

"The picture gallery?"

"Yes, that's right—the picture gallery."

"The Royal Picture Gallery?"

"Yes, yes—the Royal Picture Gallery."

"I don't know."

Anna was amazed that the man should ask so many counter-questions when he didn't know the answer after all. But for Dostoyevsky the episode was merely fresh proof that there was no point in having any dealings with this people: "It's unbelievable how stupid they are, these Germans!"

When they entered the gallery he immediately took Anna to see Raphael's *Sistine Madonna*, in his eyes "the loftiest revelation of the human spirit." He could sit for hours in front of this image of the Mother of God. She seemed to come soaring through the air toward him, the Christ Child in her arms. Her face was strangely imprinted with "sorrow," while the face of the Son was "devoid of childlike traits." What confirmation he found here of his own statement in a letter of his youth that "gods were created under Raphael's brush." Even later in his life, when on his birthday in 1879 he received a copy of the painting as a gift from Countess Sofya Tolstaya, he would often lose himself in contemplation of this picture. "When Dostoyevsky woke up in the morning, his first glance would always go to the gentle countenance of this madonna," his daughter related. "He considered her his female ideal." Yes, a picture by Raphael was like a miracle. But at the same time there was something frightening about this miracle. "Beauty is a fearful and dreadful thing," says Mitya in *The Brothers Karamazov*, "eerie because it cannot be defined, because God has only given us riddles."

Other Renaissance paintings also made an overwhelming impression: *The Treasure Mint* by Titian, *Mary with Child* by Murillo, *Night* by Correggio, *Christ* by Annibale Carracci—not to mention *Acis and Galatea* by Claude Lorrain, a depiction of "The Golden Age" which is mentioned several times in Dostoyevsky's works. "All the impressions of art keep soul and character alive," he declared in a letter to Maikov. It was probably under the influence of the Renaissance painters' cult of the beautiful person that he now acquired the idea for his new novel, *The Idiot*, in which "the completely beautiful person" was to occupy a central position.

But his work was going slowly. Just before the departure he had promised to write a long article about his acquaintance with Belinsky. But now he suddenly discovered how difficult it was to write abroad. Inspiration, mood, ideas—all were lacking. His ambivalent attitude to the subject also played a part. Certainly he had great respect for Belinsky as a critic. He had also much to thank him for. But he found it hard to forgive Belinsky for his contemptuous attitude toward religion and felt himself moving further away from the radicalism of his youth. We do not know how he finally managed to balance these conflicting impressions. By the time the manuscript was finally sent to the printer, the publisher had gone bankrupt, and the article has not been discovered since. There are, however, few grounds for supposing that Dostoyevsky's portrayal of Belinsky was any more positive than the one he gave in his letters from abroad. There Belinsky emerges as a rootless, typically European phenomenon, "a scabby mongrel," who ends his days as a regular participant in all kinds of revolutionary congresses abroad.

Another reason why Dostoyevsky's work was making such slow progress was that there was as yet no pressure on him. At that time the ruble was hard currency: for one ruble they received almost one thaler and more than three francs. Anna's tight-fisted mother was therefore of the opinion that they could live on twenty-five kopecks a day while they were abroad. This soon proved to be impossible, in spite of Anna's economies. They found it necessary to quit the hotel and find less expensive lodgings. In Johannesstrasse they finally managed to rent a three-room apartment from a Mme. Zimmerman, a Swiss lady who also put bedlinen and crockery at their disposal.

Here the couple soon settled into a monotonous daily routine. Anna was decidedly the early bird of the two. Not until eleven o'clock did she wake her husband to a simple breakfast with coffee. While he remained at home working, she would take a walk to one of the town's many museums, or perhaps make an excursion to the surrounding countryside. At three o'clock in the afternoon they liked to meet for the main meal of the day in Das italienische Dörfchen, or Die Brühlsche Terrasse—both with excellent views over the Elbe. Then followed their daily promenade in Der Grosse Garten. Here they would frequently take afternoon tea at Die Grosse Wirtschaft, but this was by no means always to the writer's taste: either the tea was too weak, or it was served without jam.

They invariably went to listen to the music played by the military band:

Mozart, Beethoven, Mendelssohn-Bartholdy. But when it began to play Wagner, the writer would take his hat and leave. He could not stand "that tiresome German scoundrel in spite of all his fame." Oh, how he hated these puffed-up Germans! Sour and peevish, he would return home and complain to Anna: why are these Germans alleys always so confoundedly rectilinear? And why was this stupid pond situated here, of all places?

Evenings were spent at home in the apartment. Dostoyevsky liked to read some Russian book that was banned in his homeland, especially the works of Herzen, while she carried on with her shorthand and wrote in her diary. Worn out after the day's tourist activities, she went to bed early, while he would continue to stay up writing. Not until two A.M. would he wake Anna in order to say good night, and the hour of loving talk that followed was for both of them the high point of the day.

Only occasionally did any changes occur in this routine, as, for instance, when they took a walk in the Deer Park or ventured into the Tivoli Gardens, where good Germans stood target-shooting. Anna said she thought *he'd* never be able to do that sort of thing. She had forgotten that Dostoyevsky was an "ex-lieutenant" in the Russian army. With irritation, he accepted her challenge. "Well, what do you say to that?" came his triumphant reply when he hit several bull's-eyes. Wasn't it just as he had always said—that a wife is her husband's natural enemy?

On the whole he had a rather unflattering view of women. Time and again Anna tried to bring up the "woman question" as a subject for discussion. She herself was an eager defender of women's rights and women's independence. But after his experiences with Polina the writer had had enough of that kind of talk, which was for him merely the fruit of the era's nihilism. Woman was unquestionably man's inferior, since she had none of his tough strength of character and stubborn perseverance when it came to attaining a preconceived goal. Anna was understandably hurt by talk like this. When all was said and done, there was little doubt about who in the Dostoyevsky menage possessed the strength of character.

A greater problem was, however, presented by the couple's mutual jealousy. Dostoyevsky was hardly enthusiastic when Anna took part in a professional conference arranged by German stenographers. And there was even something about it in the newspaper! He wanted her to have no more of such things in the future. Anna, for her part, found it difficult to put up with her husband's continued correspondence with Polina. Shortly after his arrival in Dresden he had written to tell her about his marriage to "a young, quite pretty twenty-year-old girl, of good family and with an excellent diploma." Polina's reply was intercepted by Anna, who in her despair pretended it was from Sonya:

> For a long, long time he sat reading the first page. It was as if he could not grasp what he was reading. Then finally he read it all and turned flaming red, his hands trembling. I pretended I knew nothing about the letter and asked what Sonechka was writing about. He replied that the letter was not from Sonechka, and gave me a sort of bitter smile as he said it. I had already seen him smile a smile like that before. There was a kind of contempt or compassion in that smile, I don't really know what, but it was in any case wretched and helpless. Afterwards he grew dreadfully confused and had scarcely any idea of what I was talking about.

Precisely what the writer got so confused about, we do not know, as Anna later burned all Polina's letters. During the whole of the sojourn abroad she was terrified that Polina would turn up and take her husband from her. Indeed, what if they were already meeting in secret?

Anna's suspicions appear to have been groundless. In reality, the Dostoyevsky couple lived in complete "twosomeness." They took no part in the town's famous theater life; neither were they to be found in the Greek-Catholic Chapel in Wienerstrasse. The writer had just as little time for Russians abroad as he had for foreigners. They probably believed they could only be happy if they forgot they were Russians. "How can a Russian live abroad at all? To have lost one's home—dreadful! I need Russia, I need it for my work, for my writing, for being able to live at all. Here I feel like a fish out of water."

His patriotism grew steadily stronger. When word came that the Tsar had been the subject of a new assassination attempt, he immediately rushed to the Russian legation in order to express his abhorrence. Of course it was a Pole who had been the culprit—that "louse Berezowski."

After three weeks had passed, Dostoyevsky began to harp on making a journey to Homburg in order to try his luck at roulette. Anna had no faith that he would win anything, but even so it was better to let him make the trip than to have him going around sour and peevish. On May 16 he finally set off via Leipzig. Once again he began his restless hunt from one gaming room to the next, driven by "a morbid longing for giddiness, by 'vertigo,' by a desire to lean over the abyss," to quote Stefan Zweig.

Dostoyevsky set off with the intention of returning home again in two or three days' time. Such good intentions always caved in, however, in the proximity of roulette. The visit lasted ten days, and at the end of it he was broke. He described his activities in his letters to Anna:

Homburg, May 18

Imagine—I began gambling in the morning, and by lunchtime I had already lost sixteen imperials. I had only twelve left, together with a few guilders. In the afternoon I went back with a firm intention of gambling with caution. And God be praised—I won all my money back again, and one hundred guilders *to boot*. I could actually have won three hundred, I already had them in my hand, but then I gambled again and lost. Yes, here one must be made of marble, *superhumanly* cold and cautious—then there is *no doubt* that one can win *as much as one wishes to*. One must merely have plenty of time, many days, and if one is not lucky, one must content himself with small winnings and not try too hard. One of my fellow-gamblers has held out for several days, always gambling with terrible, *inhuman* coldbloodedness and calculation. Now the bank is beginning to fear him: he rakes the money towards him in great piles and goes home each evening with at least one thousand guilders. In short, I shall do my utmost to gamble as carefully as possible. On the other hand, I have not the strength to remain here very long. To be frank, Anna, all this is repellent. It is so foul that I would prefer to run away from myself, and when I think of you, I am drawn to you with the whole of my being. Oh, dear Anna, I knew in advance how sorely I need you! When I think of your radiant smile, of that warm, happy smile that streams into my heart whenever you are present, yes, then I am drawn to you with irresistible force. . .

May 21

Listen: I have finished gambling, I want to come back as quickly as possible. Send me immediately, as soon as you receive this letter, the sum of *twenty* (20) imperials. The same day, at once, instantly, do you hear? First I must redeem the watch I have pawned (I cannot possibly let them get it for sixty-five guilders), then I must pay my hotel bill, and finally I must buy a ticket home. Whatever is left over I shall bring home with me, do not fear, I shan't gamble any more. . . . For God's sake remember to give the banker the right address, write Homburg, not Hamburg on the document!

May 24

Anna, my beloved friend and dear wife—forgive me, do not call me a scoundrel! I have committed a crime, I have gambled away all the money you sent, all of it, to the last schilling! Anna, how will I be able to look you in the eye now, what will you think of me? Yes, there is only *one thing* that now drives me to despair: what will you say now, what will you think? It is your judgment alone that I fear. Will you be able to respect me after this, will you be able to find it in yourself to respect me? For what is love without respect? Our whole marriage stands or falls by virtue of that respect! Oh, my dear friend, do not judge me too harshly! I hate this gambling—not only today, but also yesterday and the day before yesterday I cursed roulette. When I got your money, I immediately went into the gaming room in order to win back at least something of what I had lost. Yes, I actually believed I would make a small win. To begin with I lost a little, and then I really began to lose in earnest; I wanted to win back what I had lost, but then I lost even more. And then I simply *had* to go on playing, in order at least to get money for my homeward journey. And then I lost everything—everything! Anna, I don't ask for your sympathy— just try to be a little impartial. I am in any case dreadfully afraid of what you will say. For myself I am not in the slightest afraid. Quite the contrary— after a lesson like this I am quite tranquil as regards my future. Now I have only one way out: to work. I shall show what stuff I am made of!

Once again he had gambled himself away "to the bone." There was no more money to be borrowed. And then came the guilt feelings and the sense of gratification—and the need to create. The cure in Homburg had worked—not for nothing were the gaming halls called "cure-halls!" He only wished that his humiliation had received even greater nourishment. "Oh, if only I could have seen you as you read that letter!" he concluded his greeting to Anna. Yes, then the cure would certainly have been complete.

When, dusty and watchless, he at last returned to Dresden, he realized nevertheless that he had not done enough gambling. The inspiration did not seem to want to come. He had not yet quite hit bottom. Consequently he began to fuss, saying that they ought to continue on to Switzerland via the casino town of Baden-Baden. A few weeks of careful systematic gambling there would perhaps bring a welcome increment to their travel funds. And when at the end of June Anna told him she was pregnant, he felt an even stronger need to make the great win. Think if it should be a girl—soon he would have to pay a large dowry!

They set off at the beginning of July. Their itinerary lay through Frankfurt am Main, Darmstadt, Heidelberg, and Karlsruhe. In Baden-Baden they rented two tiny rooms above a smithy. But it was mostly Anna who was tormented by the noise—he spent the greater part of the time sitting at roulette in the Conversationshaus. "In the course of three days I won four thousand francs with the greatest of ease," he bragged in a letter to Maikov. But what good was it, when he was burdened with an impetuous temperament? "Everywhere and in everything I have to overstep the limit—that is how it has been all my life." The seven weeks in Baden-Baden were soon to become a hell. The initial winnings disappeared in one go, and then Dostoyevsky came creeping home to Anna to beg for more money. If he did not get more to gamble with, he would go insane! Anna immortalized one of these scenes in her diary:

> I had been asleep for quite a long time, and when I opened my eyes, I saw Fedya standing by the side of my bed. He was dreadfully perturbed. I understood at once that he had lost the ten gold pieces I had given him. I tried to calm him and asked him if he wanted more money. He asked for five more gold pieces. I brought the money, and he thanked me profusely, it was as if I had done him a great kindness. . . . He promised to come back as soon as possible. . . . But it was not until eleven o'clock that he returned, once again in a dreadfully perturbed state. He begged and implored for forgiveness, God knows for what—said that he was a villain and I an angel, and so on ad infinitum. It was almost impossible to make him quiet down.

On the street Dostoyevsky chanced to meet the writer Ivan Goncharov, who had also come to Baden-Baden in order to try his fortune. But he gambled cautiously, only with silver pieces. "I am sure that he condemned me in the sternest fashion: how could I gamble away everything, not merely half, as he did?"

From Goncharov he heard that the day before he had been observed by Turgenev, who had now taken up permanent domicile in Baden-Baden. Dostoyevsky had long shrunk from paying him a call. The old debt of fifty thalers was still not out of the way, and now he had nothing to pay it with. It was in any case unfair that he should owe anything to this man who received fees that were double his and who had not the half of his commitments.

On July 10 he made himself pay a visit nonetheless. It was a stormy meeting, during which Dostoyevsky immediately attacked Turgenev's admiration for Germany and his scornful criticism of his homeland. "If Russia were to disappear from the face of the earth, humanity would suffer neither loss nor grief." Yes, that was the message of his latest novel, *Smoke*.

How could a Russian make such an assertion? "A book like that ought to be burned at the hands of an executioner!" Dostoyevsky maintained, bitterly. "You hate Russia and have no faith in the country's future!" His rage grew extreme when Turgenev began to hold forth on the subject of how one ought to bow in the dust before the Germans and that it was stupid to develop a peculiarly Russian character. It suddenly became clear to him that Turgenev had lost all feeling for the old country. "I advised him that for the sake of his convenience he ought to procure a giant telescope from Paris," we read in a report to Maikov. "Why so?" Turgenev asked. "Russia is so far away," Dostoyevsky replied. "You will need to observe us through a good telescope—otherwise you won't be able to make out anything."

The next day Turgenev came to see Dostoyevsky at ten o'clock in the morning, well aware that he would not yet have risen, and that he would for this reason avoid meeting him. Turgenev left his visiting card, and there began the most celebrated feud in the history of Russian literature. From now on they greeted each other only when they were forced to and even then only barely.

Life did not improve when Dostoyevsky took his wife along with him to the gaming table. Soon the losses came and, with them, the humiliating journey from pawnbroker to pawnbroker. Her wedding rings were the first to go; they were followed by her wedding presents and finally her clothes— it was just as well that the weather was so mild. Anna's diary entry for July 6 is moving: "I took off my earrings and brooch and looked at them. Perhaps this was the last time I would ever see them—it was so hard, so hard. I loved these things—I had after all been given them by Fedya, they were my dearest possessions. . . . Fedya said it was hard to look at me, hard to take these things from me. But what was he to do? We had known all along that it would turn out this way. In secret I said farewell to my things and kissed them."

Scenes like these must have done much to strengthen Anna's frugality in money matters, an evidently essential quality when living with Dostoyevsky. But when this prudence turned into greed, it had dire consequences.

When everything had been pawned, a small win would follow, or a small remittance from Russia would allow them to redeem one or two of the pawned items. But soon everything was lost again, and once more the way led to the pawnbroker. Soon Anna could no longer show her face on the street, as both her dress and her shoes were worn through.

Dostoyevsky was growing gloomier and gloomier. He placed all the blame on his fellow gamblers. They distracted him, sometimes by their elbowing, sometimes by their overuse of perfume. And once again he began to bicker and quarrel. Within a short time he had become notorious over the whole gaming hall. "He was red all over his face, with bloodshot eyes, exactly like a drunkard," Anna noted in her diary.

Finally, to cap it all, his credit ran out. Not even Goncharov would advance him a fresh loan. Weeping, "poor Fedya" returned home to his wife: "I have taken the last of your possessions, have robbed you of them and have lost them all."

On August 23 they left Baden-Baden and headed for Geneva. They stayed for a short time in Basle in order to see *The Dead Christ in the Tomb* by Holbein the Younger. Concerning her impression of this shocking picture, Anna writes:

Generally Christ is portrayed after death with a face that is distorted by suffering, but with a body that shows no signs of the tortures it actually received. Here, however, he is depicted with an emaciated body, his ribs are visible, his arms and legs bear the marks of wounds, swollen and with a strongly bluish appearance, just like those of a corpse which has already begun to decompose. His face is also dreadfully tortured, with half-closed eyes which cannot see and which express nothing. His nose, mouth, and chin are bluish; taken as a whole, the image has so much in common with that of a dead man that I would never dare to remain alone with it. While it may be strikingly true to life, it is not aesthetic, and the picture aroused merely repugnance and horror in me. But Feyda was filled with enthusiasm; he even climbed up onto a chair in order to take a closer look at the picture.

"A picture like that could make one lose one's faith," was Dostoyevsky's verdict. His mouth was distorted, his face quivered nervously—he looked as though he was going to have an epileptic attack. Later he was to put those words into the mouth of Prince Myshkin in *The Idiot*, when the latter sees a copy of the picture at Rogozhin's house. How could one ever believe in the resurrection of this rotting corpse? And how could the laws of death be overcome when not even he could overcome them? Perhaps Christ was not divine after all? Perhaps God did not exist? Once again the question of God's existence became a matter of pressing urgency for Dostoyevsky. Now even more strongly he felt the inspiration for his next great novel, *The Idiot*.

They arrived in Geneva with only eighteen francs and had no option but to visit one of the town's pawnbrokers forthwith. Finally they managed to rent lodgings in the home of the sisters Raymondin, on the corner of rue Guillaume-Tell and rue Philibert-Berthelier. The spacious room had a fine view of Île Rousseau and the bridges over the Rhône. On the whole Geneva made a sympathetic impression on them initially. The town was French-speaking, and so here they could make themselves understood much more easily than in Germany. It was also renowned for its skillful doctors, and this too was a plus in view of Anna's forthcoming delivery.

The fact that Geneva contained a nest of Russian émigrés was, on the other hand, of little particular significance for Dostoyevsky. It was true that he might now and then run into Herzen in the street, and occasionally he paid a visit to the radical poet Nikolai Ogaryov, especially when he was in need of money. But for the most part the couple kept to themselves; by thus doing, they at least avoided the distasteful experience of constantly being taken for father and daughter.

Not that going out was anything much to write home about, in any case. The writer's friends were unable to grasp that it was possible to become bored with the divine Mont Blanc right outside one's windows. What was more, the weather was having a deleterious effect on his health. The north wind—*la brise*—was particularly trying. "It blows at gale-force all the time, and what is more it can change as many as three to four times a day. And this I have to put up with—I with my hemorrhoids and my epilepsy!"

He soon lost all respect for the self-satisfied Swiss. He had never seen so many bellicose and loud-voiced drunkards, not even in London. This town was proud of its freedom, but its freedom merely consisted in everyone being able to drink themselves silly and stagger around the streets bawling ditties. Stupidity, wretchedness, and vulgarity were everywhere. "In this vile republic philistinism has reached its acme," he wrote resignedly to Maikov. "If only you knew how coarse the customs are in this town, if only you knew what is regarded here as good and bad! This spiritual and cultural *bas-niveau*, this eternal drunkenness, these petty villainies of everyday life which have almost become enshrined in law!'

No, in this "tedious, gloomy, and Protestant-stupid town" one could only work, and then only just. The writer hurled himself anew into the study of Balzac, Hugo, Dickens, and George Sand, and in the middle of September he also made a start on the preparations for *The Idiot*. But the work went disappointingly slowly. He could already feel the danger of staying too long abroad. "In our craft reality is the main thing, but here reality is

Swiss!" he complained to Sonya. A little later he described his monotonous existence in the following terms:

> I get up late, light the fire (it is dreadfully cold here), we have coffee, and then I sit down at my work table. At four I have dinner at one of several restaurants, for two francs, including wine. Anna Grigoryevna prefers to eat at home. After that I have coffee at a café where I read *The Moscow News* and *The Voice* from front page to last. Then I walk around in the streets for a while in order to get a little exercise, and after that I go home in order to work again. I bank the fire up, then we have tea, and then I get on with my work again. Anna Grigoryevna assures me that she is wonderfully happy.

A welcome break in the monotony was provided by the Peace Congress organized by the Ligue Internationale de Paris de la Paix et de la Liberté during the days of September 9–12 in the Palais Electorale. Alarmed by the threat of a new war between Germany and France, a thousand pacifists from fifteen different countries were gathering together—liberals, anarchists, and revolutionaries.

The honorary president of the Congress was Garibaldi, no less, greeted by the crowd of participants as "the hero of democracy and freedom." Dostoyevsky was himself a witness to Garibaldi's colorful arrival, but he felt out of place among these people. They were almost like ghosts from his own revolutionary past. When he learned that it cost only twenty-five centimes to get in, he nevertheless went along with Anna to a meeting on September 11. Garibaldi had by that time left Geneva, after making a full-blooded attack on the papacy as a political institution. Contrary to the assertions of some of his biographers, Dostoyevsky also missed a chance to hear Bakunin, "the famous Russian revolutionist," who the day before had attacked the lack of freedom in Russia and had supported the establishment of a United States of Europe.

Even so, there were enough radicals left. For two hours the Dostoyevskys were bombarded with phrases and platitudes. According to contemporary accounts, most of the speeches were given "with an indescribable vividness of expression." Voices trembled and tumblers were smashed, while the reactions of the audience shifted rapidly from "*bravos longs*" to "*murmures*." The chairman had his hands full keeping tempers in check with a little bell, just as had been done in the Petrashevsky circle. All in all the meeting gave a good idea of the conflict that prevailed at this Peace Congress. "What the speakers proclaimed was not peace, but war," Anna noted. Her husband was even more condemnatory in his account:

> The flood of lies which the socialists and revolutionaries, whom here I met in the flesh for the first time, poured out over the heads of their five thousand spectators simply defies description! It is impossible to imagine the self-contradictions and cosmic absurdities that were produced here. And it is this headless rabble that is stirring up the ill-fated working masses! The wretches! They began by explaining that the condition for attaining peace on earth was to eradicate the Christian faith. All large states must be destroyed and be divided up. All capital must be confiscated, everything be declared common property and be apportioned out according to need, etc. And all this was put forward without the slightest argumentation, all that they had learned twenty years ago they now regurgitated in the same old way, word for word. Their chief concern is the fire and the sword— they believe that only when everything has been destroyed will there be peace on earth.

If the radicals were now repeating the same things they had said twenty years earlier, Dostoyevsky at any rate had undergone a major change since the days when he had frequented the Petrashevsky circle. The developments of recent years had done a great deal to reinforce his Slavophile sympathies. More and more frequently now he swung the lash over the Western-inspired reforms of Peter the Great. "Our constitution rests on the monarch's love for the people and the people's love for the monarch," he wrote in a letter to Maikov. "Here abroad I have become where Russia is concerned decidedly a monarchist. . . . The people, the real people, have given and continue to give all our Tsars their love; they hope and trust exclusively in him. For the people this is a mystery, a sacrament, something consecrated and an-nointed. The Westernizers don't undertand a word of it. They boast that their world outlook is based on facts, but they have overlooked the most important and most powerful fact in our history."

The most important fact in the life of the Dostoyevskys was, however, poverty. True, from time to time small sums of money did arrive from friends and relatives, and then the writer could dash out and buy pears, raisins, crawfish, perhaps also a new garment or two. "One must spend as long as one has money," he announced, to Anna's despair, "for when the money runs out, one has neither money nor clothes." Such a philosophy made everyday living a torment to them both. There could never be any question of going to the theater, for example, and Dostoyevsky flew into a rage when Anna received unstamped letters from her mother—this meant an extra expense of ninety centimes. Worst of all were these confounded begging letters from his sister-in-law Emilia Fyodorovna and from Pasha. Had he not done enough for them? They doubtless thought it was his *duty* to help them! He had better draw up his will as soon as possible; otherwise Anna might suddenly find herself without any means one of these days.

When things looked their blackest, Dostoyevsky made an excursion to Saxon-les-Bains in order to win something so that he could pay the rent. Anna had long ago realized that protests were useless. What was more, the gambling was a good means of keeping a hold over him: she knew that in the end he would come creeping back to her. She had no confidence in his assertions that one day he would make the big haul. The letters she received from Dostoyevsky the gambler became ever more pathetic reminders of his tragic addiction:

Saxon-les-Bains,
Sunday October 6, 1867
8:30 P.M.

Anya, beloved friend, I am an ass—no, worse than an ass! Yesterday evening at ten I made a net winning of thirteen hundred francs. Today I don't own a single kopeck. I have gambled it all away—all of it! And this for the sole reason that a scoundrel of a waiter at Hotel des Bains failed to wake me in time for me to catch the eleven A.M. train to Geneva. I slept until half past eleven. There was nothing to be done about it, and it was five P.M. before I could set off. And so I went to the roulette—and lost everything, everything. I have only fourteen francs left—precisely enough for the journey home.

Saxon-les-Bains
Monday November 18, 1867

Anya, my beloved, I have gambled everything away, everything! Oh, dear angel, don't be sad, don't be apprehensive! Rest assured that the day will soon come when I shall at last be worthy of you, when I shall no longer rob you like a coarse, filthy thief! Now the novel, the novel alone must save us. Oh, if only you knew what hopes I have of it! Be sure that I shall reach my goal and earn your respect. I shall never gamble again, never. Exactly the same thing happened two years ago in Wiesbaden. The situation was desperate then, too, but my work saved me. I shall now take up my work with hope and love—and in two years' time you shall see!

Once again the medicine worked. The agony of guilt he had inflicted on himself at the green table manifested itself in an uncontrollable zest for work. When he returned to Geneva, he sat down and wrote a hundred pages of *The Idiot* in twenty-three days. This novel, more than any of his other works, became a rescue bid, a penance for the crushing sense of guilt he felt for his self-destructive passions.

But now there quickly followed an event that put even the novel in the shade: Anna's delivery. In the middle of December they rented a spacious apartment in the house of Mme. Josslin in rue du Mont-Blanc, next door to the English Church. Both of them waited in excitement. If it were a boy, he was to be called Mikhail after the writer's brother; if it were a girl, she was to be called Sonya after his niece and the heroine of *Crime and Punishment*. A midwife had already been contacted. Every day now Dostoyevsky practiced the route so as to be able to get her to Anna in the shortest possible time.

At last, at two o'clock on the morning of March 5, the infant came into the world. The birth was a difficult one: Anna was in labor for more than twenty-four hours, but she managed nevertheless to note her husband's reaction:

> He knelt for a long time before my bed and kissed my hands. For the first ten minutes we were so stunned with happiness that we did not know whether we had been given a boy or a girl. First we heard a woman's voice saying, "It's a boy, isn't it?"—and a little later another, saying, "It's a girl, a charming girl!" The midwife said that never in all her many years of practice had she seen a father so beside himself with joy over his newborn child. Again and again she shook her head: "Ah, these Russians, these Russians!"

Dostoyevsky's wonder at the "angelic soul" which had come to him is reflected in Shatov's words in *The Possessed*: "They were two, and suddenly there came a third person, a perfect creation, a new thought and a new love. It is so miraculous, almost ineffable. There is nothing in the world more lofty." And imagine: Sonya resembled him "to an improbable, indeed, a ridiculous degree." "The child is only a month old, but has already acquired my facial expression, my physiognomy through and through, right down to the wrinkles on my forehead—there she lies, as if she were working on a novel!"

Their joy was short-lived, however. One day when she was three months old, they took Sonya out for an airing in her pram: she caught pneumonia and died. "He wept and sobbed like a woman in despair," Anna related. "He bent over the cold body of his little beloved and covered her small, pale face and her little hands with hot kisses. Never again did I see him in a state of such wild despair." Dostoyevsky's own words to Maikov also bear testimony to this despair:

> She was beginning to recognize me, to love me, and whenever I came over to her, she would smile. When I sang for her in my comical voice, I could see that she was listening with pleasure. When I kissed her, she would keep a straight face, and when I went over to her, she would stop crying. And now they try to console me by saying I will have more children. But Sonya! Where is Sonya? Where is this little being for which I would willingly have suffered death on the cross—if only she had been allowed to live?

Sonya was buried in the children's cemetery at Pleinpalais. The period that followed was almost unbearable. The couple wept, and the neighbors would beat on the walls in an attempt to make them stop. What a heartless attitude people had to the grief of others here in the West! Dostoyevsky was never able to forget the way his daughter had followed him with her gaze when he had gone out to read the newspapers just before she died. "O God, when a child looks at one with those beautiful, small, birdlike eyes, so happy and trustful, one can feel only shame at deceiving them," says Prince Myshkin in *The Idiot*.

From Russia there was a steady flow of bad news. Dostoyevsky's brother-in-law Aleksander Ivanov died, and his relatives reminded him of the Ivanov loan he had received. His stepson Pasha proved to be unemployable in the service of the state and was continuing his parasite's existence. Emilia Fyodorovna was complaining about insufficient maintenance. Stress and worry made his epileptic attacks once again increase in violence. Anna was desperately afraid that he might swallow his prosthetic appliance and choke to death. In addition to the fear of death came even stronger premonitions of insanity. "He complained that he was almost certain to end up in the madhouse," Anna wrote. "If this disaster were to befall him, I was not to leave him, but bring him home to Russia."

Was he really to end his writer's career as an idiot?

III

The creeping fear of dementia and spiritual darkness is by no means the only feature that unites Dostoyevsky with the hero of his new novel. *The Idiot* is perhaps the most autobiographical of all his books.

Prince Myshkin's background as the son of an impoverished nobleman and a merchant's daughter, his religiosity and epilepsy are clear reminders of Dostoyevsky himself, as are his beautiful handwriting and his great love of children. Moreover, both writer and hero undergo a four-year "cure"— in a Siberian penitentiary and a Swiss clinic, respectively. The writer has the Prince describe his own experiences on the scaffold and places him between two of his own women—Polina (Nastasya Filippovna) and Anna Korvin-Krukovskaya (Aglaya). And as if this were not enough, he makes his hero the mouthpiece for his own ideas about art and religion, such that we can follow them almost word for word in his correspondence from the time when the book was written.

The fact that *The Idiot* goes a long way toward presenting an idealized self-portrait also gives at least a partial explanation for why it was so difficult to write. In Dostoyevsky's notebooks we find a labyrinth of involved and somewhat confused variants. Each day he struggled with "six different plans," and his head gradually began to resemble "a windmill." Most of all he feared mediocrity: "If a work is not *entirely* good, it might as well be pure trash. A mediocrity of thirty to forty printed sheets is an intolerable and unforgivable thing." His desperate financial situation only increased his distaste at having to write "to order and by measure." When Anna later described his manner of working, *The Idiot* cannot have been far from her thoughts:

> If only these harsh critics knew under what circumstances Fyodor Mikhailovich had to write. It could happen that the first three chapters of the novel were already printed, that the fourth was in the process of being printed, that the fifth had just been sent off, and that the seventh was being written, while the continuation had hardly yet been given any thought.

How often was I a witness to his honest despair when he would suddenly feel that he had ruined the idea which was so dear to him, and that it was no longer possible to correct the mistake.

The poet's struggle with drafts and variants has been often described. Here we shall merely confirm that his aim was from the very first to portray a positive hero. In *War and Peace* Tolstoy had attempted to solve a similar problem. He had described the good-natured Pierre Bezukhov's laborious passage of refinement toward moral perfection, the way in which, through his encounter with a simple Russian peasant, Pierre conquers his egotism and discovers a faith in life and the powers that command it. Being the ambitious man he was, Dostoyevsky doubtless felt himself challenged by this Tolstoy—an example. He, too, now considered himself strong enough to portray the Russian character the way he wanted it to be.

Dostoyevsky, however, proceeded in a manner different from that employed by other authors who have set themselves the difficult task of portraying a positive figure. He did not endow his hero with goodness by making him comical or by arousing our sympathy, as Cervantes had done with Don Quixote or Victor Hugo with Jean Valjean. Nor did he find it possible to portray a process of resurrection, as Tolstoy had done. The "law of personality" that Pierre is supposed to have overcome through his encounter with the Russian people was in Dostoyevsky's eyes insuperable. Only Christ had been capable of overcoming the ego and thereby of loving his neighbor as himself.

The model for Dostoyevsky's "absolutely good person" was thus Christ or, more correctly, the holy Russian "fool"—*yurodivyy*. Characteristic of this saintly "fool in Christ" is that he voluntarily feigns idiocy in order to be able to vanquish his spiritual pride. The result is that he exposes himself to the humiliations of the surrounding world. His apparent weakness, humility, proves, however, to be an "unprecedented strength." It is precisely by means of his innocent humility that this holy fool wins through and displays his prophetic gift.

Dostoyevsky was, of course, perfectly aware of the difficulties in transposing a Christ-inspired figure to an earthly, everyday existence. He wrote about this to his niece:

The novel's central idea is to portray the absolutely good person. There is nothing more difficult than this in the whole world, especially in our time.

All authors—not only ours, but also all the European ones—who have attempted a portrayal of the *absolutely* good person, have always given up. For this task is an infinitely difficult one. The good is an ideal, but neither among us nor in civilized Europe has the ideal yet acquired form. In the whole world there is only one absolutely good person: Christ, and consequently the very existence of this one infinitely good being is in itself an ineffable miracle. The entire Gospel according to St. John came into being over this thought: it sees the whole miracle in the appearance of the good, in the incarnation of the perfect in flesh and blood.

From this quotation it emerges clearly how important the Gospel according to St. John became for Dostoyevsky's vision of Christ. In the preliminary sketches for the novel we encounter the catchphrase "The Prince is Christ" immediately after the note "Gospel according to St. John." A study of the underlinings in Dostoyevsky's copy of the New Testament confirms the significance of the St. John scriptures. Out of 177 markings, six are in the First Epistle General of John, sixteen in Revelation, and fifty-eight—or one-third—in the Gospel according to St. John. (By comparison it may be mentioned that the St. Matthew Gospel has to content itself with thirteen markings, St. Luke seven, and St. Mark only two.)

Dostoyevsky's Orthodox faith yields at least a part of the explanation for his interest in the St. John scriptures. It has been stressed by several observers that St. John has had an especially great significance for Orthodoxy. Thus, in his *Short Narrative about the Antichrist*, Vladimir Solovyov represents Catholicism, Protestantism, and Orthodoxy by Pope Peter II, Professor Ernst Pauli, and Starets Ioann respectively. The three different types of Christianity are each thereby made to refer to their apostle: Catholicism to St. Peter, Protestantism to St. Paul, and Orthodoxy to St. John.

But we may also suppose that there were more personal reasons for Dostoyevsky's preference. He was especially attracted by the doctrine that it is Jesus in whom the ultimate revelation of God encounters mankind. It was also important for him that this Gospel recognizes only one commandment, the commandment to love, and that sin is defined as a rejection of Jesus.

The concept of Jesus as God probably came late to Dostoyevsky. In the Petrashevsky circle he had learned that Jesus was an ethical ideal, a precursor of an imminent changed order of society—a noble dreamer, a reformer, but hardly a God. The metaphysical dimension in his image of Christ was far in the background. Only during his term in prison did he realize how much depended on his recognition of this metaphysical dimension. Later he perceived that the Aryan heresy—the denial of Jesus's divinity—was the first stage in the European process of secularization which he saw as his mission to counteract. From then on the doctrine of the divinization of Jesus became in his eyes the central point of all Christianity. "It is not the morality of Christ, not the teaching of Christ that will save the world, but the belief that the word became flesh."

The tendency in the underlinings from the St. John scriptures is plain. It is not the good action which Dostoyevsky emphasizes, and not at all the absence of evil. For him the decisive factor is the message of love. More than any of the other Evangelists, St. John sees the miracle in a Christ who proclaims love to an evil world. In particular we may observe the writer's emphasis of the following passages:

> A new commandment I give unto you, That ye love one another; as I have loved you, that ye also love one another. (John 13:34)

> This is my commandment, That ye love one another, as I have loved you. (John 15:12)

> He that loveth his brother abideth in the light, and there is none occasion of stumbling in him. (I John 2:10)

> Beloved, let us love one another: for love is of God; and every one that loveth is born of God, and knoweth God. (I John 4:7)

> No man hath seen God at any time. If we love one another, God dwelleth in us, and his love is perfected in us. (I John 4:12)

> We love him, because he first loved us.
> If a man say, I love God, and hateth his brother, he is a liar: for he that loveth not his brother whom he hath seen, how can he love God whom he hath not seen?
> And this commandment have we from him, That he who loveth God love his brother also. (I John 4:19–21)

In our time it may be worth observing that this message of love excludes sensuality. The same is by and large true of the message's application in the novel. Prince Myshkin, we learn, lacks any experience with women. He is decidedly one of the 144,000 who are described in a marked section of Revelation (14:1–7). "These are they which were not defiled with women," Dostoyevsky underlines, "for they are virgins. These are they which follow the Lamb whithersoever he goeth. These were redeemed from among men, being the firstfruits unto God and to the Lamb." Indeed, as one reads of the female characters' enthusiasm for the Christ-inspired Lev Nikolayevich Myshkin, it is tempting to call to mind the characterization given by Ernst Renan of Jesus and women: "He was surely loved more than he himself loved." It is at any rate understandable that the ageing Lev Nikolayevich Tolstoy was very enthusiastic about his namesake in Dostoyevsky's novel.

The message of love was conceived by Dostoyevsky first and foremost as a message about sympathy, compassion. "Compassion is the whole of Christianity," he wrote aphoristically in his sketches for *The Idiot*. In the novel's final redaction this idea becomes even more strongly marked: "Compassion is the most important and possibly the only law for the whole of human life."

If we are now to compare Dostoyevsky's vision of Christ with the portrait we are given of Prince Myshkin, we can hardly fail to observe the similarities. Even in the hero's external appearance there are features that recall the Christ we find in Russian icons. We learn that Myshkin is "of slightly above average height, very fair, with thick hair, sunken cheeks, and a thin little pointed, almost white beard." Like the Christ of the Gospel according to St. John, he comes "from above," from mountainous Switzerland to flat Russia. His past in Switzerland also has certain Christlike features. We hear that he used to gather the children around him and be a teacher to them. His attitude towards the "sinful" Marie is clearly inspired by the story of Mary Magdalene and the woman taken in adultery. Finally we hear of his love for the donkey, a creature with clearly Biblical associations centering on humility.

Of more importance, however, is Myshkin's behavior in St. Petersburg. Here, right from the first moment, Dostoyevsky's "Christ the Prince" becomes a teacher and father confessor. This is not because he goes around performing miracles or good deeds. It is because he is different, a mysterious outsider, a stranger in this world, like the Christ of the St. John Gospel. He represents attitudes rather than actions, and in his attitudes he is a representative of a world with a new disposition. He is as innocent as a lamb, an "idiot" who believes in the Kingdom of God on earth. Passions like greed and jealousy are deeply alien to him. Unlike the people around him, he is not preoccupied with asserting his "right" to money and power. He belongs to "the pure of heart"—he feels compassion without hatred and love without cruelty, he makes sacrifices without feeling pride. His chief virtue can best be characterized by the Russian word *smirenie*, the subjugation of passion for the sake of humility and spiritual peace. It therefore denotes the opposite of the Greek *hubris*, which stands for pride, self-assertion, and spiritual revolt. In Prince Myshkin we encounter a virtue that is *passive* and that can be attained only through humility and suffering.

By proclaiming an ideal that sets more store by attitude than by action, in which action is subordinate to the feeling with which it is carried out, Dostoyevsky made himself the spokesman for a conception of Christianity that may appear alien to the Western reader. While theologians have stressed first and foremost the value of the good deed and the importance of desisting from the bad one, Dostoyevsky places the chief emphasis on the individual's attitude toward his neighbor—or to put it in the words of St. Paul's Epistle to the Romans, underlined by Dostoyevsky in his copy of the New Testament: "Be kindly affectioned one to another with brotherly love; in honor preferring one another." (Romans 12:10)

The idea that action is of less significance than attitude has, of course, important implications for the concept of sin. The formalistic concept—that sin is the transgression of commandments—must take a back seat to the notion that sin is the absence of compassion. It follows that sinful actions are more forgivable than sinful states of mind. While we are accustomed to tolerate all kinds of attitudes and ideas at the same time as we generally condemn the actions themselves, in Dostoyevsky's eyes the actions are merely a necessary consequence of the attitudes and hence less blameworthy.

Once again there may be many who have difficulty in following Dostoyevsky here. Is the prodigal son less blameworthy than his envious brother? Or, to push the point to its extreme—is a man who commits murder with a prayer on his lips less guilty than a man who does so without saying a prayer for forgiveness? Dostoyevsky seems to answer both questions with a *yes*. The first category of sinners has at least a *will* to believe in God.

The Idiot well expresses these aspects of Dostoyevsky's outlook. The writer reserves his wrath for bellicose nihilists and hardened atheists, who to him are lost souls who believe only in themselves and have no faith in God. They have not accepted Christ's injunction to show love toward God and men. The underlinings in his New Testament leave no doubt that this "sin of omission" is in Dostoyevsky's view the real deadly sin. His condemnatory view is witnessed by the following marked passages, among others:

For it had been better for them not to have known the way of righteousness, than, after they have known it, to turn from the holy commandment delivered unto them.

But it is happened unto them according to the true proverb, The dog is
turned to his own vomit again; and the sow that was washed to her wallowing
in the mire. (2 Pet. 2:21–22)

Though I speak with the tongues of men and of angels, and have not
charity, I am become as sounding brass, or a tinkling cymbal. (1 Cor. 13:1)

Even him, whose coming is after the working of Satan with all power
and signs and lying wonders.

And with all deceivableness of unrighteousness in them that perish;
because they received not the love of the truth, that they might be saved.
(2 Thess. 2:9–10)

If any man love not the Lord Jesus Christ, let him be Anathema Maran-
atha. (1 Cor. 16:22)

On the other hand, Dostoyevsky is extremely tolerant to thieves, rowdies
and drunkards, people who are generally considered riffraff but who are
really doing nothing worse than committing evil actions. In Dostoyevsky's
world, as long as people are using their fists and shoulders and not their
thoughts, there is always a possibility that life may go on. Like his prototype,
Prince Myshkin is a friend of publicans and sinners. He feels more at home
with the boorish clown Lebedev and the drunken thief Ivolgin than he does
with the magnificent pillar of society General Yepanchin. And it is no social
or moral fastidiousness that makes him place the pure Aglaya higher than
the sullied Nastasya Filippovna. His choice between these two women is
determined rather by his own estimation of which of them needs him more.
His attitude toward Nastasya Filippovna's dubious past is very indulgent.
His stance is evidently inspired by Christ's attitude toward the female sinner
in the house of the Pharisees, yet one more Biblical passage underlined by
Dostoyevsky in his copy of the New Testament: "Wherefore I say unto thee,
Her sins, which are many, are forgiven; for she loved much: but to whom
little is forgiven, the same loveth little." (Luke 7:47)

This brings us to another important concept in this profoundly religious
book, namely that of *forgiveness*. Not surprisingly, we find among Dostoyevsky's marked Biblical passages the words of Christ in Matthew 18:22
which urge us to forgive one another not "Until seven times: but, Until
seventy times seven." Prince Myshkin also forgives everything—cuffs on the

ear, derision, and slander. He finds reasons for everything; for him there is scarcely any sin that cannot be forgiven. Dostoyevsky's own distinctive features are also, however, expressed in this complex of problems. While we strive to forgive one another, Dostoyevsky's characters struggle with the much harder task of forgiving themselves.

This is Nastasya Filippovna's problem. From her surroundings and, in particular, from the man who has seduced her, she has received a deep spiritual wound, yet all she wishes in retribution for this wound is to be wounded again. First she punishes herself for the first offense with her sense of guilt, and then death becomes the final wound she inflicts upon herself in order to punish herself for her guilt-feelings. She loves her shame and guilt more than the forgiveness which Prince Myshkin can give her, and seeks Rogozhin's knife as a final vindication of her contempt for others and herself.

The finale, in which the Prince attempts to console Rogozhin by the bedside of the murdered Nastasya Filippovna, is beyond question one of the most powerful in world literature. Yet most critics have interpreted it as a proof of the total defeat of the Prince's ideals in the world of earthly passions. Indeed, what has he really achieved by refusing to allow himself to be insulted, by living out his ideals of love, humility, and forgiveness? Nastasya Filippovna has been murdered. Aglaya has had her happiness destroyed: her marriage to a dubious Pole and quest of sanctuary with a Catholic priest must seem to Dostoyevsky's eyes like a fate worse than death.

It is, however, arguable that we may be applying too pragmatic a viewpoint when we approach the Prince for not being able to bring about a measurable improvement in his surroundings. "It's the results that count!" people often say. But this is said by people who put action before attitude, people who assert that human intercourse must be organized on a rational basis, and who can only shake their heads when Dostoyevsky has the poor peasant woman come to Father Zosima with a gift of sixty kopecks for "someone who is poorer" than herself, for, they say, there is no item in the social welfare budget that can be covered by sixty kopecks! Naturally enough, these critics have little understanding of the Prince's disturbing guest appearance in St. Petersburg. If only he had remained in his Swiss clinic, everything would have gone fine for both Aglaya and Nastasya Filippovna!

Dostoyevsky obviously found it difficult to conduct a polemic with his rationalist critics. In *The Idiot* he and they talk past one another, as they do in *The Brothers Karamazov*. But it would be premature to put down this novel with a feeling that human goodness is insufficient, that the world needs only actions, that attitudes are without significance. Of course it can be argued that Prince Myshkin is a failure, just as Christ was a failure, if we are to treat him according to the results he achieved. Neither Christ nor Prince Myshkin could fend off the insults human beings inflict on one another; all they could do is give people an image of the best in themselves. But if we put the main emphasis on the power of attitude and example, then this acquires great value. It is true that the Prince is unable to change the world, but what about a world full of Princes? An ideal may be unattainable, but to strive after anything less is not worth the trouble. Perhaps it is here that the message of this book lies.

Anna Grigoryevna, Dostoyevsky's
second wife. Photograph 1863.

One of the gambling casinos in Wiesbaden.

A casino in Bad Homburg.

A gambling table in Baden-Baden.

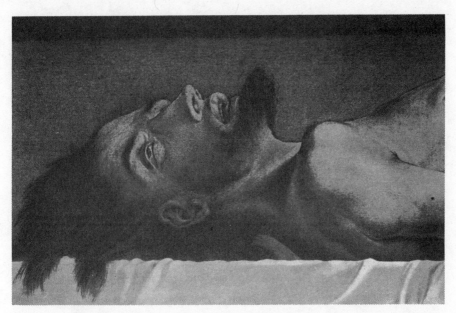

The Dead Christ in the Tomb. *Holbein the Younger, 1521.*

Peace Conference in Geneva.

9

EXILE

"I yearn terribly. If only I could get away from Western Europe!
Here I go around staring at everything like a savage. . . .
Yes, this is probably worse than my exile to Siberia.
If you only knew what hatred I have conceived for the West
in the course of the past four years."

S oon after the death of his daughter, Dostoyevsky began to find life
in Geneva intolerable. He wanted desperately to disappear forever
from this accursed Switzerland, where the weather and the people
were so impossible. If only he could take Anna to France with him! But
their travel funds were virtually exhausted, and at the beginning of June
1868 they opted instead for Vevey, a well-known French Swiss watering
place a little farther along Lake Geneva where Gogol had once worked on
Dead Souls. "I shall never forget the sad day when, having put our luggage
aboard the ship, we visited for the last time the grave of our child and laid
our farewell wreath before its cross," Anna wrote.

The crossing to Vevey took place in a gray, misty weather that was
perfectly in tune with their state of mind. Dostoyevsky was seized by a
profound depression, and was no longer able to hold back his bitter sense
of grievance at life:

> He described the loneliness and joylessness of his youth after the loss of
> his dear mother; he recalled the crude insults he had received from his
> fellow writers, the same who in the past had greeted his talent enthusias-
> tically. Dark and wretched memories from his years of penal servitude came
> to the surface again, sad recollections of his unhappy marriage to Maria
> Dimitrievna, who with her "strange, distrustful, and morbidly imaginative

temperament" had not brought him the family happiness he yearned for, or any children either. And now, when he had at last experienced "the great and unique joy of being given a beloved child" and in addition the opportunity of fully acknowledging that joy and of benefiting from it, that his ill fate should have wrested this treasured being from him! This was the only occasion on which he ever talked about the bitter wounds that life had inflicted on him.

Dostoyevsky had hoped to find a quiet place in which he could finish *The Idiot*. In Vevey they took lodgings on the corner of rue Simplon and rue du Centre. He did at least admit that the view was magnificent. "Not even in the most elegant ballet could one find settings such as one finds here on the shore of Lake Geneva; not even in one's dreams could one ever hope to see anything more beautiful." But what did it matter that the town had "one of the finest views in Europe" when the weather got on his nerves, the lake gave him toothache, and there was not a single Russian newspaper to be found in any of the cafés? What was more, Vevey was filled to overflowing with stupid and unreliable Swiss. "The Germans are, of course, worse, but even they are not half so bad as the Swiss!"

This summer in Vevey was perhaps the most difficult period of their marriage. Dostoyevsky's longing to leave Switzerland was intensified by his grief for Sonya, and it helped little that Anna's mother came to console the couple. "It was as if life had come to a standstill for us," Anna wrote. "All our thoughts and conversations centered solely on one theme—Sonya and the happy time when she had illuminated our lives. Each child we encountered on the street reminded us of our loss; and in order to escape from these reminders we went for long walking tours in the mountains."

Dostoyevsky continued to work on *The Idiot*, but not even this brought him relief. More and more he began to miss the sights and sounds, the living impressions of his homeland. Here on the streets of Vevey there was scarcely ever a single wretched Russian émigré to be seen. Worst of all, letters from Russia were becoming ever more infrequent. Could it really be that the Third Department was holding back his mail? He had long had a suspicion that the Russian priest in Geneva was in the pay of the secret police, and at the end of July he received an anonymous letter informing him that he was still under police surveillance.

It transpired that only a year earlier a "secret instruction" had gone out from the Third Department to all frontier crossing points, stating that when

Dostoyevsky returned from abroad, he was to be made the subject of "the most thorough investigation." If he were found to be in possession of unlawful material, the instruction went on, he was to be arrested without delay and brought to the headquarters of the Third Department.

Dostoyevsky did not know whether to laugh or to cry. The idea of arresting him, an archpatriot who loved his Tsar so dearly that he had even betrayed the convictions of his youth! "This is repugnant," he burst out, trembling with indignation, in a letter to Maikov. "Are they really not aware that the nihilists and liberals on *The Contemporary* have been slinging mud at me for more than five years, that I broke my ties with them long ago, that I hate these wretched Poles and love my fatherland above all else in the world? The villains!"

A little later, he happened to come across a book that had recently been banned in Russia, *Mysteries in the Palace of the Tsars under Emperor Nicholas I.* The book had been written by a gutter journalist who went by the name of Paul Grimm. Its principal action took place in the year 1855, and to his great consternation Dostoyevsky discovered that he himself played one of the leading roles. Having served his term in prison, he returns to St. Petersburg and takes part in a new conspiracy against the Tsar. When he refuses to inform on his comrades, he is subjected to corporal punishment and confined in the Peter-Paul Fortress. His wife, Natasha, persuades the Tsar to grant him a pardon, but the pardon comes too late: Dostoyevsky has already died on his way to a second Siberian exile. The book ends with his wife entering a nunnery and the Tsar committing suicide.

With its crazy plot, the book aroused great excitement. Isolated and suspicious, Dostoyevsky connected this with the rumors about his being under surveillance. This must be a new provocation! It was, at all events, extremely unfortunate that his biography should have been used to serve anti-Tsarist ends. For a while he contemplated replying to this shameful slander, but in the end he opted simply to ignore the book.

As autumn gradually drew close, it became clear to the Dostoyevskys that they would have to get out of Switzerland as soon as possible. Anna's health was failing—the frequent boat trips over to Sonya's grave were taking a toll on her vital energies. And the work on the novel was going far too slowly. Being a Russian, Dostoyevsky was accustomed to broad horizons; the mountains around Lake Geneva seemed to lock him in. "They have an oppressive effect on me and narrow down the scope of my thoughts," he complained to Anna. "I can write nothing of value in this country." It is significant that it is here, in Switzerland, where the mountains shut in gaze and intellect, that Stavrogin loses his faith in *The Possessed*.

The couple decided to spend the winter beneath the sunny skies of Italy. At the beginning of September they set off, with Milan as their provisional destination. The shortest route lay over the six-thousand-foot-high Simplon Pass. As the post chaise crawled up the inclines at a snail's pace, the couple tackled the footpaths and picked alpine flowers in the fine autumn weather. Their route took them through the wildest gorges of the Alps, with white waterfalls and precipitous mountains on both sides. "Not even the liveliest imagination could describe the beauty of the mountain road across the Simplon," Dostoyevsky declared in a letter to his niece.

Anna had learned a little Italian, and when they reached Domodossola she had a chance to act as interpreter. Dostoyevsky went into a boutique to buy a necklace for her, but when the owner of the boutique claimed that the necklace dated from imperial times and demanded three thousand francs for it, even Dostoyevsky had to oblige with a smile.

Later, Anna remembered this journey with affection. The weather was glorious; it was as if life were smiling upon her once again, as if they had left all their sorrows on the other side of the Alps. The change of climate and the constantly changing travel impressions had a beneficial effect on Dostoyevsky. He arrived in Italy in the best of moods: the inhabitants of Lombardy even reminded him of Russian peasants. They seemed to have the same gentle, patient gaze, the same sense of humility and resignation.

In Milan they took lodgings in a street so narrow that people could talk to one another across it from window to window. It was a far cry from the Nevsky Prospekt. The street led right up to the impressive cathedral— il Duomo—which Dostoyevsky never grew tired of admiring. "The only building of note in this town is the famous Cathedral," he wrote to Sonya, "a mighty marble construction in Gothic style, open and fantastic as a dream." Another glory was the view from the cathedral tower, with all its Gothic sculptures.

All this notwithstanding, Milan was hardly a place in which to stay for any length of time. The cold autumn rain meant that Dostoyevsky could no longer take his customary walks, and there were no Russian newspapers to be had here, either. Half a year had passed during which he had not read a single Russian book. Soon perhaps he ought to follow the advice he had given Turgenev—buy a giant telescope so as to be able to keep an eye on what was happening in the fatherland.

His only consolation came in the form of letters from Russia, from Sonya, Maikov, and Strakhov. With joy he greeted the news that his friends were planning a new journal—*Dawn*. The journal was to have the same liberal-Slavophile tendency as *Time* and *Epoch*. Once again the journalist in Dostoyevsky woke to life. He wanted to take part in this venture, but first he had to finish *The Idiot* for *The Russian Messenger*. He was becoming more and more dissatisfied with his realization of the book's ambitious idea, but each month he managed, in spite of everything, to produce some fifty pages or so.

Having shivered their way through two or three rainy autumn months in Milan, they moved south and took lodgings in Florence.

In Dante's native city, at that time the capital of the new Italy, the sun still had warmth to offer. In midwinter, during walks in the Boboli Gardens, they rejoiced at the newly opened roses. Yes, Florence on sunny days was "almost like heaven." "It is impossible to imagine anything more glorious than the impression of this sky, this air, and this light. . . . The sun and sky and all these *miracles of art* are quite beyond belief."

From their small apartment on via Guicciardini it was only a short distance to the Pitti Palace, where they often stood in wonder before the art treasures. Dostoyevsky was particularly enthusiastic about Raphael's *Madonna della Sedia*. "I had earlier spent a whole week studying this picture, but it is only now that I have really seen it," he wrote. He was also a frequent visitor to the Uffizi, where the *Medici Venus* captivated him. A statue of genius!

On the whole, he now derived more from the art treasures of Florence than he had done on his first visit there. He was especially delighted by the ecclesiastical architecture: the Gothic Cathedral of Santa Maria del Fiore and the old marble-covered Baptistery Chapel with its three famous bronze doors. The second door, the work of Lorenzo Ghiberti, filled him with enthusiasm, and he could understand Michelangelo's assertion that it deserved to be called "The Gates of Paradise." Were he ever to become rich, he would obtain a large photograph of this door and hang it in his study, he said. He never did become rich, and the photograph got no farther than Versilov's study in *A Raw Youth*.

In January 1869 Dostoyevsky finally completed *The Idiot*. But in spite of its effective final scene, the novel was not a success, and he soon perceived that it would be difficult to obtain any decent fee for it in book form. All the while the couple were amassing debts. Now and then he would still joke about his finances—he would describe himself and his wife as "Mr. and Mrs. Micawber"—but their destitution only grew more acute. Now he would have to set to work on a new novel that would assure him the same success as that enjoyed by *Crime and Punishment*.

Once again Dostoyevsky became a regular visitor to the Gabinetto Scientifico-Letterario di G. P. Vieusseux, an excellent lending library which had earlier numbered such famous names as Heine, Lamartine, Longfellow, and Cooper among its members. He grew particularly absorbed in the writings of Voltaire and Diderot. He wanted to write a major work to be entitled *Atheism*—"a true poem"—about an agnostic Russian who, after many religious aberrations, at last finds his way to the Russian Church and Russian soil. But although it was possible to do some of the preliminary studies for this work abroad, it was becoming ever clearer to Dostoyevsky that it required a thorough knowledge of life in his homeland. "It is absolutely imperative that I return to Russia," he wrote in a letter to Sonya dated early February 1869. "Here I shall soon be unable to write anything at all. I lack material, I lack the Russian people, the Russian reality which alone can furnish me with the necessary ideas."

The plan for *Atheism* was gradually to merge with that for *The Life of a Great Sinner*, a large-scale work "of at least the same dimensions as *War and Peace*." In this book he wished to portray a middle-aged man who one day suddenly loses his faith in God and must then struggle his way through great sufferings toward humility. "The theme that goes through each part of the novel is the one that has tormented me, conscious or unconsciously, throughout the whole of my life, namely that of God's existence." Dostoyevsky was never to write this novel. The form of the intended epic was alien to the type of dramatic, suspense-saturated novel form he favored. But the principal idea and certain of the characters were nonetheless to have a stimulating effect on his subsequent novels.

Toward the end of the winter it became clear that Anna was pregnant again. They were both filled with joy. Dostoyevsky was convinced that this time it would be a boy, but he had a girl's name at the ready, too, just in case. If only it went well! His concern for Anna reached such proportions that he removed from their copy of *War and Peace* the pages in which Tolstoy describes the death of Princess Bolkonskaya in childbirth. "I wait in fear and trembling, hope and apprehension," he wrote to Strakhov.

"Dostoyevsky was no believer in making casual travel acquaintances," Lyubov wrote in her book about her father. "If he liked someone, he would give that person his whole heart and become his friend for life; but he could see no point in wasting his friendship on passersby." During their time in Florence, the Dostoyevskys lived in splendid isolation, separated not only from the Italians but also from the populous Russian colony. Not a single Russian has left an account of meetings with the writer at this time. As a consequence of their isolation, the couple drew even closer to each other, but their solitude became a source of anxiety as the birth gradually approached. How was impractical Dostoyevsky to make arrangements for a midwife and a nurse when he knew not a single person in Florence and could not even make himself understood in Italian?

In May they received a visit from Anna's mother, who had come to lend a helping hand. Their need for more space brought them to a new apartment on Piazza del Mercato Nuovo. Here, however, it was quite impossible for Dostoyevsky to do any work. People shouted and sang all night long. No sooner had he gone to bed at around five A.M. than the marketplace woke to new life, with people crying their wares and donkeys braying. The city never seemed to sleep!

They would have to go north again. But where would they head? France was out of the question, it was far too expensive. And they did not want to go back to Switzerland—it was colder than Lapland there! They did, on the other hand, feel attracted to Prague, which at that time was a center for the Slavophile movement in Europe. Dostoyevsky had long been keeping an eye on the attempts to create a stronger ideological unity among the Slavic peoples, and was sorry that he had been unable to take part in the great convention of Slavists that had taken place in Moscow in the summer of 1867.

How interesting it would have been to become more closely acquainted with the new ideas about the special character and mission of the Slavic peoples! In *Dawn* he had rejoiced over the first chapters of Nikolai Danilevsky's historo-philosophical treatise *Russia and Europe*, an attempt to rebuild the Slavophile doctrine on a new foundation. He well remembered its author from the Petrashevsky circle. Now this erstwhile "rabid Fourierist" had conceived a genuine love for the soil and essence of his native land and had thus proven himself to be a "person of consequence."

In his sensational monograph, Danilevsky distinguished among four different cultural-historical types, each with its own representatives: the religious (the Jews), the cultural (the Greeks), the political (the Romans), and the socioeconomic (contemporary Western Europe). Now it was the turn of the Slavic people, which represented a much broader cultural-historical type. Only the Slavs were in a position to create a culture that would be capable of developing these four aspects and thereby of attaining the highest degree of development in every sphere. By reason of their special qualities, the Slavs were called upon to replace the cultural type that was at that time represented by Western civilization.

Dostoyevsky was captivated by these ideas, but interpreted them in accordance with his nationalistic and religious convictions. Among other things he thought that Danilevsky would be unable to demonstrate the central aspect of the Russian calling, which was "to reveal the Russian Christ whom the world does not know and whose origins lie in our native Orthodoxy." He was convinced that the historical mission of the Slavs could be realized only through a recognition of Russian supremacy. "Through the Russian idea a great renewal is now being prepared for the whole world," he announced to Maikov. "I have a passionate belief that this will come about in the course of a century or so. But in order that this great cause may be crowned with triumph, it is necessary that Great Russian law and Great Russian hegemony be recognized throughout the whole of the Slavic world."

The couple had hoped to be able to move early in spring before the heat set in. But the money from Russia that was to pay for their journey did not arrive, and meanwhile the temperature rose and rose. The closed-in marketplace seemed like a baker's oven. "It was like lying on the uppermost tier of a Russian bathhouse," Dostoyevsky wrote. Poor Anna! To make matters worse, they received a visit from a poisonous spider, a *piccola bestia*, which appeared and then disappeared into the mattress. "It was not found and killed until the following morning," Dostoyevsky later recalled. "But I spent nearly the entire night in a state of uncomfortable certainty that a *piccola bestia* was passing the night in my bedroom. A tarantula's bite is supposed to be seldom fatal, but I knew of one case from my time in Semipalatinsk when a Cossack paid with his life, in spite of receiving medical treatment." Was it not Svidrigailov who pictured eternity to himself as a small, grimy bathhouse in the country, with crawling spiders in every corner?

When July gave way to August, the couple was at last able to depart, but not before Anna had received a thorough medical examination. It was a long way to Prague—more than a thousand kilometers—and they took plenty of time in getting there. Their first stop was Bologna, where they went to see Raphael's *St. Cecilia*. "He was happy to see this wonderful painting in the original," Anna wrote. "I almost had to tear him away from it by force so that we should not miss the train." Venice made a deep impression on Dostoyevsky the student of architecture. For four days he wandered around the Piazza San Marco and stood for hours in front of the cathedral—"wonderful, quite incomparable."

The boat journey from Venice to Trieste was less enjoyable. Dostoyevsky was anxious during the rough sea crossing, but Anna coped perfectly. Vienna found favor—he thought the city "more beautiful than Paris." They were also enthusiastic about Prague, where they arrived ten days after their departure from Florence. But here a great disappointment awaited them. After three days they gave up trying to find a reasonably furnished family apartment, yet to buy their own furniture and utensils for only half a year would have been far too expensive, and so they opted to travel back to Dresden, where they knew their way around. With that, their circumnavigation of Europe came to an end.

II

When they returned to Dresden in mid-August 1869, they succeeded in finding a roomy apartment in the city's English quarter at Victoriastrasse 5. A short time later Anna's mother arrived to help during the forthcoming birth.

The Dostoyevskys' daughter Lyubov was born on September 26. Her name means "Love"—she herself later adopted the name "Aimée"—the beloved. Once again the writer was granted the joy of being a father. How she resembled him! To Maikov, who on this occasion too was requested to be godfather, he wrote in an excess of happiness: "Three days ago I received a daughter, Lyubov. Everything went well; the girl is healthy, a real beauty!" The comment made by the mother of the newborn infant was not entirely without irony: "One would indeed have to have the eyes of one besotted in order to see a 'real beauty' in this lump of pink flesh."

But Dostoyevsky was the most loving of fathers. He never tired of looking after the little one; he bathed her, carried her about in his arms, and rocked her to sleep. "Ah, ah, have you really never thought of marrying and having children, dear Nikolai Nikolayevich?" he wrote to Strakhov in elation. "I can assure you that three-quarters of the happiness of human beings rests in this, and that the other quarter is hardly of much consequence!"

The new addition to the family had its difficult aspect. For one thing, they had to sell and pawn clothes in order to pay the midwife—they were by now long accustomed to such painful necessities. Even worse trouble was caused by bureaucracy, and by memory. His landlord told Dostoyevsky that he must register with the authorities without delay. His visit to the police station was extremely trying: he could not for the life of him remember his wife's maiden name! The police officials looked at him with some mistrust but allowed him to go home and ask her what it was.

"What's your name?" he asked her irritably when he arrived home. "My name? My name is Anna," she replied in astonishment. "No, I know that. It's your maiden name I need to know." "Why do you want to know that?" "It's not I but the police. These Germans are a strange lot. They simply must know what you were called before you married me and I have completely forgotten."

Anna advised him to write the name down on a piece of paper so he should not forget it again. Dostoyevsky complied and triumphantly produced the piece of paper in the presence of the Saxon authorities.

After a life of the most intense isolation the Dostoyevskys now came into closer contact with the local Russian colony. It was true that he was still skeptically disposed toward these rich families who had chosen to leave Russia in order to "take advantage" of European civilization. But, on the other hand, he had a weakness for praise and appreciation, and had no objection to his Russian admirers making a fuss over him. After Sunday service he usually went along with Anna to the home of Dresden's Russian priest, where they had an opportunity to meet most of their fellow expatriates for conversation and discussion.

Now, as earlier, Dostoyevsky was living his life in the world of fictional composition. After completing *The Idiot*, he had begun work on a short story for *Dawn*, resting on his laurels while he awaited inspiration for *The Life of a Great Sinner*. Gradually, however, the story grew into a full-fledged novel about the nature of jealousy, one that shows the touch of a master from beginning to end.

In its outward form *The Eternal Husband* is a story about a love triangle. It has been claimed that the work takes up where *Madame Bovary* leaves off. But Dostoyevsky's novel brings a new element to this complex of problems: man cannot escape from his guilt; sooner or later his past actions will come home to roost and demand expiation.

The former man-about-town Velchaninov suddenly falls prey to painful memories concerning the many wrongful deeds of his youth. His moral sickness begins as a vague anxiety, apparently lacking foundation, and then appears in the form of a man in mourning; his guilt is in some strange way connected with this man, his erstwhile friend Trusotsky. Ten years earlier Velchaninov had lived in Trusotsky's house and become his wife's lover. Now she is dead, and Trusotsky has turned up in St. Petersburg with a daughter who is really the child of Velchaninov. Trusotsky has come in order to kill his rival without really knowing that that is what he wants.

The story of how retribution is exacted is full of spiritual terror, but also shows how the principal characters are bound to one another. Trusotsky and the eternal lover have both been prisoners of the same woman; the lover is in danger of being degraded to the level of the eternal husband, and the eternal husband perceives in his rival an ideal which he cannot attain.

Thus the cuckold, the comic figure of literary tradition, acquires new, tragic dimensions. And the tragedy is not in any way diminished by the fact that the book's entire action takes place on an inner level. In this respect there is a clear connection between The Eternal Husband and The Double. Both works portray the fantastic reality of people's inner world, and in both works we encounter the individual's sense of being persecuted. The entire narrative is bathed in a ghostlike half-light which indicates that Velchaninov's dreams are really projections of his own sense of guilt. Perhaps it was the writer's painful memories of his relationship with Maria that lay at the base of this short novel, a relationship in which he himself had been both lover and cuckold.

As Lyubov gradually grew older, the couple was able to resume the activities they had indulged in during their previous stay in Dresden. Once again they visited the art galleries, went to concerts at Die Brühlsche Terrasse and took promenades in Der Grosse Garten. "Since I cannot sleep at night and therefore work instead, I do not rise until one o'clock in the afternoon," Dostoyevsky wrote to Sonya. "I work from three to five. Then I take a half hour's walk to the post office and then return home through the Royal Park—always the same route. We eat our main meal of the day at home. At seven P.M. I again take a walk, and again return through the Royal Park. At home I have tea and begin work at around ten-thirty. I work until five o'clock in the morning. Then I go to bed, and as soon as the clock strikes six I fall asleep. There you have my entire life."

During these walks Dostoyevsky could hardly have failed to notice a Norwegian author who was later to become a warm admirer of his talent. This was Henrik Ibsen, who at this time lived nearby, visited the same cafés, and walked in the same park. But there is nothing to indicate that these two reserved gentlemen ever had any contact with each other.

On only one isolated occasion was there a slight variation in this monotonous existence. One day the couple visited the auction of a deceased duchess's property and effects. Among the costly items on display Dostoyevsky found a magnificent crystal dinner service. This they must have! True, he could not afford the whole service, but he immediately made an arrangement with a French lady that they should each buy half of it. Then the bids began to fly. The careful Germans contented themselves with trifling offers, while the writer each time increased his bid by a whole thaler. With horror, Anna watched his gambling fever set in. What if the French lady were suddenly to withdraw from the arrangement? Dostoyevsky's gambling instincts were not satisfied until his bid had been accepted.

Now, however, he would have to hurry if he was to pull off a major haul at the gaming tables. He would certainly have known that the authorities had long ago taken a decision, not yet implemented, to shut down all the casinos in Germany. But the following spring, he set off with Anna's blessing and 120 thalers in his pocket. His mother-in-law was informed that he had had to go to Frankfurt "on a literary errand," but there is no doubt about his true destination: in the *Bade-Blatt für Wiesbaden* for April 22–29, 1871, we read that "v. Dostoiewsky, Hr., Dresden" has moved into the Hotel Taunus. This was to be his last stay in the casino town.

The money he had brought with him vanished as soon as he entered the casino. Then, with trembling hand, he sent Anna the usual telegram: "Schreiben Sie mier"—his command of German orthography was never one of his strong points. This was a prearranged signal that he had lost everything and that she must send him more money. Anna sent it, thirty thalers, together with an expression of her concern over how matters were going.

Her words had a powerful effect on Dostoyevsky. He did not *want* to gamble this money away. What was more, the previous night he had dreamed about his father—a bad omen. In spite of this, he found himself inexorably drawn toward the gaming hall. To begin with he made do with staking his money in thought only. And it went swimmingly! Ten times he guessed the correct numbers, even including a zero. But when, encouraged by this trial run, he went over to playing in earnest, his money vanished in a trice.

Later that evening he came stumbling out onto the street. "A gambler would gamble even before Jesus dying on the cross," he had once read in Zschokke's book of family prayer in his days at the Academy of Engineers. Now he intended to pay a call on the town's Russian priest—not in order to take confession, but to ask him for a small loan. He had received priestly help on similar occasions in the past. In his excitement he lost his way and suddenly discovered that he arrived outside Wiesbaden's synagogue. "It was like having a pail of water thrown over my head," he wrote to Anna. "No, I shall not go to the priest, never, not as long as I live—that I swear!" Consequently Anna must send him another thirty thalers so that he could pay for his hotel room and travel home third class. No, of course he would not gamble the money away. She must have such a low opinion of him. He would leave Wiesbaden as soon as he received the funds. And if her mother was dismayed when she went to pawn her clothes, all she had to do was to say that he had ruined a mattress during one of his epileptic fits and therefore needed some extra money.

At the beginning of May, after slightly more than a week of gambling, he returned to Dresden hungry and crestfallen, without money or cigarettes, but as always with renewed energy for his work. Once again he had "strengthened his nerves."

In her memoirs Anna makes the following remarks about her husband's gambling mania:

> To begin with I thought it strange that Fyodor Mikhailovich did not have sufficient strength of will to gain mastery of himself and stop at a certain limit when his losses grew too severe, and that instead he would risk his last thaler. He had, it is true, been through many sufferings—imprisonment, the scaffold, exile, the deaths of his beloved wife and brother. Indeed, I even thought that this was degrading to his noble character, and it pained and offended me to discover such weakness in my dear husband. But I soon realized that this was no ordinary lack of willpower, but was rather a passion, something elemental which even a person of strong character would be powerless to resist. It was something to which one had to resign oneself, something one had to view as an illness for which there was no cure. . . .

Here I must add in parenthesis that I never used to reproach him when he lost. I never quarreled with him about it, and he appreciated that. Without a murmur I would give him the last of our money, well aware that my pawned effects would fall into disrepair and go missing, and that our landlady and creditors would come to lay claim to all that I possessed.

But it was dreadful to see how Fyodor Mikhailovich suffered during this gambling. Pale and exhausted, he would return home and beg for more money. It was all he could do to stay on his feet. Then he would go back again, but after half an hour he would return even more depressed, and thus it continued until he had gambled away all that we owned.

When he had nothing left, Fyodor Mikhailovich would pass into a state of such despair that he would begin to weep, throw himself on his knees, and beg forgiveness for having tortured me in this fashion. Then I would always have to try to convince him that the situation was, in spite of everything, not entirely hopeless, that there was after all a way out.

Anna's memoirs make painful reading, and there is no doubt that she was a major support for her husband when his passion for gambling was at its height. But when later on she claimed that he was suddenly cured of the sickness for which she herself says there was no cure, she was surely being a little premature. True, Dostoyevsky wrote from Wiesbaden: "Anna, my dear guardian angel! A great happiness has fallen to my lot. The ugly dream which has *tormented* me for nearly ten years is now at an end. For ten years, or ever since I was overwhelmed with debts after the death of my brother, I have followed this dream of a great win with seriousness and passion. But now it is all over! This was the *last* time!"

But he had made similar assurances before. Moreover, we know that he himself always denied that the aim of gambling was to win and that he "cracked" every time he went near a casino. In actual fact, his passion for gambling probably went somewhat deeper than this. It was a part of his need to suffer and punish himself, and it could not simply be eliminated by an effort of will. His abstention from gambling during his later cures in Germany is not to be attributed to any "recovery," but rather to the fact that all the gaming halls in Germany were shut down in late 1872 and early 1873. (They were not reopened until Hitler came to power.)

What irritated Dostoyevsky most of all during his last stay in Wiesbaden was the Germans' unrestrained celebration of their recent victory over France, with concerts, fireworks, and beer-drinking. His sympathies had been with the French—this had been a contest between "the brute strength of the

Germans" and the "national spirit" of the French. When the stupid German professors demanded that "Paris be bombarded" he recalled the words of the New Testament about those who live by the sword and die by the sword. At the same time he followed the process of Russian rearmament with growing interest. "Can we manage to build enough railways and fortresses? Can we manage to procure another million rifles?" It was truly essential to be wary of Germany. There were already rumors that Russia was to be her next victim! The Franco-Prussian war had certainly not made him into a pacifist: "Without war human beings stagnate in comfort and affluence and lose the capacity for great thoughts and feelings, they become cynical and subside into barbarism."

The establishment of the Paris Commune must have come as a shock to him. What if the atheistic West were to form the basis of a new society without Christ? What good would Russian messianism be then? But the Paris Commune fell, and once again Western civilization demonstrated its inability to solve the problems that beset humanity. No, the new world could not be built on reason alone. The Paris Commune was merely the final death-throes of Western civilization. At last the way lay open for Russia's "new idea," the only idea that could put humanity on the true road to renewal. "Russia's entire mission rests in Orthodoxy, in *The Light from the Orient*, the light that will flood the people of the West, the people who have lost Christ. All of Europe's misfortune, all, all of it is due solely to the fact that Christ was lost with the Church of Rome, and that people discovered they could manage without him."

Ever more powerful grew Dostoyevsky's yearning to return to the fatherland in order to preach Russia's mission. "If only we could get back to Russia as soon as possible!" he burst out in a letter to Anna. "If only we could have done with this accursed exile and these dreams! Oh, with what hatred I shall remember this time."

Their hope of an early return home had remained alive throughout, but every time it had been crushed by money worries. Now the war led to a sharp rise in the price of everything, and it was no longer possible to obtain credit anywhere. In consequence, the Dostoyevsky family frequently suffered outright deprivation. Their daughter's christening had to be postponed because they could not afford to pay for the ceremony, and it sometimes happened that Dostoyevsky lacked money to send his manuscripts to the printers, and that he had to pawn his trousers in order to get money to send a cable.

What if he were forced to spend the rest of his life among these idiotic Germans? Then he would assuredly be lost, then he would no longer be able to write. *The Idiot*'s lack of success seemed to him a bad omen. Had his creative powers begun to decline? Would he soon be as devoid of talent as Turgenev—"the most written-out of all written-out authors"? Shivers ran down his spine at the very thought. Each new work that came from Turgenev's pen was the purest scandal! It was not that he was afraid of turning into a German, as Turgenev had done. His hatred of the Germans was far too strong for that. No, he needed Russia in order to go on writing. And in order to get back to Russia he needed money.

Shortly after his arrival in Dresden a couple of opportunities for extra earnings, earnings that might perhaps make the dream a reality, had disclosed themselves.

From St. Petersburg he received word that Stellovsky had published a separate edition of *Crime and Punishment*. According to the terms of the contract, he was thereby obliged to pay the author a considerable sum of money, but was flatly refusing to shell out. Pressure from the writer's friends was to no avail. Maikov advised Dostoyevsky to make a quick trip home in order to attend to the matter. Being the mistrustful person he was, however, Dostoyevsky interpreted the cable as a trap. What if Stellovsky were trying to have him put in debtors' prison, with the intention of then paying the fee with old, paid-up promissory notes? That would be perfectly in character! In the end, Dostoyevsky engaged a lawyer, but it was to be many years before Stellovsky fulfilled his obligations.

Not even the hope of a small inheritance from Aunt Kumanina came to anything. Alexandra Fyodorovna, his mother's rich sister, had long been ill, and when she died in 1869 it was learned that she had donated forty thousand rubles to a monastery. Dostoyevsky was outraged. A will written in her insane condition could not possibly have legal force. Giving money to a monastery when he was suffering deprivation in Germany! True, he had already had ten thousand rubles of the inheritance paid out to him in advance, and indeed he had been given to understand that he had thereby forfeited his right to any more. But this money had been spent on financing his brother's journal! No, legal proceedings would have to be instituted in order to have the will declared void. "Aunt's oldest and most entitled heirs are the Dostoyevsky family."

The struggle for the Kumanin money was to be a hard one, of long duration. Old bonds of friendship were little by little more or less severed, especially those that bound him to his brother Nikolai and his sister Alexandra, both of whom lived in great poverty. Most painful of all was the break with his niece Sonya, whom he loved as one of his own children, "and perhaps a little more, too." He had dedicated the serial publication of *The Idiot* to her; but when, a few years later, the book edition appeared, the dedication was removed. An echo of this unpleasant quarrel, which had both juridical and moral aspects, is to be found in one of the plots of *A Raw Youth*.

By April 1871 they had spent four years abroad. The news from Russia grew steadily worse: Anna's house was in the process of falling into disrepair. She was expecting another child later in the summer. If they did not get home now, they might have to spend yet another year abroad. An intolerable thought! Finally, at the end of June, a large sum from *The Russian Messenger* arrived. They were able to redeem their pawned effects, pay their debts, and pack their bags.

On the evening of July 17 they boarded the train to Berlin. The customs inspection at the frontier was notorious all over Europe. Any unfamiliar reading matter found by Russian customs officials was usually confiscated. Everything was examined, even umbrellas and coat-linings. Although Dostoyevsky did not go around with a revolver, like the Danish critic Georg Brandes, he nevertheless feared the examination, and burned several of his manuscripts. "Why should I surrender my papers to the police? I shall simply lose them," he reasoned. "No, it is better to burn them myself!" The customs examination also nearly made them miss the train to St. Petersburg. Fortunately Lyubov came to her father's assistance: she began to cry so persistently that not even the zealous customs officials could bear it.

"We had to spend yet one more tiresome day in the stifling compartment," Anna recalled. "But our awareness that we were now traveling on Russian soil and were surrounded by our own people, by Russians, had such a stimulating effect on us that we forgot all the troubles of our journey. In our joy we had to keep reassuring each other that we really had at last returned to Russia, so fantastic did it seem that our long-cherished dream should at last have come true."

Their exile was over, long years of yearning and privation, filled with xenophobia and homesickness. But it had also been a rich and fruitful period, one which had given Dostoyevsky calm in which to think through most of

what was to form the basis of his future work. From Strakhov we have the
following evaluation of the significance of Dostoyevsky's time abroad:

> I am quite convinced that these four years which Fyodor Mikhailovich
> spent abroad were the best ones of his life. The writer matured in deep
> and pure thoughts and feelings. He worked with burning zeal and often
> suffered bitter deprivation, yet managed to maintain a quiet and happy
> family life far from everything that might have disturbed his thinking and
> spiritual absorption. The birth of their children, the care of them, the
> couple's self-sacrificing participation in each other's sorrows, even the death
> of their first child—all these were pure and ennobling experiences. It is
> beyond doubt that the Christian tendency, which was the distinguishing
> characteristic of his spirit, was able to develop abroad to its fullest extent,
> especially under the conditions which he endured there. When he returned
> to St. Petersburg, this great change became evident to all who knew him.
> He would always steer the conversation onto a religious plane. Even his
> manner of speech had altered. His facial expression, too, bore signs of his
> new outlook, and a tender smile would often come to his lips . . . the
> finest Christian feelings were now alive in him—the same feelings which,
> with ever greater frequency and clarity, found expression in his works. In
> such manner did he return from abroad.

What had facilitated this return was the fee Dostoyevsky had received
for his new novel, *The Possessed.*

III

The letters that Dostoyevsky wrote from abroad bear clear testimony to his
homesickness. We have more than a hundred of them, and they are mostly
very long. All have the same complaining note: Western Europe bores him
beyond all limits. While his fellow writers show at least a certain curiosity
during their sojourns abroad, Dostoyevsky's attitude toward what he saw was
at best indifferent and often downright negative. The magnificent natural
surroundings of Switzerland were swept aside in a few lines; so also the art
treasures of Florence. And when the great searcher of the soul did occasionally apply himself to the study of the people around him, his characterizations were disappointingly superficial: the Germans are stupid, the

Swiss are self-satisfied, the Italians are noisy, and so on, as if that were all there was to say about them.

Western Europe seemed only to interest him insofar as it had some connection with Russia. There, by contrast, all was of interest: intellectual life and court cases, the military and the construction of railways, crime and political unrest. Each month he received two journals through the mail, and in his Dresden *Stammkafé* he read three Russian newspapers every day—"from first word to last." In addition he read the foreign newspapers, where he often found material that could not be printed in the Russian ones.

If he kept such a close eye on what was happening in his homeland, it was not the least because of his unease concerning the spiritual development of Russian youth. Was that youth disposed to preach "the Russian idea" to the arrogant folk of the West, or was it allowing itself to be seduced by the godless message of Western socialism? He thought with horror of what might happen if contemporary youth were to make the same fateful mistakes he himself had made in the 1840s.

The portents were not good. In the autumn of 1869 the family received a visit from Anna's younger brother, Ivan Snitkin. As a pupil at the Moscow Agricultural College he was able to tell of unrest among the students there. One of his student friends was a sympathetic fellow by the name of Ivanov, who had been very helpful during the preparation for the Dostoyevskys' trip abroad.

Dostoyevsky was deeply shocked when, some weeks later, he read that this Ivanov had been murdered in a park near the Agricultural College. The murder had been carried out by five men, two of whom had lured the victim into a grotto, where the rest of the gang was waiting. One of them seized his arms; another gripped him in a stranglehold. A third man shot him in the head. Ivanov managed only to bite an assailant's finger before his body was weighted with bricks and thrown into one of the park's ponds. Shortly thereafter, his corpse was discovered in a transparent block of ice.

The person behind the murder of Ivanov on November 21, 1869, was the young student Sergei Nechayev, one of the many nihilists of the period, only much more dangerous than the others. He had recently returned from abroad, where he had been one of Bakunin's most devoted pupils. Armed with a mandate from Bakunin's fictitious "Alliance révolutionnaire européenne," he succeeded in organizing a series of "groups of five" for a terrorist organization he called The People's Justice, which had an ax as its emblem.

His intention was to bring about an uprising throughout the whole of Russia on February 19, 1870, the ninth anniversary of the abolition of serfdom. The "groups of five" operated independently of one another, but it was Nechayev who pulled the strings. Ivanov had evidently been killed because he would not play along with Bakunin's dictatorial inclinations. After the murder the leader succeeded in escaping abroad. "The raging tigers of the government have not managed to catch hold of me," he wrote in a manifesto entitled *To the Russian Students*. "Fate wills that I should survive this rotten government! Russia's future lies in our hands." Not until 1872 was he arrested in Zurich and handed over to the Russian authorities.

It was probably together with Bakunin that Nechayev prepared *Catechism of a Revolutionary*, which contained the movement's entire program. According to this "catechism" all the ruling classes were to be liquidated, if they could not be exploited to the advantage of the revolution. As examples the book names "a multitude of highly-placed simpletons or persons who are remarkable by virtue neither of their intelligence nor of their energy, but who because of the positions they occupy enjoy wealth, connections, influence, and power. They must be exploited in every possible manner; they must be entrammeled in their own nets, their ideas confused and their dirty secrets appropriated wherever possible, so that they be made slaves." There should also be exploitation of "empty-headed, insignificant, and soulless women"—they ought to be particularly easy to compromise, Nechayev considered.

Dostoyevsky saw at once that he had been given his life's calling. For many years now he had been struggling against the sickness of nihilism. Evidently with good reason! The horrible death that had taken place in the darkness of an autumn night was no chance occurrence. Once again the abandonment of the people's religious faith had led to the disintegration of the personality, to murder and crime. In *Crime and Punishment* he had unmasked nihilism at a personal level. Now it was time to take issue with it as a social evil. He would write a political novel about "the greatest and most important problem of our time," a political pamphlet against the revolutionary movement "with whip in hand." "Let the nihilists and Westernizers howl that I am a reactionary! The devil take them—now I shall speak my mind about everything—to the very last word." Yes, if only he could get two or three years to himself he would write a novel that would be read for hundreds of years to come.

In his previous novel, Dostoyevsky had portrayed a repatriate Russian distinguished by his humility and compassion, his *smirenie*. *The Possessed* also describes repatriated Russians. Most of them have, however, long since lost their Russian virtues. Possessed by foreign ideas, they have rejected the Russian *smirenie* and substituted for it Western hubris—the proud belief that man can cope without God, that he is called to rebel against all that is *holy*. "As long as God exists, man is a slave," that Swiss Bakunin had written. "Man is rational, just, free—consequently there is no God." After this, is it surprising that Kirilov becomes obsessed by the idea of taking the principle of self-assertion to its ultimate limit, by killing himself and thereby becoming a "man-god"? Yes, where did these ideas about the free, godless man really lead to? "I begin by proposing unlimited freedom, but end in absolute despotism," Shigalyov, the theoretician of the nihilists in *The Possessed*, admits.

It is these "possessed" folk whom Dostoyevsky wanted to describe in his book. In his copy of the New Testament he underlined the story in St. Luke about the way Jesus drives the evil spirits out of a possessed man. The marked passage was also to serve as the novel's epigraph:

> And there was there an herd of many swine feeding on the mountain: and they besought him that he would suffer them to enter into them. And he suffered them.
> Then went the devils out of the man, and entered into the swine: and the herd ran violently down a steep place into the lake, and were choked.
> When they that fed them saw what was done, they fled, and went and told it in the city and in the country.
> Then they went out to see what was done; and came to Jesus, and found the man, out of whom the devils were departed, sitting at the feet of Jesus, clothed, and in his right mind: and they were afraid.
> They also which saw it told them by what means he that was possessed of the devils was healed. (Luke 8:32–36)

"That is exactly the way it has gone with us," Dostoyevsky explained in a letter to Maikov.

> The evil spirits have come out of the Russians and have entered into a herd of swine—Nechayev and his peers, in other words. They have either already drowned or will do so in future, but he who is cured, he whom the evil spirits have left, sits at the feet of Jesus. Indeed, that was how it had to be. Russia has vomited up the swinishness with which it has been

fed, and in these vomited-up scoundrels there is of course nothing that is Russian left. And mark this, dear friend: he who loses his people and his nationality loses also the faith of his fathers and his God. That is also the theme of my novel. It is called *Evil Spirits*, and is a description of how these evil spirits have entered into a herd of swine.

Dostoyevsky's interpretation of St. Luke shows that the murder in the cave was something more to him than a mere crime. In his eyes Nechayev's evil deed was a fresh sign that Russia had entered the apocalyptic age of socialism. The terroristic actions of the Paris Commune only strengthened his conviction that a reckoning was close at hand. "Communism will conquer one day, irrespective of whether the communists are right or wrong," he noted. "But this triumph will stand very far from the Kingdom of Heaven. All the same, we must accept that this triumph will come one day, even though none of those who at present steer the world's fate have any idea about it at all."

This tendency to perceive earthly events from a spiritual and divine perspective was probably reinforced by Dostoyevsky's study of Swedenborg's doctrine of correspondences. The doctrine proceeds from the underlying idea that the visible world operates in a fashion parallel to the spiritual world and is permeated by it. The physical is merely a reflection of the spiritual, and the spiritual is in its turn only a reflection of the divine. Swedenborg concluded that each individual "natural" object must have its own particular spiritual and divine correspondence; each object is a shadow-image, a "representation" of a spiritual object, and this is again a reflection of the original divine image. This doctrine becomes the point of departure for Swedenborg's allegorical interpretation of the Bible, which presupposes that the Bible's words have an underlying symbolic meaning of which it is possible to gain knowledge through the doctrine of correspondences. Our entire physical world is merely a symbol of the spiritual. And from the mid-1860s on Dostoyevsky had an ever-increasing need to see human beings and their actions in terms of the Bible's divine perspective.

A large number of the underlinings that he made in his copy of the New Testament relate to his work on *The Possessed*. This is particularly true of the underlinings in that part of the New Testament where the correspondences between the original divine image and the terrifying present seemed to emerge with especial clarity, namely *Revelation*. For Dostoyevsky, *Revelation*, far from being merely a consolatory epistle to first-century Christians during the persecution they suffered, was first and foremost an eschatological prophecy that was being fulfilled in his own time. In the grip of apocalyptic moods, he also found in this book the prototype of the false prophet in *The Possessed*. His comment in *Revelation*'s margin is a laconic one: "Social!"—evidently an abbreviation of "Socialism."

Yes, such is he, the socialist Peter Verkhovensky! Like the "other beast" of Revelation, he has "come up out of the earth" among the children of the world. He has two horns and thus is powerful, even though he cannot measure up to the first beast of the Apocalypse, the beast from the sea with "seven heads and ten horns." The Lamb is also mentioned—he evidently seeks to imitate Christ—and with lies this false prophet seeks to lead souls astray under an appearance of humility and meekness. To the characters of the novel he is known, aptly enough, as a "wonderful peacemaker," but he gives himself away by his lies. Beneath the temperamental resemblance to Christ lies concealed his dragon's temperament, the temperament of the Devil.

He first appears toward the end of the first part of the novel in the chapter entitled "The Cunning Serpent." His physiognomy is very similar to that of a snake. His face has a pointed look, his forehead is high and narrow, he has small, piercing eyes, a short nose, and long, thin lips. "His head looked as though it had been pinched together at the sides," the narrator observes, "and the back of it was disproportionately large." Even his movements are like those of a snake—"swift and energetic, though never hurried."

His eloquence is initially disarming, his words seeming "forever ready to go into service." But his incessant verbal flood—we read that the words "come showering out of him like smooth grains of corn"—soon begins to seem repellent. "In the end we start to believe that his tongue must be unusually long and thin, fearfully red, and with an extremely sharp and perpetually dancing tip."

Thus Peter Verkhovensky, the socialist who is modeled on the second beast of the Apocalypse, speaks with a serpent's tongue; he is a child of the dragon, a Son of Satan. But this minor devil does not become a central character. In the revolutionary movement he is neither an ideologist nor a theoretician—he has to make do with being the movement's practical man.

The book's leading figure is without question Nikolai Stavrogin. And he in his turn is modeled on the *first* beast of Revelation, the beast from the sea. (Even his name contains the Russian word for *horn*, *rog*—and it is Peter Verkhovensky's dream to adorn his head with the crown of the

Tsarevich Ivan.) This beast has "seven heads and ten horns, and upon his horns ten crowns." It is "like unto a leopard, and his feet were as the feet of a bear, and his mouth as the mouth of a lion. . . . All the world wondered after the beast."

These words accord with the portrait we are given of Stavrogin. Several times we hear of Stavrogin's might and strength. He has killed a man in a duel and shot another, crippling him. He is well capable of fighting a bear with nothing but a knife and would not be afraid to go among the robbers of the woods.

When Dostoyevsky describes Stavrogin's "ungovernable wildness" and "superhuman strength" he does so by using verbs that connect his character with beasts of prey. He "grabs hold" of the highly respected Gaganov's nose, he "sinks his teeth" into the governor's ear and "rips" the iron grille from the prison window. Also typical is the chronicler's repeated observation: "Suddenly the beast showed its claws!" In Dostoyevsky's sketches for the novel Stavrogin is also called "a beast of prey."

That everyone "wanders after" "the bloodthirsty Stavrogin" is made manifest even in relation to the four women he subjugates. But Stavrogin's most faithful follower is Peter Verkhovensky: "I am entirely at your service. . . . You are magnificent, Stavrogin, you are the leader! You are the sun, and I am merely a worm!" Characteristically, it is Peter Verkhovensky who introduces us to "the leader." Just as the second beast of *Revelation* is at the service of the first beast and prepares the way for the first beast's might, so too does Peter Verkhovensky function as a kind of "minister of propaganda" for his leader. For example, he spreads rumors that Stavrogin is in contact with highly-placed persons in St. Petersburg and that he has come to the city with an important mission.

Revelation tells us that the second beast "doeth great wonders, so that he maketh fire come down from heaven on the earth in the sight of men." In the novel, this is manifested in the arson fire that Verkhovensky sets. We are told that the fire bewitches the spectators with its "intoxicating" beauty, that it fills them with sweet *Schadenfreude*. "We must disseminate the gospel of destruction and bring people up to be arsonists," says Verkhovensky. With his fire he not only creates a parody of the "great works" of *Revelation*, but also gets rid of Stavrogin's wife and thereby carries out his function of preparing the way for the first beast.

Finally, we read in *Revelation* that the second beast has been given power "to cause that as many as would not worship the image of the beast

should be killed." These words find their corresponding echo in Verkhovensky's staged murder of Shatov, the man who has lost his faith in the
cause of socialism and who is cleared out of the way in order to bind the
"group of five" together with a tie of blood. "This democratic rabble cannot
be relied upon," Verkhovensky complains. "What is needed is an idol—a
single, strong, despotic will."

In *The Possessed* it clearly emerges that it is Stavrogin, the man with
the "unusual gift for crime," whom Verkhovensky has designated to be the
man of lawlessness. The whole of his Satan-inspired "mighty undertaking"
is directed toward the crowning of this "strong, despotic will." Great, therefore, is his disappointment when the graven image, Stavrogin, neither wishes
to lead nor is capable of leading the revolutionary movement. "You were
to have been the ship of discovery that was to have borne us forward. But
you resemble more a rotten barge that is fit only to be broken up for timber!"

Revelation tells of "the great whore" who sits "upon a scarlet colored
beast" with "seven heads and ten horns." "And on her forehead is written
the name Mystery," we read in Dostoyevsky's translation. The writer underlined the word *Mystery* twice. This word best characterizes the beast on
which the "great whore" sits: Stavrogin.

Even as a boy Stavrogin had experienced "the first dim premonition
of the eternal, holy longing," we read. "He who has once felt that longing
will never exchange it for the cheap joys of life. Indeed, there are some
who would not exchange it for complete satisfaction, if they could attain
it." We are given more precise information about this longing in Stavrogin's
"Confession," which among other things depicts "the dream of the golden
age" as it is awoken in him under the influence of Claude Lorrain's painting
Acis and Galatea:

> This painting it was which I now dreamed about—not as a painting,
> however, but as reality. Just as in the painting, I saw a segment of the
> Greek island world, while at the same time feeling myself transported back
> three thousand years in time. I saw blue, affectionate waves, islands and
> hills, a flowering coastline, a wonderful panorama in the distance, the
> setting sun enticing and calling—it cannot be reproduced in words. In this
> image European mankind has recognized its cradle, and the thought of it
> filled my soul, too, with a love like that which I feel for my homeland.
> Here, once upon a time, lay the earthly paradise of mankind: the gods
> stepped down from heaven and mingled with human beings. . . . Oh,
> wonderful people lived here! They rose and lay down happy and innocent,

meadow and woodland resounded to their songs and cheerful cries; their great excess of unused energies found its outlet in love and simple joy. The sun bathed them in light and warmth and rejoiced at its beautiful children. . . . A wondrous dream-vision, the exalting illusion of mankind! The golden age, most improbable of all dreams mankind has ever had, yet men have given the whole of their lives and energies for it, prophets have gone to their deaths for its sake, and without it the peoples of the earth cannot live, nor even die. In the dream it was as if I had lived through the whole of this feeling; the sea and the mountains and the oblique rays of the setting sun—all this I seemed still to see when I awoke and opened my eyes, which were quite literally wet with tears. I remember that I felt joyful. A sense of the happiness I had earlier known filled my heart almost to the point of pain; it was love for the whole of mankind.

Later this "chosen one" who bears the sign of the Cross in his name (the Greek *stavros* means *cross*) must have felt himself called to take the burden upon himself by letting his fellow human beings share in his vision of the millennium. His tragedy is that he has not been able to carry this burden. Not that he has collapsed under it but, rather, that he has refused it. Instead, he has given himself up to cynical experiments with his fellow human beings merely in order to intoxicate himself with the baseness of his actions. When he falls prey to boredom, it is due not to shame at the base deeds he has committed, but to shame at feeling remorse. He is seized by what Kierkegaard calls "demonic reserve": the sin of despairing over his sin. He who despairs over his sin really wishes to live in despair.

In contrast to Raskolnikov, this "great sinner" has developed downward, not upward. When he appears in *The Possessed* he is already empty. He is sickened by his baseness, which shows itself most clearly in his seduction of a young girl—the worst of all sins, to judge from Dostoyevsky's Bible underlinings. "After this I experienced a great revulsion at life," Stavrogin writes in his confession. Revulsion—not a burning desire for rebirth. Stavrogin is a burnt-out case. In his arrogance he has stifled the voice of his conscience and has ended up on the nihilistic ground beyond good and evil. Silent and reserved, he wanders around like a Mephistopheles, like Speshnev in the Petrashevsky circle. His early enthusiasm has given way to a cold rationality that reveals an evil power: "It seemed rational, and was thus the most repulsive and the most horrible that can be imagined."

Tortured by his feelings of loathing and emptiness, Stavrogin joins the revolutionaries. But he despises them most of all. This man of doubt no longer even has any faith in the evil cause. "If Stavrogin believes, then he does not believe that he believes. But if he does not believe, then he does not believe that he does not believe." From this "lukewarm" man, who has lost all connection with the common people and the soil of his homeland, there can come no renewal. The author pronounces his judgment over this candidate for suicide by quoting *Revelation*—yet another passage he has underlined in his New Testament:

> And unto the angel of the church of the Laodiceans write; These things saith the Amen, the faithful and true witness, the beginning of the creation of God;
> I know thy works, that thou art neither cold nor hot: I would thou wert cold or hot.
> So then because thou art lukewarm, and neither cold nor hot, I will spue thee out of my mouth.
> Because thou sayest, I am rich, and increased with goods, and have need of nothing; and knowest not that thou art wretched, and miserable, and poor, and blind, and naked. (Rev. 3:14–17)

In his worldly indifference Stavrogin shuns both faith ("hot") and atheism ("cold"). That he has no faith is something that cannot be helped; what is much worse is that he cannot be bothered to be an atheist. What, then, is the reason for this gifted man's tragic fall? His downward development from a servant of God to a servant of Satan manifests itself in the novel as a result of the great "falling away."

In a passage from the second chapter of Paul's second epistle to the Thessalonians that Dostoyevsky underlined, allusion is made to three phases in the events connected with Christ's return: the great falling away, then the reign of the lawless (Antichrist), and finally the struggle and triumph of Christ. In *The Possessed* the great falling away is manifested in the figure of Stepan Trofimovich, Stavrogin's teacher and the father of Peter Verkhovensky. Trofimovich is depicted as a typical representative of the 1840s generation, a liberal idealist with the charming but deadly stock-in-trade of utopian socialism. "If you are going to write about our Russian nihilists, please remember to direct the main thrust of your attack against their fathers, for they were even worse nihilists than the children," Dostoyevsky wrote some years later. "Our secret villains may at least possess a certain repulsive ardor, but among the fathers one finds only agnosticism and indifference, and that is even worse."

With his high-flying ideas, Stepan Trofimovich is certainly capable of wakening "the eternal, holy longing" in his pupil Stavrogin. But these semi-atheistic ideas can scarcely form a bulwark against the demonic forces of the human mind. Indeed, they merely create the growing conditions for nihilism. What during the great "falling away" were only dreams become in "the reign of the lawless" a terrifying reality.

Stepan Trofimovich is the first to admit his fatherly responsibility for this state of affairs. "It is the very idea we dreamed of carrying into action," he says in his commentary to Chernyshevsky's novel *What Is to Be Done?* "We ourselves sowed the seeds of it. It is we who have done all the work of clearing the way." It is probably the perception of his own guilt that later creates his fear of being devoured by the beast he himself has taken a hand in creating. When at the end of the novel he is changed into a bearer of Dostoyevsky's faith that Russia will one day be cured of its sickness, we hear that "he was forever having dreams about a violently gaping maw with large fangs," and that these "tormented him sorely."

This open maw with its huge fangs gives us a true picture of the reign of the lawless. Significantly it can seem almost a parody of itself: the revolutionaries want to organize the world but can't even organize a meeting; they want to fight religion but make do with putting a mouse in an icon and slipping pornographic pictures into the stock of an itinerant female Bible-seller. Yet it is precisely this apparent harmlessness that creates proselytes among ordinary people. One must, after all, show indulgence, give the young a helping hand, stop them at the edge of the abyss!

It is not least against this naïve flirtation with the dregs of Western civilization that Dostoyevsky directs his satire in *The Possessed*. In their boundless naïveté these unreflecting people are unable to see through nihilism, unable to perceive the contempt for humanity that lurks beneath the outer shell of "harmless" scandals. Precisely by their indulgent attitude "ordinary people" contribute to the furtherance of this false civilization's designs on holy Russian soil.

Dostoyevsky's commentary on Chapter 17 of *Revelation* appears to lend support to such an interpretation. In this chapter an explanation is given of what is meant by the seven heads of the beast. "And here is the mind which hath wisdom," we read in verse 9. "The seven heads are seven mountains, on which the woman sitteth." Beside the word "mountains" Dostoyevsky put a small cross, and in the margin wrote the following comment: "of civilization [*tsivilizatsii*]. The great whore thus sits on 'the mountains of civilization.' " Rome with its seven hills, or what is usually thought of as the seventh, anti-Christian empire, becomes in his eyes a "seat" of civilization for the great whore. Western civilization is a source of infection which threatens the Russian faith. "Is it really possible to have faith when one has become civilized, that is to say, a European?" Dostoyevsky asked in one of the sketches for the novel.

The many who have become infected by this contagious civilization create the basis for a further spreading of nihilism. "And the beast that was, and is not, even he is the eighth, and is of the seven, and goeth into perdition." To this mysterious account in verse 11 Dostoyevsky added the word *obschechelovek* (*man in general*). Thus "ordinary people" are associated with the Antichrist: they acquire responsibility for his evil deeds, since they have not actively involved themselves in combating them.

What of the third phase of the Apocalypse, the struggle and victory of Christ? As might be expected, Dostoyevsky was forced to recourse to hints. In his copy of the New Testament he marked the following words from *Revelation*:

> And I saw thrones, and they sat upon them, and judgment was given unto them: and I saw the souls of them that were beheaded for the witness of Jesus, and for the word of God, and which had not worshipped the beast, neither his image, neither had received his mark upon their foreheads, or in their hands; and they lived and reigned with Christ a thousand years. (20:4)

The only character in *The Possessed* who refuses to worship the beast or his image is Shatov. He not only refuses to worship Stavrogin but challenges him, rises up against him in open rebellion. By means of the cuff on the ear he inflicts upon the beast the wound described in *Revelation*, which Dostoyevsky several times dwelled on in his sketches for the book. Because of this challenge Shatov has to forfeit his earthly existence. But in return, on the day of judgment he will live and will receive admission to the millennium.

Shatov may from many points of view be viewed as an idealized self-portrait of the author. Like Dostoyevsky, he too once joined the revolutionary movement and took charge of a secret printing press. Again like the author, his socialist convictions were replaced, during an absence from Russia, by a new faith in Christ.

In Shatov's view, socialism is a shoddy invention. It is based upon reason and science, and thus bears atheism in its womb. Reason and science have only a secondary, subservient role to play in the lives of people. In reality, a power of an entirely different order shapes and moves the peoples of the earth, a power that lives in the human yearning to reach the end of the road and at the same time to deny that there is any end. The artist calls this "yearning for beauty," the philosopher "moral instinct." As for Shatov, he prefers to call it "God-seeking."

> Each people seeks a god, *its* god, precisely its *own* god, and for that people its faith in that god is the only true faith. When a people wishes to share its god with other peoples, this merely signifies that the decline of that people has begun. When the gods become the common property of the earth's peoples, the gods die. Then faith in them dies, too, and the peoples themselves die. Is it really true that I debase God by making Him an attribute of the people? No, on the contrary, I exalt the people into a god. The people is the body of God. . . . A truly great people may believe that it— and it alone—is in possession of the truth. It may believe that it alone is called to wake other peoples to new life and to lead them to the truth. . . . But there is only one truth, and consequently only one people can have found the only true God. This "unique," "God-bearing" people is ourselves. It is the Russian people!

In this Russian messianism, in this great call to proclaim "the Russian Christ," lies the hope of the Russian people that it may become cleansed of the "evil spirits" of nihilism, and also the Russian people's certainty of finding its place "at the feet of Jesus." To reveal the Russian Christ, to remind the Russian people of its God-bearing mission, this too became one of the writer's most important tasks upon his return to his homeland.

Florence. The Boboli gardens.

Anna Grigoryevna in Dresden.
Photograph, 1871.

Sergei Nechayev.
Photograph from the 1870s.

A *page from the notes on* The Possessed.

The end of April 1871:
"Hr. v. Dostoyevsky" has come to play roulette in Wiesbaden.

IO

BACK ON
RUSSIAN SOIL

*"I have an ardent love of life, I love life for its own sake. . . .
That is the most important feature of my character,
and possibly of my work as well."*

When on July 8, 1871, Dostoyevsky returned to St. Petersburg, he had barely ten years left to live. He had long been a recognized author with a large and grateful readership. The critics had been more cautious in their judgment—they still found it impossible to rank him beside Turgenev or Tolstoy—and his greatest fame was yet to come, in the final decade of his life.

When the couple drove past the church where they had been joined in matrimony, they said a silent prayer, while little Lyubov looked at her parents and crossed herself.

"Well, dear Anya, so we have managed to get through these four years abroad, in spite of all our trials and tribulations. But what now? Our entire future lies swathed in mist. . . . We must still face many immense difficulties before we set firm soil beneath our feet. I can only hope for God's assistance!"

The first difficulty made its appearance in the form of a great happiness: Anna's delivery. This time it had to be a boy! Dostoyevsky had calculated that the birth would take place on July 15 and wanted to give the baby the name Vladimir, since July 15 was St. Vladimir's day. But the boy did not arrive until the 16th, and in accordance with the wish of his mother he was given his father's name. Fyodor, or Fedya, turned out to be a sturdy young fellow who was soon to bring the writer much happiness. Could there be anything more fascinating than children, the future generation of Russia?

A short time later the Dostoyevsky family moved into a four-room apartment on Serpukhovskaya Street, near the Technological Institute. Once again the struggle for existence began. During their stay abroad they had lost most of their possessions. Furniture, kitchen utensils, clothes, and books—everything had been either sold or stolen. They had to rebuild their home from scratch.

Fortunately Dostoyevsky's family had now become less troublesome— otherwise Anna would certainly have taken care to postpone the return home still longer. But their creditors were just as insistent, and as soon as newspapers reported the writer's arrival home, creditors came with their threats and pleas, their promissory notes and their demands. Had it not been for Anna's energy and business sense, Dostoyevsky would certainly have been ruined.

In the course of her life with Dostoyevsky Anna had undergone a great change. The young girl who had earlier been so lively had now become an imposing woman with the ability to fight for her family. She understood immediately that the struggle would be a difficult one. Her husband's debt had reached twenty-five thousand rubles. She had longed to pay it off by the sale of her house in Peski, but it now transpired that the tenant had neglected to pay his taxes and duties, and the house had to be auctioned off for a song.

The siege continued—several times Dostoyevsky was made the subject of legal proceedings. His creditors were planning to have him put in a debtors' prison in the hope that he would be bailed out by the Literary Fund. It was at this point that Anna took up the fight. First she managed to secure for herself the publication rights to her husband's works. Then she began to negotiate with the creditors to repay the debts in reasonable stages. In her memoirs she describes her negotiations with one of the most insistent of the creditors:

"Cash on the table, otherwise everything you own will be pawned and sold within a week! And your husband will go to a debtors' prison!"

"The apartment is in my name," I replied calmly. "The furniture is being bought on the installment plan and cannot yet be pawned."

I showed him the rent book and a copy of our agreement with the furniture dealer.

"And as for your threat of debtors' prison," I went on, "I shall see to it that my husband serves his full term. I will take lodgings near the prison, come and visit him together with our children, and help him with his work. That way you will not receive a single kopeck. You will, on the contrary, be compelled to pay for his keep. I promise you that you will live to regret your inflexibility."

In the end, Anna got her way. But the situation was still critical. It would still happen that Dostoyevsky had to pawn his watch in order to meet his most urgent expenses. Not until late 1876 and early 1877 was he finally able to note that "nothing has been pawned." His old plan of making a trip "to the East"—Constantinople, Athens, and Jerusalem—was hardly realistic under such wretched conditions.

In spite of all the unpleasantness with his creditors and the constant struggle for his daily bread, Dostoyevsky experienced great joy at his homecoming. He renewed his acquaintance with old friends like Maikov and Strakhov and soon made a number of new ones. He placed possibly the greatest value on his friendship with Vsevolod Solovyov, an elder brother of the philosopher Vladimir. Vsevolod was later to be of great significance in the development of his ideas.

The twenty-three-year-old Vsevolod had long been an admirer of Dostoyevsky's. As soon as he learned of the return to Russia, he sat down and wrote his "teacher of genius" a long letter. In his discussions with positivistic fellow-students who wanted to "repudiate that which cannot be repudiated," he had time after time found confirmation of his own religious convictions in Dostoyevsky's writings. "You have a very great influence on my life. In your works burns the flame of genius, and I bow down in deference and love."

Ever since the publication of *Crime and Punishment* Dostoyevsky had had to put up with criticism and abuse from Russian youth, and his enthusiastic welcome of this "ardent soul" should therefore not surprise us. At last he had found a young man who in his moral quest came close to his own view of life. A few days later, Solovyov visited Dostoyevsky's cramped and miserable study. "Before me stood a short, thin man who was nonetheless quite broad-shouldered. He looked much younger than his fifty-two years. His beard was reddish, his hair had begun to thin but was not yet gray; his eyes were small and brown, and at first glance his face produced an unremarkable impression." There seemed to be something morbid about this face—its skin was pale, as if made of wax. Earlier Solovyov had seen faces like that only on Old Believers who had been locked up for many years. He always remembered this face, marked as it was by "rare spiritual life."

Solovyov relates that Dostoyevsky would occasionally fall into a black mood. Then he would sit with knitted brows and bitten lips, his eyes glittering in the pale, waxen face. But when he thawed out he would talk with burning enthusiasm while he rolled and smoked his fat, "dreadful cigarettes." Other stimulants also came and went on his writing desk: "strong tea and even stronger coffee." He would also occasionally treat his young guest to sweet things: prunes, marmalade, raisins, and grapes—of these he always had a plentiful supply.

More important for Dostoyevsky's literary career was his acquaintance with several of the most influential men in Russia. Among these were Prince Vladimir Meshchersky, publisher of the weekly newspaper *The Citizen*; the Slavophile church politician Tertiy Filippov; and Konstantin Pobedonostsev, the future head of the Russian Holy Synod, who was soon to be a major influence on Dostoyevsky's development in a conservative direction. Dostoyevsky was elected to the Society of the Friends of Spiritual Enlightenment and to the Slavic Beneficent Committee. He resumed his visits to Yelena Stakenschneider's aristocratic salon, attended the evangelistic sermons given by Lord G. V. Radstock at the home of Yulia Zasetskaya, and then gradually began to gain a foothold at court. At the beginning of 1873, probably at the instigation of Pobedonostsev, he sent a copy of *The Possessed* to the Tsar-to-be Alexander III, who had long been one of his admirers.

Another testimony to Dostoyevsky's ever-increasing degree of public recognition was a request from Pavel Tretyakov, asking him to agree to have his portrait painted for inclusion in Tretyakov's renowned art collection. Dostoyevsky agreed, and in the spring of 1872 he received a visit from Vasily Perov, one of Russia's foremost artists. Perov took his time, studying him in the most varied moods, stimulating him and seeking to catch his most characteristic facial expressions. This portrait of the artist, in which he seems to be looking into himself "in the moment of creation," became a masterpiece that aroused great interest when it was exhibited a year later along with a number of other portraits of Russia's foremost authors.

"The mighty head, the high-vaulted forehead, the closed mouth with its painfully trembling and twitching lips beneath the thin, scanty, unkempt beard . . . everything in this self-absorbed, ravaged, and emaciated countenance bears the seal and imprint of agonized thought and self-consuming ecstasy," Carl Nærup wrote enthusiastically of this portrait.

The prophet's smoldering, self-consuming ardor burns and stares from these facial features—the stiff, far-seeking gaze of a reclusive seer, a soul whose inspiration and passion were world-embracing, a heart which felt to their depths all human woes, which understood all vice, all ignominy and degradation, as well as all piety, goodness, and puremindedness. Could this sealed mouth open, and these silently speaking, restless lips impart to us their secret, they would say: "I have the same feeling for the lofty as for the low, for the sacrificial lamb and the saint of duty, as for the despised and punished evildoer, for the unbelievers and the wayward as for those whose faith is good and true."

Georg Brandes, too, found in Perov's portrait a complete expression of all that lived in this writer:

Behold this face! Half that of a Russian peasant, half that of a criminal, with a flattened nose, small, piercing eyes with lids that quiver with nervosity, a long, thick, unkempt beard and light-colored hair, the forehead of a thinker and writer, large and thoroughly formal, and the most expansive mouth, which even though closed speaks of torments without number, of abysmal melancholy, of unhealthy desires, infinite compassion, passionate envy, restlessness, and anguish!

The winter went by, and in the late spring of 1872 the Dostoyevsky family began to look for a place to spend the summer. Their choice fell on Staraya Russa, a little watering place some thirty kilometers from Lake Ilmen, which was renowned for its healthy air and curative salt baths. Even though the spot was not far from St. Petersburg, it was difficult to reach. The first time they visited it they took the train to Sosninka, then a boat along the river Volkhov as far as Novgorod, and then across the placid Lake Ilmen, which reminded them of the lakes in Switzerland. The trip was a great experience of nature. "Come up on deck, Anna, and see how pretty it is!" Anna described their encounter with Novgorod:

It was a glorious spring morning. The riverbank lay there in the brilliant morning sunshine; above the town the Kremlin raised its white, crenellated walls, crowned by the gold cupolas of St. Sophia's Cathedral. Through the cold air the bells were chiming for morning prayers. Fyodor Mikhailovich, who loved and understood the beauty of nature, was seized by a strange morning mood which began to affect me, too. For a long time we sat silently beside each other, as if we were afraid to break the magic spell. This joyful mood lasted all day—it was a long time since we had felt so happy.

On their arrival they rented a villa from Ioann Rumyantsev, one of the town's priests. They had hoped to be able to rest after the exertions of the winter, but that was not to be: a few weeks before their departure, Lyubov had fallen and hurt her arm, and what the doctor had thought was only a sprain now turned out to be a broken bone. Their daughter had to be brought back to St. Petersburg to be operated on. Uneasy and depressed, Dostoyevsky sat in Staraya Russa reading the doctors' reports: "Life is difficult and troublesome. Were it not for little Fedya, I should have lost my reason. . . . We live the life of gypsies—sad and depressing, without the slightest joy, only torments and more torments!" The family's holiday was not resumed before Anna's sister died of typhus. Fresh misfortunes lay in store: Anna herself was brought to death's door as a result of a malignant boil on her neck. "I have never known such a time of misfortunes," she wrote in her memoirs.

The misfortunes led to further delays on *The Possessed*. Another reason for the work's taking so long was that *The Russian Messenger* had refused to print Stavrogin's confession—the story of his seduction of a young girl. Not until the end of 1872 were the final chapters published serially. The book was a great success among Dostoyevsky's readers, but it also made him enemies among people who thought he had once again produced a distorted image of Russian youth.

During his entire stay in Staraya Russa, Dostoyevsky was under constant police surveillance. At the end of May the mayor of St. Petersburg had alerted the governor of Novgorod to his shift of location, asking him to take the necessary precautions. The instruction was passed on to the chief of police in Staraya Russa, who spied on Dostoyevsky day and night. When Dostoyevsky left, the chief of police sent a report to the governor: "Dostoyevsky has led a sober life; he has avoided intercourse with others, and has even sought to use the least-frequented thoroughfares; each night he has sat at his desk until four in the morning."

In Staraya Russa the Dostoyevsky family lived inexpensively and at a safe distance from their creditors. Their return to St. Petersburg once again brought financial worries. In order to help with paying their bills, Anna wanted to take a job as a stenographer, tempted by an offer of work at a conference in Poland. Reluctantly Dostoyevsky accompanied her when she went to get information about the conference from one of its participants, a fiery Caucasian nicknamed "The Wild Asiatic." When the young man "with curls, protruding eyes, and full-blooded lips" planted a passionate kiss on Anna's hand, Dostoyevsky's jealousy came seething forth:

"Is there a decent hotel in your town where a young woman might find lodgings?"

The young man gave him an enthusiastic look and replied with cheeks ablush: "If Anna Grigoryevna so wishes, I can lodge in the same hotel, even though I had really planned to stay with a friend of mine."

"Do you hear, Anya? This young man is willing to live with you! That is mag-ni-ficent!"

Fyodor Mikhailovich struck his clenched fist on the table so that his tea-glass fell to the floor and smashed to pieces. The lady of the house came running in to save a swaying lamp—he himself rushed into the entrance hall, snatched his overcoat, and ran out into the street.

Anna had better luck as the publisher of her husband's works. The wretched offers she had received for the publication of second editions had led her to undertake the printing and binding herself. "The Dostoyevsky Publishing Company" was born, and in January 1873 the book edition of *The Possessed* was offered for sale. Booksellers had to call at Dostoyevsky's apartment in order to collect their copies, and all sales were in cash. Many booksellers complained about the publisher's harsh terms and demanded to speak to the author, but Anna would refuse to wake him. He might have written the books, but it was *she* who sold them! Before the year was out she had sold three thousand copies, and then it was the turn of his other books. "I was naturally glad of the money," wrote the zealous publisher, "but the main thing was that here I had found a job which interested me: the publication of my husband's works." For his part, Dostoyevsky had complete faith in Anna's financial arrangements: "She would make an excellent Minister of Finance!" he noted.

Still, their major expenses had to be covered by the writing of new works. After finishing *The Possessed* Dostoyevsky was so exhausted that he did not have the strength to begin a new novel. Instead he started to turn over in his mind the notion of publishing an independent monthly journal with the title *Diary of a Writer*. The plan required capital, however. To begin with, it would be best to publish the *Diary* in an already existing periodical. An opportunity of this kind presented itself at the end of 1872, when he assumed responsibility for the publication of Prince Meshchersky's weekly newspaper *The Citizen*.

In the summer of 1873, Anna took the children with her to Staraya Russa, where they rented a summer cottage from Lieutenant-colonel Alexander Gribbe. Once again, Dostoyevsky remained alone in the heart of St. Petersburg in order to work on *The Citizen*. He kept having dreams that the children were exposed to all kinds of danger—that Lyubov had hurt herself or that Fedya had fallen out of the window. He would convince himself that what he had dreamed was true and would be unable to rest until Anna had persuaded him that everything was all right. It was hard for him to restrict his married life to a few hectic summer visits. "Dearest, now I should like to have you here," he writes in mid-July. "Do you understand? Is it really true that you see me in your dreams? Perhaps it's someone else you're seeing. I kiss your feet and *everything*. Passionate kisses."

Through his work on the newspaper, Dostoyevsky had abundant opportunities to feel the pulse of Russian life, and these were to stand him in good stead as a writer. The publicity the newspaper afforded him was also important. Polemical articles brought his name to everyone's lips. Even so, he did not intend to become a full-time journalist. In the spring of 1874 he took his leave of *The Citizen*. Inspiration had once again begun to awaken in him. He wanted to write a long *Bildungsroman* to be called *A Raw Youth*.

One day he received a visit from his old friend Nikolai Nekrasov, who wanted to print *The Possessed* in *Notes of the Fatherland*. The offer was a tempting one: two hundred and fifty rubles per sheet—a hundred more than he usually got at *The Russian Messenger*. And since Katkov had already obtained the rights to *Anna Karenina* and was unable to pay a sufficient advance, Dostoyevsky agreed—not, however, without some misgivings. How would he ever be able to come to an agreement with the publishers of Russia's most radical journal, men who since the 1860s had been his literary opponents? And how would this agreement be received by his conservative friends?

Dostoyevsky's departure from his editorial post was necessary because of his ill-health. Even though his epileptic attacks had grown less frequent, his resistance to them had diminished also. He was increasingly troubled by coughing and breathing difficulties, the first signs of the lung disease that was to send him to the grave. In addition to compressed-air treatment with Dr. Simonov in St. Petersburg, the doctors recommended a visit to a spa abroad. But where was he to go? Professor Dmitry Koshlakov thought Ems would be the right place, while Dr. Yakov von Bretzel suggested Soden. To Dostoyevsky they were all the same: the casinos had been closed down, after all, and he had little faith in any cure other than roulette. In the end he settled for Bad Ems, an attractive spa resort on the River Lahn in Hessen-Nassau, which ever since Roman times had been noted for its numerous mineral springs.

When in mid-June Dostoyevsky arrived in Berlin, he had himself examined by Professor Frerichs, one of the world's foremost lung specialists. The examination lasted for two minutes and ended with the illustrious practitioner referring him to another specialist. "Here is the address of a doctor in Ems. Say that you were given it by Frerichs." Dostoyevsky was exasperated by this superficial treatment, and later wrote a magnificent satire on medical specialists. "And this way you have of referring people to specialists!" the Devil in *Brothers Karamazov* bursts out. "If it's nose trouble you have, you're sent to Paris: there they have an important specialist in nasal disorders. You go to Paris and he examines your nose. 'I can only cure your right nostril,' he tells you—'I don't want to have anything to do with your left nostril. It doesn't fall within my area of specialization. But after you've been treated by me, you can go to Vienna. There you will find another specialist who will be able to treat your left nostril.' "

Dostoyevsky's letters from abroad dating from 1874 are surprisingly positive, initially at least. The old masters in Berlin's royal museum made a strong impression on him, as expected. (For the fashionable painter Wilhelm von Kaulbach, on the other hand, he has no respect: in him he saw "cold allegory and nothing besides.") And he waxed lyrical about the route from Berlin to Ems: "What is Switzerland, what is Wartburg compared to the last part of the journey to Ems? A fantastic landscape, gentle and bewitching; hill-ridges, mountains, and towns such as Marburg and Limburg with their enchanting towers, this alternation of mountains and valleys! I have never seen the like! And it was thus right until we drove into Ems one warm, brilliant morning."

Faithful to his custom, Dostoyevsky made straight for the hotel that was situated closest to the railway station, the Hôtel de Flandre. But his room there was so small that he could hardly turn round in it, and it lacked the most essential furniture. He left immediately in search of better lodgings.

On Fürst Blücherstrasse there was a room which he managed to price down by haggling to twelve thalers per week. But not even this was any place to stay in: the landlady—"a cunning old crone"—gave him food that got worse and worse, and not a week passed without quarrels over the rent. It was sheer highway robbery! In the middle of July his patience ran out. He moved to the Ville d'Alger, where one Mme. Bach took him in.

Soon Dostoyevsky found himself in the hands of one of the town's many doctors—not Dr. Gutentag, as recommended by Professor Frerichs, but Dr. Orth, an up-and-coming luminary recommended by Dr. von Bretzel. After making a thorough examination the doctor confirmed that Dostoyevsky was suffering from acute catarrh. This they would get rid of, just as soon as he would begin to drink the town's excellent mineral waters. Dostoyevsky procured a "Kurtax-Karte" priced at four thalers and began to drink mineral water twice a day. His daily routine changed totally—he rose at 6 A.M. and by 6:30 was standing in line at the spring along with a thousand or so other cure residents. "The band is playing in the park; they usually begin with a tedious Lutheran hymn to God; I cannot imagine anything more artificial and insipid than this dirge." Another extremely annoying feature was the pushing and shoving inside the Kurhaus, where the mineral water was served. People elbowed and jostled, slurped and slopped; time and time again he had to give his fellow residents a course in rudimentary human etiquette: "The sight of all these people is intolerable," he wrote. "I have become so irritable that, particularly in the mornings, I regard each single man jack of this motley crew as my own personal enemy—indeed, I should quite frankly be glad if it came to a fight." No wonder that, within a short time, Dostoyevsky had acquired the nickname of "the surly Russian."

Even the cure itself made him sour-tempered and irritable. Among the other residents, apart from the lyrical poet Konstantin Sluchevsky, only Princess Shalikova had pity on him. He had met Shalikova earlier at the home of Katkov, and now they made short excursions into the surrounding countryside together. But there weren't many places to walk quietly: each year twelve thousand people descended on the town. Dostoyevsky consequently spent most of his time sitting in his hotel room reading Pushkin. It was futile to attempt to communicate with these stupid Germans. At the post office they thought his name was "Tostoevsky," and when they made music all that came out was "oompah, oompah." "The way they pronounce their words is dreadful, and they suffer from a total inability to listen." The

only German with any style was Kaiser Wilhelm—"a tall old man with a
worthy appearance."

Dostoyevsky's letters to Anna are filled with longing. "Anya, beloved
Anya—I kiss you, *all* of you, do you understand?" If only she knew how
seductively she appeared to him at nights. Oh no, there was no danger of
his being tempted by other women—she was the only one who could tempt
him! How were the children? Were they safe and well, had they any friends
to play with? Each time he heard the sound of a child crying he was gripped
by evil forebodings.

The irregular passage of the mail brought him repeatedly to the point
of despair. Not until April 1875 did he receive confirmation of his suspicion
that his letters in 1874 lay for days on end in the post office at Staraya Russa
to await reading by the chief of police. In the eyes of the police he was still
a state criminal. "How many lawbreakers they close their eyes to," he burst
out, "while me they watch with suspicion and an eagle eye, a man who is
devoted to the Tsar and the fatherland with all his heart and soul. It is an
insult!"

There was little to begin with to suggest that the cure would do any
good. Dostoyevsky was troubled by a dry cough, and the cigarettes he smoked
only made it worse. Only after several weeks, when Dr. Orth began to
prescribe a new mineral water—Kesselbrunnen instead of Kränchen—did
he seem to make any progress. If only the weather were not so peculiar! It
was cold in the mornings and hot through the day. In the course of each
twenty-four hours he had to change his shirt several times. An epileptic
attack made him even more depressed; his head felt "like porridge." He
could understand the author of a Russian handbook who counseled epileptics
against drinking mineral water. Luckily, his appetite was normal: that must
be a sign that the cure was having the desired effect.

By the end of his stay he was perishing of boredom. He wanted to leave
this "accursed hole" before the end of the cure. He felt like a dessicated
mummy; not even Anna's seductive portrait was capable of arousing him.
The noise got on his nerves: residents shouted and yelled, knocking on the
doors and thumping up the stairs, while from the adjacent room came the
plunking of a piano and the babble of women's voices. And the prices! A
Frenchwoman was demanding two thalers for a little pomade. "I began to
wrangle and haggle, and at last I got it for one thaler. A hellish place—no
worse place is to be found in all the world!"

Dostoyevsky had thought of going to Paris to buy a pretty dress for Anna, but he did not have enough money. Instead, he made a quick excursion to Geneva and fetched a couple of fronds from the cypress tree on Sonya's grave. A pressed flower from the grave is still to be found inside his copy of the New Testament in the Lenin Library—he could never forget his firstborn.

During his stay in Ems Dostoyevsky had begun to make notes for *A Raw Youth*, in defiance of the doctor's orders that all intellectual effort was harmful to the cure. The work went slowly; it looked as though his epilepsy might rob him of both imagination and memory. "Now and then I am visited by a melancholy thought: what if I am no longer capable of writing? Well, we must wait and see."

When Dostoyevsky came back to St. Petersburg at the end of July 1874, there were not many months left before Nekrasov was due to start printing the first chapters of *The Possessed*. So that her husband should have peace for his work, Anna suggested that they should spend the winter in Staraya Russa. There their living expenses were lower than in St. Petersburg: General Yevtikhy Leontiev's villa was actually available for a rent of twenty rubles per month! Dostoyevsky mumbled something about the importance of taking part in the capital's social life, but in the end his "Minister of Finance" got her way.

The winter of 1874–1875 was a good time for the Dostoyevsky family. The children stayed healthy and brought the writer many joys. "Never have I seen a person with a greater capacity for entering into the world of children," wrote Anna. He put plenty of time aside for chatting and playing with them, and invariably kept a small surprise waiting in his desk drawer—caramels, raisins, and nuts. When he was in a really good mood he would even dance the mazurka with the family. "He danced as beautifully and with as much enthusiasm as a fiery Pole," Anna declared proudly.

Once again he got back into his usual working rhythm. He could only write at night, when silence reigned and there was no one to disturb him. One day he was observed by a priest who was on his way to morning service. "You're up early this morning, Fyodor Mikhailovich!" he remarked. "I haven't been to bed yet," was the gloomy reply.

When Dostoyevsky woke up in the morning he was generally confused by the night's thoughts and dreams. At such times it was best to leave him to himself for an hour or so. During morning coffee he would liven up, however, and when he began to dictate to Anna at around two o'clock in the afternoon, he would be at the top of his form. Then it was time for reading, usually the life of some saint, or a French novel. In mid-afternoon he would set out for his daily walk, and at five, refreshed by a small dram of vodka, he would sit down at the dinner table with his family. After an hour of storytelling to the children, it was time for an evening stroll with Anna. Then he would read the newspapers while Anna played solitaire, and by ten o'clock the house was quiet. The night's work could begin.

The favorable working conditions that prevailed in Staraya Russa meant that Dostoyevsky was able to make speedy progress with *A Raw Youth*. During a trip to St. Petersburg in February 1875, he received a visit from Nèkrasov who was in ecstasies over the first sections of it. "I was so thrilled that I sat up all night reading it. . . . Such freshness! Not in the work of any of our other authors does one find such freshness of description. In Tolstoy's latest novel I merely found repetitions of what I had read earlier—with the sole difference that previously he used to express himself better."

This visit must certainly have awoken memories of Nekrasov's enthusiastic reception of *Poor Folk* thirty years earlier. The comparison with Tolstoy must also have warmed Dostoyevsky's heart. He also considered *Anna Karenina* a "rather tedious" work. What was the public so wild about? Think of all the important questions in Russia that awaited solution—yet, here one was asked to show interest in a young officer who had fallen in love with a married woman! And why should Tolstoy be getting five hundred rubles per sheet when he, Dostoyevsky, had to make do with half that amount? It was unfair! Yes, he had to admit that he envied Tolstoy his advantageous working conditions, his being able to write when he felt like it and receive the price he asked for. But was it not also an advantage to be forced to complete a piece of work on deadline—would he not otherwise fall into lazy habits, Solovyov inquired? "Yes, of course, but if a writer grows lazy and writes nothing, that probably means he has nothing to say."

An unpleasant experience of this sojourn in St. Petersburg concerned Dostoyevsky's clash with the police. Immediately upon his arrival he was summoned to the chief of police, who confiscated his old temporary passport and demanded that he produce a permanent one forthwith.

"Where shall I get it?"
"That is not our affair."

"In St. Petersburg there are over twenty thousand people going around without passports, and you arrest a well-known author as though he were a common vagabond!"

"Yes, we know that you are well-known all over Russia, but we must observe the law. Why are you getting so worked up about it? Tomorrow or the day after tomorrow you will receive a residence permit, isn't it all the same?"

"Confound it, why couldn't you have said that in the first place, instead of starting to wrangle with me?"

The police had only wanted to show their zeal for power! The end of the story was that Dostoyevsky was allowed to keep his old passport. And not only that: in the summer of 1875 his police surveillance was brought to an end. He did not learn this, however, until 1880, when he applied to the Minister of the Interior concerning the surveillance. "Twenty-five years have now passed since I was pardoned and had my civil rights restored," he wrote. "In hundreds of pages I have given an account of my political and religious convictions. I truly hope that these convictions are of a type such that they do not give the authorities grounds to suspect my political morality, and permit me therefore to ask that I be released from police surveillance."

On his return to Staraya Russa, Dostoyevsky discovered that Anna was once again pregnant. His happiness at the prospective addition to the family tempted him to indulge in some surprising practical jokes. One morning he emerged from his bedroom looking gloomy. Did he feel unwell? No, everything was all right, except that there was a mouse in his bed! "I woke up with something scratching and scrabbling in my bed, and when I threw the blanket aside I caught sight of a mouse. Ugh, how horrible it was!" Anna gave instructions for the room to be searched from top to bottom, but without result. "It's the first of April, Anna—April Fool!" the writer cried merrily.

The first spa treatment had in spite of everything proved to have long-lasting good aftereffects. His cough had lessened in severity, and Dostoyevsky was in better condition than he had been for a long time. For this reason, in the summer of 1875 the doctors advised him to return to Ems.

This time he installed himself in Hotel Luzern, under the care of a Mme. Meuser, a tall, emaciated lady. "I do not know whether I shall manage to remain here," he reported in a letter home. The overcrowding in the Kurhaus was the same as before. The band in the park was even worse, now they mostly played the "Ems-Pastillen Polka." The place was swarming with Russians. Dostoyevsky knew none of them—neither did he wish to know these people who "idolize the Tsar and despise the Fatherland." The weather was terrible, the rain poured down without cease, the cure residents went around like wet chickens. In groups of twenty they stood gargling twice a day. "You should have heard that band!" His only consolation was the letters he received from Anna. "I must be the happiest person in the whole world," she wrote. "In my eyes our family, for all its individual disagreements, is wholly and fully exemplary."

The unaccustomed daily routine and the strenuous mineral-water drinking made it difficult for Dostoyevsky to complete *A Raw Youth*. "What pains me most is that I cannot get on with my work," he complained to Anna. "Here I sit suffering torments of doubt and loss, unable to find the strength to begin. No, this is not the way to write literary works—on order, under the whip; one must have time and freedom."

On the way home he met Pavel Annenkov, a close friend of Turgenev's, and asked him to deliver fifty thalers to his old rival. For more than a year now he had gone in fear that Turgenev might take revenge for the malicious character-portrait of Karmazinov in *The Possessed*. What if Turgenev were to hold him up to scorn in his new novel for not having paid a debt of honor? But Turgenev contented himself with protesting about the amount: was it not a *hundred* thalers he had lent him in Wiesbaden ten years ago? No, said Dostoyevsky; he had, it was true, *asked* for a hundred, but had *received* only fifty! Fortunately Anna succeeded in unearthing the letter, so that Turgenev was left disappointed.

A beautiful late summer awaited Dostoyevsky when he returned to Staraya Russa at the end of July. His son Aleksei entered the world on August 10. The birth went easily, and it was not long before Anna was once again able to help him with the conclusion of the novel. Not until the middle of September did they leave their summer abode, and by that time *A Raw Youth* was almost finished.

II

Dostoyevsky's editorship of *The Citizen* was of brief duration, from January 1873 until March 1874. It was, however, in this weekly newspaper that he began to publish *The Diary of a Writer*, the work that gradually won him influence on the life of Russian society.

The Citizen was Prince Meshchersky's personal property. The prince, an amateur writer and a grandson of Nikolai Karamzin, had friends at court and was well-known for his reactionary views. He considered, among other things, that it was now time to put an end to all liberal reforms in Russia. Because of his elevated position in the state he could not act as editor of the newspaper himself. Nevertheless, no article in it was printed without his approval, and his relations with the editorial department were not always of the best. In the autumn of 1872 the editor had resigned, and the prince was therefore on the lookout for a big name who could help to increase circulation.

Dostoyevsky's offer to assume the editorship was received with instant enthusiasm. The newspaper's aims—"to defend the monarchy and the authority of the Church, to unmask all the excesses of liberalism"—seemed to fit the author of *The Possessed* like a glove. "Never in my life have I met a man more conservative than Dostoyevsky," the prince wrote in his memoirs. "He was a loyal monarchist and a passionate adherent of the autocracy, and yet he had managed to end up in Siberia because of political crimes!"

Might not this man be the right person to take over the position of editor of *The Citizen?* the prince wrote to the head of the Third Department. Dostoyevsky had, after all, now become "deeply religious and profoundly devoted to the state." No one had known how to ridicule the stupidities of nihilism as he had. The secret police finally gave their reluctant consent, "but," they said, "the Third Department will under no circumstances accept responsibility for this person's future activity as editor."

In addition to fees for articles contributed by himself, the editor's post carried a monthly salary of two hundred and fifty rubles. But Dostoyevsky was soon to regret having accepted it. The work was hard and unpleasant. He himself had to correct all the articles and to be accountable for his co-workers. As the paper came out on Mondays, the weekends usually had to be spent in the editorial office. What was more, the censors were constantly at his heels. After only four weeks he had committed an indiscretion that brought him to the attention of the law.

It was, nevertheless, even more painful to observe how young people reacted to his appointment. So the author of *The Insulted and the Injured* had gone into the service of the reactionaries, had he? A turncoat, that's what he was. Well, now this "mystic" had really lost his wits. Was it not as they had said all along—that Perov's portrait showed an insane individual who belonged in a madhouse?

The work on the newspaper gave Dostoyevsky an excellent opportunity to get to know Russian reality "in the most minute detail." As a realistic writer he felt the need of this knowledge, and set eagerly to work. The newspaper's proofreader, the twenty-two-year-old Varvara Timofeyeva, has left an account of her first meeting with her superior:

> He was very pale, and looked tired and ill. . . . His face was somber and emaciated; it was as if each muscle in his sunken cheeks and high forehead was animated by thoughts and emotions. These thoughts and emotions sought constantly to break to the surface, but were forever held in check by the iron will of this thickset, gloomy, and unassuming man. He seemed entirely closed up—he made no movements, not a single gesture, except for the nervous and convulsive motion of his bloodless lips whenever he spoke.

A similar portrait of a taciturn, reticent man was given by Mikhail Aleskandrov, the newspaper's senior typesetter. It was hard to get close to him, Aleskandrov related, trying to explain why Dostoyevsky was so suspicious of strangers. Everyone knew that he had been in prison, but only a few knew *why* he had been sent to Siberia. Heaven only knew what people thought of him. What if they supposed he was a murderer or a rapist? Best to keep one's distance! "He laughed very rarely," Varvara noted.

As an editor he was without mercy. Pity the poor fellow who made alterations to his manuscripts! "Every author has his own style and consequently his own grammatical rules," he instructed his proofreader. "I put commas where I deem them necessary, and where I deem them unnecessary others must not put them!" The senior typesetter was lectured in a similar manner: "Remember that I never use superfluous commas: Never add or remove a single one!" His demand that the editorial staff should serve him with "the faithfulness of a dog" drew its aggrieved attention. Within a short space of time he had acquired the nickname "Spitfire."

Even so, he was not *always* difficult and irritable. According to Varvara, he possessed a decided charisma as he sat at his desk with his manuscripts and cigarettes. "He smoked almost continually," she related. "I can still see his thin, pale hands with their knotty fingers—around his wrists there were hollows, possibly the marks left by the prison manacles. I can still see him stubbing his 'dead men' out in the sardine can he used as an ashtray."

Dostoyevsky conceived a similar fondness for Varvara. There was something "exalted and inspired" about her, he thought, a striving toward the highest ideals that reminded him of his first wife. The fact that she had radical opinions merely increased his interest in her. What a stimulating task—to be the preceptor of this charming young girl! They began to make presents of pears and óranges to each other, and soon Dostoyevsky wanted to know what was her aim in life.

"I want to write . . . to do literary work," I managed to stammer out. And to my great amazement Fyodor Mikhailovich did not burst out laughing.

"You want to wri-ite? I see!" he said, drawing the words out. "And what do you want to write about? I mean, what do you plan to write—a novel, a tale, or perhaps some articles?"

"Something psychological . . . about people's inner lives," I mumbled anxiously, feeling an utter idiot.

"Do you suppose it is an easy matter to describe people's inner lives?"

"No, I don't. I am preparing myself to that end."

"There is in the entire world only one female author who deserves the appellation," he continued, grandly. "And that is George Sand! Do you really suppose that you can do as well as her?"

I froze with dismay. He had taken from me all my hopes for the future. . . . And beside myself, as in a dream, I repeated senselessly:

"I want to write! . . . I feel I must. . . . That is all I live for!"

"Really?" he inquired earnestly. "Well, then you must begin to write. But remember my advice: Never try to make anything up—neither plot nor narrative. Use what life itself gives you. Life is so infinitely richer than any of our inventions! Imagination can never give you what life can, however ordinary and everyday it may appear. You must show respect for life!"

Varvara also witnessed Dostoyevsky the creator at work. "Before he wrote his dialogues he would always rehearse them aloud or in a whisper five times over, accompanying the words with suitable gestures," she wrote admiringly. "It was as if he could *see* the character he was protraying." It comes as no surprise, therefore, to learn that during his walks Dostoyevsky once suddenly pointed at a passerby, saying: "Look, here comes my Raskolnikov!"

On the other hand, Varvara found it difficult to sympathize with her superior's strange views, as, for example, when he began to hold forth on the subject of the Russian people's "holiness" as opposed to the peoples of the West. If only she knew what offers he had received on the streets of Naples and Rome, sordid propositions from young lads, children, almost! That kind of thing would be unthinkable in Russia, he opined. Here the whole nation would condemn it as a sin. But in Western Europe immorality had quite simply become a habit.

"And this is the civilization which they wish to impose upon our people! Never will I give my consent to that! I shall fight them to the end of my days, and not give way one iota!"

"But it's not *that* kind of civilization they're seeking to bring us, Fyodor Mikhailovich!"

"Yes, it is! For there is no other kind of civilization. That is how it has always been, everywhere. And that is how it will be with us, if they start transplanting Europe over here by artificial means. The Roman Empire, too, perished because it began to import Greece. . . . Such transplantations always begin with luxury, fashions, scholarship, and art—and invariably end in sodomy and universal corruption."

It came as no surprise to Dostoyevsky to learn that the radical Varvara had some difficulty in accepting ideas like these. These liberals had no understanding of the apocalyptic age that had now begun.

"These people do not even understand that the end of the world is near . . . that there will soon be an end to their chatter about 'freedom' and 'progress'! They even fail to understand that the Antichrist was born long ago . . . and is on his way to us!" He said this with an expression which made me feel that he was announcing a great and dreadful event. Then he looked at me and asked me sternly:

"Do you believe me? I'm asking you a question—reply! Do you or do you not believe me?"

"I believe you, Fyodor Mikhailovich; I simply wonder whether you are not a little too eager and are therefore exaggerating a little. . . ."

He slammed his fist on the table and, raising his voice, wailed like a mullah from a minaret: "The Antichrist is coming! He is on his way! And the end of the world is near, nearer than people suppose!"

These speculations on recent history led to Dostoyevsky's developing a keener eye for the actual disparities in Russian life. There was nothing that indicated he had lost his concern for the insulted and the injured.

One day he told of an encounter he had had with two young law students who were returning home, happy and contented, from a merry evening at a restaurant, all the while declaiming Schiller's *Ode to Joy*. In their elevated mood, "with the ideal living in their souls," they caught sight of a prostitute, and they suddenly felt such abhorrence for this "creature" that they spat in her face. "What knowledge of the 'exalted ideal' can such people have when they are capable of doing something so base and vulgar! . . . And afterward they defend their 'lawful rights' by referring to legal theory!" To think that these wretches might have spat in Varvara's face, instead! A proud and pure girl making her way home from a night of work at *The Citizen*! A tremor passed through Varvara; she had to hide her face in her hands.

"You know," he concluded suddenly, with a convulsive, almost tortured smile, "I actually wish that had happened to you. What a defense I should have prepared for you! How I should have flayed those exalted, noble idealists who spit on a woman while they declaim Schiller after a merry evening at Dussot's!"

He could also be friendly and obliging when young writers brought him their manuscripts. "This thin, nervous man with the penetrating gaze in his gray eyes was able to read people's souls and to exert a powerful influence," wrote the twenty-year-old literary novice Alexander Kruglov. "You should avoid the political parties," Dostoyevsky admonished him. "It is Russia whom writers should serve, and no one else. The cause of the Russian people—that is the goal. A Russian writer must be a believer, for Christ alone is the true way."

A moralizing index finger is also evident in Dostoyevsky's articles for *The Citizen*. Together they constitute an entire volume in his collected works and display a wide range of concerns, from comments on foreign policy to discussions of literary works.

The most important contributions went into *Diary of a Writer*. In this peculiar one-man journal Dostoyevsky realized his dream of creating a new form for literary-philosophical journalism. His aim was to come into contact as closely as possible with his readers, to carry on an honest and straightforward discussion with his public and let it participate in his thoughts and plans.

The form of *Diary of a Writer* is free and unforced. One often has the impression that one is reading a personal confession, not merely a diary. "In this diary I want to talk to myself and let things come as they will," he wrote in the introduction. "What is it I wish to talk about? Everything that strikes me or that gives me cause for thought."

It has been asserted that Dostoyevsky was a better artist in his articles than he was a thinker in his novels. While this may be so, the writer whom we meet in the diary articles is a different person. It is true that both literary artist and journalist were inspired with ethical seriousness and a burning sense of commitment. But in his articles Dostoyevsky spoke more directly to his readers. He became a preacher rather than a doubter, and therefore also more vulnerable to counterarguments. As one reads these arguments, it is easy to be provoked. Some of them are melancholy examples of how chauvinism can make the most profound thoughts splash about in shallow, muddy waters. Not least, one is irritated by his tireless assertion of Russia's excellence, and by his bitter complaints that this excellence cannot be understood by Western Europeans.

"Russia can never be comprehended by reason." These words of the poet Fyodor Tyutchev might stand as a motto over most of Dostoyevsky's reflections on the distinctive qualities of the Russian character. Frequently, however, his choice of examples is unfortunate. Russians have no difficulty in understanding Western Europeans, he claimed in an article about the great Russian art exhibition of 1873—just consider their phenomenal grasp of foreign languages! Western Europeans will, on the other hand, forever lack comprehension of the Russian contribution to world culture. Russian poetry is untranslatable, and what qualifications does a Western critic possess for the understanding of a painting such as *Barge-haulers by the Volga*? Dostoyevsky did not even dare to imagine how these pictures would be received at the World Exhibition in Vienna.

Dostoyevsky's concern had little foundation in reality. The Russian painters received an effusive welcome in the West. Russia took twenty-nine medals, as many as England, and more than Denmark, Norway, and Sweden put together. Henrik Ibsen, one of the members of the jury, commented:

> The exhibition teaches us that in every sphere of the plastic arts Russia unquestionably stands upon the very heights of modernity. The most astringent and the most vigorous national self-perception is here allied to an unsurpassable technical skill, and it is in no way to be construed as a delusion, founded upon the striking impression conveyed by the unusual motifs, when I assert that Russia possesses an Academy that is fully the equal of that possessed by Germany, France, or indeed any other land.

The idea that the Russians were an entirely unique people soon became an important tenet of Dostoyevsky's preaching. Many would say it is a shaky tenet, for how could he reconcile it with his conviction that the Russians were capable of bringing about a fraternization among all the peoples of the world? When Dostoyevsky was later confronted by this paradox, he never managed to get beyond its initial postulate. He was quick to nip discussion in the bud, the French diplomat E.-M. de Vogüé recalled. "We possess the genius of all peoples and have in addition our own Russian genius. Consequently we are able to understand you, but you are unable to understand us!"

Dostoyevsky the publicist was considerably more penetrating when dealing with social and moral problems. One of the results of his articles was a lengthy correspondence with his readers, who in their turn provided material for fresh utterances. Politics, ethics, child abuse, the judicial system, the prevention of cruelty to animals, drunkenness, new trends in art and literature—there was scarcely an issue that was alien to this committed social thinker, and his reflections also frequently produced literary works of high caliber.

In an article entitled "The Environment" (1873), we encounter the central motifs of Dostoyevsky's thinking: the problems of crime and punishment, of human beings' responsibility for their own actions and those of others.

True to form, Dostoyevsky takes as his point of departure Russian reality, or, to be more precise, the new jury courts that had been introduced following the abolition of serfdom. The reform was intended to do away with the old corruption of the Russian judicial system, and Dostoyevsky was among those who welcomed it. At the same time, however, he saw that the new order might easily be abused by clever defense attorneys. It became a sport to see who could get the greatest number of clients acquitted. The question whether the accused were guilty or not seemed often to be only secondary. Indeed, when one read the sensational acquittal verdicts of the time, one could be forgiven for supposing that there were no culprits at all! All the blame was placed on the social environment.

Dostoyevsky gave an example of the harmful consequences of this attitude in A Raw Youth. In it, he has his pilgrim, Makar Ivanovich, tell of a soldier who confesses to committing a crime but is nonetheless acquitted. The attorney, or "bad conscience of the nation," has as usual made a splendid effort: all blame is to be placed on the brutalizing military environment. "Innocent" is the jury's verdict. But one cannot with impunity rob the individual of his right to expiation. For the soldier, the acquittal is a catastrophe. "When he was released he began to brood and fret; he neither ate nor drank, and did not talk to a soul. On the fifth day of his freedom he went off and hanged himself. 'That is what it is like to live with a sin on one's conscience,' Makar Ivanovich concluded."

For Dostoyevsky the ex-prison inmate, the theory based on the influence of the environment was quite unacceptable. To assert that crime did not exist, that there was no sin requiring expiation—that could only be done by people who had no God. It was true that Christianity preached mercy toward sinners. But Christianity also taught that it was the individual's moral duty to combat evil. It was precisely by making the individual responsible for his actions that Christianity acknowledged the individual's freedom. We must call evil by its name, Dostoyevsky wrote, but as we do so, we must not fall into Satanic pride and suppose that we ourselves are blameless. We bear a personal responsibility. If we had been better, the crime might perhaps not have taken place. Instead of exulting over the unfortunates who have committed crimes, we must feel pain in the consciousness of our own blame for those crimes.

Dostoyevsky's "crime report" thus became a powerful protest against the determinism of utilitarian philosophy. His theory of the individual's universal sin and guilt, which implies that each individual is guilty with regard to everyone and everything, became a few years later a cornerstone of Father Zosima's preaching. At the same time the article extended to another of Dostoyevsky's favorite ideas: that suffering has a purifying value for the individual.

The writer returns to this subject in *Vlas*, the story of the village lad who is seduced into taking a potshot at the communion bread and ends up seeing the Cross and the Crucified. Never did Dostoyevsky plumb the depths of the Russian soul more deeply than in this astonishing tale. Here we encounter the Russian need for self-abnegation and self-effacement, and also an ardent longing for penitence and salvation. Here is the great sinner who in remorse and atonement raises himself from degradation. Dostoyevsky knew this Russian. He too had gone to the utmost limit; his hosanna, too, had passed "through the blast furnace of doubt."

The novella *Bobok* bears witness to the *Diary*'s range. Here Dostoyevsky deals with an unsuccessful fellow writer who has recently been declared mad—"declaring other people mentally ill is something we are very good at here in Russia; yet none of us has yet displayed the power to make people saner." On a superficial level the story of the deceased man's "internment" and the conversation at the cemetery are full of burlesque humor. But gradually the laughter begins to stick in one's throat. Dostoyevsky had often thought before about "how without Christ everything upon earth would have become sinful and dirty." In this frightening metaphysical vision of shamelessness and depravity, he describes with great power the putrefaction of atheistic man. The soul stinks worse than the body in this *danse macabre*.

Even though with contributions like this Dostoyevsky enjoyed great success with the public, it soon became clear to him that he would have to move on from *The Citizen*. Throughout the autumn his clashes with the newspaper's owner grew more frequent. Prince Meshchersky found it difficult to accept that the editor should meddle with his manuscripts, and Dostoyevsky was strict about the type of reactionary utterances he was willing to print. When Meshchersky began to put forward the idea that rebellious students in the universities should be herded together so that they could more easily be kept under surveillance, Dostoyevsky quickly got out his blue pencil: "I have a certain reputation as an author, and what is more, I have children," he wrote to the prince. "For me to print this would be equivalent to suicide. Added to which, I feel the deepest revulsion at your views."

Not that his own political articles were that much more liberal. The pieces he wrote on foreign policy in the autumn of 1873 all stay safely within the official guidelines laid down by the Tsarist government, with well-aimed kicks at rebellious Poles and a glorification of Russia's "altruistic" foreign policy. "Russia is not afraid of people in Western Europe getting to know it better," he asserts, à propos of Prince Alfred's marriage to a Russian princess. If only the West could now have some trust in the Russians' self-sacrificing foreign policy and stop suspecting the Tsar of laying insidious plans against European civilization!

The paper's friendly attitude to Tsardom was nonetheless ineffective in preventing the censor from becoming steadily more troublesome. A cautious editorial intimation that the authorities were not doing enough to end the catastrophic famine in the province of Samara immediately led to the paper's being banned from the streets for seven weeks. Dostoyevsky had to promise to do better in the future. For a man with an enthusiastic disposition like his, it was frustrating to have such declarations of loyalty wrested from him by force. When in mid-March 1874 the paper received a warning for its deprecatory remarks about the Russified Germans in the Baltic provinces, he thought it prudent to tender his resignation. When he later resumed publication of *Diary of a Writer*, the project took the form of an independent one-man journal.

Understandably enough, it was with relief that Dostoyevsky reported at the end of March 1874 that his time as an editor was at an end. "It is as though a stone had been lifted from my soul. I want freedom. Now I have begun to work on *my own stuff*."

First, however, he had to "comply with the demands of the law" and atone for his "editorial peccadillo." Back in June 1873 he had been served with a summons for publishing an article in which Prince Meshchersky had quoted some of the Tsar's words without having obtained permission from the Court Minister. The sentence prescribed for this offense was two days' imprisonment, but Anatoly Koni, the liberal public prosecutor at the St. Petersburg District Assizes, had agreed that Dostoyevsky could put off serving it until it was convenient for him to do so.

On March 23 he was finally arrested and taken to the prison at the Haymarket. He certainly received no maltreatment. The jailer knew him, and he passed the time with *Les Misérables*. An excellent book, incidentally, he thought. Imagine that Tyutchev had said that his novel about Raskolnikov was so much better! On the following evening he returned home, pleased and satisfied, with toys for the children. Papa had been on a little excursion to Moscow. . . .

"Oh, what a good time I had in prison!" he exclaimed afterward. It had almost been like being back in Siberia again. "You really ought to serve a prison term!" he told Vsevolod Solovyov enthusiastically, when Solovyov visited him in jail. "But Fyodor Mikhailovich, you surely don't think I ought to go out and kill someone just to go to prison?" The writer smiled. "No, of course not. . . . You'd have to do something else. But quite seriously, a spell in prison would be the best thing that could happen to you." He expressed the same wish for Vsevolod's brother Vladimir: "A spell in a penitentiary would make you into a good and true Christian."

Dostoyevsky's comeback as a publicist was to be of great significance. Without his journalistic experience he would hardly have been able to become the novelist we know today. The *Diary* became a laboratory in which he tried out his ideas concerning the most important questions of the day. Not least, it gave him ever new material for literary works. Now he was already at work on a novel about rootless young people from "casual" families.

III

In the early spring of 1874 Varvara Timofeyeva came to see Dostoyevsky and told him that she had sat up all night reading *Notes from the Underground*. "I cannot free myself from the impression it has made on me. . . . What a terrible thing is a human soul! Yet at the same time, what a fearful truth!"

Dostoyevsky smiled and told her that Apollon Grigoryev had considered the book his masterpiece and had advised him always to write in this genre. "But I do not agree with him," he added. "The book is far too gloomy and disheartening. I have already overcome this attitude. Now I am capable of writing something that will be lighter and more reconciling. Yes, now I am working on a new book."

He was referring to *A Raw Youth*. In this *Bildungsroman* he wanted to give his version of the contemporary clash of the generations, and show that Russia's hope lay in the striving of young people to find their way to a "strengthening and binding idea" for their own lives and for the life of the fatherland.

True enough: compared with the gloomy finale of *The Idiot* and the apocalyptic atmosphere of ruin that characterizes *The Possessed*, the message of *A Raw Youth* does seem "lighter and more reconciling." Like *The Brothers Karamazov*, it is a novel of hope. But it too takes its starting point in the shadowy sides of Russian society. The country was in a state of upheaval— socially, because the aristocracy was threatened with disintegration, and morally, because more and more people had begun to take their own lives. Social unrest, suicide epidemics, and rootlessness—this was how reality appeared to Dostoyevsky from the editorial office of *The Citizen*.

In this uncertain era of conflict, when all norms were being questioned and in which there was no longer any common idea binding "fathers and sons," his greatest concern was for the younger generation.

Children had always been close to his heart, and now he himself had become an educator and paterfamilias. "The novel is to be about children, only about children, and about a hero who is very young," we read in one of the earliest notes. In the spring of 1874 he asked Anatoly Koni if he might be allowed to visit a prison for juvenile offenders in St. Petersburg. What would become of these unhappy young people who had been left completely to themselves, who came from "casual families" that lacked spiritual solidarity among their members? What if they were already going about dreaming of revenge on the society that had punished them? Or what if what they really wanted was a firm anchoring and spiritual guidance? "The novel's central idea is that the raw youth seeks a governing idea for his behavior, an idea of what is right and wrong. . . . In our society there is no such idea. But he thirsts after it, seeks it intuitively, and this is what this novel is intended to show."

How different this uncertain future was from the secure and attractive life of the aristocracy in the novels of Tolstoy! In *War and Peace* not even the Napoleonic wars can shake the foundations of the Rostov family. There the older generation serves as a loving but firm mentor of the younger, which in its turn provides a continuity with the succeeding generation. One generation follows the next, and all is characterized by solidity, stability, order, and calm. But, in reality, how relevant was this "landowners' literature" to contemporary Russia? "This literature has said all that it has to say," Dostoyevsky wrote in 1871. "Tolstoy has done an excellent job of reproducing the word of the aristocracy. But this word was also the last, and the new word which will succeed this landowners' word has not yet arrived."

A Raw Youth has aptly been called an "artistic polemic" against Tolstoy's portrayal of family life, the beautiful life-form that is proper to his aristocratic heroes. Dostoyevsky, on the other hand, wished to write "about disintegration." As a working title for his novel, he chose the word *besporyadok*, best translated as *disorder* or *chaos*. And indeed, the novel developed into a very chaotic book. He himself admitted he had "combined four novels into one"—and this is certainly no exaggeration. It is nevertheless possible to distinguish two "principal novels": the youth's own novel and the novel about his father, Versilov.

The book takes the shape of a chronicle written by the twenty-year-old Arkady Dolgoruky, a "casual member of a casual family." The first-person narrative helps to make the portrait of the central character intimate but also demonstrates its weaknesses in a work of such large proportions. Arkady has constantly to keep running around in search of information about what is going on; eavesdropping behind doors and curtains are the order of the day. The narrative's nervous, at times fussy tone is worsened by the compression in time: the principal action takes place in the course of three months, of which two weeks receive an exhaustive description.

Arkady Dolgoruky bears an illustrious name: Moscow itself was founded by a prince by the name of Dolgoruky. But Dostoyevsky's hero is far from being of princely origin. His lawful father, Makar Dolgoruky, once did service as a gardener on the estate of one Versilov, an aristocrat. Shortly after Makar's marriage to the serf-girl Sonya, Versilov visited his estate and seduced her. Makar had to accept that his master should take a serving-maid as a mistress in this way. Humbly, he withdrew and became a devout pilgrim. Versilov, for his part, began a restless wandering among Russian émigrés in Western Europe, where he almost forgot both Sonya and the two children he had had by her, Arkady and Liza.

The novel describes the events that take place when Arkady is only nineteen and considered a "raw youth." In Dostoyevsky's view, the transition from nineteen to twenty is of especially great significance in the life of a young man (he also addressed it in Alyosha in *The Brothers Karamazov*). One may surmise that a biblical model lies at the basis of this attitude. In the Old Testament, too, the importance of this "transitional age" is emphasized, the age at which a man must learn to distinguish between good and evil. Then, as Arkady begins his chronicle, Versilov has just summoned the young man to St. Petersburg, where after a long sojourn abroad the aristocrat has once more resumed his silent union with Sonya. Arkady is full of bitterness toward his father. Right from birth he has been, as it were, "farmed out" to strangers. He has only seen his father once, when he was ten years old.

He has a better memory of his mother's icon-like appearance. "Her face bore traits of naïveté, but not in any sense of stupidity; it was pale and anemic. Her cheeks were very thin, almost hollow, and her forehead was already covered in wrinkles; there were, however, no wrinkles around her eyes, which were large and open, and which always shone with a gentle and exalted light." His mother had once visited him at his boarding school in Moscow dressed like a poor peasant woman. Arkady can still remember nearly refusing to admit to his highborn schoolmates that she was his mother, and afterward feeling ashamed of himself and crying in his sleep. Confronted with the portrait of Sonya's faded beauty, even Versilov must stop short: "Russian women burn themselves out quickly . . . when they love they surrender everything at once—both the moment and their fate, their present and their future—they do not know how to economize, they do not save so as to have something in reserve, and they give their beauty to the man they love."

Arkady would prefer to avoid having anything to do with his father. He feels deeply wounded and betrayed by this Versilov who cannot even remember where he grew up. Being spiritually fatherless, he refuses to call him "father." But at the same time, his lack of spiritual contact has the effect of making Versilov seem fascinating and mysterious. Gripped by a strange love-hatred, he finds himself being drawn toward his father. His urge to solve the enigma of Versilov becomes irresistible.

When Arkady comes to St. Petersburg he is still obsessed by his great "idea"—that of becoming a second James Rothschild, who had recently left behind him the fabulous sum of one thousand seven hundred million francs. He considers that it should be possible to realize this idea by means of application and careful roulette-playing, and that then he will at last free himself from his environment and lord it over others. Through the power of gold he will compensate for his humble origins: money makes all men equal. Yes, money will bring him revenge for the humiliations he has suffered.

Characteristically, this idea vanishes on his arrival in St. Petersburg. In his quest to understand himself, Arkady finds his way into a society where the struggle for wealth and power is carried on devoid of controlling principles or great ideas. Yet he cannot avoid being influenced by this society. The aging Prince Nikolai Sokolsky tells him, "The life of every woman is an eternal quest for submission"; equally cynical is the young Prince Sergei Sokolsky, who has insulted his father, seduced his sister, and ends up in prison for forging stock certificates. Other strata of this society are also in the grip of moral anarchy. The poor girl Olga advertises for private pupils and meets up with a businessman who offers her fifteen rubles—"and if I find complete virginity, I will give you forty rubles more."

He discovers an alternative to this corrupt society in a revolutionary circle that is trying to bring about a spiritual revolution among the masses. But their collective lifestyle is alien to the loner Arkady. He refuses to love a humanity of the future. He prefers to "live for himself." Even without his great "idea" he feels the allure of consciousness of power. What value there is, for example, in the letter in his possession in which Princess Katerina Nikolayevna consults her lawyer about the possibility of having her father, Prince Nikolai, interned in a madhouse! If the contents of this letter were to become known to her father, he would quite certainly deprive her of her inheritance. And what would happen then to this "earthly queen" by whom both he and Versilov have been so charmed?

Dostoyevsky was to return to the theme of rivalry between father and son in *The Brothers Karamazov. In A Raw Youth* it is principally the psychological analysis of Versilov's character that demands attention.

Versilov bears an affinity to Stavrogin in *The Possessed*. They both originate with the "greedy, grasping type" of the great sinner. In both, the "low" element is identified with the unconscious or the insufficiently conscious. When Stavrogin commits his base deeds, he can never find justification for them. In *A Raw Youth* Dostoyevsky, apparently reaching back to the works of his youth, names the base impulse "the double." When Versilov suddenly destroys Makar's icon, when he suddenly insults his beloved in the coarsest fashion and even threatens her life, it is the double who is at work.

"Yes, it really is true that from a psychological point of view I am two people, and that makes me immensely afraid," he writes in a description of his double nature. "It is as though my double stood beside me. One is sane and sensible, but this double will stop at nothing to commit some meaningless action or other—sometimes even a practical joke—and God knows for what reason. One does it reluctantly, one resists it with all one's energies."

"What is a double, really?" Arkady asks. He too attempts to provide a reason for the stain on his father's character:

> The scene at my mother's house, that time he smashed the icon, unquestionably took place under the influence of the double. But it keeps occurring to me that there was a certain malicious symbolism behind his mode of conduct. There was manifested a certain hatred of the expectations of these women, a kind of rage at the fact that they had rights and could sit in judgment over him; and so, in a pact with his double, he had smashed the icon. Look, the rest of you—that is how your expectations will be smashed, too!

The fact that a person can see the folly of a decision is by no means an obstacle to that person's going ahead and, fully conscious, putting it into action. There need be nothing wrong about this—quite the contrary. There can be no synthesis without an antithesis, no salvation without sin. When the "double" finally disappears from Versilov's life, when in the epilogue he lies licking his wounds and lets Arkady's mother stroke his cheeks, he is only "a shadow of the former Versilov," a broken and burnt-out man.

But not even in the intensity of his contradictions is Versilov capable of being a spiritual mentor to Arkady. As an aristocrat he has become a victim of the upper classes' moral disintegration. And, since he himself lacks a moral center, he can give his son no firm foundation, either. Tormented by spiritual hunger, Arkady must be satisfied with abstract arguments and fine words. Versilov is really a representative of the liberal values Dostoyevsky himself had flirted with a generation earlier—the idea of culture as a substitute for God, of virtue without Christ. The sin of the fathers lies in their belief in a divine kingdom which has no heaven, no God.

If Versilov did ever once possess faith, he has at any rate long ago lost it. All that remains in him is a vague yearning for God, but his beautiful illusions are contradicted by his human person. He is, to be sure, wise, and, to be sure, he has performed many good deeds. But at the same time he illustrates that good deeds without God must forever remain egoistic and consequently evil. He wants to marry the mentally retarded Lidia, who has been seduced by Prince Sergei. He even assumes responsibility for their children but solely in order to irritate Katerina Nikolayevna, who by rejecting him has wounded his pride.

Instead it is the devout pilgrim Makar who becomes Arkady's mentor. In this embodiment of the Russian people's religious faith, the raw youth finds what Versilov cannot give him—an ideal of moral beauty. And the destruction of Makar's icon illustrates Versilov's despair at being unable to attain Makar's degree of religious insight.

Makar is a descendant of Prince Myshkin and also points forward to Father Zosima. While the eternal émigré Versilov is rootless and isolated, Makar the pilgrim is securely anchored in the spiritual communion of the Russian people. He has a fixed point in life to cling to. "Go your way, sell whatsoever you have, and be a servant to others," he says, quoting Christ to his avaricious age:

Then your days and hours will be multiplied a thousandfold, for you will not want to miss one single minute—you will want to enjoy each single one of them in your heart. Then you will gain learning not from books alone, but will stand face to face with God Himself, and the earth will shine more brightly than the sun, and there will no longer be any sorrow or sighing, but only one single incomparable paradise.

In the fact that even young people in Russia had begun to listen to words like these, Dostoyevsky saw the "lighter and more reconciling message" of A *Raw Youth.* "For from young men the generations grow," he wrote, concluding his novel.

*Perov's famous painting of
Dostoyevsky, 1872.*

*Konstantin Pobedonostsev.
Caricature, 1907.*

Dostoyevsky's house in Staraya Russa.

Dostoyevsky's "Kurtax-Karte," 1874.

*The Hotel Ville d'Alger,
where Dostoyevsky lived
in 1874, 1876, and 1879.*

*Nikolai Nekrasov.
Photograph from the 1870s.*

II

THE PROPHET

*"Lift up your minds and formulate your ideal.
You have sought the ideal before, have you not?"*

The year 1876 began in a hair-raising fashion for Dostoyevsky. Both his son and his daughter came down with severe attacks of scarlet fever. Fedya only barely survived. The father followed the progress of his children's illness with the greatest anxiety. If a note by Anna is anything to go by, he even said that he would have taken his own life in despair if his son had died.

This statement is characteristic not only of Dostoyevsky's love for his own children, but also of his concern for children in general. Shortly before Christmas 1875, he had met a little beggar boy in the street. The writer took the boy in hand and made him tell him about his life. His encounter with with this "begging boy," together with a visit to a Christmas tree party for children of the wealthy inspired him to write the moving short story "A *Christmas Tree Party and a Wedding*," which is a Russian version of Hans Christian Andersen's "The Little Match Girl." At the same time he began to visit children's homes and children's prisons. With great interest he asked his acquaintances to tell him all they could about their children's habits, language, and view of life, and soon concluded that in many respects children are a good deal more sensible than grown-ups.

Dostoyevsky also carried on this exhaustive study of the life of children during his sojourns abroad. He had a predilection for stopping in front of schools, listening to the conversation of the schoolchildren, and studying their playground games. He was well acquainted with the boys in the streets of Ems. One of these, a cobbler's son, he discussed in a letter to Anna. The boy was in great pain; his eyes were bulging and inflamed because his miserly father would not fork out a few kopecks for medicine and treatment.

The question of the adult maltreatment of children soon became one of the principal themes of *The Diary of a Writer*, the publication of which Dostoyevsky resumed in 1876. Here, with great passion, he discussed criminal cases in which parents were accused of having tortured their children— of having scalded them, beaten them until they bled, smeared them with their own excrement. And these very same parents were usually acquitted to tumultuous applause from the public! Stronger and stronger grew his desire to write a novel "about the Russian children of our time and their parents, about the mutual relationship between them." It is clear that even at this stage he had already begun to formulate many of the ideas that were later to form the basis of *The Brothers Karamazov*. If one were going to contest the way in which God had ordered the world, the sufferings of children were the best argument against that order. In this, Dostoyevsky was in agreement with the narrator of "The Legend of the Grand Inquisitor."

Whereas Dostoyevsky's novels generally appeared in book editions of two to three thousand copies, single volumes of the *Diary* were sold in more than double these quantities. And each month the journal in which it was serialized was distributed to nearly seven hundred different addresses across the whole of Russia. None of Dostoyevsky's other books received such a lively response. Indeed, his success tempted several people to forgeries.

One direct consequence of the *Diary* articles was a protracted correspondence with the readers. Dostoyevsky received several hundred letters each year, most of them filled with praise. "You are the poet of suffering, you are the most sympathetic, the most profound of all our writers!" one woman wrote. "May I be allowed to write to you again? Please say yes!" As he was not especially fond of writing letters, the pile of unanswered mail soon became a burden. "If I go to Hell, I will surely be condemned to write ten letters a day for my sins." Still, the readers' letters were a source of great joy. "It is always more welcome and more important to a writer to hear a few kind and encouraging words direct from a sympathetic reader than it is for him to read laudatory reviews of his work in the press. I really do not know why this should be so, but when the praise comes straight from the reader, it somehow rings more true," he wrote to one of his correspondents.

Most of Dostoyevsky's other replies have been lost, but the readers' letters of gratitude for his responses give us some idea of what they were like. He tried to help in whatever way he could, with money, services, and recommendations, but first and foremost with words of consolation amid life's trials. A striking number of appeals for assistance came from young women. One had failed her exams, another was in doubt as to which school she should choose, a third wanted advice concerning her prospective marriage. Dostoyevsky's replies were not particularly original: get yourself an education, be kind to your parents, don't marry without love. But occasionally, he gave his young correspondents something to think about, as for instance in calling attention to the moral superiority of giving and the moral inferiority of demanding: "A Christian says: 'I must share my property with my neighbor and serve my fellow human beings;' but a communard says: 'Yes, share your property with me, and serve me, who am poor.' The Christian is right, the communard is wrong."

There is a plainly Christian tendency in these instructions and suggestions. "The principal thing is to promote the moral sense," he noted in one of his letters, and one could best do this by setting a good example to others: "Believe me, to set a good example, even if only in a limited sphere, is of great importance. A firm desire to lead a righteous life without falsehood sows confusion among the frivolity of other people and exercises an influence on them."

Soon young people began to visit "the prophet." It might be a young theology student who had seen him praying devotedly in church, and who now came to confess to him his doubt in God's existence. Good heavens— had unbelief now gained a foothold even in the seminaries? Was it not as he had always said: men of the cloth were particularly tempted by atheism? But what would happen if people began to live "without God, without Christ, without faith in the only-begotten Lamb and His redeeming blood? No, that will never come to pass—never, never!" he decided, casting an enigmatic gaze into the distance. "In the most difficult hours of my life, when I felt abandoned by everyone and everything, I always found a support in God. From my own experience I know that there is nothing worse than unbelief. Let all who wish to be convinced of the truth of this make a visit to the *ostrog*. If they do not commit suicide, they will return believers."

Materialism and miserliness could, in his eyes, never be an alternative to faith. "In our time people believe that freedom consists in having enough money; in reality this is not freedom, but slavery to money. The most exalted freedom consists, on the contrary, in abstaining from the amassal of wealth, in sharing what one possesses with all and going out to serve them. If everyone were to do that, all men would be brothers. And where there is brotherhood there is also equality."

The young teacher Khristina Alchevskaya came all the way from Kharkov in order to meet the publisher of *The Diary of a Writer*. "When one saw his suffering-filled countenance, his deepset, narrow, lifeless eyes, the deep wrinkles, each of which seemed to have its own biography, it immediately became plain that this man had thought much, suffered much, and endured much," she wrote in her memoirs. "It was as though life had almost been extinguished in this infirm body." But it was not easy to pursue discussions with someone who dismissed *Anna Karenina* with a wave of his arm and who valued the Great Russians far above Ukrainians. When she refused to answer his inquiry as to whether she believed in God, he grew bewildered. "So you don't believe! That is not good! We must have a serious talk about this another time!"

Dostoyevsky was now acquiring a more positive opinion of Russian youth. The girls who visited him were a far cry from the nihilists with their closely-cropped hair; they were wonderful young people, magnanimous, full of a sincere desire to live for others and be of use to society. "Such simplicity, such naturalness and frankness of feeling, such purity of heart and mind; the most genuine seriousness and the most genuine humor!" Yes, he felt the greatest respect for this new Russian youth, especially since the young men had begun to enlist as volunteers in the war against the Turks. Enthusiastically he wrote to the friend of his younger days, Stepan Yanovsky:

> Mark my words—the prospects here in Russia are not at all so bad as they once seemed. The principal thing is this: everything points to the fact that in wide circles of society there exists a sincere striving for a new and authentic life, that there exists a deep faith in a speedy turnaround in the mode of thinking prevalent in the intellectual world, a mode of thinking which in its lack of understanding has always been alien to our people.

It is probable that Anna was not always indifferent to the admiration of young girls for her husband. When she thought it was becoming too much of a good thing she had a sure method of giving her "Papa" a mental nudge—playing on his ungovernable jealousy.

Some of these escapades were rather ignominious and could easily have had catastrophic consequences. In the spring of 1876, for example, Anna sent her husband an anonymous letter. "As soon as your wife thinks you are gone, she behaves like a dove which, out of joy at being able to spread its wings, frolics beneath the free sky with no thought of returning to its nest," the letter says. "And should you doubt the truth of my words, just take a look at the medallion she wears around her neck, and there you will learn who it is she carries in her heart."

How would "Papa" react to an anonymous epistle of this kind? What if he were to throw it in the wastepaper basket? But no—Anna was not disappointed:

I sat down at my usual place at the writing desk and began the conversation with a few questions. He maintained a sullen silence, striding to and fro about the room with heavy, measured paces. I could see that he was seething inwardly, and suddenly felt sorry for him. To break the silence, I said:

"Why are you so bad-tempered today, Fedya?"

He gave me an angry look, took another few paces around the room, and stopped in front of me: "Are you wearing your medallion?" he asked, breathlessly.

"Yes."

"Let me see it."

"Why? You've seen it many times before."

"Let me see your medallion!" he shouted at the top of his voice. I realized I had pushed the joke too far and undid my collar in order to pacify him. But I did not manage to take the medallion off myself. Fyodor Mikhailovich was unable to control his rage any longer. With all his strength he tore from my neck the thin chain he had bought for me in Venice. When he found the medallion he went quickly over to the writing desk; bending over the medallion, he began to study it. I saw that his hands were shaking so badly that he almost dropped it.

"It's all very well for you to laugh, Anna," Dostoyevsky said, when he finally discovered that the medallion merely contained a picture of Lyubov and himself. "But just think what a misfortune might have come of this! In my rage I might have strangled you by mistake!"

Nevertheless, Anna did not keep her promise never to provoke his jealousy again. A few months later, when she had just had an encounter with her former fiancé, she could not restrain herself from making the following outburst in a letter to Ems: "Whom do you suppose I have met? Him!!! Yes, now you can be jealous and guess who I mean. Details will follow in my next letter." "Yes, just give me the details," Dostoyevsky replied, gloomily. "Even so, you probably have something to hide. What dress were you wearing? But don't suppose that jealousy increases love, or that it helps to torture a man with jealousy."

The spiritualistic séances that Dostoyevsky attended in St. Petersburg during this time were another stimulating experience. He was by no means lacking in appreciation of the era's quest for "the fourth dimension," and followed the experiments with delight mixed with alarm, to begin with, at any rate. Gradually the rumors concerning dancing tables and mysterious knots became so fierce that the foremost scientist in the land, Professor Dmitry Mendeleyev, was asked to appoint a commission of inquiry. The report concluded that spiritualism was nothing but fraud and superstition. Dostoyevsky was not entirely satisfied with this easy conclusion. It would surely be better to inquire how such a phenomenon could arise—it could hardly be eliminated by means of "mathematical proof." His preoccupation with occult matters is mirrored in Father Zosima's reflections on the possibility of contact with "other worlds." But for Dostoyevsky, too, spiritualism was in the last analysis an unacceptable phenomenon that stood in contradiction to the Church's teaching. No, he simply *would* not believe in this —it was worse than atheism. Anna was of the same opinion; after her husband's death she disassociated herself completely from the attempts of the spirtualists to establish contact with him.

It was probably during these séances that Dostoyevsky came into contact with Aleksander Aksakov, Emanuel Swedenborg's great prophet in Russia. There is reason to believe that he had considerable sympathy for Swedenborg's theory of correspondences and his biblical interpretations. But when the Swede reported his conversations with people who had long ago died, Dostoyevsky gave up. "That his book about heaven, hell, and paradise is sincere and not mendacious, there can be not the slightest doubt—but there can be no doubt either that it is the fruit of a morbid hallucination."

A loan from Anna's brother meant that in the spring of 1876 they were able to buy the summer cottage that for several years they had rented in Staraya Russa. It occupied a beautiful site on the bank of the River Pererytitsa, and was equipped with a bathhouse, stable, and barn. A corner room on the second floor had been converted into a study. Dostoyevsky found these rural surroundings thoroughly congenial. He was very fond of animals, and had an especial liking for feeding pigeons. To get milk for the children they used to rent a cow from some peasants, and many were the tales of how Dostoyevsky would wander about the streets looking for it when it failed to return home at the usual time. It was in this "cattle town" that he later set the action of *The Brothers Karamazov*. The house itself (which has now been turned into a museum) has many points of similarity to Fyodor Karamazov's in the novel.

Dostoyevsky's increasing social contacts and the demanding nature of his work on *The Diary of a Writer* were taking an ever greater toll on his nervous strength. Even though his epileptic attacks were no longer so violent or so frequent, they were nonetheless extremely troublesome, and in addition his breathing was becoming more and more difficult because of his bronchial catarrh. In the summer of 1876, therefore, he set out once again for Ems.

As usual, the journey was unpleasant, and this time the unpleasantness began while he was still on Russian soil. Dostoyevsky traveled in the company of a merchant who sat spitting all the time—eventually there were "whole lakes" in the compartment. It was not merely abroad that people lacked culture and breeding! And yet the *Diary* boasted several thousand readers! His mood became even gloomier on his arrival in Germany, where he shared a compartment with six Germans who kept making offensive remarks about the sorry state of the Russian army. What, only six cartridges to each soldier? Dostoyevsky flew into a rage and said he thought they ought to beware of underestimating the Russians' strength. But the Germans merely sat complacently, smiling at this stuttering hothead.

On July 19 he reached Berlin, where in the zoo he saw a real live orangutan. The high point of his visit was, however, a lady who had strayed into the gentlemen's toilet. "She saw everything—literally everything—for no one had a chance to conceal anything!" he relates enthusiastically. "I don't know whether she managed to find the ladies' room afterward. If she was English she must surely have died from mere prudery alone. But there was no suggestion of laughter. The Germans merely kept sullenly silent; at home everyone would have roared with applause."

Dostoyevsky's most reasonable offer of board and lodging came once again from Mme. Bach at the Ville d'Alger. She had, it transpired, become a widow in the interim, and now sat with a suitor on the bench in front of the hotel. Dostoyevsky advised her to marry quickly.

This was his third stay in Ems. People smiled and nodded to him in the street when they recognized him. "There goes Dostoyevsky!" He, in turn, began to take a less embittered view of the Germans. He could not help admiring the girl who served him his mineral water. She always remembered the dose he was supposed to have. And the like of the serving-maid at the hotel, who drudged from five in the morning until half past ten at night, was not to be found in Russia. "Here everyone has a job to do," he writes in the *Diary*. "Here everyone works, not just the serving-maids but also the hotelier."

Dr. Orth was able to reassure Dostoyevsky that he still had many years ahead of him, and prescribed Kränchen with milk morning and evening, in addition to gargling with Kesselbrunnen. The writer felt wretched, with a dry cough and persistent throat spasms. Concerning his daily program he wrote to Anna:

> I get up at six and begin my drinking at seven. It takes an hour and a half. The band plays to an audience of six thousand. At half past seven I have coffee and biscuits; the coffee is dreadful, but I have a good appetite. . . . At one I am given a wretched dinner: two plates of soup, beef, potatoes, and compote (at a price of two marks). But the drinking leads to increased appetite, so I eat as though I were having dinner at Dussot's. At five o'clock I drink mineral water again while I listen to the band. Then I go for a walk, and at eight I have tea and beef, before finally retiring to bed at around ten.

He had hoped to write something for the *Diary*, but as usual it was difficult to find peace for work; there was tramping on the stairs, the banging of doors, howling and baying from the room next door. His reading did not go much better. In the town library he got hold of Emile Zola's latest novel, *Le Ventre de Paris*. "God, what filth! The whole thing is so repulsive that it is only with difficulty that I can bring myself to read it. And yet back home people are going around shouting that Zola is a celebrity, a master of realism!"

It was just as well that he had letters from his "angelic wife." Next time he would damn well take her with him. First they would take a trip to Munich's famous "Wunderfrau," especially since she almost never took payment for the treatment she offered. And if that did not work, they could always return to Ems for the waters. His letters to Anna grew more and more ardent—now she had become his "alpha and omega." "I worship each single atom of your body and soul, I kiss the whole of you, the *whole* of you, for all this is *mine, mine!*" As soon as he gets home he will devour her! In spite of Anna's blushing deletions, the letters display a sensuality of unusual power.

Compared to Anna, the ladies of Ems were meager fare. "There are a number of attractive ladies down here, all in exquisite dresses, but I don't even give them a glance," he asured his "sovereign." With one of them, the wife of the radical critic Yeliseyev, he formed an enmity when she rose against one of his bitter attacks on the nihilists. Not even at the spas could these damned socialists control their materialistic instincts: they even drank the waters according to the formula "the more the better!"

Dostoyevsky appears not to have been a particularly assiduous church-goer during this visit. He wrote not a word on the subject of the newly built Orthodox St. Alexandra's Cathedral, to which a year earlier he had donated three thalers.

It was at least gratifying that Dr. Orth seemed pleased with the way his treatment was progressing. To Dostoyevsky's query as to whether his illness had now run so far that it must be nearing its conclusion, the doctor merely laughed and told him he could easily hope to live for another fifteen years— "always, of course, presupposing a good climate and a careful diet, and assuming that you do not catch cold and do not abuse your energies." The hardworking writer probably did not know whether to laugh or to cry.

Progress was also made with the distribution of Dostoyevsky's works. In the summer of 1876 excerpts from *The Diary of a Writer* had been published in the *Journal des Débats*. On his return to Russia the writer was instructed by Pobedonostsev to send the *Diary* to the Tsar. "I have long dreamed of the happiness of being allowed to bring my work before your Imperial Majesty," Dostoyevsky's letter declared. "Your Majesty, forgive me my outspokenness, do not judge with too much severity one who loves you so passionately: let him continue to send you the monthly issues of *The Diary of a Writer*." Great must have been his joy when a short time later the Court Marshall was able to report that the Tsar had graciously consented to become a free subscriber to the *Diary*.

Now that Dostoyevsky had started to gain a foothold at court, the circle of his acquaintances soon began to expand considerably. From the winter of 1876–77 onward he was a regular guest in the salons of St. Petersburg— in the homes of the radical Anna Filosofova, of the gifted Countess Sofya Tolstaya and, most importantly, of his friend Yakov Polonsky, where he was able to meet celebrities such as the politician Count Witte, the journalist Aleksei Suvorin, the musician Anton Rubinstein and the painter Ilya Repin. "Everywhere he was cordially received, not only as an outstanding intel-lectual personality, but also by reason of his good-natured disposition," Anna writes. But he did not fit very well into this high-born society. Even a good friend such as Yelena Stakenschneider was forced to admit that he had much in common with a "petty bourgeois." It is, however, certain that he made an impression. "Once one had seen him, one never forgot him," E.-M. de Vogüé remarks. "He was a mirror-image of his works, of all that he had experienced. . . . His lips, his eyebrows, every fiber in his face quivered, as from a nervous illness. But when this face blazed up in anger one was always sure that one had seen it in the prisoner's dock or among street mendicants. On the other hand, his face also expressed on occasion the melancholy gentleness of the saints in the old Slavic icons."

Anna preferred to stay at home with a good book while her husband went out—it was not so easy for her to find a dress that was suitable. When he returned home at around one o'clock in the morning, she would have tea ready, and then he would have to tell her about the evening's discussions with counts and princes. Not all of these were equally agreeable, but in Anna he always found a ready consoler for the distress he had been caused in the course of the evening. "How petty were these attempts to wound Dostoyevsky's self-esteem!" she exclaimed in her memoirs. And Dostoyevsky would thank his wife for her support by showering her with presents: dresses, chemises, earrings and bracelets, for as long as the money held out and their prospects looked good.

This hectic social life soon began to have serious consequences for Dostoyevsky's health. In March 1877 alone he had at least five attacks of epilepsy. His head felt like lead, and he was also tormented by a strange nervous laughter. "His seizures usually began with a terrible, inhuman shriek," Anna said later in a newspaper interview. "When after much exertion I came running into his study—the room between us was filled with books—his legs could barely carry him, and his face was distorted with pain. I managed to take hold of him from behind and lay him down on the floor." As a rule, the attacks occurred at night, and so Dostoyevsky lay on a wide divan, so that he should not fall and hurt himself. When he came to himself, he would remember nothing of what had happened. "An attack?" he would say in a mournful, pathetic voice. "I have them so often." After that he would fall into a shallow sleep. A sheet of paper falling from the writing desk would be enough to wake him, and then he would jump up and begin to mumble words which no one could understand. After severe attacks he would be incapacitated for several days. Possessed by a strange terror, he would wander around the apartment in a daze, looking for his wife.

The discussions that winter were principally concerned with the Russians' responsibility for the Slavic peoples of the Balkans, who were now being pressed ever harder by the Turks. Was it not time to help these brothers in need? "There are tasks that cannot be measured in rubles," Dostoyevsky opined. Katkov's bellicose leading articles in the *Moscow Gazette* received his full support, and at the beginning of 1877 he wrote on behalf of the inhabitants of St. Petersburg a letter to the Tsar on the subject of the sufferings of the Slavs. "We are ready to lay our lives and our property at Your Majesty's feet in this cause," the letter declared. When on April 12 the Tsar made his declaration of war, Dostoyevsky immediately went to the Kazan Cathedral to pray for the Russian armed forces. "I knew that at important moments he usually prayed in silence and solitude," Anna wrote. "Half an hour later I found him in a remote corner of the cathedral. So affected had he been by his prayers that he scarcely recognized me." At last the Russian people themselves, with the Tsar at their head, had risen to the struggle for their Slavic brethren!

Instead of making his annual cure-trip to Ems, in the summer of 1877 Dostoyevsky traveled to Maly Prikol, an estate in the province of Kursk that belonged to Anna's brother. The doctors were of the opinion that a spell of taking the waters there would do him good. Because of the troop transports, the journey was an arduous one. Dostoyevsky shortened the train time by strolling around the cars and treating the heroic soldiers of the fatherland to cigarettes.

Later he had to return to St. Petersburg to get out the summer issue of the *Diary*, while Anna went on a pilgrimage to Kiev together with the eldest children. It was a sad separation. Immediately after his arrival in the capital he was knocked to the ground by a violent attack that made "his soul dark." Why did Anna no longer write that she had dreamed of him? "After all, if you don't dream of me, you must dream of someone else." And he who prayed to her as though she were an icon! She could be damned cold, this angel; cold and mysterious—that was what she was.

A brief excursion to Darovoye, the estate on which he had spent his childhood, was an exhausting experience. The train took ten hours to cover 150 kilometers. "Everyone knows the motto of the Russian railroads," he complained in *The Diary of a Writer*. "It is not the railroads that exist for the public, but the public that exists for the railroads."

The re-encounter with Darovoye brought him happiness nevertheless. In only a few days he revisited all the places that he remembered so well from his childhood years. The peasants invited him to tea; several of them could still recall the helpful little Fedya they had known in summers long ago. He spent a lot of time sitting on a tree stump making notes, the peasants reported afterward. Perhaps it was here that he conceived the idea of sending Ivan Karamazov to buy forested land in Cheremoshnya?

On receiving the news of Nekrasov's death at the end of December, Dostoyevsky once again sat down to read his poems. In spite of political disagreements, he clearly felt a sense of kinship with the "wounded heart" that had sung its unprecedented words about the great sufferings and bitter fate of the common Russian people. "In this respect he deserves a place in Russian poetry just beneath Pushkin and Lermontov," he said in his funeral oration. "Above, above!" said Georgy Plekhanov, who together with a large group of armed revolutionary comrades had come to salute the radical poet. Pushkin and Lermontov had, after all, been mere "Byronists." "Not above, but certainly not beneath Pushkin!" was Dostoyevsky's slightly irritated response. There was a limit, after all!

At about the same time, Dostoyevsky was elected a corresponding member of the Russian Academy of Science, a distinction that only the most important writers are accorded. When in February 1878 he was offered the Latin diploma, he hastened to accept. With his "modest and insignificant contributions" had he really deserved this honor?

By virtue of *The Diary of a Writer*, Dostoyevsky's name was now known all over Russia. His awareness that he was starting to become a power factor that could have influence on Russia's historical development gave him the idea of expanding his publicistic activity. During the marketing of his journal he kept a lookout for "men of steadfast character with a clear view of the cause." "In my journal I could, perhaps, gather together all the sincere and honorable people who love Russia," he wrote.

More and more often now he received letters from young Russians who asked him to be their "flagbearer" and "leader." At last they had found a man who not merely talked about the people, but knew them from his own experience. "What he writes and feels is a fact," the subsequently famous physiologist Ivan Pavlov wrote to his fiancée, who also experienced Dostoyevsky's ability to pentrate the soul's "mysterious, unconscious depths."

He never forgot, however, that he was first and foremost a *writer*. Soon readers learned that he wished to take a rest from the *Diary* so as to work on his new novel, *The Brothers Karamazov*. He felt that as a writer he still had much ground to cover. On Christmas Eve, 1877, he wrote a "memo for the whole of my life," which reads as follows: "1. To write a Russian *Candide*. 2. To write a book about Jesus Christ. 3. To write my memoirs. 4. To write the epic *Requiem*. NB: All this, in addition to my new novel and the planned issues of *The Diary of a Writer* will take at least ten years' work, and I am already fifty-six."

An important source of inspiration for Dostoyevsky's last novel was the lectures that Vladimir Solovyov gave at the beginning of 1878 on the subject of the "God-man." In this young religious philosopher Dostoyevsky recognized features of the friend of his youth, Shidlovsky—it was as though Shidlovsky's soul had taken up residence in him. With Solovyov he discussed Nikolai Fyodorov's ideas about the resurrection of the fathers. The awakening of dead men to life was for Fyodorov a "project" that could probably only be realized when human beings had begun to live together in brotherhood, in a great family united in active love. With his speculative cast of mind, Dostoyevsky had considerable sympathy for these daring thoughts. "The resurrection of our forefathers depends on us," we read in the notes for *The Brothers Karamazov*. At the same time he stressed that this philosophy did not necessarily have to conflict with the teachings of the Church. "Solovyov and I believe in a real, literal, personal resurrection, one that will take place here upon earth," he wrote in a letter.

Later, in the spring of 1880, Dostoyevsky attended Solovyov's doctoral disputation, where he took special note of the following remark by the candidate: "I am deeply convinced that humanity is in possession of considerably greater knowledge than it has so far managed to express by means of art and science." Was this not what he himself had felt during his work on *Karamazov*—that he had managed to express only a twentieth of what he wanted to say?

In politics it was easier to express oneself, and in this field he made no secret of his opinions, either. He was certainly no maker of compromises. He declared his views coarsely and intransigently, without playing to the gallery. People were not to think he was one of those who "save hearts, free souls, and dispel sorrow." "I am not adept at singing cradle songs, even though I may have made attempts in that direction. There are plenty of people in our time who need to be lulled to sleep."

Many of his utterances in the times to come were to prove extremely unpopular. When in the spring of 1878 Vera Zasulich was indicted for her sensational attempt to assassinate the military governor of St. Petersburg, he horrified his conservative friends by coming out in favor of her acquittal.

The revelations concerning the military governor's brutality had made a strong impression on him, but here first and foremost he wanted to emphasize his attitude to sin and expiation: "Punishment will do no good in this case. What the courts ought to say to the accused is: 'You have a sin on your conscience; you wanted to kill a person, but you have already atoned for your sin, so go your way and do not do anything like this ever again . . .' "I know that we have no such legal formula," he added, when the acquittal was a fact, "but now she will merely become a heroine, and that is not good."

He viewed with great concern the unrest that followed in the wake of Zasulich's acquittal. The authorities annulled the verdict and hardened their attitude toward the students; antipathy toward radicals spread to the common people. When students came to Dostoyevsky and complained that the city's butchers had given them a thrashing, he reproached them for having broken with the people: "The forces of democracy have always, everywhere, been *for* the people. But in our country the intellectuals have thrown in their lot with the aristocracy and have gone *against* the people. They go out to the people 'in order to do them good' but they have contempt for the people's customs, for their entire ideological foundation. And contempt cannot lead to love!"

Soon there came evidence of even greater recognition. The Tsar asked Dostoyevsky to hold conversations with the Tsar's youngest sons and thereby influence their spiritual development. Even after the first meeting Dostoyevsky thought he could confirm that Paul and Sergei were in possession of "good hearts and rare intelligence." He also became acquainted with the Tsar's brother, General Admiral Konstantin, and his son, Grand Prince Konstantin Romanov, who had himself begun to write. "A haggard, sickly-looking man with a long, thin beard and an unusually melancholy and thoughtful expression on his pale face"—thus does Dostoyevsky figure in Konstantin's diary.

Dostoyevsky's groveling admiration for the Tsar and his family has often aroused wonderment among his readers. Had he not been banished by the Tsar, had it not been he who had exposed the Tsar's "houses of the dead"? When the famous English correspondent Donald Mackenzie Wallace asked such questions after listening to Dostoyevsky's respectful utterances about Tsar Nikolai, the following reply came from the Slavophile Ivan Aksakov: "For you foreigners this is doubtless difficult to comprehend, but for us Russians it is perfectly simple—it is a national characteristic."

In the spring of 1878, Dostoyevsky was invited to an international conference about authors' rights being held in Paris. In a letter signed by the organizing committee's president, Edmond About, he was described as "one of the most celebrated of our foreign colleagues." Dostoyevsky willingly accepted the invitation. Nothing would please him more than to take part in a conference under the chairmanship of Victor Hugo, "the great writer who with his genius had such powerful influence on me even as a child." He would certainly have done his utmost to get to the conference, but fate decreed otherwise.

A few months earlier, Dostoyevsky had sought out one of St. Petersburg's fortune-tellers, one Mme. Field. From her he received two prophecies: that he would soon attain a degree of celebrity such as he could scarcely imagine, and that within a short space of time he would lose one of the members of his family.

The writer's son Aleksei had long been plagued by convulsions. On May 16, 1878, he died after an attack that lasted for more than two hours. "Fyodor Mikhailovich kissed the little one, made the sign of the cross three times over him, and burst into tears," Anna related. "He had loved Alyosha with a strange, almost morbid love, as though he had had a premonition that he would die young. His pain was made all the worse by the fact that the child died because it had inherited his epileptic illness."

Instead of going to the conference in Paris, Dostoyevsky now undertook a pilgrimage with Vladimir Solovyov to Optina Pustyn, where he had three meetings with the venerable monk Ambrosius, the prototype of Father Zosima in *The Brothers Karamazov*. The pious monk made a deep impression on him, and the consolation Father Zosima gives the grieving peasant woman in the novel is in reality a greeting from Ambrosius to the inconsolable Anna Grigoryevna:

> "Yes, thus did Rachel weep over her children; she would not be consoled, either," said the elder Zosima. "That is the lot of mothers upon earth. You will not allow yourself to be consoled. Be inconsolable then, and weep! But every time you weep, you must know that your little boy is one of God's angels. He sees you from heaven and is happy because of it. He sees your tears and draws God's attention to you. In your great sorrow you will continue to weep for a long time to come. But in the end your sorrow will be transformed into quiet, humble joy. Then you will attain the purity of heart that delivers from sin. But I shall remember your little boy during the prayers for the dead. What was his name?"

"Aleksei."

"A handsome name. Is he called after the servant of God Aleksei?"

"Yes, father, he is."

"A great saint! I shall remember you in my prayers. I shall also pray for your husband."

After his pilgrimage to Optina Pustyn, Dostoyevsky also felt that he had attained "the purity of heart that delivers from sin." It was his gentle eyes that were now his most striking feature, the seventeen-year-old Anatoly Aleksandrov related concerning his meeting with the writer in Staraya Russa. "He had very lively and wakeful eyes, it was as if he could see through one's soul, with all its secret loops and bends. But there was no stern condemnation, no malignant irony in this gaze. No, he looked at one affectionately and encouragingly, creating openness and trust. His voice was also uncommonly sincere and cordial."

When the family returned to St. Petersburg later that autumn, they could no longer bring themselves to go on living in their old apartment, where everything reminded them of little Alyosha. They moved into a new six-room apartment on the corner of Yamskaya Street and Kuznetsky Lane, right next door to the Church of St. Vladimir. Dostoyevsky had once lived here earlier, at the very beginning of his literary career. The circle was complete: in this apartment he would also end his career. (Today the house is the site of one of the Soviet Union's seven Dostoyevsky museums.)

When he woke in the afternoon, he would first do a little morning gymnastics, and then take a bath. He liked to wash himself thoroughly, and if he was in a good mood he would usually break into a short aubade:

> Never awaken her at sunrise,
> when she is still sleeping so sweetly;
> the morning is breathing on her breast,
> reddening her cheek so lightly . . .

After this, he would begin to dress. His clothes must be clean and neat; if they were not, Anna would have to attend to them. "Stains upset my concentration," he would complain. "I cannot work in clothes that are stained; I keep thinking about the stains, instead of about my work." When he had got his clothes on and had said his morning prayers, he would come into the parlor in order to have tea and greet the children.

He liked to read aloud to them, but not from his own works. It did happen occasionally that they were allowed to be present at readings he gave, but he made it clear he did not consider himself a children's author. What was more, he did not enjoy the same success his father had had as a reader at the hospital. Lyubov and Fedya would sometimes fall asleep during his reading of Schiller's *The Robbers*. "They are still too young to understand this play," he would say sadly. The children's interest was more aroused by visits to the opera, but their father was not inventive in his choice of spectacles—they mostly went to performances of Glinka's *Russlan and Ludmilla*. As might be expected, he took an active role in the children's religious education, often led family prayers, and from the time when they were very young, took the children with him to church.

Even so, he had far too little time for his children, and his work was an obstacle to his taking a deeper concern. Not seldom he had to make do with simply giving them caramels. (He was convinced that sweet things were good for children, and he was in the habit of quoting medical opinion in this regard.) Maria Stoyunina, one of Anna's schoolfriends, related that Fedya ran around the apartment in rags while Anna had her hands full trying to organize her husband. Little by little he had become completely dependent on her. When he finally managed to go out for his walk, he would sometimes suddenly return in complete consternation: Anna had forgotten to give him his handkerchief!

Even though Dostoyevsky had now taken a temporary break from publishing the *Diary*, he continued to take a lively interest in political events of the day. Copies of a few of the newspapers he read have been preserved. They are full of notes and underlinings that show he closely studied Russia's political development. But even this study was disturbed by the trivial concerns of everyday living. "I must get my suitcase repaired, " he notes in his copy of *New Time* for April 21, 1879.

Full of pride he greeted the victory of the Russian forces over Turkey. He was especially pleased that several of his old companions from the Academy of Engineers had distinguished themselves. With one of the war heroes, General Mikhail Chernyayev, he sat for hours discussing the future unification of the Slavs. He was, of course, outraged by the "treachery" of the Western powers during the Congress of Berlin. So bitter was he about this "peace" without honor that he even supported the idea that Russia should recall her diplomats in Western Europe. Oh, that accursed West! Vogüé became quite alarmed when this "cross between a bear and a hedgehog," as he called him, suddenly began to make prophecies concerning the fate of his native city: "One night a prophet will come into the Café Anglais. In letters of fire he will write three words on the wall, and that will be the signal for the collapse of the old world. Paris will come crashing down in blood and flames, with all her pride, her theaters, and her cafés."

Yes, what had these Frenchmen really given humanity, after all, apart from "the French disease," the guillotine, and their cuisine? And what about the Germans? The Germans had never created anything new! What could the Germans put alongside a masterpiece such as *The Sistine Madonna*? Holbein's *Madonna*? "But that is no Madonna! It's a baker's wife! A petit-bourgeois madam! Not one iota more! And Goethe's *Faust*! It's a mere rehash of the Book of Job; read Job, there you will find everything that is important and valuable in *Faust*." Harangues of this sort must have created a rather painful impression in the cultivated salons of St. Petersburg.

There were, on the other hand, scarcely any limits to the enthusiasm with which Dostoyevsky was received as a public reader. He was especially active during the two last winters of his life. As a rule he selected well-known scenes from his own works, but he was also famous for his readings of Pushkin's poems, in particular *The Prophet* which derives its subject matter from the Book of Isaiah. His interpretation of the poem's last line—"Go out and burn the hearts of people with the word!"—made an overwhelming impression. "It was as though his eyes emitted a lightning that burned the hearts of people, his face shone with the most exalted power of inspiration!" wrote one visitor of his meeting with "the prophet" Dostoyevsky. The well-known literary historian Semyon Vengerov was no less impressed by the writer's mastery of public reading: "Dostoyevsky looked like a prophet in the full meaning of the word. . . . From the moment he mounted the podium all his listeners were completely in the hypnotic power of this thin and inconspicuous man. Each person in the auditorium was spellbound by his penetrating, strangely burning gaze that stared far out into an indeterminate remoteness."

His female audience was particularly enthusiastic: "Bravo, prophet! The prophet Fyodor Mikhailovich!" And indeed, they had much in common, this prophet and Dostoyevsky. Pushkin's prophet "dragged himself around in the wilderness," while Dostoyevsky suffered in the wildernesses of Siberia. And just as an angel appeared to the prophet and pointed the way he should follow in order to serve the people, so Dostoyevsky, too, after his prison term, began to "burn the hearts of people with the word." "People are probably under the impression that I read with my voice," Dostoyevsky would say with a smile. "Oh no! I read with my nerves, with my nerves!"

"When he began to read, he resembled an Old Testament prophet," we read in one of many reports:

> It was as though he had been created in order "to burn the hearts of people with the word." Every word he spoke was charged with such a profound conviction in what he was saying that this conviction also rubbed off on his listeners, who might otherwise have had quite different ideas. This deep conviction in the rightness of what he was saying, coming from an author who had never bowed either to people or to circumstances, together with his certainty about all he had been through in the course of his suffering-filled life, aroused a sense of deep respect and sympathy even among the most impassioned opponents of his ideas.

"He read wonderfully well," another listener recorded. "I have never experienced the like of such reading since. Though really one cannot call it reading or acting, either—it was life itself; a sick, epileptic fever fantasy."

The audience was best pleased when Dostoyevsky read from *The House of the Dead*, which better than any other work corresponded to the notions people had about him. But he resisted: "It looks as though I am standing there complaining all the time! It is not right to make such complaints, is it? Consequently I have stopped giving readings from this work, so that the public must not say I am continuing to whimper when it has long been time to stop!"

From the spring of 1879 on, several of these reading soirées took on the aspect of duels with Turgenev, who was still considered Russia's foremost author. But in altercations with Dostoyevsky, Turgenev invariably lost. When he later accused Dostoyevsky of being "a spiteful person, envious of other people's success," he can hardly have been thinking of these encounters, for it was always Dostoyevsky who received the flowers, even on those occasions when Turgenev was a guest of honor. An eyewitness has given this depiction of the protagonists just before one of their duels: "Dostoyevsky paced silently up and down the room, sipping lemon tea; Turgenev was trying to keep calm, but his jocular tone when he spoke to the girls who surrounded him was not very successful."

This situation was not significantly altered by Turgenev's allying himself with the famous actress Maria Savina—the fact was that he only had old-fashioned works from the 1850s to offer. "Each single word you utter is as carved from ivory," Dostoyevsky said smilingly to Savina during one of the intermissions, "but that old fellow of yours just stands there lisping all the time." He, on the other hand, could serve up new scenes from *Karamazov*, a work that was being followed with excitement by the entire Russian reading public. He must certainly have shaken his head at the sight of his elegantly dressed, cigar-smoking rival. Was it not as he had always said: that Turgenev had long ago written himself out? He had really caught the old man's likeness in that Karmazinov caricature he had done of him in *The Possessed*!

Anna was often a support to him during these reading soirées. If he was nervous, she would quickly come to the rescue with the sugar water she brought with her, and she made sure that he was not seated with his enemies; if he got too excited during the discussions she had to divert his attention. He liked to observe the public ovations he received, and kept an exact count of how many times he was called back to the podium.

At the same time, however, Anna often found herself in difficult situations because of her husband's "scenes of baseless jealousy." The twenty-five-year difference in their ages was beginning to tell. He saw red each time any man made so bold as to kiss Anna on the hand: "Men who kiss women on the hand view them as slaves and console them for this by treating them as queens." Each time be began one of his readings he would peer out over the auditorium to see whom she was sitting with. Perhaps it was a young guards officer she had got hold of? Anna could be really sharp about his suspiciousness:

> "Listen here, my dear friend: if you start peering around for me this evening I shall get up and leave the hall at once!"
> "And I shall jump down from the podium and run after you to see where you go!"

Dostoyevsky's encounters with Turgenev became more and more difficult. On occasion his rival would extend his hand in greeting, but he would refuse to shake it. It was no wonder that Polonsky was afraid to leave them in the same room together! During a festive dinner held for Turgenev in 1879, the guest of honor gave a speech in which he looked forward to the day when the "Tsar Liberator" would "crown his work." Everyone understood that he had in mind the plans to give Russia a constitution, but Dostoyevsky seethed with anger. "What does he mean—'crown his work'?" he asked in a loud, challenging voice. Expressions of displeasure from the dinner guests meant that he had to defend himself, but his defense did not sound very convincing: "I actually have a high opinion of Turgenev—look, I have even come in white tie and tails." A few days later an attempt was made to reconcile the two protagonists by introducing them on the stage hand in hand.

"He spoke little," an observer wrote of Dostoyevsky's behavior in the St. Petersburg salons, "but the expression on his lively, nervous face told everyone that he was giving careful thought to each single sentence."

There must, nonetheless, have been many who wrinkled their noses at some of these sentences—especially, perhaps, among his female listeners. For Dostoyevsky was long an irreconcilable opponent of women's emancipation. "Science can manage perfectly well without you," he lectured his female admirers, "but your families, your children, your kitchens cannot. Women have but one calling in life—to be housewives and mothers. They have no other; women have no calling in society, cannot have one—all that is stupidity, chimeras, the purest nonsense."

When later, however, he became a witness to the heroic role played by Russian women during the war against the Turks, he revised this negative perception. "In Russian women lies our only hope, one of the guarantees of our renewal," we read now in the *Diary*. "If we were with complete sincerity to set about providing women with higher education, with all the rights it gives, Russia would once again overtake Europe in the struggle for the regeneration of mankind."

As a partner in conversation Dostoyevsky could be sour-tempered and quite unpredictable. For the most part he sat alone and contented himself with watching the other guests mistrustfully out of the corner of his eye. Then suddenly he would become worked up over nothing. A single word that displeased him brought forth a flood of insults. Delicate society ladies would be told that they were unequal to "the lowliest peasant"; some women who were unfamiliar with St. Petersburg geography were given the rudest of dressing-downs. And why could that stupid professor not get it into his head that it was better to cultivate fruit than to waste one's time pottering around in a little kitchen garden? Why did that doctor describe the heart as a simple muscle—did he not know that the heart was a "spiritual and moral force"? When on one occasion the writer Pyotr Boborykin began to talk about the Paris Commune, he was brusquely interrupted by an angry outburst from Dostoyevsky: "Why the devil are you sitting here talking about that confounded Delescluze? Why do we have to listen to such rubbish?" The guests would stiffen with horror when he erupted in this manner. What if he were about to have an attack of epilepsy which would spoil the dinner?

Angry and sour-tempered utterances were indeed often a consequence of his attacks. In such phases of depression he could be something of a strain on those around him. "He would sometimes come into my study like a thundercloud," Vsevolod Solovyov wrote. "Indeed, sometimes he would even forget to greet me at all, and seek every possible pretext to snap and scold. He would interpret everything as an attempt to offend him and irritate him. Now my room would be too light, now it would be too dark; if he was given strong tea, he would complain that he had been given beer, and if his tea was weak, he would say he had been given hot water!"

Fortunately, bad times did not last forever, not even for Dostoyevsky. "An hour later he would be in the best of spirits. Only the pallor of his features, the flashing in his eyes, and his heavy breathing gave any hint of his morbid state. But if he chanced to meet strangers, things at once grew more complicated." Even so, it sometimes happened that strangers, even foreigners, were able to find favor in his eyes. The young Finnish-Swedish officer Georg Fraser was even permitted to borrow the keys to his summer cottage!

The common people could, at any rate, invariably rely on Dostoyevsky's benevolence. When in March 1879 he was assaulted by a drunkard, he refused to take the case to court. For one thing, he was not sure that the police had arrested the right man, and for another he found it impossible to believe that any healthy man could bring himself to give his neighbor a thrashing. "If he could, he must be abnormal, i.e., sick . . . and a sick man must be cured, not punished." When the man was nevertheless found guilty, the writer gladly paid his fine of sixteen rubles.

Single-mindedly, Dostoyevsky had consolidated his position, and now the dream of his youth, that of being famous, was starting to come true. As late as 1874, it was possible for him to be written off with a few lines in a new encyclopedia. Turgenev received six times the space. Four years later, Dostoyevsky was elected a member of the board of the Slavic Benevolent Society in St. Petersburg, and in the summer of the following year he was included in the honorary committee of the Association Littéraire Internationale, which described him as "one of the most famous representatives of contemporary literature." There were a good many important names on this honorary committee: Victor Hugo, Ivan Turgenev, Paul von Heyse, Alfred Tennyson, Anthony Trollope, Henry Wadsworth Longfellow, Ralph Waldo Emerson, Lev Tolstoy. Dostoyevsky, who was almost as ambitious as Ibsen, was surely flattered. In his letter of thanks, he wrote: "The literary congress has accorded me an exceedingly great honour in electing me as a member of the honorary committee. I thank it with all my heart. Can one do other than feel pride at figuring among so many well-known names, in the same category as the most eminent celebrities in contemporary literature?"

Meanwhile his health was steadily deteriorating. It was now three years since he had been at Ems. At the beginning of August 1879, he visited the spa for the fourth and last time, with his suitcase full of strong Russian cigarettes. Dr. Orth was of the opinion that his pleural emphysema was still only in its early stages. While it was true that it was no longer possible to cure the illness, one could at least fight it "with some degree of success." After five weeks of mineral water therapy he would certainly feel much better! The right diet was also important: plenty of meat and wine. Dostoyevsky quickly moved to the Ville d'Alger—wine was cheapest there.

Dostoyevsky counted every day of those five weeks. Never had he been so bored. He would give anything to be able to get out of "this damp hole" as quickly as possible! "Crowds of people, overcast weather; it rains day and night. I exist in the most profound loneliness, take my walks to the same places and am nearly dead of tedium." This time he met scarcely a single Russian. "Not a soul I know, only strange, foreign mugs." Again and again he declared that he had felt much better in the penitentiary. Quietly and monotonously the days dragged on:

> I rise at 6 o'clock. At 7 I drink mineral water, and at 9 I return to drink coffee. An hour for coffee and rest, and it is already 10 o'clock. From 10 to 12 I work. At 12 I look in at the post office and take a walk. At 1 I eat my main meal of the day. From 2 to 4 I write letters, or go out and read newspapers. From 4 to 5:30 I drink mineral water again. Then I take another walk—it is quite essential. By 8 it is completely dark; I light the lamps and drink tea, and at 10 I go to bed. There you have my entire day.

On the way to Ems he had dictated the following to one of his acquaintances in Berlin: "With 'The Legend of the Grand Inquisitor' Fyodor Mikhailovich has attained the high point of his creative work." Now he was going to follow up that success with his story about the Elder Zosima. Would he be able to repudiate Ivan's accusations against God's creation? He felt a heavy sense of responsibility: "Never before have I written with greater seriousness." If only his energies had not begun to fail him! "When one is bored, even work becomes a torture," he complained. Now he could only manage to write for two hours a day. What was more, he was increasingly tormented by his cough, the mineral water made him sour-tempered and irritable, and at night he had attacks of sweating and nightmares—he saw his brother before him with slashed veins. . . .

From time to time he was overtaken by thoughts of death. "I sit here and think that I shall soon die—well, let us say in a year or two, and what will happen to the people I leave behind me then?" he asked in a letter to Pobedonostsev. An echo of these worries may also be found in his copy of the New Testament. "For the children ought not to lay up for the parents, but the parents for the children," he underlined in a passage from Second Corinthians, 14.

Filled with such moods, he began to turn over in his mind the same idea his father had once had: that of buying a small estate in order to secure the family's future. "A village is a capital that will have tripled its value before the children have grown up," he declared to Anna, "and those who own land also have a say in the running of the state." A few days before his death he began to talk of this plan again.

Anna was not enthusiastic. Who would manage the estate? Nevertheless, in her husband's absence she traveled to the province of Ryazan in order to secure for the family a part of Aunt Kumanina's estate. As a result, Dostoyevsky received five hundred acres of forest and two hundred and fifty acres of arable land—in itself a handsome dividend, although Anna had to endure violent reproaches for all the "secretiveness" in this affair. "It was always a torture for me to have to conceal something from him," she wrote, defending herself in her memoirs. "But from time to time it was necessary in order to preserve his peace of mind and to spare him unnecessary excitement, which always carried with it a great risk."

She attempted to set his mind at rest by assuring him that she kissed him "hundreds of billions of times." But that was quite impossible, Dostoyevsky objected. She ought to write "a thousand times," the way he did, as that was feasible. His letters to Anna maintain the high temperature: "It is not simply that I love you—I am still in love with you, you are the only mistress of my soul, and this after twelve years!" She has also kept her power of attraction "in the most earthly sense," for when a woman is thirty-two she is still in her full flower. Anna was doubtless of the opinion that her husband was apt to overdo things in this respect, and she was not above complaining a little about it to her female friends. But in his eyes sexuality was the fundamental condition for the relationship between man and woman. "You think perhaps that this is only one aspect of the matter, the coarsest one even. But there is nothing coarse about it; everything else is dependent on it." There was also no need to worry that their letters were being read by strangers: "Let them envy us!"

He had, in any case, to put up with the fact that his fellow writers envied him for *The Brothers Karamazov*. But with the publication of each separate installment in the *The Russian Messenger* the enthusiasm of his readers only mounted. "This book brought me almost to the point of madness," one of his female readers recalls. "I could hardly sleep at nights and wept constantly. But how sweet it is to shed tears over a great work of art!"

The book's tumultuous reception was due not least to its exciting plot. Who was the murderer? "The old Karamazov is murdered by his servant Smerdyakov," was the writer's reassuring reply. Ivan has merely permitted him to do it. The readers must understand that Dmitry could not have done it; otherwise he would not have been able to climb back over the fence in order to express his sympathy with the servant Grigory! "It is not merely the novel's action that is important," he instructed one of his readers. "Every author must be allowed to expect that the reader has a certain insight into the human soul."

Dostoyevsky had originally planned to complete the novel during 1879, but the work continued right up until the autumn of 1880. Dostoyevsky probably felt that the book was going to be his last, and was pleased with its reception. "The novel is read everywhere, I constantly receive letters about it . . . to judge by the impression the book has made, I have never had a success like it." A high point in this triumph came when Dostoyevsky himself presented the heir to the throne with a copy of the novel.

II

Of *The Brothers Karamazov*, Dostoyevsky wrote that he had spared no effort to "hone it all finely, jeweler-fashion." He was never able to spend as much time on his journalistic works. If the censor was strict, it sometimes happened that he had to rewrite a whole issue in a matter of two or three days. Even so, it was the *Diary* just as much as the novel that made him famous, and thanks to it that he acquired the reputation of being a "teacher of life." Yekaterina Junge must have given voice to many people's reaction to this one-man journal, which stands alone in all of world literature, when she wrote: "During the war, when everything was difficult and one's strength often seemed to fail, *The Diary of a Writer* was the only book that was capable of bringing me consolation. I would sometimes sit thinking: all this is mere utopianism. And yet all the same I would feel something sweet and consoling seeping into my soul, for I observed a loving heart, a soul that understood everything, even the necessity of faith."

If today one reads the five volumes of Dostoyevsky's collected works that contain the monthly issues of the *Diary* for 1876 and 1877, one is struck first and foremost by the breadth of his interests. With courage and independence he took count of most of the social questions then being debated. In the midst of the multiplicity of topics, it is nevertheless possible to pick out the main complexes of problems: crime and punishment, and Russia's mission in the history of mankind.

Of these, it is probably the first which has the greater interest for us today. Here we also meet Dostoyevsky the humanist, just as fiercely committed and just as passionately disarming as in his finest literary works. A good example of his commitment may be found in the issue of the *Diary* for February 1876. Here he deals with the so-called Kronenberg case, which had just been in the St. Petersburg courts.

Stanislav Kronenberg stood accused of child abuse, in Dostoyevsky's eyes the most pernicious of all crimes. In the Franco-German war Kronenberg had fought for France, which had awarded him the Légion d'Honneur for brave conduct in twenty-five battles. Upon his return to his home city of Warsaw he was told that he had become the father to a daughter who was now in a Swiss children's home. Kronenberg accepted paternity and later took his daughter to St. Petersburg, where he settled down with a new wife. He was seldom at home; his daughter was maltreated and kept locked in her room. One day it was discovered that she had stolen a prune from a box belonging to her stepmother. The brave lieutenant, who had been in the habit of inflicting corporal punishment on his seven-year-old daughter, now felt once again that his paternal authority was threatened. Resolutely he went off and fetched his rod, which was made of nine thick rowan switches. A witness asked him to take out one of the switches, but he refused: "There is more power in my rod when all its switches are in place."

The punishment lasted for a quarter of an hour, until the war-hardened lieutenant himself was nearly dead from exhaustion. The only thing he could remember afterward was that the rod had become noticeably shorter.

He was reported to the police by a concierge's wife who had come rushing in when she had no longer been able to endure the girl's screams of "Papa! Papa!"

As might be expected, the case aroused much attention. People were interested in its relevance to the question of parental authority: some felt compelled to admit that in this case the authority of the parent had been abused; but many considered that there had to be limits to the right of society to meddle in people's private lives and in the way parents brought up their children. This last view was defended with great bravura by Kronenberg's defense attorney, a liberal professor named Vladimir Spasovich, possibly Russia's most eminent trial lawyer and one of the prototypes of Mitya's defense attorney in *Karamazov*.

With impressive eloquence this "bad conscience" set about proving that Kronenberg was innocent. Had he not magnanimously accepted paternity of the child, and this in spite of the fact that she had not even recognized him when he had come to take her with him to St. Petersburg? And had not the girl herself stood up in court and admitted that she was both a thief and a liar? A truly naughty little girl, she was! So she had stolen a prune from her stepmother, had she? What if she had stolen money, too? That would be quite in character for her! The punishment was well-deserved; a father must be allowed to act in such a fashion. Torture? Far from it! The medical experts had not even been able to establish that her father had broken a single one of her bones. There would be no end to the applause if Kronenberg were to be acquitted. Another victory for the liberal courts of Russia!

Dostoyevsky saw the case differently. He could tell the jury a thing or two. In Siberia he himself had been present at floggings with rods of the type that had lain as evidence on the court table. Most of the prisoners had collapsed after a few hundred strokes. What pain, what agony must a seven-year-old girl have endured during flogging that had almost done in the executioner?

Quivering with rage, Dostoyevsky addressed the defense attorney in his article:

Listen, do you know what it means to violate a small child? A child's heart is full of innocent, almost unconscious love, and such blows evoke merely sorrowful wonderment and tears that are seen and counted by God. For the child will never be able to perceive its own guilt. Have you ever seen or heard tell of a small child who has been tortured? Have you ever seen a child hide itself away in a corner in order to weep in secret, one who contorts its little fists (yes, *contorts*—I myself have seen it) and beats its breast without understanding its guilt, without understanding the reason why it has been punished, but with a strong feeling that its parents no longer love it?

There are several such pleas for the defense of children in the *Diary*. In the most exact detail Dostoyevsky depicts the adults' crimes; sometimes the wealth of detail becomes so nauseating that readers have wondered whether some trauma may be lurking here. Why does he constantly return to these depictions of the physical, mental, and, not least, sexual maltreatment of children by adults? Is there some biographical foundation for these depictions, or are we possibly dealing with a fresh manifestation of his sadomasochistic urges?

Let it be clear at once that there is not the slightest proof that Dostoyevsky ever at any time in his life abused children. That is not the aim of our inquiry; if it were, one can easily dismiss the question in the words of one Danish scholar as "downright infamous rubbish." But when one reads the numerous accounts of seductions and rapes, all the way from *Poor Folk* to *Karamazov*, one sees that the matter cannot be brushed aside, either. Dostoyevsky must have experienced this problem personally and tried to write it out of himself.

"I want to relate this so I shall not forget it," he stated in the December issue of the *Diary* for 1876. And then followed an "anecdote" about a girl of twelve—that "extremely interesting age in girls." The girl grows bored with school and runs away to the city. This time things go well: she soon returns to her mother. But what captivates Dostoyevsky most of all is the girl's thoughts as, weary and exhausted, she wanders through the streets of St. Petersburg dreaming that a "good man" will come and invite her home. Such thoughts bear witness to the girl's innocence and lack of maturity, the narrative informs us. But think how easily this dream could have come true—the streets of St. Petersburg are, after all, filled with such "good men!" And what would have happened to the girl then? The morning after? Would she have found a hole in the ice? Would she have felt shame over what had happened? Perhaps after a while she would have trained herself to live with her memories, perhaps she would have forgotten everything, perhaps she would soon be seized by a desire to repeat the experience, and then "all the rest" would follow as a matter of course.

That Dostoyevsky was obsessed by this subject, not merely by the dirty thoughts in the minds of the "good men," but also by the young girl's "desires," emerges even more clearly in the novels. In *Crime and Punishment* the voluptuary Svidrigailov imagines that he sees the smile of the *Dame aux Camélias* on the lips of a five-year-old girl; in *The Possessed* we find the seduction scene between Stavrogin and the twelve-year-old Matryoshka. This latter scene is depicted with an intensity that made a number of Dostoyevsky's contemporaries suspect the authenticity of lived experience, all the more so since he was constantly going around reading it aloud.

Certain factors indicate that at moments of provocation Dostoyevsky attempted to relive ideas like these, on a verbal level, at any rate. Valery Bursov is one of the few people who has dared to write about this, in a section of his book about the writer which he had to leave out of the final version: "If one could with certainty say that Dostoyevsky was familiar with the rumors that he had committed Stavrogin's crime, one could with no less certainty say that he did nothing to repudiate them." Thus we have Turgenev's well-known story concerning Dostoyevsky's "shameless propositions" to a French governess who was out walking with a twelve-year-old girl. When Turgenev was about to throw him out after he had made this "confession," Dostoyevsky turned in the doorway and said: "Ivan Sergeyevich, do you not understand that I invented that story merely to entertain you a little?"

Not even Turgenev had any doubt that the "old satyr and hypocrite" had invented the story. Even worse is Strakhov's notorious account in a letter to Tolstoy a few years after Dostoyevsky's death: "He had many swinish proclivities and bragged about them all," we read here. "Viskovatov once told me how he had boasted that he had [. . .] with a little girl in a bathhouse; he had persuaded the governess to bring the child with her."

This story has been interpreted as a vengeful reply to a few insulting lines that Strakhov found in Dostoyevsky's papers during the work on his biography. Anna Grigoryevna for her part tried to repudiate Strakhov's "slander" by pointing out that Dostoyevsky could not possibly have had access to the kind of money he would have needed to bribe the governess. Neither explanation seems wholly convincing. Even if most people would hardly go further than Tolstoy, who felt obliged "almost to believe" Strakhov's story, it seems clear that we are here in the presence of a running sore in Dostoyevsky's personality.

A lack of biographical information makes it difficult to locate the causes of this sore. Its roots may possibly extend back into the writer's childhood, to the time Fyodor learned that the girl who was his friend had been raped and murdered in the hospital garden. In the course of a soirée at the home of Anna Filosofova at the end of the 1870s he returned to this horrible childhood experience. The guests were discussing what ought to be accounted the greatest sin. Some thought it was parricide, others murder with intent to rob—what was Dostoyevsky's opinion? "The most fearful crime is to rape a child," the writer said quickly and nervously. "To take life—that is dreadful, but to destroy faith in love's beauty is an even more dreadful crime." And then he related the episode at the Hospital for the Poor. "All my life I have been haunted by that memory, which was the most dreadful crime, the most fearful sin, a sin for which there exists no forgiveness and which cannot be forgiven. It was with that crime that I punished Stavrogin in *The Possessed*."

Seen in this light, it becomes less interesting to discuss how much truth there was in Turgenev's assertion that Dostoyevsky was a "Russian Marquis de Sade" or in Strakhov's secondhand story about Dostoyevsky as child seducer. We must remember that for him the evil intention was at least as sinful as the evil action. With his unique capacity for penetrating the criminal psyche and the infinite sense of guilt which was a consequence of his epilepsy, he would in any case be disposed to identify with the practitioners of this "most dreadful sin." Those who cry "slander" as soon as this question comes up seem to overlook the writer's profound need to slander himself.

Many of the articles in *The Diary of a Writer* are permeated with Dostoyevsky's faith in the Russian people and its religious destiny. For him the peasant spirit was the same as the Christian spirit. He liked to recall that the Russian words for *peasant* (*krestyanin*) and *Christian* (*khristianin*) are etymologically related. More and more, his articles on this theme took on a kind of mystical populism. The peasant's teacher in questions of faith, Dostoyevsky maintained, is the soil itself, the Russian land. The peasant's creed is inborn, secured in his heart together with life. "It is possible that the people know Christ, their God, better than we do, even though they have never attended any school. The people know Him as a consequence of all the sufferings they have had to endure throughout the centuries, and in their sorrow they have even to this day heard about this God—their Christ—from their saints."

In an article entitled "About Love of the People" dated February 1876, Dostoyevsky gave an example of the purifying and consoling power of the

Russian peasant. Not that he regarded the peasant as an ideal in any moral sense. "The people are immoral," he emphasized in the *Diary*. "But the main thing is that they do not consider their vices to be anything good. We, on the other hand, view all the filth that has gained entry to our hearts and minds as the alluring aspect of culture and want the people to come and learn from us." For all their dark instincts, the Russian people are in possession of the highest spiritual education, and this is something that the enlightened strata must also obtain, by reconciling themselves with the people in humility. "Who is better—the people or ourselves?" he asked. "Should the people follow us, or should we follow the people?" Similar questions were raised by Tolstoy, and both writers replied in favor of the people.

Against the simple, God-fearing peasant Dostoyevsky set representatives of the intelligentsia who renounced Russian ideals in favor of West European ideas. There is no justification for following people like these, for they are probably only contemplating suicide, he thought. In several articles he came to grips with the growing suicidal tendency among the intellectuals. In five years the suicide figure had trebled! At the same time, he was a master at depicting these despairing people's bitterness about life. The publication of a suicide's farewell letter created consternation among his friends. This was tantamount to exhorting people to kill themselves! Perhaps he was an atheist? The letter was, after all, written with the greatest conviction! "No, I am a deist, a philosophical deist!" Dostoyevsky replied. "People have simply failed to understand me. . . . I merely wished to show that one cannot live without Christianity."

Dostoyevsky saw faith in the immortality of the human soul as a necessary condition for being able to acquiesce in life. Love for others is not something that is implanted in human nature, he wrote—human nature is supernatural and presupposes a faith in the soul's immortality. This faith in immortality was for him something more than a conception about the reward of the good and the punishment of the wicked in the world to come. In his view it is by virtue of being immortal that human beings have absolute dignity. To deny the immortality of human beings is equivalent to denying human beings themselves, as the suicide does. Either human beings are immortal, or they are the passive product of their surroundings and therefore lack inner worth.

In "A Simple But Difficult Case," Dostoyevsky returned from philosophical speculations such as these to the question of the courts' treatment of criminals. Here, however, one no longer sees the demand for tougher sentences. In the case of Yekaterina Kornilova, a pregnant young woman who had thrown her small stepdaughter out of the window in a fit of rage at her quarrelsome husband, he took the side of the accused. Not that he had given in to the "environmental theory." His intervention in the Kornilova case was due first and foremost to his knowledge of the human soul, his awareness that it is possible to act in full consciousness without at the same time being accountable for one's actions. By means of a deep analysis of the woman, he succeeded in convincing the jury that the crime had been committed in a state of morbid excitement brought on by her pregnancy. The case was reopened and ended in the woman's full acquittal.

The presiding judge warned members of the jury against allowing themselves to be influenced by "certain talented authors." At this time Dostoyevsky was also the target of violent attacks in the press. Was he not sorry for the victim, Yekaterina's six-year-old stepdaughter? These attacks made Dostoyevsky uneasy, and he promised to re-examine the case. Then, in the summer of 1878, he received a letter from Yekaterina's husband, saying that she had suddenly died. The suspicion of suicide must have given him an unpleasant time. Had he, on this occasion, fallen prey to sentimentalism? Whatever the facts of the matter, Dostoyevsky's involvement in this case fails to lend any support to Nikolai Mikhailovich's assertion that the writer was a "cruel talent."

Another piece of testimony to Dostoyevsky's compassion for the unfortunate is the story "Krotkaya"—one of the most moving narratives about human despair that has ever been written. True to form, he dubbed the story "fantastic." But nothing was more fantastic to him than reality, and it was another contemporary event that formed the basis of the narrative. In a newspaper, he had recently read a brief report concerning a poor seamstress who had thrown herself out of a window hugging an icon. "This holding-on to an icon—such a strange and outlandish feature in connection with a suicide!" he exclaimed in his *Diary* commentary. "This was a remarkably gentle and peaceful suicide. There was no trace of 'complaining,' of directing reproaches against anyone. She had simply found it impossible to go on living, it was 'no longer God's will,' and so she went to her death saying her prayers."

What had driven the girl to this act of despair? Here it could not be a question of a lack of faith in the immortality of the soul—human hard-heartedness and cruelty must have been the deciding factors.

Little by little the tragedy is unfolded to us through the stuttering words of the girl's husband over her bier. Like many of Dostoyevsky's heroes he is gloomy and withdrawn, with a boundless, wounded *amour propre*. He feels that he has been disowned by his fellow men and wants to take revenge on society by means of power and wealth. The gentle Krotkaya becomes one of the means to this end. Nowhere has Dostoyevsky given such a concentrated depiction of the unrestrained domination of a weak but proud character by a despotic one. Krotkaya dies because her husband has killed her love. And when love does finally break through in him, it is too late. The narrative runs out in a despairing illustration of the great poet Arnulf Øverland's words:

> No one can spend his days,
> standing by a grave lamenting.
> The day has many hours.
> The year has many days.

"A story of this kind would not pass unheeded in the literature of any country," wrote one contemporary critic. Knut Hamsun was among those who noticed the story. "There is, for example, a little story entitled 'Krotkaya.' A tiny little book. But it is too great for us all, too unattainably great. Let everyone acknowledge that."

"The Dream of a Queer Fellow" is another "fantastic story," which Dostoyevsky published in the April issue of the *Diary* for 1877. Here again "the fantastic" is portrayed within a realistic framework, and again the violation of a helpless girl is decisive for the narrative's outcome.

Once again we meet an intellectual nihilist who suddenly feels that nothing any longer has meaning, that it is a matter of indifference how things work out. As he makes his way home to his revolver, however, his feeling of compassion for a little girl whom he has refused to help awaken to life. These feelings, strange in one who has condemned himself to death, restrain him from suicide and give him instead a vision of an earthly paradise where humanity dwells in universal and harmonious brotherhood. It is true that sinful man brings about the downfall of paradise. But the vision of the "child of the sun"—brought into being by compassion for a human being who has been violated—lives on in the "queer fellow." He refuses to believe that evil is the normal condition of mankind. From now on it is the millennium which he wants to proclaim. "For I have seen the Truth and know that people can be beautiful and happy without losing their ability to live upon earth."

What Dostoyevsky has created here is a piece of utopian poetry. At the same time, the story is also a key to the whole of his religious philosophy, a synthesis of his entire world outlook. Life is a paradise—if only we understood that, we should instantly be in paradise, he has Father Zosima proclaim in *The Brothers Karamazov*. For Dostoyevsky, paradise was something more than the bliss enjoyed by bodiless souls in the beyond. He believed in the millennium, when humanity would finally be united in brotherhood and love upon earth.

In the realization of the millennium, in the evolution of this human fellowship, *Russians* had their historic mission. Not the intellectual Russians who had broken with the people and eaten of the tree of materialism, but the ordinary Russian people, who lived according to the ideals of compassion and humility and therefore possessed the ability to understand other peoples. This is how he pictured the Russians' historic, saving task.

> At the head of the united Slavs our great Russia will proclaim to the world its new, healing, and hitherto unprecedented word. This word will bring tidings of the good and true association of mankind in a new, brotherly, universal union, conceived by the Slavic spirit, and principally by the spirit of the Russian people, which has suffered so much and which for centuries has been condemned to silence, but which has always possessed a great ability to resolve and settle many of the bitter and fatal misapprehensions in Western European civilization.

In his story about Foma Danilov, dated January 1877, Dostoyevesky shows us one such representative of the Russian people. Foma lets himself be tortured to death rather than renounce his Christian faith. For him the truth about Christ is more precious than riches and worldly glory. He becomes a Christian martyr, a martyr without a martyr's crown. "But among the people this great death will of course not be forgotten," Dostoyevsky asserts. "In this hero who has suffered untold agonies for the sake of Christ, the people will always see a great Russian."

Dostoyevsky's Russian messianism, as we encounter it in a series of articles about the "eastern question" dating from 1877, has quite understandably been the subject of violent attacks by posterity. From messianism it is a short distance to chauvinism, which soon led him on to anti-Semitic diatribes, both in the *Diary* and in *The Brothers Karamazov*: "Alyosha, is it true that the Jews steal children at Easter and eat them?" Liza asks. "I don't know," the hero replies.

An unpleasant impression is also created by Dostoyevsky's open glorification of war. Dostoyevsky's war-fever emerges in naked rancor, forming a strange contrast to the gospel of love that is to be found on other pages of his *Diary*. Disguised as "Paradoxist" he let off the following salvo in the April issue for 1876:

> A political, international war is useful in every respect, and is therefore also entirely necessary. . . . During long intervals of peace human beings lose all nobility of vision, and in its place cynicism and boredom come sneaking in. . . . War elevates the spirit of the people and its sense of its own dignity. War makes everyone equal and reconciles master and servant in the loftiest manifestation of human dignity—by sacrificing life for a common cause, for everyone, for the fatherland.

The *Diary* for 1877 abounds in such provocative remarks. True, these statements were made during the war against the Turks, one of the bloodiest of all wars. It was not only Dostoyevsky who found it difficult to be a pacifist when fathers were being flogged, mothers raped, and infants impaled on bayonets in their parents' sight.

Was Dostoyevsky an imperialist? If we are to employ the customary definition of the word—supporter of a policy based upon the acquisition of colonies and the exploitation of their resources—then the answer must be no. Not even his most provocative claim—that "Constantinople must be ours"—can provide any foundation for such a charge. The background to this remark was that back in the sixteenth century Russia had introduced the two-headed eagle as its national emblem. "With this act it was as though the country had assumed an obligation," Dostoyevsky wrote:

> From the earliest times until the present day the Russian people has been fond of calling its Tsar "Orthodox"—the "Orthodox Tsar." By allowing the people to call him by this name, the Tsar has as it were sanctioned the destiny that it contains: that of protecting and unifying Orthodoxy and —when God sounds the command—of freeing every part of Christendom that professes Orthodoxy from the barbarism of Islam and the heresy of the West.

In making its declaration of war it seemed quite clear that Tsardom had political aims. Russia wanted to strengthen its influence in the Balkans in order to increase its international prestige and divert attention from burning political questions at home. But Dostoyevsky had little sense for such practical political considerations. He was in no doubt that the Russians had been acting unselfishly when they had decided to declare war on the Turks. "Russia has no plans to expand its territory at the expense of the Slavs, no plans to annex their lands and make them into Russian provinces," he wrote in the *Diary*. In his view the war was evidence that the Russians felt obliged to *sacrifice themselves* for their Slavic brethren. For him this was a "holy" war.

In *The Possessed* he had spoken of the "god-bearing" people. By this he intended the opposite of what was later to be called a "master race." The task of such a people is not to subjugate but "to create a large and powerful organism composed of united fraternal peoples, not by means of political might, not by fire or by sword, but through the persuasive example, through love, light, and unselfishness." A "god-bearing" people, by the very nature of its burden, cannot wage a policy of oppression.

What Dostoyevsky dreamed of was a voluntary amalgamation of the Slavic peoples, a spiritual union in the name of Christ's truth, for the defense of all who were weak and oppressed. In a time filled with aggressive nationalism he could make the following declaration: "We wish to show ourselves as a people with no wish to coerce. We do not want to make Poles into Russians. If the Poles or the Czechs truly want to be our brothers, we will grant them the right to self-determination. This will not destroy our connection with them—they will reach out their hands to us as to a friend, an elder brother, a great center. Love and the cause of true enlightenment. That is my utopia."

The conviction that the world, in spite of all its aberrations, is moving toward a society built on a foundation of love and brotherhood—that is the exalted ideological level on which Dostoyevsky's thought operates, the level that gives his work its passionate, optimistic coloring.

But his faith in a happy future for mankind dwelt alongside visions of an impending catastrophe. To find the way to moral principles that could ward off this catastrophe—in this he saw his main task as a publicist. To him, the radical theories of his time were faulty because they tended to ignore the moral aspect of things and had a merely utilitarian conception of liberty, equality, and fraternity. "Their socialism is a false and desperate idea," he wrote of his opponents. The "god-bearing" mission of the Russian people must be to prevent the building of a new Tower of Babel.

So how could Russia come to the aid of materialistic and atheistic Europe and bring ultimate reconciliation? By virtue of its suffered-through ideals, by virtue of brotherly love, by virtue of "the Russian Christ." With this latter formulation Dostoyevsky had in mind the image of Christ that was still alive among the ordinary Russian people. And when he came to describe this Russian Christ, he usually fell back on the words of the poet Tyutchev:

> These poor settlements,
> This meager nature—
> Native land of long endurance,
> Thou land of the Russian people!
>
> The proud gaze of the alien
> Will not understand and will not perceive
> What shines and secretly glimmers
> In your humble nakedness.
>
> Weighed down by the burden of the cross,
> The Prince of Heaven, dressed as a slave,
> Traveled your length and breadth, O native land,
> And blessed you.

Nicholas Berdyayev has written, with justification, that there is much in *The Diary of a Writer* which is inconsistent with the spiritual depths we find in Dostoyevsky's novels. Dostoyevsky was no politician and never succeeded in elaborating a program for the realization of his ideals. His pronouncements of political questions can sometimes appear both naïve and self-contradictory, colored as they are by the struggles of the moment. On the other hand, he possessed something many politicians lack: a great vision of mankind united in brotherhood, and a burning faith in the value of the ideal in a materialistic age. It is from this faith that his last novel, too, derives its power.

III

Is an unworthy and unloving father entitled to the love and respect of his sons? How can the notion of a good, heavenly Father be reconciled with the suffering and injustice in the world He has created? *The Brothers Karamazov* is a didactic, sermonic novel. Dostoyevsky has a message he wishes to communicate to his readers.

The didactic novel is probably as old as literary history itself. But the genre became especially widespread in the seventeenth and eighteenth centuries, when the didactic message was expressed principally in the utterances of the characters, usually in the form of letters, reminiscences, and diary entries, outside the plot of the novel proper. Dostoyevsky also used this technique in the "Legend of the Grand Inquisitor," for example, and in the teachings of Father Zosima. But in his novel the didactic material is more intimately connected with the development of the narrative itself. The didactic teachings are given as conclusions that the reader himself must draw from the action of the novel.

Our frequent difficulty in arriving at clear, unambiguous conclusions is due to the fact that Dostoyevsky was from many points of view himself a doubter. He was certainly a Christian writer, but his Christianity was far from conflict-free. "His faith is moving, full of doubt, uncertain, and ardent," wrote Albert Camus. Dostoyevsky was a god-seeker who struggled with his doubt. This aspect of his character set its mark on the type of novel he created. Using musical terminology, Mikhail Bakhtin has characterized his art as "polyphonic," arguing that Dostoyevsky thinks not in ideas but in points of view, in voices that belong to characters who are equal participants in a great dialogue.

Dostoyevsky ranges opinions against other opinions that are both his own and not his own. "He never does violence to the distinctive qualities of his characters in order to make them serve his message," Ronald Fangen has observed. "He is always such a great writer that he is completely in the power of his creative invention." It is by letting contradictory voices and opinions fully unfold that he could approach his vision of the truth.

The obscurities and self-contradictions in the dialogic struggle that takes place in Dostoyevsky's novels also have deep roots in his view of writing itself. He disagreed with the notion that everything in a work of art must be easily comprehended and pleasantly obvious at whatever price. An author must have the right to keep certain things concealed in the mystical and obscure. "Let the readers do some of the work themselves," he would say, defending his right to produce books that were difficult and intricate.

Dostoyevsky offers no conclusive answers to the questions he poses in his didactic writings, partly because he could not give conclusive answers, and partly because he thought it up to his readers to draw their own conclusions. In this respect he obviously differed from Tolstoy, who in his tendentious novels had a clear message that he attempted to sell his readers by means of logical argument. Those who go to the novels of Dostoyevsky in search of solutions to life's problems will be quickly disappointed. Dostoyevsky writes rather for those who wish to know what things are worth thinking about. This is possibly the reason why his books possess such vital energy. Answers and solutions easily go out of date, while the most important questions about man's existence always preserve their actuality.

Dostoyevsky's attitude toward the characters he creates is also quite different from Tolstoy's. Both are typically autobiographical authors who write about their own experience. But while Tolstoy's heroes—Pierre and Levin, for example—significantly increase our sympathy for the writer, the same cannot really be said about those of Dostoyevsky. In his books we not infrequently encounter the most repulsive people in the main roles, not just "positive" characters such as Sonya or Alyosha. In a letter to his publisher Dostoyevsky characterized Stavrogin as a "gloomy person" and a "villain." Typically, however, he added: "I took him from my heart." He might well have said the same about several of the characters in The Brothers Karamazov. Even the villains are close to him in the sense that they are "taken from his heart." To old Karamazov he gives his first name, to Smerdyakov he gives his epilepsy. Indeed, he even had no difficulty in identifying with the Devil when shortly before his death he noted: "My hosanna has passed through the great purgatory of doubt—that is what the Devil says about himself in my latest novel."

While Tolstoy never spends much time beating about the bush when it is a question of condemning an unsympathetic character, Dostoyevsky always tries to "find the human being in the man," even in the most blunted and worn-out individuals. In him, sternness is intimately connected with compassion. And it is because he himself feels an affinity with his negative heroes that he so often allows them to have their say.

Dostoyevsky's characters have been called "embodied ideas." Although such a designation fails to take sufficient account of his power to portray the human being behind the ideas, it is nonetheless true that his characters are fused to an extraordinary degree with the ideas they represent. Ivan Karamazov is a good example of this. In Book Seven his nihilistic ideas are portrayed in their abstract form. But as Sigurd Fasting perceptively remarks, Ivan also *lives* his ideas—they are made concrete through his destiny:

> Like Raskolnikov, Ivan is only willing to accept the twentieth part of his being that is his reason, and therefore exists in a state of deep, inner conflict.

Like a true Karamazov he is possessed of a violent, instinctive appetite for life and an infinite love of it, but this irrational side of his being stands in conflict with his reason, which tells him that life is meaningless and makes him into a rebel against God—and in reality also a denier of God. After he has finished telling Alyosha his legend, Alyosha says of the Grand Inquisitor that his secret is that he does not believe in God at all—and that is also Ivan's secret. Ivan is not only an "anti-theist" but an atheist. That is a thought which Ivan does not quite dare to admit to himself, for he knows what it implies: that he himself is a god, that everything is permitted. This aspect of his soul is embodied by the lackey Smerdyakov, who in order to serve his "grand inquisitor" murders his father, the old Karamazov, whom Ivan hates. Ivan's inner conflict is thereby made even more acute, and he arrives at the verge of losing his reason. But then something happens to him that is similar to what befalls Raskolnikov: in spite of his own reason and his own theories he admits in court his moral guilt and accepts responsibility for the murder he has indirectly exhorted Smerdyakov to commit.

Ivan's story is that of how the nineteen-twentieths win over the twentieth part that is respresented by reason. And just as he does in the case of his spiritual relative Raskolnikov, so here Dostoyevsky shows the painful struggle that takes place in Ivan between his heart and his reason. This struggle sets its mark on his thoughts, his words, and his actions. Person and idea are fused together.

The ability to fuse person and idea is also connected with the fact that Dostoyevsky lived through the same problems that he has his heroes face. We also meet ideological caricatures such as some of the revolutionaries in *The Possessed* and Miusov, Rakitin, and Smerdayakov in *Brothers Kara-mazov*. But the most important of Dostoyevsky's characters are those who in Dmitry Chizhevsky's formula are "equal in world outlook." This means that the author never paints his opponents all black, but seeks rather to justify their opinions by means of the strongest and most convincing arguments. Not infrequently his novels give the impression of a battle over problems that he has not yet solved. We are confronted with depictions of philosophical and religious quests that remain inconclusive.

A good example of this is the "Legend of the Grand Inquisitor," in which Ivan raises problems that Dostoyevsky found particularly bewildering. Even if the character of Ivan is intended as a warning of the dangers of a Western-influenced, atheistic youth in Russia, there can be no doubt that

Ivan's pathos and eloquence in Book Five derive in several respects from the fact that Dostoyevsky shared his ideas. In the chapter "Revolt," it even seems as though the author is taking over from his hero and relating experiences from his own life. Even cruel people can be fond of children, Ivan declares—"In prison I knew a robber who loved children to an inordinate degree." Here Dostoyevsky has so identified himself with Ivan that he inadvertently commits an error: unlike Dostoyevsky, Ivan has never been in prison.

As a modern atheist, Ivan is little concerned with the question of whether God exists. He is quite prepared to accept God's existence. But this does not make his revolt any the less—quite the contrary. He only accepts God in order to be able to reject Him. What he cannot accept is the world God has created. For how can suffering be the most dominant feature in a world that is supposed to have been created by a merciful God?

Ivan's main argument against the way God has ordered the world is *the suffering of children*. In his conversation with Alyosha he produces a long string of authentic accounts of innocent children subjected to cruel maltreatment by their fathers, torn to pieces by bloodhounds, or impaled on bayonets in the sight of their mothers. Ivan's conclusion is unambiguous: if the Devil does not exist and man invented him, he probably created him in his own image. What is the purpose of these sufferings? he asks. That one day an "eternal harmony" shall be established in the world? If the fulfillment of God's universal plan depends upon the sufferings of innocent children, he would rather forego eternal life: "It costs too much to gain entry to the world of eternal harmony. We cannot afford to pay such an exorbitant entrance fee. Consequently, I want to return my entrance ticket as soon as possible. That is simply the only right course of action for an honorable man to take. I do not repudiate God, Alyosha. I show him complete respect. I am merely returning my ticket, that is all."

Alyosha, who is portrayed after models from the Russian heroic tales, attempts to counter his brother's sacrilegious argument by pointing to Christ. Man cannot forgive, but *he is forgiven*. Christ also suffered innocently, but He did not therefore give himself over to cursing existence. On the contrary, He loved life and human beings in spite of their evil ways.

For Ivan it is clear that all this suffering cannot be forgiven. It is little help to him that a good God can see a reason for everything when he himself, as a human being, cannot see one. But instead of discussing Christ's right to forgive, or the meaning of forgiveness, he suddenly changes his tactics. In place of logical proof he introduces a myth; instead of taking as his starting point the concrete reality that surrounds him, he has recourse to a legend that is set in sixteenth-century Spain. "The Legend of the Grand Inquisitor" has thus become much more than a contribution to a discussion about Christ's right to forgive the sufferings of the innocent. We are in fact faced with a genius-inspired attack on the whole of God's world order. The legend also contains Ivan's vision of a new world order.

Seen from a technical point of view, "The Legend of the Grand Inquisitor" is a novella inserted into a novel. Ivan himself calls it a "poem," and he is its author. "Of all Dostoyevsky's heroes Ivan Karamazov is the only one of them who could have written his novels," observes Leonid Grossman.

When in December 1879 Dostoyevsky read the "Legend" to the students of St. Petersburg University, he wrote a brief introduction in which he explained his view of the poem:

> An atheist who is suffering in his unbelief writes during a spell of misery a curious, fantastic poem, in which he portrays Christ in conversation with one of the foremost priests of the Catholic Church—the Grand Inquisitor. The author's sufferings are so intense because in this priest he sees a true and genuine servant of Christ, even though the priest has a Catholic world outlook which has clearly grown remote from the orthodoxy of the old Apostolic faith. The Grand Inquisitor is really an atheist. What the poem is saying is that if the Christian faith is combined and corrupted with the objectives of this world, then the meaning of Christianity will perish. Human reason will abandon itself to unbelief, and in place of the great ideal of Christ a new Tower of Babel will be built. Where Christianity had an exalted view of mankind, under the new order of things mankind will be viewed as a mere herd, and behind the appearance of *social* love there will arise an open contempt for humanity.

The stage is set in the fearsome era of the Inquisition and the religious persecution that accompanied it. After fifteen hundred years Christ has returned to earth. In Seville He strolls around performing miracles and being greeted by the people with great acclaim. On the orders of the Grand Inquisitor, an old man of ninety, the most powerful cardinal of the Roman Catholic Church, He is, however, placed under arrest and thrown into prison. When night comes, He is visited by the Grand Inquisitor, who delivers Him a stark reprimand. Indeed, he even threatens to have Him burnt at the stake. By coming back, Christ has created an obstacle to the necessary mission of the Catholic Church here upon earth. Christ remains silent as the Grand Inquisitor makes his accusations, rejecting the entire teaching of God. Ever since Christ's resurrection the Church has had to strive to correct that teaching, to make it more applicable to human beings.

According to the Grand Inquisitor, where had Christ gone wrong? Principally, in rejecting the temptations in the wilderness. By so doing, He gave man freedom instead of happiness. He did not reflect that human beings would actually prefer death to the freedom to choose between good and evil. He also erred when He refused to turn stones into bread. If He had, mankind would have rushed after Him an obedient and grateful herd. And He declined to throw himself from the temple—he wanted to win the free trust of human beings and was unwilling to bind them by a miracle. He desired that people should serve Him of their own free will and not as slaves of external authority.

Because of Christ's poor knowledge of human nature, the Catholic Church has been compelled to "improve" his teaching. In the name of love of humanity the Grand Inquisitor has accepted the temptations of the Devil and made miracle, mystery, and authority into the cornerstones of His future world empire. Christ overestimated human beings, the Grand Inquisitor complains. By giving them freedom of conscience He asked too much of them. Human beings are weak, wretched creatures who prefer bread and circuses to freedom. The freedom to choose between good and evil is a gift that is far too burdensome for ordinary people. They long for someone who will relieve them of this freedom, someone who will accept the responsibility for their sins and give them bread:

> In the course of a few centuries humanity will have reached a point where through the mouth of its wisdom and science it will declare that there is no longer any crime, and consequently no sin, either. There will be only hunger and the hungry. Then human beings will rise up against You, and on the banner of the rebels will be written: "Give us food! Only then can You demand virtue of us!" Under this banner they will conduct a rebellion against You, and Your temple will collapse into rubble. Where it stood, a new building will be raised—a new and fearsome Tower of Babel.

The Grand Inquisitor and his helpers have set themselves the goal of completing this Tower of Babel. By satisfying people's material requirements and robbing them of their freedom they wish to create an earthly paradise, in which everyone will be happy except the small ruling minority who know the difference between good and evil.

The "Legend" may be viewed as a protest against Christ in which the Grand Inquisitor represents Ivan's vision of God. This is what God would be like if He were to rule justly: commanding but wise and loving, compassionate toward all the weak human wretches who have at last been liberated from the burden of freedom.

Never has the *problem of freedom* been raised with such vehemence as in "The Legend of the Grand Inquisitor." We stand before a mighty confrontation between two great, irreconcilable forces: Christ and the Devil. The Great Inquisitor represents the Antichrist . . . "the negation of the Christian idea. Atheistic socialism has always reproached Christianity for not having made people happy, for not having given them peace and food," Nicholas Berdyayev wrote. "But if Christianity has not made people happy, has not given them peace or food, it is because it addresses man's freedom and awaits from it the fulfillment of the word of Christ. It is not Christianity's fault that mankind has not wished to fulfill that word and has betrayed it: the guilt lies not in the god-man, but in man."

But at the same time it is clear that Dostoyevsky's Antichrist possesses a dangerous charm in his concern for the weaker members of society. Many, therefore, are the critics who defend the Grand Inquisitor and claim that Dostoyevsky bit off more than he could chew in his attempt to refute him.

Among these is D.H. Lawrence. "And we cannot doubt that the Inquisitor speaks Dostoyevsky's own final opinion about Jesus," he writes. "The opinion is, baldly, this: Jesus, you are inadequate. Men must correct you. And Jesus in the end gives the kiss of acquiescence to the Inquisitor, as Alyosha does to Ivan." Taking the part of the Grand Inquisitor, Lawrence places himself on the side of darkness and unfreedom. He does it reluctantly, it is true: he would much rather that man were different. But he must give the Grand Inquisitor his due, in that man's nature *is* weak and slavish. And for this reason the Grand Inquisitor is also right that Christ was too severe in wishing to raise the average person to ideals that only the chosen few would be able to follow in their lives. Thus Christianity merely becomes a utopian dream about man as he ought to be.

A characteristic of many of the Great Inquisitor's defenders is that they are determined to pull Dostoyevsky over to their side. One of the principal theses in Lev Shestov's treatise on Dostoyevsky and Nietzsche is that the Russian writer takes the part of his godless hero. Vasily Rozanov, who wrote a scholarly study of the "Legend," is likewise not in the slightest doubt that Dostoyevsky is on the side of the Grand Inquisitor: "When Dostoyevsky died, he did not take the secret of his soul with him. Before his death he gave us, as though he were exposing his soul by some kind of instinct, a sensational scene in which it clearly emerges that Alyosha's words to Ivan: 'and you are with him' can also be applied to the author himself, who so clearly stands on his side."

But for anyone who knows Dostoyevsky's intention with the "Legend," such a placing of the writer among the adherents of the Grand Inquisitor must seem like something approaching sacrilege. The Grand Inquisitor wants to adapt the ideal to fit man, he attacks the ideal because man is not strong enough to live up to it. Does not this imply the most profound contempt for man?

There is no shortage, either, of well-meaning attempts to free Dostoyevsky from the suspicion of being in league with the Grand Inquisitor. It has been claimed that the Grand Inquisitor's attack is self-contradictory, that it is founded on empty rhetoric and cheap tricks. But in reality it is difficult to find weak spots in his argument. When Konstantin Mochulsky writes that the Grand Inquisitor is mistaken because he argues from love for man and yet portrays man as a weak, slavish creature, it can justifiably be objected that it is perfectly possible to love the weak and the wretched. Here there is no contradiction: the Grand Inquisitor loves man for what he is and not for what he is not. And he accepts that man is weak quite simply because that is a fact.

Our contempt for the Grand Inquisitor's view of mankind should not allow us to attack it on false premises. The adherents of the Grand Inquisitor would also prefer Christ's strength, beauty, and freedom. But the "Legend" has demonstrated that it is not a question of what man wishes to be but what man is and is capable of being. Even the Grand Inquisitor is willing to admit that Christ's view of mankind is more attractive than his own. But that is no proof that Christ's view of mankind is the correct one.

In order to reply to the Grand Inquisitor, Dostoyevsky needed a new dimension. He found it in the figure diametrically opposed to the Grand Inquisitor: that of the pious monk Father Zosima.

Book Seven bears the title "A Russian Monk." Like "The Legend of the Grand Inquisitor," this section also lies outside the central plot, since it principally contains Father Zosima's recollections and teachings. Only at its very beginning and at its end does Book Seven follow the novel's true time span.

We witness Alyosha's last conversation with Father Zosima. The old monk, mortally ill, says that Alyosha will be sorely tested, but through his suffering will be made happy. He will come to bless life and will help others to bless it. This is a central theme in Dostoyevsky's work: purification through suffering.

On the same evening, Father Zosima delivers his last sermon to the monks. Alyosha copies it down, complementing it with earlier pronouncements. It is significant that Father Zosima's sermon takes place on the same evening that Alyosha has listened to Ivan's confession: the antithesis between the two utterances is thrown all the more strongly into relief. Dostoyevsky's intention was that Father Zosima's sermon should refute Ivan's indictment of God in Book Five. It is characteristic that he should have called both books "the climax of the novel."

In all of world literature, there can scarcely have been an author who had such exalted ambitions as Dostoyevsky. He himself was under no illusions as to the difficulty of the task he set himself. "I had the plan of giving an answer to this *atheistic* side of my work in Book Seven, with the title 'A Russian Monk,' " he wrote in a letter. "Now I am afraid that this answer will not be *sufficient*, particularly as it does not refute the objections that are raised in the 'Grand Inquisitor' and earlier in the work point by point, but merely constitutes an indirect reply. It manifests itself as a world outlook that stands diametrically opposed to these postulates, not point by point, but as an artistic portrait."

To demand that Dostoyevsky should give a "sufficient" reply to the problem of evil would, as Erik Krag has pointed out, be the same as to demand a solution to the riddle of the world itself. But if we view his reply as an "artistic portrait," we will find it hard to reject it as unsuccessful.

Nicholas Berdyayev has given the following résumé of the writer's view of the problem of evil in the form of a paradox: "The existence of evil is a proof of God's existence. If the world consisted solely and exclusively of goodness and justice, God would not be necessary, for then the world itself would be God. God exists because evil exists. And this means that God exists because freedom exists."

What Dostoyevsky did in his reply was to transpose the problem to the super-rational plane. With his vast knowledge of human nature he considered he had a right to do this. In *Notes from the Underground*, he had shown that man is not a rational being, and in *Crime and Punishment*, Raskolnikov's attempt to find a rational basis for morality had ended in total defeat. Ivan's struggle to find a rational solution to the problem of suffering is a product of his "Euclidean" intelligence, an intelligence that is closed to everything that lies outside the province of reason and experience. With this intelligence he stands a long way from the deep perception to which Dostoyevsky had fought his way, namely that it is only by *loving life* that man can grasp its meaning.

The idea of love as a precondition for a true understanding of life's meaning is one of the main themes of *The Brothers Karamazov*. We meet it above all in Dmitry's and Father Zosima's hymns to God and his creation. As suffering human beings they have both been compelled to seek an answer to the problem of life's meaning that is different from the one arrived at with theoretical arguments. The way they have found consists in opening themselves to life and letting it speak to them. Concerning this way of love, Father Zosima says in his sermon:

> You must love all that God has created, both his entire world and each single tiny sandgrain of it. Love each tiny leaf, each beam of sunshine. You must love the animals. Love every plant. If you love all things, you will also attain the divine mystery that is in all things. For then your ability to perceive the truth will grow every day, and your mind will open itself to an all-embracing love.
>
> Love is the best teacher we have, brethren. But it does not come to us of its own accord. It is dearly bought. It often demands many years of persevering toil before a person can reach the point where he is able to love—not merely for a moment, but for eternity.

Erik Krag has the following to say about this "way of initiation":

> This is the way of the mystic, and it is also the way of the artist. Every true artist must be something of a mystic. And, seen from this point of view, all people have the chance of *becoming artists*. For this way is open to all. What matters is not that something "be produced"; what matters is one's relation to things and the experience of reality which this brings with it. The only "mystical" aspect of this way of initiation is the *experience* that whoever approaches things with openness and sympathy ("love") will also receive an *answer*. The world is not a lifeless machine. Things will begin to talk to him, to speak within him.

But in that case, is the power of love applicable and efficacious in all situations? Father Zosima thinks it is:

> One may often be in doubt as to what is right, especially when one observes how much sin there is in the world. And many ask: "Should the sinner be chastised with harshness or won over with contrite love?" You should always attempt the path of contrite love. If you once resolve to do it, you will have acquired the ability to win over the entire world. Contrite love is stronger than anything else. There is nothing like it. . . . Instead of passing judgement on others, you must suffer for their misdeeds—as if you yourself had performed them. You must take suffering upon yourself voluntarily. Then you will gain peace of mind, and will perceive that you yourself are guilty. You ought to have been a shining example to these people. But you were not, were you? If you yourself had shone, you would have lighted the way for others, too, and then perhaps they would not have performed any misdeeds.

Father Zosima does not give us examples of specific crimes, but when we consider the moral position he adopts, we must accept that his message must also be applicable to the cases of the child abuse reported by Ivan. Here Dostoyevsky forces his thesis concerning the power of love to what may appear to be an absurd conclusion. But, as Sven Linnér has pointed out in his major study of Father Zosima, this interpretation of the monk's words is nonetheless preferable to the alternative: that Dostoyevsky allow Ivan's question to hang in the air unanswered.

A concise summary and interpretation of Father Zosima's message has been given by Sigurd Fasting:

> The kernel of Father Zosima's teaching is contained in the two commandments he inherited as a child from his brother, who was converted on his deathbed. The first of these is: "Life is a paradise, and we are all in paradise. We simply do not want to acknowledge it. Were we to acknowledge it, we should be in paradise tomorrow." This irrational love for life and for the earth as God's creation unites all human beings in a sense of universal solidarity, and creates Christian brotherhood, which is built upon Father Zosima's second commandment: "You must be aware that each person is guilty before all, and of everything." For Father Zosima, this maxim solves the relatively simple *social* problem, and it also solves the most difficult of all problems—*the problem of suffering*. Through his feeling of guilt before his neighbor, suffering acquires for Father Zosima a di-

mension that is quite different from the one it possesses for Ivan. Father Zosima's indirect reply to Ivan is the scene in which he ecstatically quotes from the book of the Bible that is dearest to him, the Book of Job. Job's laconic justification of suffering is something that is obvious to him, in that he believes in a Divine Providence and in the redeeming and spiritualizing function of suffering in man. Suffering raises man to the level of God, and so it is not an injustice, but a completion—it does not destroy life's harmony, but is one of the necessary elements of life. Man goes the way of suffering as Christ did, and thereby realizes himself as God-man. Dostoyevsky sees suffering as the *ennobler*, not the *squanderer* of that which is valuable in man—and with this vision he rejects his century's ideal of progress in all its forms.

For a modern reader it is probably this vision of suffering that is the biggest stumbling block to acceptance of Father Zosima's philosophy. In Western theology suffering has been portrayed as a negative result of sin. This point of view has acquired an acute form in the slogan of the charismatic movement: "Believe more, and suffer less!"

For Somerset Maugham, too, suffering is an evil, and no more than that. He wrote in a polemic against Dostoyevsky: "So far as physical suffering is concerned, my experience is that long and painful illness makes people querulous, egotistic, intolerant, petty, and jealous. Far from making them better, it makes them worse."

In Dostoyevsky's view, however, suffering is something more than "long and painful illness." The capacity for suffering is a moral quality that drives man to self-understanding and gives him the chance of purification and transformation. Suffering is, moreover, the price we must pay in order not to end up in the Grand Inquisitor's herd. If man wants to be free, to live in accordance with his dignity as a free individual, he must also accept suffering. "The way of freedom is the way of suffering," Berdyayev wrote. "It is always tempting to free man from suffering after robbing him of his freedom. Dostoyevsky is the defender of freedom. Consequently he exhorts man to take suffering upon himself as an inevitable consequence of freedom."

Suffering is equally necessary as a means of curbing the self-assertion and pride that create man's rebellion against God. Dostoyevsky's own sufferings during his period of imprisonment had given him a new perception, a new truth. They had helped him to attain a true comprehension of life's meaning. "Suffering contains an idea," we read in *Crime and Punishment*. And in the sketches for the novel Dostoyevsky touched on what this idea is: "Happiness does not consist of comfort, happiness must be bought with suffering. That is the law of our planet, but this direct perception that is felt in the process of life itself is a joy so great that one can pay for it with years of suffering. Man is not born to happiness. He earns happiness, and always through suffering."

If for Dostoyevsky suffering is a result of sin, then it is at least a *positive* result. Suffering becomes a necessary psychological condition of obtaining forgiveness for sin. By voluntarily submitting, man atones for his sins and thereby attains happiness.

Many readers have had difficulty in following Dostoyevsky on this point. Sin creates suffering, suffering leads to happiness—therefore sin is both necessary and productive. "Love man even in his sin," Father Zosima instructs. In the sketches for the novel the message is pushed to the extreme: "Love sin!"

An illustration of the idea that sin brings man to suffering, and that suffering leads him to deliverance, is given by Father Zosima in his story of how as a young man he struck his servant in the face— "with all my might, so that the blood came." This bestial cruelty, which causes Zosima endless shame and mortification, leads him straight to his conversion. The reason for this is not that he attains forgiveness from the man he has offended, but that through the suffering his action causes him he attains *the right to forgive himself*.

Thus forgiveness becomes a process in the conscience of the sinner, and this forgiveness can only be won by freely seeking suffering and by submitting to it of one's own free will. Raskolnikov obeys Sonya's urging, and takes suffering upon himself in order to atone for his crime. Tikhon teaches the great sinner Stavrogin that he can "forgive himself and win forgiveness for himself in this world through suffering." And Dmitri takes upon himself the suffering that will free him from the painful consciousness of having sinned by wishing for his father's death.

The portrayal of man's penchant for evil is characteristic of Dostoyevsky. But his conception of sin is different from the one expressed by St. Paul: "The evil which I would not, that I do." For Dostoyevsky, sin is more than a lapse from good intentions. In his view, the problem of sin lies in the *will* of human beings to do evil. We are dealing with a kind of *nostalgie de la boue*. In *The Brothers Karamazov* this receives unpleasant illustration in Liza's fantasy of watching a child being tortured to death while she herself sits eating pineapple compote.

At the same time, however, man's awareness of his nature's baser instincts becomes in Dostoyevsky's novels a key to man's deliverance. Through the antithesis of good and evil man can attain the divine synthesis. Here we have the origin of Dostoyevsky's "dangerous" ideas about man's search for deliverance through sin, and his acceptance of suffering in order to redeem himself from sin. D. H. Lawrence described this doctrine as "sinning one's way to Jesus," but that is a crude oversimplification. Even if man is enabled to grow by his tragic experience of evil, this does not mean that Dostoyevsky concedes man the right to rest content with his evil actions. The good that comes of evil is attained only through suffering and through the rejection of evil. Freedom opens the way of evil to man; evil is a proof of freedom, and man must pay the price that lies in suffering. We should, moreover, observe that the sin which for Dostoyevsky leads to deliverance is not to any significant degree the personal sin that has played such an important role in Protestant theology. As E. H. Carr has pointed out, we are confronted rather with a theory that can best be described as "communism in sin" and that expresses itself in man's *common sense of guilt*.

The idea of personal participation in the guilt of all is deeply embedded in the work of the great Russian writers. At the basis of the Russian power for compassion, which in Tolstoy's novel *Resurrection* manifests itself in the weeping women as they see the prisoners on their way to exile and hard labor in Siberia, lies the circumstance that instead of judging their neighbor they perceive *their share in his guilt*. That compassion ousts condemnation is also demonstrated by Sonya's words when Raskolnikov admits his double murder: "Then you are the unhappiest man on earth."

Dostoyevsky's conception of man's will to sin and crime is of major significance to our understanding of the murder of Fyodor Karamazov. The murder can be viewed not simply as a consequence of Dmitri's desire and Smerdyakov's plan, but also as a consequence of the latent wickedness that distinguishes a number of the novel's characters. By adopting this point of view Dostoyevsky succeeds in illustrating one of the book's principal theses: that "all are guilty before all and for all."

That it is so difficult for the law to deal justly with the case against Dmitri is due to the lack of clear boundaries between good and bad, moral and immoral. Some observers have seen here an opposition between Dostoyevsky and Plato. According to Plato's ethics, good is the opposite of evil. Thus the idea of the good cannot include evil. Dostoyevsky is of another opinion. Father Zosima wanders along the paths of God, but it is a criminal who has led him there. Tormented by doubt, Alyosha goes to the "sinner" Grushenka, but it is with her that he regains his inner equilibrium: "You have raised up my soul from the depths." In Dostoyevsky's novels good and evil cohabit. Both the evil and the good must exist, so that man can make a choice of his own free will.

In *The Brothers Karamazov* Dostoyevsky demonstrates how evil becomes the starting point for the growth of good. He shows us life not merely as decay but also as *resurrection*. The decay is a prerequisite for the liberation of life's energy. In Kant we find the idea that every object has its price, but only man possesses dignity. These words could have been written by Dostoyevsky. But when from this proposition Kant concludes that it is better for a person to die than to stain his moral conscience, we must see this as a result of the German philosopher's abstract idealism, which is alien to the Russian writer. Of great significance here is the novel's epigraph: "Verily, verily I say unto you, Except a corn of wheat fall into the ground and die, it abideth alone: but if it die, it bringeth forth much fruit" (John 12:24).

These words, which were later carved on Dostoyevsky's gravestone, may be said to contain the novel's principal idea. The central event of the book—the murder of Fyodor Karamazov—is the clearest expression of life's decay. But at the same time the murder is a condition for the possibility of new life. The epigraph applies first and foremost to Dmitri: his fall and suffering become a necessary precondition for his rebirth. But a number of other characters in the book are also included in the epigraph's message: Father Zosima, Ivan, Alyosha, and, not least, little Ilyushka.

The death of Ilyushka unites the boys in brotherhood and makes them solemnly promise *to remember*. The book's final chapter, "Ilyushka's Funeral. The Speech by the Tombstone," opens up Christian connotations for many readers. Around Ilyushka's coffin Alyosha finds "a dozen" boys— and our thoughts go to the twelve apostles for whom he will from now on act as spiritual father. We hear of the breadcrust that is crumbled for the birds, and of the resurrection: that all shall rise up from the dead and see one another again. The color symbolism is also significant: the blue church, the blue doves, the white coffin, the white rose, the snow. Finally, Alyosha's speech to the boys sounds like a synthesis of Father Zosima's message of love for life: "O boys, O my dear young friends, do not be afraid of life! How beautiful life is as soon as you do something that is good and right!"

Dostoyevsky. Photograph, 1876.   *Anna Grigoryevna. Photograph, 1878.*

A *page from the notes for* The Brothers Karamazov.

The Grand Inquisitor.
Ja. Turlygin, 1906.

Starets Zosima.
B. Rybchenkov, 1932.

The Conversation Between Ivan and Alyosha
in The Brothers Karamazov. *M. Royter, 1956.*

12

TRIUMPH AND DEATH

"I intend to live for another twenty years. . . .
It is all just in its beginning."

After many years of financial worries, things were now beginning to go better for Dostoyevsky and his family. The first edition of *The Brothers Karamazov* quickly sold out, and the hardworking Anna also busied herself with the distribution of more and more new editions of the writer's other works. Thus a popular success like *The Insulted and the Injured* appeared in 1880 for the fifth time.

Together they worked "like oxen," and little by little they managed to pay off the irksome debt. But Anna still had to strain to make ends meet. Their growing circle of acquaintances meant that they had to spend increasing amounts on entertainment. On Sundays there were often dinner parties at the Dostoyevsky home. Dostoyevsky's tailoring bills were also increasing—as a guest in the homes of counts and princes he had to be impeccably dressed. Igor Stravinsky tells us that he received the impression from his parents that Dostoyevsky was always hard up.

Chief among the family's expenses was Dostoyevsky's generosity. Each month he sent, in the greatest secrecy, a hundred rubles to one of his young admirers, Orest Miller. Whenever he set off for his afternoon walk, he had to have at least ten rubles in his pocket. While he wandered pensively about the streets, most of the money would disappear into the hands of the beggars who knew his route and waited for him. On one occasion Anna put on an old kerchief and took up a beggar's pose with their daughter. "When Father drew near," Lyubov tells us, "Mother said in a whining tone: 'Kind sir, have pity on us! I am a sick woman with two children to look after.'

Dostoyevsky stopped, looked at Mother and gave her some alms. When she
began to laugh, he grew offended. 'How could you play a trick like that on
me!' he said, bitterly. 'And in the presence of your child, too!' "

As a rule it was she who complained about him. While he was discussing philosophical problems in Yelena Stakenschneider's salon, she would
sit in a corner complaining to the landlady. Any stranger could invariably
count on getting a few rubles out of Dostoyevsky. Sometimes the beggars
came several times a year. The family received particularly frequent visits
from an old nursemaid. "You must give her three rubles," Dostoyevsky
would say. "The children must give her two each, and then I shall give her
five." Anna sometimes had to take out her handkerchief as she sat complaining about her husband's irresponsibility in money matters. "Yes, that's
how it is for us. And what if something were to happen—what would we
do then? What would we live on? We're poor, after all! We don't even get
a pension!"

As there seemed little likelihood of keeping their expenditures down,
Anna began to examine the possibilities of obtaining extra income. At the
beginning of 1880, she set to work on a new project: "F. M. Dostoyevsky's
Bookstore." The idea of this mail-order business was to promote the sale of
the books published in St. Petersburg to readers and institutions in the
provinces, principally those who subscribed to *The Diary of a Writer*. Dostoyevsky had to obtain a business license, and within a short time Anna had
succeeded in building up a small circle of customers who each month sent
in orders for newly published books. They received from fifty to ninety
rubles a month from this bookselling.

The young lad who worked for them tells of constant quarrels about
money between husband and wife. On the whole, Dostoyevsky was not
always very kind to his wife, the hired lad reports. He attached great importance to a good dinner and complained that Anna never served him a
proper game meal. When on one occasion she herself had bought a quantity
of tasty goods, there was an instant and terrible row. "Papa" let out a yell
and, stamping his feet, shouted: "I suppose you never get enough, you're
always playing poor!" He always insisted on his rights, and she "always
yielded to him in everything."

While Anna looked after the book orders, Dostoyevsky busied himself
with politics and work connected with various associations. On February 3,
1880, he was elected vice-president of the Slavic Benevolent Society. Two

days later an explosion in the Winter Palace almost killed the Tsar. The terror tactics of the nihilists were becoming bolder and bolder, and the net around the "Tsar Liberator" was being drawn ever tighter. On Dostoyevsky's initiative, the Slavic Benevolent Society voted to send a declaration of loyalty to the Tsar on the occasion of his forthcoming Jubilee. The Tsar quickly replied that he had never suspected *this* society of supporting the nihilists.

As a result of this latest terrorist action, Count Mikhail Loris-Melikov, one of the heroes of the war against the Turks, was appointed head of an Extraordinary Committee that was to attempt to damp down the unrest by making various concessions. Dostoyevsky welcomed this "dictatorship of the heart" but was nonetheless anxious as to how the liberal "vice-Tsar" would fare. His fears proved not to be unfounded: only five days after his appointment to the post, Loris-Melikov came close to death after being shot by a young revolutionary named Ippolit Mlodetsky.

On the same day, Aleksei Suvorin came to visit Dostoyevsky. In his diary he described the writer's mood in these troubled times:

> He sat in the parlor rolling cigarettes at a small round table. His face was red and sweaty; it was as though he had just come down from the uppermost tier in a bathhouse. I expect I was unable to conceal my astonishment, for having caught sight of me and greeted me, he suddenly said:
>
> "I've just had an attack. How nice of you to drop by."
>
> He continued his rolling.
>
> Neither he nor I had yet heard about the assassination attempt. But the conversation quickly turned to the subject of political crimes and the explosion in the Winter Palace. Although Dostoyevsky condemned this act, he was also preoccupied by the public reaction to this type of crime. It seemed as though most people felt sympathy for them, or perhaps more correctly did not know how they ought to react.
>
> "Let us suppose that we are standing outside Daziaro's, looking at paintings. Beside us there is a man who is pretending to look at the pictures. He seems to be waiting for something, for he keeps looking round. Suddenly a man comes up to him and says: 'In a little while the Winter Palace will be blown up. I have just set the fuse.' As we stand there, we hear this. Imagine, these people are so excited that they can't even keep their voices down. What would we do? Go to the Winter Palace and warn of the explosion, or report these people to the police in order to have them arrested? Would you have done that?"
>
> "No, I would not."
>
> "Neither would I . . ."

Why would he not have gone and warned people of the crime? Was it the former revolutionary's abhorrence of all that smacked of informing that was manifesting itself here? Was it that his loyalty to the social status quo was not as firmly-rooted as it seemed? Did he still perhaps feel desperately attracted by the vengeance of the revolutionaries for the sufferings of the insulted and the injured? Or was the reason quite simply his instinct for self-preservation? "The liberals would never have forgiven me something like that," he concluded. "They would have hurled themselves on me, brought me to the point of utter despair. . . . I should like to write something about this. I could have said much that would have been good and useful for society and the government, but it is unfortunately not possible. In this country it is forbidden to talk about those things which are of most importance."

It was possibly at this time that he had the idea of writing a sequel to *The Brothers Karamazov* in which Alyosha would appear as a revolutionary and be executed for a political crime. Suvorin's account of this plan is, however, far from being authenticated. Recent studies of his diary have set a question mark over the word "executed," and indeed such a denouement would have been quite uncharacteristic of Dostoyevsky.

It is at least certain that two days after this conversation with Suvorin he went to attend the execution of Mlodetsky. "I did not like this," we read in the diary of Grand Prince Konstantin Romanov. "I myself would have felt revulsion at witnessing an inhuman act of this kind; but he explained that he was interested in all that concerned human beings." "I was present at the execution," Dostoyevsky said when he visited Polonsky that same evening. "Nearly fifty thousand people had turned out to watch." If he had hoped that this time, too, a miracle would happen, he was disappointed. "Mlodetsky was hanged on Semyonovsky Square at 11 A.M.—all is quiet," the Tsar noted in his diary.

As usual the social season went quickly. Dostoyevsky was continually on the go, now off to a princely reception, now to a public reading. His renown as an interpreter of Pushkin was steadily growing, and in the spring he was invited to give one of the many celebratory addresses on the occasion of the unveiling of Aleksander Opekushin's Pushkin Monument in Moscow.

The plan of erecting a monument in honor of the national poet was quite old. In a materialistic age, when even literary critics announced that a pair of boots were of more value than the foremost poet, assembling of the necessary materials took quite some time. It was almost a generation and a half after the poet's death before the Society of Lovers of Russian Literature was able to send out invitations to the unveiling of the monument.

Everyone sensed that this would be far more than a literary event. It would be a struggle between Westernizers and Slavophiles. Who was he, this Pushkin? A master of form who had courageously promised the Western torch of freedom in the Tsar's dark empire? Or a profoundly national writer who had prophetically announced his people's mission in world history? The two camps in Russian intellectual life gathered their forces for a decisive battle; celebratory speakers began work on their speeches. Dostoyevsky left the salons of St. Petersburg for his ramshackle writer's cottage in Staraya Russa; Turgenev came back from Paris and sought refuge in his stately home in Tula. Tolstoy was one of the few who refused to attend: a celebration of this type was in his view a great sin, the more so because he believed the people were completely indifferent to this aristocratic poet.

The unveiling of the monument had originally been set for Pushkin's birthday on May 26. As a delegate from the St. Petersburg Slavic Benevolent Society, Dostoyevsky thought it best to arrive a few days in advance. He had to obtain an admission card and buy wreaths for the arrangements; it might, moreover, be advantageous to do a bit of reconnaissance before the great battle.

Anna was not allowed to accompany her husband on this occasion. Dostoyevsky had no confidence in the nursemaid at Staraya Russa; if Anna came, the children would have to come too, and it would be too expensive, particularly if she also had to buy a new dress. The decision came as a hard blow to Anna. How would he manage without her? What if he were to have an epileptic fit and be locked up in one of the city's madhouses? She got back at her husband with a succession of irritable, snappish letters. As for him, he wrote her long bulletins about what was going on, both officially and behind the scenes.

On his arrival in Moscow on May 23 he was met at the railroad station by some twenty or so writers. From there they repaired to one of the best hotels in town, the Loskutnaya on Tverskoy Boulevard.

As a consequence of the death of the Tsarina, the unveiling was postponed indefinitely. Dostoyevsky was afraid of the expense and would have preferred to go right home, but the Slavophiles would not hear of it. His stay would be financed by the municipality, they maintained, and moreover "all Moscow" would be disappointed and offended if he were now to withdraw before the battle had been fought. Everyone who had bought tickets wanted to know if Dostoyevsky was to appear!

A few days after his arrival a fine dinner was held for him, with speeches and telegrams. "They spoke of my 'great' importance as a 'world-famous' artist, as a publicist and as a Russian," he wrote home proudly. Everyone came up to drink his health, and he replied with a brief speech of thanks which aroused great enthusiasm. "Kiss the children from me, and tell them about papa," he concluded his report to Anna.

A promising beginning! It seemed that he had done the right thing in staying, after all. If his celebratory speech were to be a success, he would be as famous as Tolstoy and Turgenev, he explained in another letter.

But it was tiring. Every day admirers appeared at the hotel, and then there were social calls to make, and gatherings to attend until late into the night. He could not even manage to make his usual assurances of affection. "I have noticed the evident coldness in your letters," Anna wrote sharply. "I hope you will celebrate in moderation and not pay the young ladies too much attention, I cannot tolerate that. . . . Admit that you cannot live without me!"

Worst of all, however, were the intrigues. Why, even a month ago that damned disciple of Turgenev's, Annenkov, had tried to blacken his name with mendacious reminiscences from the 1840s, and now Turgenev had held a meeting with the program committee and upset all his reading plans! There were even some people who did not want him to take part at all! Oh, how he hated that conceited look on the faces of his opponents: "You are just a reactionary, but we are liberals." Still, it was good to know he had the public behind him. "In the Moscow Inn there are always a lot of people, and it is seldom that they do not turn round and look at me; they all know who I am."

On Friday June 6, it was finally time for the unveiling of the monument. More than a hundred deputations had turned up for the ceremony. The complement of police and informers was a large one. After his death in 1837, Pushkin's body had been smuggled out of the capital in the dead of night in order to prevent demonstrations. Who knew what might happen now, in a time when the terrorists had almost thrown the country into a state of emergency? Perhaps there would be trouble with that libertarian poet Pushkin again!

After a moving commemorative service in the Strastny Monastery, the nearly three hundred delegates moved on to Tverskaya Square. A brass band played a march from Giacomo Meyerbeer's *Le Prophète*. Then the statue was unveiled and presented to the city of Moscow. "Dostoyevsky was surrounded by a large flock of students," Nikolay Shamin wrote in his unpublished memoirs.

> I well remember how he looked: of average height, thickset, slightly stoop-shouldered, with pallid features—a man on whom great sufferings had left their mark. He was bare-headed, and his hair and beard were blond, straggly, and somewhat flecked with gray. He walked carefully, supporting an old man of 85 who had been a servant to the Pushkin family. Later I heard that Dostoyevsky had asked the old man if he thought the monument looked like Pushkin as he had been when he was alive. "Yes, it does," the man replied. "It looks very like him, except that Aleksandr Sergeyevich wasn't nearly as tall as that."

After the unveiling the festivities resumed at the city's university, where Turgenev was presented with an honorary doctorate for his "talented mastery of Pushkin's language." The award was hardly calculated to improve Dostoyevsky's attitude; during the dinner which the municipality gave later in the day for the delegates, there were very nearly renewed clashes. Dmitri Grigorovich had been charged with the responsibility of keeping the two rivals apart. When he came into the room together with Turgenev, Dostoyevsky turned demonstratively away, and looked out of the window. "Come over here—I want to show you a fine statue," Grigorovich said, nervously. Turgenev pointed to Dostoyevsky. "Well, if it looks anything like him, please count me out."

Dostoyevsky retaliated during the evening meeting in the Noblemen's Assembly, where he read Pimen's monologue from *Boris Godunov*. The audience was wildly enthusiastic, and he received three curtain calls. "The only thing is," he had to admit in a letter to Anna, "that Turgenev got even more curtain calls, though he read altogether abominably." The explanation must be that one of his rival's friends, Professor Maksim Kovalevsky, had told a hundred of his students to "roar with applause" every time Turgenev came up to take his bow. These liberals were dastardly enough to employ *claqueurs*! How much more genuine had been the enthusiasm with which *he* had been received! With kisses and flowers that audience had thanked him for his latest novel: "You are our great prophet! We have become better people since reading *The Brothers Karamazov.*" There could be no doubt that this novel had made a "colossal impression."

On Sunday June 8, Dostoyevsky's "fateful day" arrived, on which he was to give a speech in the morning and a reading at night. Now he would bring the Pushkin celebrations to a fitting conclusion.

The great Hall of Columns in the Noblemen's Assembly was packed full. Several thousand people had arrived for the morning ceremony. Among the guests of honor were Pushkin's three daughters and two sons, Governor General Vladimir Dolgorukov, and Andrei Saburov, Russia's new Minister of Culture. One by one the writers came onto the stage and laid their wreaths at the foot of the Pushkin statue. Only Turgenev was bold enough to place his wreath on the poet's head, winning applause from the audience as he did so.

In spite of his tired and gloomy appearance, Dostoyevsky was in a fighting mood. The newspapers had begun to describe Turgenev as "first among the delegates"—Turgenev, who the day before had delivered a scandalous address in which he had not even been able to bring himself to admit that Pushkin was the Russian national poet! It was just as well that that was not to be the last word on this matter. Was Turgenev unable to understand that they were all pygmies in comparison with Pushkin?

"Fyodor Mikhailovich Dostoyevsky will now speak!"

The applause died away, all gazes were directed toward the writer as he hastily leafed through his notes on his way up to the rostrum. He did not exactly cut an imposing figure; his suit hung from him as though from a clotheshanger, his shirt was crumpled and his tie loose. He seemed to have a slight limp in one leg—the prison fetters had marked him for life.

" 'Pushkin is an unusual—indeed, the only—revelation of the Russian spirit,' said Gogol. For my own part I will add: a prophetic revelation." The hall grew silent. This was going to be something quite different from Turgenev's wordy exposition. This was going to be something heavy, something Karamazovian, which no one would be able to tear himself away from.

Prophetic revelation? Yes—even in the poetry of his youth Pushkin had anticipated today's rootless representative of the Russian intelligentsia, the vagrant who, having severed his attachment to the ideals of the people, had hurled himself into the arms of socialism in a convulsive attempt to save the world. "This Russian vagrant will not rest until the whole of humanity is happy—nothing less will do."

Pushkin had also prophesied the fate that lay in store for this proud individual. The people would reject him as a foreign body. "Humble your-self, proud man, and break your pride in pieces! Humble yourself, super-fluous man, and set to work on your home field!" The only salvation for the rootless Russian was to seek redemption in a faith in the love of the Russian people for all human beings. Only in humble union with the people could the Russian individual show his true face: "To become a real Russian, to become a Russian completely and entirely, that means perhaps in the last analysis to become a brother to all men, a *universal man*, if you like."

In Pushkin the Russian people's peculiar ability to enter into the spirit of foreign nations attained its loftiest expression, Dostoyevsky maintained. And thereby this Russian national bard has also become a prophetic figure who shows the striving of the Russian national character of universality and common humanity. In exhortatory tones he called upon the conflicting factions of his homeland to settle their differences, so that Russia could get on with its historic task: to serve and promote the idea of unity upon earth, not with violence or weapons, but with the power of brotherly love. By the end of the speech Pushkin had become a symbol of the realization of Dostoyevsky's vision of Russia's future:

> It is true that our land is poor, but through it "Jesus Christ once wandered, blessing as he went." And why should we not be able to bear His last words within us? Was He not also born in a manger? We can at least point to the universal and all-human in Pushkin's genius, to his spiritual affinity with other peoples. In his art he has given us an incontrovertible proof of the Russian spirit's striving toward universality—and this is for us an ex-hortatory omen. Even if the idea we have enunciated here is only fantasy, we still have Pushkin as a basis for this fantasy. If he had been allowed to live longer, perhaps he would have revealed the Russian soul in a way which our European brothers would have understood, and perhaps they would stand closer to us than they do today. Yes, perhaps if he had explained to them the whole truth about our endeavors, perhaps then they would have understood us better, perhaps they would have ceased to regard us with mistrust and arrogance. Had Pushkin been allowed to live longer, perhaps even among us Russians there would be fewer misunderstandings and conflicts than there are now. But God willed otherwise. Pushkin died in the flower of his youth and took a great secret with him to the grave. And now we who are left behind must try to guess what that secret was.

"You have guessed it!" came a high-pitched wail from the back of the hall. "It is you who are the prophet!"

To judge from numerous eyewitness accounts, Dostoyevsky's speech made an overwhelming impression. Everyone present, Westernizers as well as Slavophiles, was seized with enthusiasm for Dostoyevsky's burning faith in Russia's future. Even a soberminded jurist like Anatoly Koni later told Dostoyevsky's daughter: "As we sat listening to your father we were completely hypnotized. It was as though the walls in the auditorium had been replaced by a gigantic bonfire. If your father had pointed at this bonfire and said: 'Let us now rush into the flames and die in order to save Russia!' we would all have followed him as one man, happy and content to be able to die for the Fatherland."

Hysterical ladies had to be guided out of the hall; a young man managed to press Dostoyevsky's hand before passing out. There was no end to the ovations and embraces. Finally with great difficulty Turgenev and Aksakov, the leaders of factions that had previously been in such conflict, succeeded in piloting the writer out. Grigorovich went on ahead waving a handkerchief, while the President rang his chairman's bell in a desperate attempt to bring the meeting to order.

"Pale and nervous, with sunken head and eyes grown dim, Dostoyevsky sat resting," a journalist reported from the side room. "I have never experienced anything like that in all my life," Dostoyevsky said. "This surpasses all human powers . . . everything started to go round, and my legs refused to carry me. . . . I don't understand it myself. . . ." On the same evening he wrote to Anna "with shaking hands and feet":

> When at the end of the speech I called for the universal reconciliation of human beings, the public grew completely hysterical. And when I finished speaking, it was not simply a question of acclaim and enthusiasm: people sobbed and wept and threw their arms around one another, solemnly promising one another to become better, and not hate, but love one another. . . . The curtain-calls lasted for half an hour; people waved handkerchiefs; I was suddenly stopped by two old men I did not know: "We have been enemies for twenty years, but now we have embraced and made it up. It is you who have reconciled us. You are our saint, our great prophet!"

The President of the Society of Lovers of Russian Literature mounted the rostrum and announced that Dostoyevsky had been unanimously elected a member of the society. There was more applause; the mayor came up and thanked the writer on behalf of the city. When the proceedings resumed once more, Aksakov declared that he would abstain from speaking. All the points at issue had been resolved in Dostoyevsky's "speech of genius," a speech that had been "an event in our literature." At the end of the meeting Dostoyevsky was handed a massive laurel wreath by the female delegates; toward morning of the following day he laid it by the statue of Pushkin. How was he to explain such a success? No, he had certainly not expected this. . . .

Later, in the evening, the festivities concluded with Dostoyevsky's reading of *The Prophet*. The writer's eyes were "mysteriously directed toward some place outside the world," an eyewitness related. It was as though Pushkin had been thinking of Dostoyevsky when he had written about the prophet who would burn the hearts of men with his word! The Pushkin Festival had turned into a tribute to Dostoyevsky. People were still coming up to him and congratulating him. The French Slavist Louis Léger found in his deep gaze and quivering features a "martyred, defiant genius," and thought his speech would be of great interest *pour le maître*—i.e., to Victor Hugo.

Dostoyevsky was pleased. Anna wrote of the photograph Léger took of the writer the following day: "Here I found once again the expression I had seen on his face on several earlier occasions at moments of joy and happiness."

Now only Tolstoy could measure up to him! Ought he perhaps to make a quick trip out to Yasnaya Polyana? He had never been able to forgive Strakhov for not having introduced him to Tolstoy during one of Solovyov's readings. But now Turgenev was going around telling people that Tolstoy had completely lost his reason! No, it was probably safest to go home to his family.

After over three weeks' absence he was back in his cottage again, tired but happy. He barely managed to say hello to Fedya's new pet, a little foal which Anna had bought for three rubles, before sitting down at his writing desk. There would be no trip to Ems this summer. The last quarter of *The Brothers Karamazov* still remained to be written and, what was more, the storms around his Pushkin speech soon began to break.

Full of confidence in the power of the word, Dostoyevsky had been hoping that the speech would form a turning point in the struggle between the Slavophiles and Westernizers. It was high time for Russians to unite and get on with fulfilling their world-historic mission! But when a short time later the speech was published in *Moscow Reports*, his once so enthusiastic public awoke from their trance. Instead of praise, he now received criticism, both from left and from right.

Turgenev was one of the many who had let himself be swept along with the rest. Indeed, he had even embraced his rival with tears in his eyes. But no sooner was he back in Paris than he was seized with anger and revulsion at this "idiotic rubbish" about the "Russian universal man." Lies and falsehood from beginning to end—Dostoyevsky had quite blatantly seduced the entire Russian intelligentsia! A conservative thinker like Konstantin Leontyev was, for his part, annoyed that the speaker should have misused the Christian commandment to love our neighbor in order to preach international brotherhood: that was plain heresy! But the main thrust of the attack came from the liberal political scientist Aleksandr Gradovsky, who in an article entitled "Dream and Reality" accused Dostoyevsky of harboring idealized notions about the Russian people. In Gradovsky's view there were scant grounds for calling this people "great." What special qualifications did this enslaved and unenlightened people possess for leading civilized Europe onto the true path? Would it not be better instead if Russia were to begin to glean some learning from the West's progressive ideas and social institutions?

Angrily Dostoyevsky sat in Staraya Russa poring over the attacks made on him. So this was the reward for his great speech of reconciliation! They called him a "coward," an "arrogant man," a "poet" who had broken loose from the real world and had "flown away on the wings of fantasy and mystical prophecy." "There you can see how the press is falling on me for the speech I made in Moscow," he wrote to Orest Miller. "As though I had incriminated myself of deception or forgery!" He considered that this was something he must reply to, and set to work on the August issue of The Diary of a Writer, the only one to appear in 1880.

In his reply to Gradovsky Dostoyevsky rejected the argument that the Russian people must first complete its social development before it could start preaching the idea of brotherhood. Nourished on Christian soil, the Russian people already possessed enlightenment in the true meaning of the word: a spiritual light that illumines the heart and shows people the path of life. "Don't come and tell me that I don't know the people!" he warned. "Oh, I know the people all right: it was the people who saw to it that I once again received Christ, the same Christ who had been revealed to me in the home of my parents, and whom I almost lost when I allowed myself to be transformed into a 'European liberal.'"

Without Christ, Gradovsky's social institutions have no value whatever, Dostoyevsky continued. Only the spirit of Christianity is in a position to create such a sense of brotherhood. If only men will become brothers because of Christ, all other social problems will at once find their solution. A true brother cannot allow his brother to be a slave. On the other hand, no institution will be able to create brotherhood if men are not brothers. If one creates a society under the slogan "liberty, equality, and fraternity," it will soon become necessary to add two more words to the slogan: "or death." Brotherhood or death! "And then the brothers will begin to cut the heads off their brothers in order to create brotherhood through this 'civic institution.'" No, brotherhood via the introduction of foreign institutions is impossible. The starting point must be man's love for Christ: brotherhood can only be created through self-perfection. And it is precisely here that the suffering Russian people can show the way to other nations!

The unpleasantness associated with the polemics surrounding the Pushkin speech soon brought a recurrence of Dostoyevsky's epileptic fits. Yet in spite of this the fine, golden autumn in Staraya Russa was a period of rich creativity. When at the beginning of October the family finally got ready to leave, Dostoyevsky had, in addition to working on the *Diary*, also managed to complete *The Brothers Karamazov*. Altogether he had written more than three hundred printed pages in three and a half months, and this in spite of the fact that he now needed "double the time in order to write the same amount as before."

At the end of a tiring night's work he sat down and wrote a letter to one of his friends. He had just snuffed a large cigarette with his penholder and taken a gulp of tea that was strong as tar. The pair of tallow candles cast a faint radiance over the well-ordered writing desk:

> It is night now; the hands of the clock are approaching six. The town is waking up, but I have not gone to bed yet. And the doctors say that I must not overexert myself, that I must sleep at night and not sit for ten to twelve hours at a stretch huddled over my writing desk. Why do I write at night? Well, as soon as I wake up at around one, there is a ring at the door: someone has come to ask me for something, someone else wants something else, a third person comes with some request or other, a fourth demands that I shall resolve some quite unresolvable "accursed question" for him— otherwise I'll go and shoot myself, he says. (And this is the first time I have seen him.) Then delegates come from the students, from the gymnasium, from the Society of Noblemen—all wanting me to take part in evening readings. When will I get time to think, to work, to read, to live?

He seldom refused when he was asked to read from his own works but would take the stand no matter how much it taxed his energies. It was as though his cough did not dare to show itself when this "dry little peasant" mounted the rostrum. "His hoarse voice sounded like metal," the actor Vladimir Davydov recalled, describing a reading by Dostoyevsky of *The Prophet* in 1880. "The public groaned with enthusiasm; Dostoyevsky grew pale, he was evidently on the point of fainting; he had to be almost carried down from the podium."

He devoted his mastery of the art of public reading mostly to the support of various organizations—the Red Cross, The Literary Fund, The Slavic Benevolent Society. Best of all, he liked to perform before the students and gymnasium pupils. "The love of our young people is what matters most," he explained. He always chose his repertoire with great care—Nellie's story from *The Insulted and the Injured*, Raskolnikov's conversation with Marmeladov in the tavern, Olga's story from *A Raw Youth*, Alyosha's speech at Ilyushka's funeral. The *pièce de résistance*—"The Legend of the Grand Inquisitor"—was performed with such gusto that in the end the school headmasters had to put their feet down: these inspired atheistic arguments were far too dangerous for young minds!

Dostoyevsky's social life was also exhausting, but he liked to be seen in public. After his success in Moscow, his earlier embarrassment had given way to self-confident assuredness. With great effort he puffed his way up five flights of stairs to Polonsky's apartment. He had to sit down and rest at each landing, and when he finally reached his destination, he was exhausted: people frequently received an erroneous impression of him as he stood there gasping for breath. He was not as fierce as he sometimes looked. "Is it difficult for you to climb the stairs?" Yelena Stakenschneider asked. "Yes, it is," he replied. "It is just as difficult as getting to paradise. But on the other hand one feels good when one has found paradise, and that is how I feel here in your home."

The salon conversations were probably not always conducted on the highest level. The discussions did, however, occasionally touch on interesting topics, and then Dostoyevsky would always have some remark ready. Was it true that all creatures possess consciousness—not just people, but also animals? "Yes," was Danilevsky's opinion: "even a pine tree is capable of saying 'I am.' " "To perceive one's existence, to be able to see 'I am'— that is a great gift," Dostoyevsky said quietly. "But to say 'I am not'—to perish for the sake of others—whoever can do that stands possibly even higher."

He was unfamiliar with false modesty. He liked to be compared to men like Hugo and Balzac and was genuinely delighted when he learned that Tolstoy considered *Notes from the House of the Dead* "the finest work in all of modern Russian literature." Whom did he place higher—Balzac or himself? "Dostoyevsky did not laugh at my childish naïveté," related the girl who asked him this question in the autumn of 1880. "He thought for a little and then said: 'Each of us only possesses worth to the extent that we have brought something distinctive and original into literature. Everything depends on that. But one cannot compare us. I think we both have our merits.' "

He did not want to be a mentor to the new and coming generation of writers. He did, it was true, sometimes give his backing to new authors, but his judgment was usually severe. "What rubbish!" was one of his customary pronouncements. The fifteen-year-old Dmitri Merezhkovsky gives an example of how merciless he could be to writers who did not satisfy his requirements. Through Countess Tolstoya, Merzhkovsky's father had obtained an audience with Dostoyevsky for his son, in order to find out once and for all whether the boy had talent. "He listened to me in silence, irritation, and impatience," Merezhkovsky related. "It was clear that we were interrupting him. 'Weak . . . wretched . . . quite useless!' he said finally. 'In order to write well one must suffer much!' " "Well, in that case it'll be better if he doesn't write at all," the boy's father retorted.

Most of all he liked to spend his time among children and young people. Hour after hour he would sit on a bench near the Church of St. Vladimir and play with the little children there. They would make sandpies on his coattails—the pies would suddenly disappear when he had one of his coughing fits. "What's happened to the cakes, grandpa?" they would ask. "I've eaten them all, they were so good that . . ." "A wonderful age . . ." he would say, turning to a student. "As yet they have no hatred, they know no sorrow. . . . Tears are succeeded by laughter."

He was very pleased by the fact that the new generation of young people had a greater interest in and understanding of the "Russian idea" and the "Russian Christ." These young people would encircle him at banquets and balls and start to ask him questions, and he would talk to them about Christ, while the couples danced around him in merry waltz time.

Increasingly Dostoyevsky was caught up in the dazzling world of the nobility. The writer who had once depicted the worst slums and the worst degradation now regularly consorted with the foremost aristocrats of the land. He also gradually became a frequent guest in the Anichkov Palace, where he conversed with the future Tsar Alexander III and his consort Maria Fyodorovna, the Danish Princess Dagmar, who always had to take out her handkerchief when he read from his sentimental tales. But he never became a court aficionado. He cared little about court etiquette and liked to begin the conversations himself and leave as soon as he felt like it. "He used to say of the successor's consort that she was a real Women's Institute girl," his niece Maria Ivanova related. "And when he grew too heated in the course of a conversation, he never noticed that he was pulling at the buttons on her dress." Never was he in a better mood than when he came home from these receptions in an imperial carriage, piled high with presents for the children.

At the beginning of 1881, the ground had been laid for a meeting with the "Tsar Liberator" himself. But by that time Dostoyevsky's strength had given out.

II

Sometime around 1880, during one of his salon conversations, Dostoyevsky was asked about the advantages of the Russian religion over all other religious persuasions. "Go and see the peasant who is sitting in your kitchen," he replied. "Then you will surely find out." "And what can one learn from this peasant?" "How one must live, and how one must die."

It was not only the ideals of suffering and humility that Dostoyevsky had learned from the Russian peasant. He had also learned how to die in peasant fashion. "How wonderfully the Russian peasant dies!" Turgenev exclaims in A Huntsman's Sketches. "His state of mind before death can be called neither indifference nor apathy; he dies just as though he were performing a ritual, coldly and simply." Dostoyevsky had the same familiarity with death. For him, too, death had long been mentally present. He too could look death in the eye without protests or agonizing struggles. And so his death was as peaceful as that of a Russian peasant.

To many people, Dostoyevsky's death came as a great surprise. It seemed so difficult to grasp that this resilient man should fall victim to a hemorrhage. He had, after all, lived for so long in the vicinity of death, without its affecting his plans or capacity for work in any obvious fashion. He had been planning to publish his *Diary* for two years and then get on with a sequel to *The Brothers Karamazov*. Surely he would attain his goal this time, too, his friends thought. Why, he himself was going round telling everyone that he intended to live for another twenty years!

Their optimism was unfounded. People who had observed Dostoyevsky during the Pushkin festivities reported a few months later that he had become still thinner and paler. He was in fact hopelessly unfit, taking, for example, more than ten minutes just to undress himself. The pulmonary veins had become so delicate that the slightest exertion could make them burst. All effort must be avoided, the doctors told him, as they tried to keep his spirits up. A small hemorrhage need not have fatal consequences, the doctors assured him. A "pack" could form that would prevent too great a loss of blood. They could only shake their heads over his intense activity. Von Bretzel would sometimes appear at his readings in order to rush to his aid as he totteringly left the rostrum.

Even though Dostoyevsky clung to the doctors' assurances to the last moment, he knew in his heart that his days were numbered. Avoiding effort had never been something he had been good at. "I am working very nervously, amid torment and great anxiety," he wrote in the autumn of 1880. "Although I am working, I am also physically ill."

Now he was feeling the pressure of his work on *The Diary of a Writer*— the first issue was to appear at the end of January. How would the censor react to his outspoken utterances about the legislative assembly which was soon to be convened? This problem was solved when Nikolai Abaza, the chief censor no less, volunteered to read the issue through. But what would readers say? With great fervor he had urged that the people's representatives on the rural councils should have greater influence; otherwise the planned constitution would be merely a "landowners' constitution." The Tsar ought to consult the Russian peasant about what was not going right in Russia. Could he really not see that he was the father of the people?

Then there was his social life, with all the obligations that entailed. He had recently promised to attend a theatrical performance at the home of Countess Tolstoya, and he was also soon to read Pushkin at a literary evening for the benefit of poor students.

But it was neither work nor social life that sent him to his grave. His death was connected rather wih various political and financial worries.

On Sunday, January 25, the Tsar's secret police conducted a search in the apartment next door to Dostoyevsky's. They were looking for members of the terrorist organization People's Will, which a few months later was to claim the life of Alexander II. One may suppose that this disquieting search, which must have once again reminded Dostoyevsky of his revolutionary past, contributed to his first hemorrhage during the night of January 26, 1881.

Anna did not mention a word about this in her memoirs. According to her "official" version, Dostoyevsky simply lost his favorite pen on the floor somewhere and the hemorrhage came as he tried to lift a cupboard in order to find it. True, this first hemorrhage was a minor one—he did not even consider it necessary to wake his family—but when that same night he wrote to ask for the rest of his fee for *The Brothers Karamazov*, he felt all the same that this might possibly be his "last prayer" to *The Russian Messenger*.

Neither did Anna say anything about the cause of the second hemorrhage—the quarrel about the inheritance.

After a dispute that had gone on for ten years and a lot of pressure, mainly from Anna, judgment had finally been passed in the case of the Kumanin inheritance: Dostoyevsky had succeeded in inheriting a large estate. This was, however, on condition that he should pay a sum in compensation to his three sisters. As might be expected, the "minister of finance" had done little about this matter, and the sisters were beginning to grow impatient. Alexandra had long ago severed all links with her brother because of their unfortunate quarrel; Varenka, his favorite sister, wanted nothing to do with the case; it was Vera, the mother of Sonya and Masha, who was charged with the task of reminding him about the conditions of the inheritance.

On Monday, January 26, Vera arrived in order to carry out her task. Money had never been a favorite subject of conversation in the penniless Dostoyevsky family. Nonetheless, she reminded her brother about his obligations vis-à-vis his sisters. If he had no means with which to discharge them, he would have to relinquish the estate. In some irritation Dostoyevsky proceeded to explain to her the shakiness of his finances. He had no confidence that his books would become any sort of gold mine, and as he was not an employee of the state, Anna could expect no widow's pension either. The inheritance was practically all that he had to leave his wife and child. One word led to another; Dostoyevsky interrupted his evening meal and went into his study. Suddenly he noticed that his hands were wet. When he looked at them, he saw that they were covered in blood.

Anna immediately sent for von Bretzel: "My husband has had a hemorrhage—for God's sake, come at once!"

Lyubov and Fedya came running in. Dostoyevsky tried to calm them and produced a humorous drawing of two fishermen who had gotten entangled in a net and lay splashing in the water. He laughed and laughed at this drawing. But when the family doctor finally appeared, there followed a second hemorrhage, this time so violent that the writer lost consciousness. He was so weakened by the loss of blood that there was nothing to be done except to administer palliatives. Several more doctors arrived, but it was plain that his life could not be saved.

When, later in the evening, Dostoyevsky regained consciousness, he said to his wife in a whisper: "Anya, send for a priest, do you hear? I want to take confession and receive the sacrament."

The parish priest of St. Vladimir's arrived half an hour later. For a long time the writer lay taking confession.

The priest left, and Anna and the children came in and congratulated him on the holy act. Dostoyevsky gave them all his blessing and asked them to live in peace and tolerance. Then Anna had to read the story of the prodigal son. After the reading he turned to his son and daughter and said in a weak voice:

"Never forget what you have just heard, dear children. Have complete trust in God, and never doubt in his forgiveness. I love you dearly, but my love is as nothing beside God's infinite love for man. Even if you should commit a crime, never doubt God. You are His children, so humble yourselves before Him, just as the prodigal son humbled himself before his father. Ask for His forgiveness; then He will rejoice, just as the father rejoiced over the return of his prodigal son."

The children wept. "Papa, dearest papa, I shall always remember what you have just said," Lyubov sobbed. "You will be by my side all my life!"

When Dostoyevsky was left alone with Anna, he thanked her for all the happiness she had given him. "Remember, Anya, that I have always loved you dearly and have never deceived you, not even in my thoughts."

On Tuesday morning, Dostoyevsky awoke happy and cheerful. "Why are you all standing there holding a funeral over me? I'll outlive you all, you'll see!" He had had a good rest during the night and was only staying in bed because the doctors had instructed him to do so. He talked to his children in a whisper. A bright future awaited the new generation in Russia! Later in the day the proofs of *The Diary of a Writer* arrived. The issue had grown several lines too long for the whole of it to fit onto two printed sheets: Anna had to help him with some deletions.

In the meantime the news of Dostoyevsky's illness had spread across the whole town. From early in the afternoon until late in the evening the doorbell rang almost incessantly. Friends and strangers came to inquire about the writer's condition, and finally the doctor had to issue a ban on any further visits. Dostoyevsky was happy about the attention he was now being shown. But it was growing more difficult for him to speak: "He simply lay looking at us with his affectionate eyes," the hired man recalled.

Anna spent the night of Wednesday, January 28 (February 9 by the Gregorian calendar), on the floor by the side of the sofa. When she awoke at about seven, she saw that her husband was looking at her.

"Well, how do you feel today, my dearest?" she asked as she leaned over him.

"Listen, Anya," he said in a semi-whisper. "I've been awake for three hours, lying here thinking, and now it's quite clear to me: today I shall die."

"Dear Fedya, why do you think that?" Anna asked, uneasily. "You're much better now; you haven't had any more hemorrhages, and a 'pack' has probably formed. . . . For God's sake, you mustn't torment yourself with such thoughts; I assure you that you will live for a long time yet!"

When Dostoyevsky had been allowed to sleep for a few more hours he felt much better. He even sat up in bed in order to put on his socks. But this small exertion was enough to bring on another hemorrhage. Once again Anna tried to give him hope that he would live. The writer merely replied with a melancholy smile, as though to say that he had been right in his feeling that death was near. "Anya, go and fetch the New Testament!"

Anna brought the New Testament he had received as a gift from the wives of the Decembrists on his way to Siberia. "During all the four years he spent in the penitentiary he never let this book leave his side," she says in her memoirs. "Later it always lay out on his writing desk, and when he fell into thought or was in doubt about one thing or another, he would often open the book at random and read what was on its left-hand page."

Now, too, he sought clarity in his New Testament. The book opened at the Gospel according to St. Matthew, at the passage where Jesus comes to John in order to be baptized. "But John forbad him, saying, I have need to be baptized of thee, and comest thou to me?

"And Jesus answering said unto him, Suffer it to be so now: for thus it becometh us to fulfil all righteousness."

"Hear now—permit it. Do not restrain me!" Dostoyevsky said, quietly.

On page 6 of his New Testament we find, written in Anna's hand: "Opened by me and read aloud to Fyodor Mikhailovich at three o'clock on the day he died."

Friends and acquaintances continued to crowd in. One of the few people who were allowed to see the writer was Apollon Maikov. "Give him a cigar!" the sick man whispered, and pressed his friend's hand in parting. At around five in the afternoon Maikov dictated the following lines as a reply to a sympathetic letter from Countess Heiden:

On the 26th a vein burst, and his lungs were filled with blood. In the evening there was another hemorrhage, with great loss of blood and a sense of asphyxiation. For a quarter of an hour or so Fyodor Mikhailovich was quite certain that he was going to die; he took confession and received the sacrament. Little by little his breathing grew easier and the blood stopped flowing. But since the vein has not healed it is possible that there may be another hemorrhage. And then it is of course probable that death will follow. At this moment he is, however, fully conscious, but he fears that the vein may burst again.

There was great consternation when Pasha turned up and demanded that "father" should write a will. Professor Koshlakov, who was now leading the doctors, rejected this demand. Such a scene would only excite the writer. His deathbed was painful enough as it was. The mere thought that he would have to leave his family in poverty tormented him to the last.

"Fetch the children!" he whispered several times. When Fedya and Lyubov came in, he pressed them close to him. They kissed him and went out crying, followed by their father's sorrowful gaze. At the last meeting he gave his New Testament to Fedya.

Little by little his strength ebbed away. At about half-past six in the evening his chin and beard were again stained with blood. An attempt was made to stop the bleeding with ice, but to no avail. Silent and immobile the writer lay under the reproduction of *The Sistine Madonna*. Then the door opened, and all his friends entered in order to be present at his death. It was quiet in the room; only Anna and the children sat by the bedside, weeping softly. The writer's pulse grew steadily weaker, and finally the doctor confirmed that his heart had stopped beating. The time was 8:38 P.M.

"It was a true, Christian death, the kind of death the Orthodox Church wishes for all her faithful, a death without pain and without shame," Lyubov writes in her memoirs. "He only lost consciousness at the last moment, and looked death in the eye without fearing it. He knew that he had not buried his talent, and that all his life he had been a faithful servant of God. He was prepared and could without fear present himself before his eternal Father in the hope that God would reward him for all his sufferings by giving him another great work to perform, another great task to fulfill."

In the death certificate which was later issued by the Church of St. Vladimir it is stated that Dostoyevsky died of a "pulmonary hemorrhage." At this time the tuberculosis bacillus had not yet been discovered, and we can therefore scarcely ignore tuberculosis as a possible cause of death. The writer could have been infected both by his mother and by his first wife. But there are also various factors which support the diagnosis that was given by the doctors of the day—that he suffered from emphysema, a chronic lung disease which was aggravated by his extremely heavy cigarette-smoking. "January 28, 1881. Papa died at a quarter to nine," was the laconic message from the writer's daughter. The words were written on the back of his tobacco box.

The days that followed developed into an unbroken nightmare for Anna. The irretrievable loss of a beloved human being was heavy enough in itself for her to bear; the publicity and the steady influx of strangers and the curious made it even heavier. A number of coffin-makers gathered on the landings in the hope of securing themselves a fresh commission. The rooms were full of journalists, who later described the family's grief in the most intimate detail. How she wished she were now alone in her sorrow, surrounded only by her closest family!

When shortly before the death Boleslav Markevich, a journalist on *Moscow Report*, arrived in the apartment he was met by a weeping Lyubov: "Please pray for Papa, so that God will forgive him for his sins!" Anna was more preoccupied by immediate things: "He wanted so much to live a little longer, life had only just begun to smile on him, he still had so much to say. . . . We had just begun to breathe easier. . . . And then suddenly! . . . Today he said: 'All my life I have fought and struggled for my daily bread—in the hope that my children should have a good start in life, and now here I lie dying and must leave them in poverty.' "

The financial worries were, however, quickly cleared out of the way. On Pobedonostsev's initiative the Tsar gave his agreement that Anna should receive an annual widow's pension of two thousand rubles, while the children received the offer of free places in the foremost schools of the land.

After a sleepless night Lyubov found her father's body stretched out on the table according to Russian custom. In his folded hands lay an icon. "He looked as though he were asleep, gently smiling, as though he could see something beautiful," she remembered. Her mother had the same impression: "The dead man's face was peaceful; it looked as though he were not dead at all, as though he were merely asleep, smiling at the 'great truth' which had finally revealed itself to him." This impression of peace and reconciliation is also clearly manifested in the drawing to which Ivan Kramskoy put the finishing touches only when Dostoyevsky was on his bier. "In this portrait Fyodor Mikhailovich does not look as though he were dead, but rather as if he had only fallen asleep," Anna wrote. "His face is smiling, transformed, as though the secrets of the life hereafter were already being revealed to him."

Later that morning the parish priest from St. Vladimir's came to conduct the first funeral rites. In the days that followed, frequent services of mourning were held in Dostoyevsky's apartment. Even the famous choir of St. Isaac's Cathedral took part. An ever denser throng of people found its way to Kuznechny Lane. The crowding on the stairway that led up to the writer's poor apartment was terrible; there was a bad smell of cats and boiled coffee. "So this is how our famous authors live," one of the visitors remarked, shaking his head.

Upstairs in the apartment the guests stood in line to visit the bier. Some brought flowers and wreaths, to little Lyubov's great joy: "Look, look how pretty they're making my dear papa!" One day they even found two rubles in the coffin: "For hungry people in memory of God's servant Fyodor Mikhailovich, who had such concern for the poor and oppressed, from one who is not rich." The group that stood around the coffin represented every stratum of society: students and teachers, authors and princes, peasants and workers. Even Grand Duke Dmitri Konstantinovich appeared at one of the funeral services in order to say farewell to his tutor. Delegation upon delegation came from schools and institutions, underscoring the writer's great significance for Russian intellectual life. Not infrequently they brought their own choirs with them, so that their visits acquired the character of funeral services. The heat in the small, overcrowded apartment gradually became unbearable, and the candles went out from lack of oxygen.

Many of those who were present later described their last encounter with the deceased. "What a face!" Koni exclaims. "It seemed illumined by an inner light, it was as if it were saying: 'Yes! I have always believed and said that it was so, and now I see it and know it!' " "I kissed the writer's hand and preserved forever the memory of a man with whom one might disagree, but for whom one could never cease to feel the deepest esteem," writes another of those who had come to pay the writer his last respects. "The coffin was full of flowers," a female admirer writes. "And in the midst of this sea of flowers lay the little emaciated writer who for so many years had captivated people with his pen. His features were calm and peaceful, and seemed to belong to a man who was tired and exhausted, and who had now lain down to rest with pleasant dreams."

III

The news of Dostoyevsky's death was immediately circulated to every school in the city. All lectures at the university were cancelled; students and professors gathered for a memorial service. "The divine spark never once died in his breast," the university chaplain declared, "not even in the long years when he wore his prisoner's garb." All over Russia the newspapers printed obituaries; when Anna later did her sums, she discovered that almost four hundred people had written about her husband's death. Tolstoy now realized that Dostoyevsky had been "the person nearest, dearest, and most necessary" to him. "And then suddenly I read that he had died," he wrote in a letter to Strakhov. "It was as though the ground had given way beneath my feet."

Many people felt the same way. "The news had an extraordinarily powerful effect," the literary historian Alexander Borozdin recalls. "For us young folk Dostoyevsky was something more than a writer—he was a great teacher who stood forth with his mighty words and showed us the only true way for our lives and our actions." "The Russia he loved was not an idealized one," wrote Ivan Yakhontov on behalf of the students of the Moscow Spiritual Academy. "He loved Russia with all its weaknesses and all its imperfections." Dostoyevsky's pupils, the Grand Dukes Sergei and Paul, also found it natural to stress the deceased's love for his fatherland. Their telegram of condolences from Rome was worded as follows:

"Nous prenons une part sincère à votre malheur. Nous avons eu le grand avantage de connaître votre mari et d'apprécier son grand talent, son coeur si plein d'amour pour son pays et son prochain, et son influence si bienfaisante. Nous partageons la douleur générale, et nous comprenons tout ce que

vous avez perdu et tout ce que vous souffrez. Que Dieu vous soutienne! Serge et Paul."

Most remarkable of all, however, was the commemorative speech given by Vladimir Solovyov, possibly the man who had been closest to the writer in his final years, and at any rate the one who had the most profound understanding of his message. In a hitherto unpublished address delivered at the Women's University on January 30, he gives a pithy account of the writer's significance for Russia:

> In Dostoyevsky Russia has not merely lost a writer, she has lost her spiritual leader. This evil can be fought with two kinds of power: the wordly and the spiritual. Worldly power seeks to contain evil by means of evil, it combats evil with retribution and violence and thereby creates a certain outward order. Spiritual power cannot view this order as an expression of absolute truth and strives therefore to realize that truth with the aid of an inner, spiritual force, so that evil is not merely contained by outward order, but is entirely and completely vanquished by the good. And just as supreme worldly power is concentrated in a single person, namely the representative of the state, so the highest spiritual power of the people belongs to the person who has the clearest perception of mankind's spiritual ideals, who strives with the highest degree of awareness for those ideals, and who has the strongest influence on others with his advocacy. Dostoyevsky became for the Russian people such a spiritual leader.
>
> For as long as society is founded on viciousness and falsehood, for as long as the good and the true are merely striving for realization, such men will take up a position that differs from that which is permitted to the rulers of the state. Such men will rather stand forward as prophets who are often not recognized. Their lives are struggle and suffering. Such, too, was the life of Dostoyevsky.
>
> In order to demonstrate his right to be called a spiritual leader we have only to turn to his life.
>
> The first precondition of being called a spiritual leader is to perceive and feel the falsehood that is prevailing in society, and then to dedicate one's life to a struggle against that falsehood. If one tolerates the falsehood and resigns oneself to it, one can never become a prophet. If one cannot rise above material life, one cannot even become a citizen in the kingdom of the spirit, far less a leader of others.
>
> Dostoyevsky entered literature with *Poor Folk*, an original and living portrayal of society's falsehood, of the contradiction between man's inner dignity and outer conditions. But he did not stop at the depiction of reality's

falsehood, as an artist pure and simple would have done. As a prophet he not only saw more clearly than everyone else the existence of society's falsehood—he also took upon himself the task of implementing the truth, and in this lies another necessary precondition of becoming a leader and a prophet.

In his youth he became a member of a circle which strove to realize its moral ideals. We do not know what means the members wished to employ in order to achieve this end, we know only that they failed to achieve any practical results. But these people were viewed as being dangerous and were condemned to death. Only at the moment when the death sentence was to be carried out was it commuted to penal labor.

Together with his comrades Dostoyevsky was sent to Siberia. And there emerged another feature which gave him an even greater right to be called a spiritual leader of the Russian people. Dostoyevsky did not grow embittered by the violence to which he was subjected, and thereby displayed a spiritual and moral strength that is greater than all outer strength.

He returned from Siberia without resentment or hatred, but with the same sense of society's falsehood and the same striving for a moral struggle against that falsehood. In *Notes from the House of the Dead* the falsehood appears even more clearly than it did in his early stories. The heroes of this book, the outcasts who stand outside the law and society, are not only equivalent in moral worth to the majority of society's privileged and law-abiding members. On occasion they are even infinitely better than these, and not only when Dostoyevsky describes them, but also in the reality to which he always remained faithful.

In the works that followed, his central ideas acquired new depth. Now he no longer points to the outer contradiction between society and moral demands, but to the contradiction between man's spiritual strength and the actual condition of the human soul. And here Dostoyevsky becomes the advocate of the conviction that no moral fall, no moral baseness or loathsomeness is capable of sapping man's spiritual strength. He is convinced that the human soul is a part of the divine soul, and that consequently it can be born anew, freed from all baseness and all loathsomeness.

Many people have reproached Dostoyevsky for this. Why does he dwell on the dark side of life and the soul, why does he depict people who are abnormal, morally sick, and simply dissolute? Many have asserted that in his view man must pass through all this loathsomeness in order to gain moral stature. That is not correct. Did not Jesus Christ do the same when he surrounded himself with publicans and sinners? Was that not precisely the reason why the scribes and Pharisees of the day raised their accusations against him? We who are Christians do not accuse Christ of this, and consequently we ought not to accuse Dostoyevsky either. In his works it is not the necessity of falsehood that is preached, but the necessity of combating outer falsehood—and accordingly also inner falsehood—with the strength of the spirit.

In spite of all the sufferings Dostoyevsky had to endure as a consequence of his protest against falsehood, he never ceased to protest. But it was his genuine conviction that evil could not be eradicated by violence, that brute force could only be fought not with brute force but with the infinite strength of love.

Many have also taken him to task for preaching an inner self-completion instead of actively promoting the realization of the good; he has been accused of asceticism. That is unjust. Dostoyevsky was no ascetic—he did not need to be one. The martyr's crown was placed upon his head without his wishing it, and the fact that he bore it without hatred or resentment clearly demonstrates that he was above all asceticism. Dostoyevsky did not preach asceticism; he preached the spiritual rebirth of man and society in the power of infinite and all-embracing love to realize the kingdom of universal truth on earth. This he preached more powerfully, more vitally, and more unwaveringly than anyone else in his day. And it is for this reason that we must regard him as the spiritual leader of the Russian people, and as God's prophet.

The question of where Dostoyevsky should be buried had long been a subject of discussion in the family. The writer himself had expressed a wish that he be laid to rest in the Novodevichy Monastery, beside Nekrasov. The thought of lying next to his literary enemies in the writers' cemetery at Volkovo did not appeal to him. Anna had suggested the Alexander Nevsky Laura instead. "I thought only generals were buried up there," the writer replied, jestingly. "Yes, that's right," Anna retorted. "But aren't you a general in literature?"

The negotiations with the prioress at the Novodevichy Monastery led nowhere. The price she demanded for burial ground and funeral service was far in excess of what Anna could manage. "There was nothing for it but to get up and take our leave of this female usurer in nun's robes," Lyubov writes acidly in her memoirs. Fortunately the problem was solved that same evening when Metropolitan Isidor, reacting to insistent pressure from Pobedonostsev, hesitantly agreed that Dostoyevsky could be buried in the Alexander Nevsky Laura. Anna gave a sigh of relief. She had got what she wanted, without having to pay anything for it, either.

On Saturday, January 31, St. Petersburg was decked out with flowers, wreaths, and garlands. Dostoyevsky's funeral procession was the largest which had ever been held in Russia, and this in spite of the fact that everything took place spontaneously, without planning of any sort. Sidewalks and balconies were thronged with spectators. One newspaper reporter estimated that at least a hundred thousand people had turned out to show the writer their last respects. "Petersburg has never experienced anything like it."

After a final requiem in the writer's home, his bier was carried out onto the street. The master of ceremonies was Dmitri Grigorovich. Once upon a time he had greeted Dostoyevsky as a new author. Now it was time for them to say farewell.

Out on the street the dead man's autograph was distributed to those taking part as a souvenir and token of thanks. People went around selling portraits of the writer.

There was no need of a hearse. Students and colleagues would carry the coffin the two-and-a-half miles to the Alexander Nevsky Laura. Anna took her place with the children behind the gilded bier, followed by other relatives and friends. The coffin was decked with green, flowered garlands, first among which was the wreath from the St. Petersburg Slavic Benevolent Society: "To a Russian."

The bells of St. Vladimir's began to toll, the cortège began to move off, and the participants started to sing the burial psalm, *Holy Father*. "Then it seemed as though everyone, believers and non-believers alike, suddenly sensed the Godhead's presence," writes one of those who took part.

The cortège, which was over a mile and a half long, had features that were reminiscent of a triumphal procession. "This was no burial," wrote Suvorin. "It was a triumph of life, the resurrection of life."

The procession was led by the delegates from the Engineers' Academy. They were followed by nearly a hundred deputations from schools, institutions, and associations. The numerous wreaths were fastened to long poles, and their inscriptions bore unequivocal witness to Dostoyevsky's unique position: "To the poet of artistic truth," "To the defender of the insulted and the injured," "To the friend of youth," "From the students," "From the city of St. Petersburg," "From the children," "From the heart of Russia to our great teacher."

"Who is to be buried here?" a coachman wanted to know. "Some general or other, maybe?" "A general?" one of the students replied. "Oh no—an ex-convict! The Tsar sent him to do forced labor because he told the truth. Do you think we would have taken part if it was a general who was being buried?" "Because he told the truth?" the coachman asked and, taking off his cap, crossed himself. "Well, may God have mercy on him; we are also fond of the truth."

Outside St. Vladimir's there was a brief intermezzo: the police broke in and confiscated a pair of leg-fetters which the students were carrying in memory of the fact that the dead man had suffered for his political convictions. The authorities' fear of demonstrations proved to be otherwise groundless; but in the interests of security, orders had been given that a division of Cossacks should hold exercises in the vicinity of the graveyard.

The cortège took almost three hours to reach the grave. The burial psalms sung by some twenty choirs made a strong impression. Many people, particularly women, wept, "as though they had lost a beloved father or husband." "Do not forget the fine funeral which Russia is giving your father," someone whispered to Lyubov. Some people remembered the funeral scene at the end of The Brothers Karamazov. Alyosha had spoken to a handful of people, while at his death the writer himself had inspired the whole of thinking and feeling St. Petersburg.

As the bier approached the monastery, the monks, led by Simeon, their Father Superior, came out to meet the dead man, an honor which normally only a Tsar would receive. Outside the monastery gates the crowding was severe; Lyubov was almost crushed to death. Grigorovich addressed the crowd and asked them not to try to force their way into the church, as there was room for only a thousand people.

Finally the coffin was set down inside the Church of the Holy Spirit. People began to leave, but the students wanted to remain in order to watch over their teacher. When late in the evening the Metropolitan entered the church, some of them were kneeling and weeping, while others stood reading from the Psalter. "The students read in voices deeply stirred with emotion, putting their entire souls into each word," he related some days later. "People say that these young folk are atheists and that they detest the Church. Yet Dostoyevsky managed nonetheless to lead them back—he must have had magical powers!"

After much urging, Anna had consented to postpone the interment until Sunday, February 1, so that everyone could have an opportunity to say farewell to the writer.

When on the morning of that day she drove up to the churchyard with Lyubov, the large square in front of the monastery was already crammed with people. She had forgotten both entry tickets and identity papers—she only barely succeeded in getting in. "You are the sixth of Dostoyevsky's widows who has demanded to be allowed in; now that is enough!" said the chief of police, in irritation.

The flower-bedecked coffin stood in the middle of the church on a catafalque, under a baldachin of red velvet and surrounded by a large number of wreaths. To Anna's great sorrow the coffin had been closed. A long row of eminent people had turned out—Pobedonostsev, the church leader; Tretyakov, the mayor of Moscow; Saburov, the Minister of Culture; and representatives of the Court and the Academy of Science.

The liturgy was conducted by Archbishop Nestor of Vyborg, while the consecration was performed by Ioann Yanyshev, Dostoyevsky's friend of many years and rector of the St. Petersburg Spiritual Academy. In his speech before the consecration, Yanyshev touched on the subject of Dostoyevsky's Christian and ecclesiastical commitment: "Neither adversity nor suffering were able to break this writer who was so strong in spirit and so full of enthusiastic faith in the vital energy of the Orthodox idea." Even in the lowliest soul the writer had managed to find his way to that which was lofty and pure, Yanyshev stressed. "It is sufficient to recall the titles of his works in order to perceive the identity of those whom this writer portrayed, those who were closest to his heart, those who had his sympathy: *Poor Folk, The Insulted and the Injured, The House of the Dead, The Idiot.*"

Then the coffin was lifted down and carried out of the church. Slowly the procession made its way past the deputations, which formed a cordon with lowered wreaths. The site of the grave was close to those of two of Dostoyevsky's favorite writers, Karamzin and Zhukovsky. As a child, Dostoyevsky had had his patriotism aroused by Karamzin's historical writing, while Zhukovsky had with his brilliant translations given him an early confidence in the Russians' ability to enter into the spirit of foreign cultures. He had come to the right place.

By the grave there were many speeches. Alexander Palm, the friend of Dostoyevsky's youth, recalled the writer's indomitable optimism at the darkest moments of his life; Orest Miller, his preaching of man's struggle for self-completion; Konstantin Bestuzhev-Ryumin, his ardent commitment to the fight for the cause of the Slavic peoples. Vladimir Solovyov's words about his close friend drew special attention:

Above all he loved the living human soul in everything, everywhere, and he believed that we are all God's servants. He believed in the infinite strength of the human soul, the strength that triumphs over all outer force and all inner defeats. . . . The reality of God and Christ revealed itself to him in the inner strength of love and forgiveness, and it was this forgiving and blessed strength which he preached as a basis for the union of all men in one common brotherhood, in order to realize the kingdom of truth upon earth, the kingdom for which all his life he thirsted and strove. . . . As we gather together here about his grave, we can do him no better honor than to assert unanimously that Dostoyevsky's love is *our* love, that Dostoyevsky's faith is *our* faith. And as we unite in our love for him, let us do our utmost to see to it that this love can also contribute to *our* reconciliation. Only then shall we be able to give the leader of the Russian people something in return for his works and his great sufferings.

The grave was filled with earth and flowers. "Farewell, dear good and kind Papa—farewell, farewell!" The grave might have been closed, but the future lay open.

Dostoyevsky's study, where he died
January 28 (February 9), 1881.

*Dostoyevsky's last apartment
in St. Petersburg. Photograph, 1929.*

*The unveiling of the Pushkin
memorial, June 6, 1880.*

*Panov's photograph of Dostoyevsky,
1880, the last taken of the writer.*

*S. Merkulov's statue of
Dostoyevsky, 1918.*

1. *Kramskoy's drawing of Dostoyevsky on his deathbed, January 29, 1881.*

Dostoyevsky's funeral.

*Anna, Lyuba, and Fedya at
Dostoyevsky's grave, February 5, 1881.*

BIBLIOGRAPHY

The literature on Dostoyevsky is in the process of becoming impossible to survey. Every year several hundred important dissertations appear, most of them about his novels.

This bibliography has been prepared with the help of the Dostoyevsky card indexes in the Lenin Library, Helsinki University Library, and Oslo University Library. It includes only those works that I found especially useful during my work on this book; thus, for example, biographical works of a literary type are not listed. With regard to the sources, I should like to draw the reader's attention to the works listed at the end of the bibliography that refer to each of the book's chapters.

1. EDITIONS

(a) In Russian

Dostoyevsky, F. M. *Letters, I–IV.* Moscow and Leningrad. Vol. I, 1928; Vol. II, 1930; Vol. III, 1934; Vol. IV, 1959.
————. *Complete Works,* Vol. I: *Biography, Letters, and Notes from Notebooks.* Leningrad, 1983.
————. *Complete Works in Thirty Volumes.* Vols. I–XXV, Leningrad, 1972–83.
————. *Complete Works in Ten Volumes.* Moscow, 1956–58.
Dostoyevsky, F. M., and A. G. Dostoyevskaya. *Correspondence.* Moscow, 1979.
"F. M. Dostoyevsky, New Materials and Research." *Literaturnoye nasledstvo,* Vol. LXXXVI. Moscow, 1973.
"F. M. Dostoyevsky at Work on the Novel 'The Adolescent.' Working Manuscripts." *Literaturnoye nasledstvo,* Vol. LXXVII. Moscow, 1965.
"The Unpublished Dostoyevsky: Notebooks and Journals, 1860–1861." *Literaturnoye nasledstvo,* Vol. LXXXIII. Moscow, 1971.

(b) In Norwegian

The Brothers Karamazov, Vols. I–II. Translated by Thomas Christensen. Oslo, 1949–50. Vol. III, translated by Elsa Uhlen. Oslo, 1951.

The Brothers Karamazov, Vols. I–II. Translated by Olaf Broch. Oslo, 1976.

"A Confession" and Other Stories. Translated by Martha Grundt. Oslo, 1948.

Crime and Punishment, Vols. I–II. Translated by Ivar Digernes. Oslo, 1948–49.

The Devils, Vols. I–II. Translated by Thomas Christensen. Oslo, 1946.

The Diary of a Writer. Selected and translated by Geir Kjetsaa. Oslo, 1980.

The Double. Translated and with a Foreword by Peter Normann Waage. Oslo, 1980.

The Eternal Husband. Translated and with a Foreword by Marit Bjerking Nielsen. Oslo, 1976.

The Gambler. Translated by Thomas Christensen. Oslo, 1978.

The Idiot, Vols. I–II. Translated by Martha Grundt. Oslo, 1947.

"Long Ago in Constantinople the Burden Became Ours." In *The Russian Intelligentsia and the Church*. Presented and selected by Pal Kolsto. Oslo, 1982. Pp. 103–10.

Notes from the House of the Dead, Vols. I–II. Translated by Ivar Digernes. Oslo, 1948.

Notes from Underground. Translated by Gunnar Opeide. Oslo, 1973.

Poor Folk. Translated and with a Foreword by Geir Kjetsaa. Oslo, 1980.

A Raw Youth, Vols. I–II. Translated by Einar Hansen. Foreword by Erik Krag. Oslo, 1945.

"The Russian People and Tsar Peter's Reforms"; "Mankind's Capricious Will"; "When Christ Was Denied"; "Three Novels of Dostoyevsky." In *Conservatism from Hume to the Present Day*. Selected and with an Introduction and Commentary by Lars Roar Langslet. Oslo, 1965. Pp. 117–26.

Uncle's Dream. Translated and with a Foreword by Erik Krag. Oslo, 1945.

"A Weak Heart." Translated and with an Introduction by Geir Kjetsaa. Oslo, 1980.

White Nights. Translated and with an Introduction by Geir Kjetsaa. Oslo, 1975.

2. WORKS ABOUT DOSTOYEVSKY'S LIFE

Belov, S. V. "Bibliography." *F. M. Dostoyevsky in Reminiscences by Contemporaries*, Vol. II, Moscow, 1964. Pp. 478–89.

Bograd, G. L., et al. *The Literary-Memorial Museum of F. M. Dostoyevsky*. Leningrad, 1981.

Cheshikhin-Vetrinsky, V. Ye. (Cheshikhin, V. Ye.). *F. M. Dostoyevsky in*

Reminiscences by His Contemporaries and in His Letters, chaps. I–II. Moscow, 1923.

Dostoyevskaya, A. G. *Diary, 1867*. Moscow, 1923.

———. *Memoirs*. Moscow, 1925, 1971, 1981.

Dostoyevsky, as Described by His Daughter A. Dostoyevskaya. Munich, 1920.

Dostoyevsky, A. M. *Memoirs*. Leningrad, 1930.

Dragomanov, M. P. "The Biography of Dostoyevsky." *TSGALI* f. No. 1065, yed. khr. No. 3, op. No. 1.

F. M. Dostoyevsky in Reminiscences by Contemporaries, Vols. I–II. Moscow, 1964.

"The Geneva Diary of A. G. Dostoyevskaya." *Literaturnoye nasledstvo*, Vol. LXXXVI. Moscow, 1973. Pp. 167–282.

Grossman, L. P. "Chapters from the Biography of Dostoyevsky." *Uchonyye Zapiski Moskovskogo gorodskogo pedagogicheskogo instituta im. V. P. Potyomkina*, Vol. XCVIII, 1959, pp. 253–90.

———. "Materials Toward a Biography of F. M. Dostoyevsky (Dates and Documents)." F. M. Dostoyevsky, *Collected Works in Ten Volumes*, Vol. X. Moscow, 1958. Pp. 531–620.

Grossman, Leonid. *Dostoyevsky on the Road of Life: Part One, Dostoyevsky's Youth, 1821–1850*. Moscow, 1928.

———. *The Life and Works of F. M. Dostoyevsky: A Biography in Dates and Documents*. Moscow and Leningrad, 1935.

Khlebnikov, A. V. *Fyodor Mikhailovich Dostoyevsky. Biography. His Works. The Last Minutes of His Life. The Transport of the Body, the Funeral, and the Reaction of the Russian Public*. Moscow, 1881.

Lyubimov, S. "Toward the Question of Dostoyevsky's Genealogy." *F. M. Dostoyevsky Articles and Materials, II*. Leningrad and Moscow, 1924. Pp. 303–6.

Miller, Or. "Materials for the Biography of F. M. Dostoyevsky." F. M. Dostoyevsky, *Complete Works. Vol. I: Biography, Letters, and Notes from His Notebook*. St. Petersburg, 1883. Pp. 3–176.

Nechayeva, V. S., ed. *Fyodor Mikhailovich Dostoyevsky in Portraits, Illustrations, and Documents*. Moscow, 1972.

———. *The Early Dostoyevsky, 1821–1849*. Moscow, 1979.

Neufeld, Jolan. *Dostoyevsky: An Outline of His Psychoanalysis*. Leipzig, Vienna, and Zurich, 1923.

Nikolsky, Yu. *Turgenev and Dostoyevsky: The Story of an Enmity*. Sofia, 1921.

Notzel, Karl. *The Life of Dostoyevsky*. Leipzig, 1925.

Onasch, Konrad. *Dostoyevsky—A Biography*. Zurich, 1960.

Piksanov, N. K., ed. *From Dostoyevsky's Archive: Letters of Russian Writers*. Petrograd, 1923.

Rumyantseva, Ye. M. *Fyodor Mikhailovich Dostoyevsky: The Biography of a Writer*. Leningrad, 1971.

Saruchanyan, Yevgeniya. *Dostoyevsky in Petersburg*. Leningrad, 1970.

Slonim, Mark. *Dostoyevsky's Three Loves*. New York, 1953.

Strakhov, N. N. "Reminiscences about Fyodor Mikhailovich Dostoyevsky." F. M. Dostoyevsky, *Complete Works. Vol. I: Biography, Letters, and Notes from His Notebook*. St. Petersburg, 1883. Pp. 177–329.

Suslova, A. P. *Years of Intimacy with Dostoyevsky: A Biography—A Tale—Letters*. Moscow, 1928.

Sventsitsky, V. *The Life of F. M. Dostoyevsky*. Moscow, 1911.

Thomassen, Ejnar. *F. M. Dostoyevsky: Portrait of a Life*. Oslo, 1947.

Volotskoy, M. V. *A Chronicle of the Dostoyevsky Family, 1506–1933*. Moscow, 1933.

Vrangel, A. Ye. *Reminiscences of F. M. Dostoyevsky in Siberia, 1854–56*. St. Petersburg, 1912.

3. WORKS ABOUT DOSTOYEVSKY'S LIFE AND WORK

Antsiferov, N. P. *Dostoyevsky's Petersburg*. Pb. 1923.

Arban, Domenique. *Fyodor Dostoyevsky's Years of Apprenticeship*. Paris, 1968.

Batyuto, A. I. "Dostoyevsky and Turgenev in the 1860s and 1870s (Only a Story of Enmity?)." *Russkaya Literatura*, 1979, No. 1, pp. 41–64.

Bursov, B. *Dostoyevsky's Personality*. Leningrad, 1979.

Carr, Edward Hallett. *Dostoyevsky, 1821–1881*. London, 1962.

Catteau, Jacques. *Literary Creation in the Works of Dostoyevsky*. Paris, 1978.

Dolinin, A. S., ed. *F. M. Dostoyevsky, Articles and Materials, I*. Petrograd, 1922.

Dostoyevsky and His Time. Leningrad, 1971.

Dostoyevsky, Materials and Research, Vols. I–V. Leningrad, 1974–83.

Frank, Joseph. *Dostoyevsky: The Seeds of Revolt, 1821–1849*. Princeton, 1976.

———. *Dostoyevsky: The Years of Ordeal, 1850–1859*. Princeton, 1983.

Gide, André. *Dostoyevsky (Articles and Essays)*. Paris, 1923.

Gonner, Gerhard. *Fyodor M. Dostoyevsky*. Salzburg, 1981.

Gozenpud, A. A. *Dostoyevsky and Music*. Leningrad, 1971.

Grossman, Leonid. *Dostoyevsky: A Biography*. London, 1974.

———. *Dostoyevsky's Path*. Moscow, 1928.

———. *A Seminar on Dostoyevsky: Materials, Bibliography, and Commentary*. Moscow and Petrograd, 1922.

Hingley, Ronald. *Dostoyevsky: His Life and Work*. London, 1978.

Karlova, T. S. *Dostoyevsky and the Russian Court of Law*. Kazan, 1975.

Kirpotin, V. *Dostoyevsky in the Sixties*. Moscow, 1966.

———. *F. M. Dostoyevsky: Artistic Path (1821–1859)*. Moscow, 1960.

———. *The World of Dostoyevsky: Studies and Research*. Moscow, 1980.

Kjetsaa, Geir. *Dostoyevsky and His New Testament*. Oslo, 1984. (*Slavica Norvegica*, 3.)

Krag, Erik. *Dostoyevsky: The Literary Artist*. Oslo and New York, 1976.

Kuleshov, V. I. *The Life and Work of Dostoyevsky: An Essay*. Moscow, 1979.

Lagerlof, Karl Erik. *Dostoyevsky's Life and Work*. Stockholm, 1978.

Lavrin, Janko. *Fyodor M. Dostoyevsky*. Hamburg, 1981.

Leatherbarrow, William J. *Fyodor Dostoyevsky*. Boston, 1981.

Levander, Hans. *Fyodor Dostoyevsky*. Stockholm, 1963.

Magarshack, David. *Dostoyevsky*. London, 1962.

Maurina, Zenta. *Dostoyevsky*. Stockholm, 1951.

Mochulsky, Konstantin. *Dostoyevsky: His Life and Work*. Princeton, 1967.

Othman, Hans. "Dostoevsky and Reality." *Fenix*, No. 1, Argang 2 (1984), pp. 18–136.

Pascal, Pierre. *Dostoyevsky: The Man and His Work*. Lausanne, 1970.

Pokrovskyj, V., ed., *Fyodor Mikhailovich Dostoyevsky: His Life and Works: A Collection of Historico-Literary Articles*. Ch. I, Moscow, 1908; ch. 2, Moscow, 1912.

Seleznev, Yury. *Dostoyevsky*. Moscow, 1981.

Stief, Carl. *On Reading Dostoyevsky*. Copenhagen, 1965.

Yarmolinsky, Avrahm. *Dostoyevsky: Works and Days*. New York, 1971.

Zamotin, I. I. *F. M. Dostoyevsky: A Systematic Survey and Historico-Literary Analysis of Biographical Materials and Criticism about F. M. Dostoyevsky*. Warsaw, 1912–13.

4. WORKS ABOUT DOSTOYEVSKY'S WORKS

Allain, Louis. *Dostoyevsky and God: The Bite of the Divine*. Lille, 1981.

Bakhtin, M. M. *Problems of Dostoyevsky's Poetics*. Ann Arbor, 1973.

Belkin, A. A., ed. *F. M. Dostoyevsky in Russian Criticism*. Moscow, 1956.

Berdyayev, Nicholas. *Dostoyevsky*. Cleveland and New York, 1969.

Braun, Maximilian. *Dostoyevsky: Oeuvre as Diversity and Unity*. Göttingen, 1976.

Burnett, Leon, ed. *F. M. Dostoyevsky (1821–1881): A Centenary Collection*. Essex, 1981.

Dimitrieva, L. S. *The Literary-Aesthetic Conception of F. M. Dostoyevsky (on the Material of "The Diary of a Writer")*. Diss., Avtoreferat, Donetsk, 1974.

Drouilly, Jean. *The Political and Religious Thought of Dostoyevsky*. Paris, 1971.

Egeberg, Erik, et al. *Inroads into Dostoyevsky's World*. Oslo, 1982.

Fasting, Sigurd. *Dostoyevsky*. Edited and with a Foreword by Jostein Bortnes. Oslo, 1983.

Fridlender, G. M. "The Study of Dostoyevsky Today (Controversial Questions, Research, Problems)." *Russkaya Literatura*, 1971, No. 3, pp. 3–23.

————. *Dostoyevsky and World Literature*. Moscow, 1979.

Gibson, A. Boyce. *The Religion of Dostoyevsky*. London, 1973.

Grazhis, P. I. *Dostoyevsky and Romanticism*. Vilnius, 1979.

Grishin, D. V. *Dostoyevsky—The Man, the Writer, and the Myths. Dostoyevsky and "The Diary of a Writer."* Melbourne, 1971.

Grossman, Leonid. *Dostoyevsky's Works*. Moscow, 1928.

Gronbech, Vilh. *Dostoyevsky and His Russia*. Copenhagen, 1948.

Hansen, Knud. *Dostoyevsky*. Copenhagen, 1973.

Holquist, Michael. *Dostoyevsky and the Novel*. Princeton, 1977.

Ivanov, Vyacheslav. *Dostoyevsky: Tragedy, Myth, Mysticism*. Tübingen, 1932.

————. *Freedom and the Tragic Life: A Study in Dostoyevsky*. New York, 1966.

Jackson, Robert Louis. *Dostoyevsky's Quest for Form: A Study of His Philosophy of Art*. New Haven and London, 1966.

————. "The Testament of F. M. Dostoyevsky." *Russian Literature*, 4, 1973, pp. 87–99.

Jackson, Robert Louis, ed. *Dostoyevsky: New Perspectives*. Englewood Cliffs, NJ, 1984.

Jones, John. *Dostoyevsky*. Oxford, 1983.

Jones, Malcolm V. *Dostoyevsky: The Novel of Discord*. London, 1976.

Jones, Malcolm V., and Garth M. Terry, eds. *New Essays on Dostoyevsky*. Cambridge, England, 1983.

Kabat, Geoffrey C. *Ideology and Imagination: The Image of Society in Dostoyevsky*. New York, 1978.

Kantor, V. *Dostoyevsky's "The Brothers Karamazov."* Moscow, 1983.

Kirpotin, V. Ya. *The Disillusionment and Downfall of Rodion Raskolnikov: A Book about Dostoyevsky's Novel "Crime and Punishment."* Moscow, 1970.

————. *Dostoyevsky the Artist: Studies and Research*. Moscow, 1972.

————. *Dostoyevsky and Belinsky*. Moscow, 1976.

Kjetsaa, Geir. *Dostoyevsky and Tolstoy: Essays*. Oslo, 1977.

————. *Purification Through Suffering: On Dostoyevsky's "The Brothers Karamazov."* Oslo, 1980.

Kjetsaa, Geir, ed. *Dostoyevsky's Novel About Raskolnikov*. Oslo, 1973.

Linnér, Sven. *Dostoyevsky on Realism*. Stockholm, 1967.

————. *Starets Zosima in "The Brothers Karamazov": A Study in the Mimesis of Virtue*. Stockholm, 1975.

————. *Dostoyevsky: The Icon and the Mystery of Life*. Stockholm, 1982.

Losskij, N. *Dostoyevsky and His Christian Worldview*. New York, 1953.

Merezhkovsky, D. S. *L. Tolstoy and Dostoyevsky*. St. Petersburg, 1901.

Middleton Murry, J. *Fyodor Dostoyevsky: A Critical Study*. Boston, 1924.

Morson, Gary Saul. *The Boundaries of Genre: Dostoyevsky's Diary of a Writer and the Traditions of Literary Utopia*. Austin, 1981.

Nazirov, R. G. *The Artistic Principles of F. M. Dostoyevsky*. Saratov, 1982.

Neuhauser, Rudolf. *Dostoyevsky's Early Works: Literary Tradition and Social Concern*. Heidelberg, 1979.

Onasch, Konrad. *Dostoyevsky as Tempter: Christianity and Art in the Work of Dostoyevsky, an Investigation.* Zurich, 1961.

———. *The Discreet Christ: An Investigation of the Poeticization of Christianity in the Work of Dostoyevsky.* Berlin, 1976.

Rowe, William Woodin. *Dostoyevsky: Child and Man in His Works.* New York and London, 1968.

Rozanov, V. V. *Dostoyevsky and the Legend of the Grand Inquisitor.* Ithaca, NY, and London, 1972.

Rosenblyum, L. M. *Dostoyevsky's Journals.* Moscow, 1981.

Seduro, Vladimir. *Dostoyevsky in Russian Literary Criticism, 1846–1956.* New York, 1957.

Shestov, Lev. "Dostoyevsky and Nietzsche: The Philosophy of Tragedy," in Spencer E. Roberts, ed., *Essays in Russian Literature: The Conservative View: Leontiev, Rosanov, Shestov.* Athens, 1968. Pp. 3–183.

Sokolovskaya, A. I. *Dostoyevsky and Romanticism.* Diss., Avtoreferat, Moscow, 1975.

Steffensen, Eigil. *Dostoyevsky's Major Novels.* Copenhagen, 1971.

Steiner, George. *Tolstoy or Dostoyevsky?* London, 1967.

Stief, Carl. *Russian Nihilism: Background for Dostoyevsky's Novel "The Devils."* Copenhagen, 1969.

Terras, Victor. *A Karamazov Companion: Commentary on the Genesis, Language, and Style of Dostoyevsky's Novel.* Madison, WI, 1981.

Tunimanov, V. A. *Dostoyevsky's Works, 1854–1862.* Leningrad, 1980.

Villadsen, Preben. *The Underground Man and Raskolnikov: A Comparative Study.* Odense, 1981. (Odense University Slavic Studies, Vol. 3.)

Volynsky, A. L. *Dostoyevsky.* St. Petersburg, 1909.

Wasiolek, Edward. *Dostoyevsky: The Major Fiction.* Cambridge, MA, 1964.

Wellek, René, ed. *Dostoyevsky: A Collection of Critical Essays.* Englewood Cliffs, NJ, 1962.

Wikstrom, Owe. *Raskolnikov: Concerning the Divided Road to Unity in Dostoyevsky's "Crime and Punishment." A Religio-Psychological Study.* Avesta, 1982.

The Works of F. M. Dostoyevsky. Moscow, 1959.

Zundelovich, Ya. O. *Dostoyevsky's Novels: Articles.* Tashkent, 1963.

OTHER SOURCES

Chapter 1:
CHILDHOOD AND BOYHOOD

Alekseyev, G. "The House Where a Writer Was Born." *Vecherniy Leningrad*, No. 247, October 19, 1971.

Fyodorov, G. "The Drashusovys and Tushar's Boarding School." *Literaturnaya Gazeta*, No. 29, July 17, 1974.

———. "L. I. Chermak's Boarding School, 1834–1837 (According to new materials)." *Dostoyevsky: Materials and Research*, Vol. I. Leningrad, 1974. Pp. 241–54.

———. "The Little Village Darovoye." *Za novuyu zhizn'*, No. 135 (9153), November 10, 1981; No. 136 (9154), November 12, 1981.

Kachenovsky, Vlad. "My Memories of Dostoyevsky." *Moskovskiye Vedomosti*, No. 31, January 31, 1881.

Krag, Erik. "Dostoyevsky and His Childhood Home." *Frisprog*, October 11, 1958, November 8, 1958; *Org og Bild*, 72, 1963, pp. 423–31.

Nechayeva, V. "From Literature about Dostoyevsky (The Journey to Darovoye)." *Novyy Mir*, 1926, No. 3, pp. 128–44.

———. In the Dostoyevsky Family and Estate (The Letters of M. A. and M. F. Dostoyevsky). Moscow, 1939.

"Something New about Dostoyevsky." *V mire knig*, 1966, No. 9, p. 47.

Onasch, Konrad. "Dostoyevsky's 'Kinderglaube.'" *Canadian-American Slavic Studies*, 12, No. 3 (Fall, 1978), pp. 377–81.

One Hundred and Four Sacred Stories from the Old and New Testaments Chosen for the Use of the Youth of the Holy Scripture and Provided with Useful Moral Lessons, Pious Meditations and Clear Questions by Ivan Gibner and Ivan Flek; Now for the Edification of Russian Youth and for Use in Schools, Newly Translated with Corrections and Additions, chaps. I–II. St. Petersburg, 1819.

Polyantsev, V. "Literary Zaraysk." *V mire knig*, 1970, No. 11, pp. 44–45.

The Service Record of M. A. Dostoyevsky [the writer's father] 1809–1832. *GLM*, of. 4812.

Shneyder, A. P. "A Few Words in Memory of Dostoyevsky." *TSGALI*, f. No. 909, yed. khr. No. 3, op. No. 1.

Shpadaruk, Ivan. "Not Far from Pinsk." *Neman*, 1971, No. 11, pp. 187–89.

Chapter 2:
ST. PETERSBURG

Alekseyev, M. P. *An Early Friend of F. M. Dostoyevsky.* Odessa, 1921.

Annenkov, P. V. "From 'The Remarkable Decade.' " *F. M. Dostoyevsky in Reminiscences by Contemporaries,* Vol. I. Moscow, 1964. Pp. 137–39.

Antsiferov, N. P. *Dostoyevsky's Petersburg.* Pb. 1923.

Barsht, K., and P. Torop. "Dostoyevsky's Manuscripts: Drawing and Calligraphy." *Tekst i kultura: Trudy po znakovym sistemam XVI.* Tartu, 1983. Pp. 135–52.

Busch, R. L. "Dostoyevsky's Translation of Balzac's *Eugénie Grandet.*" *Canadian Slavonic Papers,* Vol. XXV, No. 1, March 1983, pp. 73–89.

Carr, E. H. "Was Dostoyevsky an Epileptic?" *Slavonic and East European Review,* Vol. IX, 1930–31, pp. 424–31.

Dostoyevsky, Z. M. "On F. M. Dostoyevsky: A Letter to the Publisher." *Novoye Vremya,* No. 1778, February 8, 1881.

———. "More on the Illness of F. M. Dostoyevsky." *Novoye Vremya,* No. 1798, March 1, 1881.

An Excerpt from the Conduct Record of the Chief Officers of the Main Engineering School for 1841, Compiled June 20, 1842. *GLM.*

Frank, Joseph. "Freud's Case History of Dostoyevsky." *Times Literary Supplement,* July 19, 1975.

Freud, Sigmund. "Dostoyevsky and Parricide." *Collected Works,* Vol. XIV. Frankfurt, 1968. Pp. 399–418.

Fyodorov, G. "Conjecture and the Logic of Facts." *Soviet Literature,* 1975, No. 10 (331), pp. 87–93.

Grigorovich, D. V. "From 'Literary Reminiscences.' " *F. M. Dostoyevsky in Reminiscences by Contemporaries,* Vol. I. Moscow, 1964. Pp. 121–36.

Justman, Stuart. "The Strange Case of Dostoyevsky and Freud: A Lesson in the Necessity of Imagination." *Gipsy Scholar,* Vol. II, 1975, pp. 94–101.

Khlebnikov, K. D. "Notes." *Russkiy Arkhiv,* 1907, Book 1, No. 3, pp. 377–451.

Kirpotin, V. "A Story Refuted." *Soviet Literature,* 1975, No. 10 (331), pp. 93–97.

Kjetsaa, Geir. "Two Legends about Dostoyevsky." *Dostoyevsky and Tolstoy: Essays.* Oslo, 1977. Pp. 16–27.

Knigge, Adolph Freiherrn. *On Association with Men.* Hanover, 1792–93.

Konechny, A. "Dostoyevsky in Reval." *Sovetskaya Estoniya,* No. 2, January 3, 1971.

———. "Dostoyevsky in the 1840s." *Dostoyevsky and His Time.* Leningrad, 1971. Pp. 280–83.

Krag, Erik. "On the Question of Dostoyevsky's Father and Parricide in *The Brothers Karamazov.*" *Studi in Onore di Ettore Lo Gatto e Giovanni Mayer.* Rome, 1962. Pp. 361–67.

Pauly, Robert. "Dostoyevsky's Epilepsy." *Journal de Médicine de Bordeaux*, No. 8, August 1948, pp. 337–45.

Pistsova, A. Z. "Unknown Letters of M. M. Dostoyevsky about His Brother, the Famous Novelist." *Vestnik Leningradskogo Universiteta*, 2, No. 1, January 1972, pp. 152–57.

Prokhorov, Gr. "Why Dostoyevsky Retired." *The Literary-Artistic Collection of the Red Panorama*. Leningrad, 1929. Pp. 46–48.

Rice, James L. "Dostoyevsky's Medical History: Diagnosis and Dialectic." *The Russian Review*, Vol. XLII, 1983, pp. 131–61.

Rizenkampf, A. Ye. "The Beginning of a Literary Career." *F. M. Dostoyevsky in Reminiscences by Contemporaries*, Vol. I. Moscow, 1964. Pp. 111–18.

———. "Reminiscences of Fyodor Mikhailovich Dostoyevsky." *Literaturnoye nasledstvo*, Vol. LXXXVI. Moscow, 1973. Pp. 322–31.

Rozental, T. K. "Suffering and the Work of Dostoyevsky: A Psychogenetic Investigation." *Voprosy izucheniye i vospitaniya lichnosti*, 1919, No. 1, pp. 88–107.

Savel'yev, A. I. "Reminiscences of Fyodor Mikhailovich Dostoyevsky." *F. M. Dostoyevsky in Reminiscences by Contemporaries*, Vol. I. Moscow, 1964. Pp. 96–104.

———. "To the Memory of D. V. Grigorovich (His Tenure at the Main Engineering Institute)." *Russkaya Starina*, 1900, Vol. CIII, No. 8, pp. 327–36.

Schmidl, Fritz. "Freud and Dostoyevsky." *Journal of the American Psychoanalytic Association*, Vol. XIII, 1965, pp. 518–32.

Semyonov-Tyan-Shansky, P. P. "From 'Memoirs.'" *F. M. Dostoyevsky in Reminiscences by Contemporaries*, Vol. I. Moscow, 1964. Pp. 201–21.

Sollers, Phillipe. "Dostoyevsky, Freud, Roulette." *Tel Quel*, 1978, LXXVI, pp. 9–17.

Stonov, Dimitry. "The Little Village of Darovoye: An Essay." *Krasnaya niva*, 1926, No. 16, pp. 18–19.

Trutovsky, K. A. "Reminiscences of F. M. Dostoyevsky." *F. M. Dostoyevsky in Reminiscences by Contemporaries*, Vol. I. Moscow, 1964. Pp. 105–10.

Yakubovich, I. D. "Dostoyevsky at the Main Engineering School (Materials toward a Chronicle of the Writer's Life and Work)." *Dostoyevsky: Materials and Research*, Vol. V. Leningrad, 1983. Pp. 179–86.

Zschokke, Heinrich. *Lessons in Devotion for the Advancement of Lasting Christianity and the Worship of God in the Home*, 1–12. Aarau, 1837–38.

Chapter 3:
DREAM AND CATASTROPHE

Bortnes, Jostein. "Christology and Novelistic Fiction—Some Problems in Dostoyevsky's Poetics." *Inroads into Dostoyevsky's World.* Oslo, 1982. Pp. 11–31.

Dolinin, A. S. "Dostoyevsky among the Petrashevtsy." *Zven'ya*, VI, Moscow and Leningrad, 1936, pp. 512–45.

Dryzhakova, Ye. "Reverie and Terrorism: Dostoyevsky's Road to the Secret Seven." *Grani*, 1981, Vol. CXXI, pp. 164–211.

Grossman, L. P., and Vyach Polonsky. *The Controversy over Bakunin: Articles.* Leningrad, 1926.

Kann, P. Ya. *The Petrashevtsy.* Leningrad, 1968.

Komarovich, V. L. "Dostoyevsky's Youth." *Byloye*, 1924, No. 23, pp. 3–43.

Letkova-Sultanova, Ye. P. "On F. M. Dostoyevsky." *F. M. Dostoyevsky in Reminiscences by Contemporaries*, Vol. II. Moscow, 1964. Pp. 379–98.

———. "Petrashevets N. A. Speshnev (For the 75th Anniversary of the Petrashevtsy Affair)." *Byloye*, 1924, No. 25, pp. 12–31.

———. *The Petrashevtsy.* Moscow, 1965.

Lutskaya, N. N. *The Feuilleton in the Work of F. M. Dostoyevsky.* Diss., Avtoreferat, Moscow, 1982.

Lyaskovsky, A. I. *F. M. Dostoyevsky: Jail, the Scaffold, Labor Camp, Exile.* Berlin, 1937.

Masaryk, Thomas Garrigue. *The Spirit of Russia, Studies in History, Literature, and Philosophy*, Vol. I. London, 1961.

Milyukov, A. P. "Fyodor Mikhailovich Dostoyevsky." *F. M. Dostoyevsky in Reminiscences by Contemporaries*, Vol. I. Moscow, 1964. Pp. 179–200.

Ovsyannikova, N. P. "A. N. Maikov's Story of Dostoyevsky and the Petrashevtsy." *Istoricheskiy arkhiv*, 1956, No. 3, pp. 222–26.

Panayeva, A. Ya. "From 'Memoirs.' " *F. M. Dostoyevsky in Reminiscences by Contemporaries*, Vol. I. Moscow, 1964. Pp. 140–43.

Poddubnaya, R. N. "The Beketov Circle in the Ideological Searches of F. M. Dostoyevsky." *Voprosy russkoy literatury*, No. 2 (24). Lvov, 1974. Pp. 3–17.

Pokrovskaya, Ye. "Dostoyevsky and the Petrashevtsy." *F. M. Dostoyevsky: Articles and Materials.* Pb. 1922. Pp. 257–72.

Prokof'yev, V. *Petrashevsky.* Moscow, 1962.

Proudhon, P.-J. *Sunday Celebration: The Complete Works of P.-J. Proudhon*, Vol. II. Paris, 1873.

Segaloff, Timotheus. *Dostoyevsky's Illness.* Heidelberg, 1906.

Segalov, T. Ye. "Dostoyevsky's Illness." *Nauchnoye slovo*, 1929, No. 4, pp. 91–98.

Shchegolev, P. Ye., ed. *The Petrashevtsy in Reminiscences by Contemporaries: A Collection of Materials.* Moscow and Leningrad, 1926.

Sollogub, V. A. "From 'Memoirs.'" *F. M. Dostoyevsky in Reminiscences by Contemporaries*, Vol. I. Moscow, 1964. Pp. 144–45.

Veslovsky, K. "Reminiscences of Several Friends at the Lycee: Mikhail Vasil'evich Butashevich-Petrashevsky." *Russkaya Starina*, 1900, Vol. CIII, No. 9, pp. 449–56.

Winther, Truls. "God and Freedom 200 Years after the Birth of Lamennias." *Morgenbladet*, No. 135, June 17, 1982.

Yanovsky, S. D. "The Illness of F. M. Dostoyevsky." *Novoye Vremya*, No. 1793, February 24, 1881.

———. "Reminiscences of Dostoyevsky." *F. M. Dostoyevsky in Reminiscences by Contemporaries*, Vol. I. Moscow, 1964, pp. 153–75.

Chapter 4:
AT THE SCAFFOLD

Akhsharumov, D. D. "From the Book 'From My Memoirs (1849–1851).'" *F. M. Dostoyevsky in Reminiscences by Contemporaries*, Vol. I. Moscow, 1964. Pp. 222–34.

Arenin, Ye. "Semyonov Square." *Smena*, No. 264, November 11, 1971.

Basina, M. *Through the Twilight of the White Nights: A Documentary Tale.* Leningrad, 1979.

Bel'chikov, N. F. *Dostoyevsky at the Trial of the Petrashevtsy*, Vols. I–III. Moscow and Leningrad, Vol. I, 1937; Vol. II, 1941; Vol. III, 1951.

"From Newspapers and Magazines." *Molva*, No. 50, February 19, 1881.

Gernet, M. N. "The Tsar's Punishment of the First Representatives of Utopian Socialism in Russia." *Sovetskaya yustitsiya*, 1940, No. 12, pp. 13–17; No. 13, pp. 14–18; No. 14, pp. 21–24.

———. *A History of the Tsar's Prisons*, Vol. II, 1825–70. Moscow, 1961.

Grossman, L. P. "The Civic Death of F. M. Dostoyevsky." *Literaturnoye nasledstvo*, Vols. XXII–XXIV. Moscow, 1935. Pp. 683–736.

———. *Dostoyevsky's Execution.* Moscow, 1928.

I. Ar-v. "From Reminiscences of Fyodor Mikhailovich Dostoyevsky." *Peterburgskiy listok*, No. 22, January 31, 1881.

Leykina-Svirskaya, V. R., ed. "A Note on the Petrashevtsy Affair." *Literaturnoye nasledstvo*, Vol. LXIII. Moscow, 1956. Pp. 165–90.

Maskevich, T. "Petersburg Dawn." *Ogonyok*, 1946, Nos. 44–45, p. 47.

Norretranders, Bjarne. *The Ways of Empires to Revolution: A Political History of Russia.* Copenhagen, 1983.

"On Dostoyevsky's Sentence." *Novoye Vremya*, No. 1790, February 20, 1881.

Shchegolev, P. Ye. *Alekseyev's Ravelin: A Book about the Downfall and the Greatness of Man.* Moscow, 1929.

Shevtsov, A. "If Stones Could Speak." *Smena*, August 31, 1969.

The Society of Propaganda in 1849: A Collection of Secret Papers and Highest Sanctions. Leipzig, 1875.
Vuich, Iv. "Diary." *Poryadok*, No. 48, February 18, 1881.

Chapter 5:
SIBERIA

A. M. (A. I. Markevich). "Toward Reminiscences of F. M. Dostoyevsky (An Eyewitness Account)." *Odesskiy Vestnik*, No. 60, March 18, 1881.
Abel'dyayev, V. "To the Memory of F. M. Dostoyevsky." *Moskovskiye Vedomosti*, No. 29, January 29, 1891.
Auezov, M. "F. M. Dostoyevsky and Chokan Valikhanov." *Druzhba narodov*, 1956, No. 3, pp. 154–55.
Aydarova, Ch. "Chokan Valikhanov." *Druzhba narodov*, 1952, No. 3, pp. 256–66.
Bogdanovich, A. V. *The Three Last Autocrats: A Diary.* Moscow and Leningrad, 1924.
Brailovsky, S. N. "F. M. Dostoyevsky and the Poles in the Omsk Labor Camp." *Istoricheskiy vestnik*, 1908, Vol. CXII, No. 4, pp. 189–98.
Cherevin, N. T. "Colonel de-Grave and F. M. Dostoyevsky (the Omsk Jail)." *Russkaya Starina*, 1910, Vol. CXLI, No. 2, p. 318.
Dostoyevsky in Omsk: A Short List of Literature. Omsk, 1972.
Fasting, Sigurd. "Dostoyevsky's Christ." *Inroads into Dostoyevsky's World.* Oslo, 1982. Pp. 32–55.
Feoktistov, N. "Lost Letters of Fyodor Mikhailovich Dostoyevsky." *Sibirskiye ogni*, 1928, No. 2, pp. 119–25.
Frantseva, M. D. "Memoirs." *Istoricheskiy Vestnik*, 1886, No. 6, pp. 628–32.
G-v, B. G. (B. G. Gerasimov). "On Dostoyevsky's Stay in the City of Semipalatinsk (On the Occasion of the 30th Anniversary of the Writer's Death, 1881–1911)." *Sibirskiy arkhiv*, 1913, No. 1, pp. 2–14.
————. "Dostoyevsky in Semipalatinsk." *Sibirskiye ogni*, 1924, No. 4, pp. 140–50; 1926, No. 3, pp. 124–44.
Gerasimov, Bor. "Where Did Dostoyevsky Spend His Imprisonment and Exile?" *Sibirskiye ogni*, 1927, No. 4, pp. 174–77.
Govorov, A. S. "On Dostoyevsky's Stay in Omsk." *Omskaya oblast'*, 1940, No. 8, pp. 49–53.
Grossman, Leonid, ed. "The First Journal: A Siberian Notebook." *Zven'ya*, VI. Moscow and Leningrad, 1936, pp. 413–38.
Ivanov, A. "A Meeting with Dostoyevsky (from My Travels Across Asian Russia)." *Turkestanskiye Vedomosti*, No. 12, February 14, 1893.
Ivlev, N., and N. Gruzinova. "They Were Friends." *Irtysh*, December 14, 1967.

K. "Among Newspapers and Magazines." *Novoye Vremya*, No. 7221, April 7, 1896.

K-n, N. "From Siberian Memoirs: F. M. Dostoyevsky in Omsk (An Essay)." *Volgar'*, No. 353, December 25, 1902.

Kats, N. F. "A Note on Dostoyevsky's Stay in Semipalatinsk." *Stepnoy Kray*, No. 21, February 17, 1896.

Kalamanovich, K. "Dostoyevsky's Kazakh Friend (Chokan Valikhanov)." *Druzhba narodov*, 1971, No. 11, pp. 284–85.

Kaydash, Svetlana. "Dostoyevsky and Fonvizina." *Voprosy Literatury*, 1981, No. 5, pp. 307–13.

Khranevich, V. "F. M. Dostoyevsky According to the Memoirs of an Exiled Pole." *Russkaya Starina*, 1889, Vol. CLXI, No. 2, pp. 367–76; No. 3, pp. 605–21.

Kirpotin, V. "Dostoyevsky in Siberia." *Literaturnaya Gazeta*, February 9, 1956.

———. "In Siberia, the Places of Dostoyevsky." *Oktyabr'*, 1959, No. 4, pp. 208–23.

Kopylov, A. N., ed. *The Decembrists in Siberia*. Novosibirsk, 1977.

Kosharov, P. "A Small Feuilleton: Reminiscence of Dostoyevsky." *Tomskiy Listok*, No. 12, August 10, 1897.

Kulikov, S. N. "Toward a Biography of F. M. Dostoyevsky (According to Materials of the Central War-Historical Archive)." *Katorga i ssylka*, 1934, No. 3, pp. 108–14.

Kungurov, G. V. "In Siberian Exile." *Vostochno-Sibirskaya pravda*, No. 316, November 12, 1971.

Leyfer, Aleksandr. "The House on the Bank of the Irtysh." *Soviet Literature*, 1981, No. 12 (405), pp. 195–97.

Lyubimova-Dorovatovskaya, V. "Dostoyevsky in Siberia: New Materials." *Ogonyok*, 1946, Nos. 46–47, pp. 27–28.

Manuilov, V. A. "Dostoyevsky's Friend Chokan Valikhanov." *Trudy Leningradskogo bibliotechnogo instituta imeni N. K. Krupskoy*, Vol. 5, 1959, pp. 343–69.

Mart'yanov, P. K. *The Affairs and People of the Century: Excerpts from Old Notebooks, Articles, and Notes*, Vol. III. St. Petersburg, 1896.

———. "From the Book 'At the Turn of the Century.' " *F. M. Dostoyevsky in Reminiscences by Contemporaries*, Vol. I. Moscow, 1964. Pp. 235–43.

Materials Relating to the Affair of Butashevich Petrashevsky and His Associates (Part 13—No. 214 the Case of Engineer-Lieutenant F. M. Dostoyevsky) 1849–1862. *GLB* f. No. 93, Dost./I, 4, 2.

Mel'nikov, V. "F. M. Dostoyevsky in Siberia: According to Archival Documents." *Tymenskaya pravda*, April 15, 1962.

Nikolayevsky, K. "F. M. Dostoyevsky's Prison-mates." *Istoricheskiy Vestnik*, Vol. LXXI, No. 1, pp. 219–24.

Novikova, O. A. "A Russian Deputy: Memoirs and Correspondence, 1880–1885." *Russkaya Starina*, 1913, Vol. CLVI, No. 11, pp. 377–91.

Orlov, P. "An Archival Windfall about Dostoyevsky (from the Materials of the Omsk Archive)." *Rabochiy put'*, April 14, 1926.

Ornatskaya, T. I. "Siberian Notebook." *Dostoyevsky: Materials and Research*, Vol. V. Leningrad, 1983. Pp. 222–25.

Ornatskaya, T., and V. Tunimanov. "By the Hand of Dostoyevsky." *Literaturnoye obozreniye*, 1981, No. 11, pp. 107–10.

Palashenkov, A. F. *The Places of Dostoyevsky in Omsk*. Omsk, 1965.

———. "In the Omsk Jail: On the Occasion of the 150th Anniversary of the Birth of F. M. Dostoyevsky." *Molodoy sibiryak*, October 17, 1970.

Pervishin, N. V. "Gogol and Dostoyevsky: Concerning a Polemic." *Novyy zhurnal*, 121, 1975, pp. 279–81.

Plotnikov, Yuri. "No. 118 Dostoyevsky Street." *Prostor*, 1971, No. 11, pp. 104–7.

Reznikov, L. "In Siberia, on the Irtysh." *Trud*, No. 265, November 11, 1971.

Roznovsky. "From Reminiscences of F. M. Dostoyevsky." *Illustrirovannyy mir*, No. 9, February 27, 1882, pp. 135–36.

Seduro, Vladimir. "All the Same a Meeting Between Dostoyevsky and Gogol Did Occur." *Novyy zhurnal*, No. 1, pp. 84–100.

Skandin, A. V. "F. M. Dostoyevsky in Semipalatinsk." *Istoricheskiy Vestnik*, 1903, Vol. XCI, No. 1, pp. 200–25.

Stepanova, Ye. K. "From Reminiscences." *Dostoyevsky. Odnodnevnaya gazeta Russkogo bibliologicheskogo obshchestva*, St. Petersburg, November 12, 1921, pp. 9–10.

Sytina, Z. "From Reminiscences of Dostoyevsky." *Istoricheskiy Vestnik*, 1985, Vol. XIX, No. 1, pp. 123–28.

Tokarzewski, Szymon. "F. M. Dostoyevsky in the Omsk Labor Camp (Reminiscences of a Convict)." *Zven'ya*, VI. Moscow and Leningrad, 1936. Pp. 495–512.

Varshavsky, L. "F. M. Dostoyevsky in Kazakhstan." *Sovetskiy Kazakhstan*, 1956, No. 2, pp. 121–25.

Vyatkin, G. "Dostoyevsky in the Omsk Labor Camp: On the Occasion of the 75th Anniversary of Dostoyevsky's Exile in Siberia." *Sibirskiye ogni*, 1925, No. 1, pp. 177–80.

Yadrintsev, N. "Dostoyevsky in Siberia." *Sibirskiy Sbornik*, 1897, No. 4, pp. 393–401.

Yakovelev, N. "A Note on Dostoyevsky's Life in Semipalatinsk." *Sibir'*, No. 80, July 11, 1897.

Yakushin, N. *Dostoyevsky in Siberia: An Essay on His Life and Work*. Kemerovo, 1960.

Yevseyev, Ye., and Aleksandr Leyfer. "Siberian Meetings." *Sibirskiye ogni*, 1971, No. 11, pp. 162–76.

Yurasova, M. "A Prisoner of 'The House of the Dead.'" *Sibirskiye ogni*, 1956, No. 1, pp. 131–35.

Chapter 6:
HOMECOMING

Ardens, N. N. "Dostoyevsky in Paris." *Pages from the History of Russian Literature: For the Eightieth Birthday of N. F. Bel'chikov, Member-Correspondent of the Academy of Sciences of the USSR*. Moscow, 1971. Pp. 45–52.

Baedeker, K. *Germany: A Handbook for Travelers*. Coblenz, 1864.

Belov, S. V. "Uncollected Letters of F. M. Dostoyevsky." *Russian Literature and the Socio-Political Struggle of the XVII–XIX Centuries*. Leningrad, 1971. Pp. 351–56.

Bem, A. "F. M. Dostoyevsky and Anna Suslova." *Nashe doba*, 1924, No. 31, ch. 5, pp. 287–91.

Birague, Charles de. *Roulette and Trente-et-Quarante, or the True System of Games of Chance*. Paris, 1862.

Boborykin, P. D. *Memoirs in Two Volumes*. Moscow, 1965.

Bykov, P. V. "First Meeting with Dostoyevsky." *Silhouettes of the Distant Past*, ch. VII. Moscow and Leningrad, 1930. Pp. 51–59.

———. "To the Memory of a Penetrating Interpreter of Human Nature (From Personal Reminiscences)." *Vestnik Literatury*, 1921, No. 2 (26), pp. 4–5.

Cherneshevsky, N. G. "My Meetings with Dostoyevsky." *F. M. Dostoyevsky in Reminiscences by Contemporaries*, Vol. I. Moscow, 1964. Pp. 317–21.

Chances, Ellen Bell. *The Ideology of "pocvennicestvo" in Dostoyevsky's Journals Vremja and Epokha*. Diss., Princeton, 1972.

———. "Literary Criticism and the Ideology of *Pochvennichestva* in Dostoyevsky's Thick Journals *Vremja* and *Epokha*." *The Russian Review*, Vol. XXXIV, 1975, pp. 151–64.

Ciriguotta, F., C. V. Todesco, and E. Lugaresi. "Temporal Lobe Epilepsy with Ecstatic Seizures (So-called Dostoyevsky Epilepsy)." *Epilepsia*, Vol. XXI, December 1980, pp. 705–10.

Corti, Egon Caesar. *The Magician from Homburg and Monte Carlo*. Leipzig, 1932.

Dershau, F. "From the Notes of a Gambler." *Russkoye Slovo*, 1859, No. 4, pp. 54–69.

Dolinin, A. "Dostoyevsky and Herzen (Toward the Study of Dostoyevsky's Socio-Political Views)." *F. M. Dostoyevsky, Articles and Materials*, I. St. Petersburg, 1922. Pp. 275–324.

———. "Dostoyevsky and Suslova." *F. M. Dostoyevsky: Articles and Materials*, II. Leningrad and Moscow, 1924. Pp. 153–283.

———. "Dostoyevsky and Strakhov." *Dostoyevsky's Last Novels: How "The Adolescent" and "The Brothers Karamazov" Were Created*. Moscow and Leningrad, 1963. Pp. 307–43.

Dorovatovskaya-Lyubimova, V. "A French Bourgeois (Materials toward an Image of Dostoyevsky)." *Literaturny kritik*, 1936, Bk. 9, pp. 202–17.

Dostoyevsky at Roulette. Published by René Fulop Miller and Friedrich Eckstein. Munich, 1925.

Dostoyevsky, Fyodor Mikhailovich. Foreign Passport Received from the Military Governor-General of St. Petersburg, *GBL,* f. No. 93, Dost./I, 4, 7.

Engelstad, Carl Fredrik. "The West as Seen in the Eyes of Dostoyevsky." *Inroads into Dostoyevsky's World.* Oslo, 1982. Pp. 71–86.

Feigen, Christian. *Gambling House Pictures: Earnestness and Merriment During the Homburg Season.* Homburg, 1911.

Fischer, Klaus. *Gambling in Baden-Baden: The Little Casino Manager.* Baden-Baden, 1981.

Gastaut, Henri. "Fyodor Mikhailovich Dostoyevsky's Involuntary Contribution to the Symptomatology and Prognosis of Epilepsy." *Epilepsia,* Vol. XIX, April 1978, pp. 186–201.

German California: Roulette and Trente-et-Quarante, a Sure Way to Make an Income of 100,000 Francs. Paris, 1862.

Grossman, L. "One of Dostoyevsky's Girlfriends." *Russkiy sovremennik,* Bk. 3. Moscow and Leningrad, 1924. Pp. 248–52.

Halliday, John, and Peter Fuller, eds. *The Psychology of Gambling.* London, 1974.

A Handbook for Travelers on the Continent. London, 1858.

Hochauer, Brigitte. *Decision-making in a Risky Gamble: A Field Study for an Investigation of Gambling Behavior at Roulette.* Diss., Salzburg, 1970.

Ivanov, A. "On the Traditional Mistake in the Evaluation of the Meetings of Dostoyevsky and Herzen." *Novy zhurnal,* 141, 1980, pp. 234–52.

Jercey (L. Hennet du Vigneux). *The Gambling Houses Ruined by Gamblers.* Paris, 1858.

Kashina, N. V. *Dostoyevsky's Aesthetics.* Moscow, 1975.

———. *The Aesthetics of F. M. Dostoyevsky.* Diss., Avtoreferat, Moscow, 1980.

Kierulf, Halfdan. *Epilepsy in the Life and Work of Dostoyevsky.* Diss., Strasbourg, 1971.

———. "Dostoyevsky and Epilepsy." *Tidssfrift for Den norske laegeforening,* 1973, No. 19–20, pp. 1303–7.

Kjetsaa, Geir. "Belles Lettres." *Dostoyevsky and Tolstoy: Essays.* Oslo, 1977. Pp. 9–15.

———. "Written by Dostoyevsky?" *Dostoyevsky Studies,* Vol. I, 1980, pp. 73–88.

Koz'min, G. "The Dostoyevsky Brothers and the Proclamation 'Young Russia.' " *Pechat' i revolyutsiya,* 1929, Nos. 2–3, pp. 69–76.

Lansky, L. "Lost Letters of Dostoyevsky." *Voprosy Literatury,* 1971, No. 11, pp. 196–222.

Lavretsky, A. "Dostoyevsky and Shchedrin." *Na literaturnom postu,* 1931, No. 24, pp. 39–42.

Leykina, V. "Reactionary Democracy of the Sixties: The Pochvenniks." *Zvezda,* 1929, No. 6, pp. 168–81.

Lishchiner, S. D. "Herzen and Dostoyevsky: The Dialectics of Spiritual Quests." *Russkaya literatura*, 1972, No. 10, pp. 53–56.

Lund, Mogens. "Dostoyevsky and His Epilepsy." *Roche Litteratur-Tjeneste*, 40, 1972, No. 10, pp. 53–56.

Makagonova, T. M. *Dostoyevsky's Journalistic Activity, 1861–1863*. Diss., Avtoreferat, Moscow, 1974.

Milyukov, A. P. "Fyodor Mikhailovich Dostoyevsky." *F. M. Dostoyevsky in Reminiscences by Contemporaries*, Vol. I. Moscow, 1964. Pp. 325–29.

Nechayeva, V. S. *M. M. and F. M. Dostoyevsky's Journal "Vremya" 1861–1863*. Moscow, 1972.

The Office of the Military General-Governor of St. Petersburg. The Secret Bureau, Passport Department. June 13, 1863, No. 1338, *TSGALI*, f. 1286, op. 24, 1863g.

Olisov, V. P. "On Dostoyevsky's Stay in the City of Tver." *Krasnyy arkhiv*, Vol. IV, 1923, pp. 398–401.

Panteleyev, L. F. *Memoirs*. Moscow, 1958. Pp. 225–26.

Petukhov, V. Ye. "From the Intimate Life of Dostoyevsky (Ap. Prok. Suslova-Rozanova)." *Izvestiya Krymskogo pedagogicheskogo institua imeni M. V. Frunze*, Vol. II, 1928, pp. 35–46 (1–12).

Pipes, Richard. *Russia Under the Old Regime*. London, 1974.

Rozanov, Vasily. Unpublished letter without date. *TSGALI*, f. No. 412, op. No. 1, yed. khr. No. 655.

———. Unpublished statement to A. G. Dostoyevskaya from 1898. *GBL*, f. No. 93, Dost./II, kar. No. 8, yed. khr. 39a.

Rozenblyum, N. G. "The Petersburg Fires of 1862 and Dostoyevsky (Censored Articles from the Journal V*remya*)." *Literaturnoye nasledstvo*, Vol. LXXXVI. Moscow, 1973. Pp. 16–54.

Schroder, Friedrich Karl. *The Religious Character of Epileptic Experiences (The Example of Dostoyevsky and Practical Clinical Experience)*. Diss., Tübingen, 1965.

Segalov, T. Ye. "Dostoyevsky's Illness." *Nauchnoye slovo*, 1929, No. 4, pp. 91–98.

Shtakenshneyder, Ye. A. *Diary and Notes (1854–1886)*. Moscow and Leningrad, 1934.

Shtraykh, S. "Dostoyevsky's 'Eternal Love.' " *Ogonyok*, 1933, No. 10, pp. 12–13.

Shubert, A. I. *My Life*. Leningrad, 1929.

Simmons, J. S. G. "F. M. Dostoyevsky and A. K. Tolstoy: Two Letters." *Oxford Slavonic Papers*, Vol. IX, 1960, pp. 64–71.

Spiridonov, Vasily. "The Direction of V*remya* and *Epokha*." *Dostoyevsky: Odnodnevnaya gazeta Russkogo bibliologicheskogo obshchestva*. Petrograd, November 12, 1921. Pp. 2–9.

Veynberg, P. I. "Literary Spectacles (from My Memoirs)." *F. M. Dostoyevsky in Reminiscences by Contemporaries*, Vol. I. Moscow, 1964. Pp. 330–36.

Wykes, Alan. *Gambling: All about the Games.* Translated by Hans Braavig. Stavanger, 1972.

Zaborova, R. B. "F. M. Dostoyevsky and the Literary Fond (According to Archival Documents)." *Russkaya Literatura,* 1975, No. 3, pp. 158–70.

Chapter 7:
YEARS OF CRISIS

Akhsyarumov, N. D. (Review of *Crime and Punishment*). *Vsemirnyy trud,* 1867, No. 3, pp. 125–56.

Chelyshev, B. "A Novel to Boot." *Knizhnoye obozreniye,* No. 52 (294), December 24, 1971.

Dolinin, A. S. "Toward a History of the Censorship of Dostoyevsky's First Two Journals." *F. M. Dostoyevsky: Articles and Materials,* II. Leningrad and Moscow, 1924. Pp. 559–77.

Fon-Fokht, N. "Toward a Biography of F. M. Dostoyevsky." *F. M. Dostoyevsky in Reminiscences by Contemporaries,* Vol. I. Moscow, 1964. Pp. 371–81.

I. R. (I. Rossinsky). "The Double: The Adventures of Fyodor Srizhov." *Iskra,* 1866, No. 12, pp. 159–62; No. 13, pp. 172–73; No. 14, p. 84.

"Dostoyevsky's Journals and Notebooks: II. Notebook 1862–1864." *Literaturnoye nasledstvo,* Vol. LXXXIII. Moscow, 1971. Pp. 171–200.

Kjetsaa, Geir. "*Crime and Punishment* in Contemporary Criticism." *Dostoyevsky's Novel about Raskolnikov.* Oslo, 1973. Pp. 138–52.

Kovolevskaya, S. V. *Memories of Childhood and Autobiographical Essays.* Moscow, 1945.

———. *Memoirs: Tales.* Moscow, 1974.

Kovalevsky, P. M. "From 'Meetings on the Road of Life.' " *F. M. Dostoyevsky in Reminiscences by Contemporaries,* Vol. I. Moscow, 1964. Pp. 322–24.

Lambeck, Barbara. *Dostoyevsky's Dispute with Cherneshevsky's Ideology in "Notes from Underground."* Diss., Tübingen, 1980.

Larsen, Alf. *The Regal Art: Essays.* Oslo, 1949.

"Literary Notes." *Nedelya,* No. 5, April 10, 1866, pp. 72–74.

Modzalevsky, B. M. "Dostoyevsky—Contributor to *Russkiy Vestnik:* Unpublished Letters of F. M. Dostoyevsky, 1866–1873." *Byloye,* 1919, No. 14, pp. 30–52.

Nechayeva, V. S. *M. M. and F. M. Dostoyevsky's Journal "Epokha," 1864–1865.* Moscow, 1975.

Ornatskaya, T. I., ed. "A. Ye. Vrangel's Letters to Dostoyevsky." *Dostoyevsky: Materials and Research,* Vol. III. Leningrad, 1978. Pp. 258–85.

Pisarev, D. I. "The Struggle for Life." *Complete Works in Six Volumes,* Vol. VI. St. Petersburg, 1905. Pp. 343–404.

Polyansky, N. N. "From Reminiscences about Dostoyevsky." *TSGALI,* f. No. 212, yed. khr. No. 301, op. No. 1.

Shtraykh, S. Ya. "An Episode in Dostoyevsky's Life." *The Kovalevsky Family.* Leningrad, 1948. Pp. 115–28.

Strakhov, Nikolay. "Our Elegant Literature." *Otechestvennyye zapiski,* 1867, Vol. CLXX, No. 2, pp. 544–56; Vol. CLXXI, No. 3, pp. 325–40; Vol. CLXXI, No. 4, pp. 514–27.

Vasil'yeva, G. "Dostoyevsky and the Korvin–Krukovsky Sisters." *Pskovskaya pravda,* No. 263, November 11, 1971.

Veynberg, Pyotr. "April 4, 1866 (From My Memoirs)." *Byloye,* 1906, No. 4, pp. 299–303.

Yeliseyev, G. Z. (Review of *Crime and Punishment*). *Sovremennik,* 1866, No. 2, pp. 263–80.

Chapter 8:
MARRIAGE AND FLIGHT

Alanen, Yrjo O. "The Idiot." *Psychiatrica Fennica,* 1975, pp. 47–67.

The Annals of the Congress of Geneva (September 9–12, 1867): Preliminaries— The Four Sessions—Appendix. Geneva, 1868.

Baden-Baden: Tourguide through the City and Its Vicinity. Baden-Baden, 1874.

The Bible, or The Holy Scriptures: The Canonical Books of the Old and New Testaments. Oslo, 1965.

Cherbuliez, Joel. *Geneva: Its Institutions, Its Mores, Its Intellectual and Moral Development.* Geneva, 1867.

Cox, Roger L. "Myshkin's Apocalyptic Vision." *Between Earth and Heaven: Shakespeare, Dostoyevsky and the Meaning of Christian Tragedy.* New York, 1969. Pp. 164–91.

Dostoyevskaya, A. G. "How I 'Was Married Off'!" *Russkaya rech',* 1981, No. 5, pp. 35–38.

Dostoyevsky, A. F. "The Sun of My Life." *Neva,* 1963, No. 12, pp. 193–95.

Dupont Lachenal, Leon. "A Russian in Saxony." *Annales Valaisannes,* 10, 1957/59, pp. 299–316.

Garshin, Yevgeny. "Reminiscences of I. S. Turgenev." *Istoricheskiy Vestnik,* 1883, Vol. XIV, No. 11, pp. 366–98.

Gor'kiy, M. *Literary Works. Articles. Notes.* (Arkhiv M. Gor'kogo, Vol. XII). Moscow, 1969.

The Gospel of Our Lord Jesus Christ: New Testament. St. Petersburg, 1823. GBL, f. 93/I, Dostoyevsky K. 5b/1.

Grieben, Theobald. *Dresden and Its Environs: An Illustrated Guidebook for Travelers.* Berlin, 1865.

Hollander, Robert. "The Apocalyptic Framework of Dostoyevsky's *The Idiot.*" *Mosaic,* VII, 2, Winter, 1974, pp. 123–39.

Illustrated Guide to Geneva. Geneva, 1888.

Jervell, Jacob. *No Greater Love . . . The Gospel of St. John the Evangelist.* Oslo, 1978.

Keller, Howard H. "Prince Myshkin: Success or Failure?" *Journal of Russian Studies*, Vol. XXIV, 1972, pp. 17–23.

Kjetsaa, Geir. "Dostoyevsky's Gospel." *Aftenposten*, May 3, 1983.

"A Letter from Dostoyevsky to the Kashins." *F. M. Dostoyevsky: Articles and Materials*, II. Leningrad and Moscow, 1924. Pp. 309–10.

"The Memoirs of A. G. Dostoyevskaya." *F. M. Dostoyevsky: Articles and Materials*, II. Leningrad and Moscow, 1924. Pp. 285–302.

Metral, Maurice. "Fyodor Dostoyevsky at the Casino Saxony." *Gazette de Lausanne*, February 2, 1964.

Meyers, Jeffrey. "Holbein and *The Idiot*." *Painting and the Novel*. Manchester, 1975. Pp. 136–47.

Milosz, Czeslaw. "Dostoyevsky and Swedenborg." *Emperor of the Earth. Modes of Eccentric Vision*. Berkeley, Los Angeles, and London, 1977. Pp. 120–43.

Onasch, Konrad. "The Hagiographical Type 'Yurodivy' in the Work of Dostoyevsky." *Dostoyevsky Studies*, Vol. I, 1980, pp. 111–21.

———. "Individuality and Suffering in the Work of Dostoyevsky." *Zeitschrift für Slawistik*, Vol. XXVIII, 1983, No. 5, pp. 712–19.

Rakusa, Ilma. *Dostoyevsky in Switzerland: A Reader*. Frankfurt a. M., 1981.

Schmidt, Aurel. "Dostoyevsky in Saxony." *Basler Magazin*, No. 41, October 14, 1978.

Schon, Robert Conrad. *Dostoyevsky's Path to Himself*. Diss., Freiburg im Breisgau, 1957.

Solovjov, Vladimir. *A Short Story about the Anti-Christ*. Translated and with a Foreword by Peter Normann Waage. Oslo, 1984.

Stakheyev, D. I. "Groups and Portraits (Pages from Reminiscences)." *Istoricheskiy Vestnik*, 1907, Vol. CVII, No. 1, pp. 81–94.

Stoyunina, M. "Reminiscences of A. G. Dostoyevskaya." *F. M. Dostoyevsky, Articles and Materials*, II. Leningrad and Moscow, 1924. Pp. 578–82.

———. "My Reminiscences of Dostoyevsky." *Vozrozhdeniye*, Vol. L, February, 1956, pp. 25–39.

Zweig, Stefan. "Dostoyevsky." *Three Masters: Balzac, Dickens, Dostoyevsky*. Leipzig, 1927. Pp. 89–220.

Chapter 9:
EXILE

Al'tman, M. "Pryzhov and Dostoyevsky." *Katorga i ssylka*, 1931, Bks. 8–9 (82–83), pp. 57–71.

Baedeker, K. *Italy. A Handbook for Travelers*. Coblenz and Leipzig, 1872.

Eritsland, Lars. *An Interpretation of The Revelation of St. John the Divine.* Oslo, 1978.

Grimm, Paul. *The Mysteries of the Tsar's Palace (under the Emperor Nicholas I).* Wurzbourg, 1868.

Il'in, N. "Dostoyevsky in the Controversy over the Kumaninsky Inheritance." *Zven'ya,* IX, Moscow, 1951. Pp. 547–59.

Izmaylov, A. "At A. G. Dosotoyevskaya's (for the 35th Anniversary of the Death of F. M. Dostoyevsky)." *Brizhevyye Vedomosti,* No. 15350, January 28, 1916.

Jonsson, Inge. *Swedenborg's Correspondence.* Stockholm, 1969.

Krag, Erik. *The Struggle against the West and Russian Intellectual Life.* Oslo, 1932.

Larsen, A. C. *The Revelation of St. John the Divine: Translated and Annotated.* Copenhagen, 1899.

Markovitch, Milan. "Dostoyevsky, Italy and Florence." *Rivista di letterature moderne e comparate,* 1958, Nos. 3–4, pp. 245–59.

Mikhail Bakunin and His Relations with Sergey Nechaev, 1870–1872: Writings and Materials (Bakunin Archives, IV). Leiden, 1971.

Moe, Olaf. *The Last Book of the Bible: An Interpretation of the Revelation of St. John the Divine.* Oslo, 1960.

Muller, Fedia. "Dostoyevsky's Stay in Vevey." *Feuilles d'Avis de Vevey,* November 11, 1960.

Oksman, Yu. G. "The Secret Instructions about Dostoyevsky (Materials from the Odessa Archival Collection)." *The Work of Dostoyevsky, 1821–1881, 1921: A Collection of Articles and Materials.* Odessa, 1921. Pp. 36–38.

Prozhogin, N. P. "Dostoyevsky in Florence." *Inostrannaya literatura,* 1981, No. 8, pp. 237–44.

———. "Dostoyevsky in Florence in 1868 and 1869." *Dostoyevsky: Materials and Research,* Vol. V. Leningrad, 1983. Pp. 204–8.

Strelsky, Katherine. "Dostoyevsky in Florence." *The Russian Review,* Vol. XXIII, No. 2, April, 1964, pp. 149–63.

Swedenborg, Emmanuel. *The Apocalypse Explained according to the Spiritual Sense,* Vols. I–VII. Paris and London, 1855–59.

The Victory of God's Church: The Revelation of St. John the Divine Explained by Dr. W. F. Engelbreth. Odense, 1855.

Weider, Bjarne O. *An Interpretation of the Thessalonika Epistles.* Oslo, 1978.

Yevnin, F. I. "The Novel *The Devils.*" *The Works of Dostoyevsky.* Moscow, 1959. Pp. 215–64.

Zink, Wolfgang Richard. *Gambling in Germany: Historical Development and Current Legal Arguments.* Diss., Mainz, 1970.

Chapter 10:
BACK ON RUSSIAN SOIL

Aleksandrov, M. A. "Fyodor Mikhailovich Dostoyevsky in Reminiscences by a Typesetter, 1872–1881." *F. M. Dostoyevsky in Reminiscences by Contemporaries*, Vol. II. Moscow, 1964. Pp. 213–56.

———. "Memoirs." *TSGALI*, f. No. 212, op. No. 1, yed. khr. No. 256.

Bel'chikov, N. F., ed. "Dostoyevsky and Pobedonostsev." *Krasnyy arkhiv*, 1922, Vol. II, pp. 240–55.

Belov, S., ed. "From A. G. Dostoyevskaya's Correspondence with Her Husband." *Baykal*, 1975, No. 5, pp. 133–41.

Brandes, George. *Impressions of Russia. Collected Works*, b. 10, Copenhagen, 1902. Pp. 293–548.

Byrnes, Robert F. "Dostoyevsky and Pobedonostsev." *Jahrbucher für Geschichte Osteuropas*, 9, 1961, pp. 57–71.

De Vogue, E. "Fyodor Mikhailovich Dostoyevsky as Psychologist." *Epokha*, February, 1886, pp. 75–96.

Germany and Austria. A Practical Tourguide. Berlin, 1879.

Girshgorn, A. *The Curative Waters of the Ems and Its Sources*. St. Petersburg, 1874.

Goldstein, David I. *Dostoyevsky and the Jews*. Austin, 1981.

Ibsen, Henrik. "Kunst-Utstillingen i Vienna." *Hundrearsutgaven*, b. XIX. Oslo, 1952. Pp. 140–45.

K. E. (Karl Yak. Ettinger). "At Dostoyevsky's Widow's." *Birzhevyye Vedomosti*, 1906, No. 9178.

Kantor, R. "Something Unknown about Dostoyevsky." *Vestnik literatury*, 1921, No. 11 (35), pp. 6–7.

Kirpotin, V. "Dostoyevsky's Alternative." *Oktyabr'*, 1981, No. 1, pp. 203–14.

Kn. V. M. (V. P. Meshchersky). "Reminiscences of Fyodor Mikhailovich Dostoyevsky." *Dobro*, 1881, Nos. 2–3, pp. 31–37.

Morson, Gary Saul. "Dostoyevsky's Anti-Semitism and the Critics: A Review Article." *Slavic and East European Journal*, Vol. XXVII, No. 3, 1983, pp. 302–17.

Natova, N. A. *F. M. Dostoyevsky in Bad Ems*. Frankfurt a. M., 1971.

Nechayeva, V., ed. "Three Original Manuscripts of Dostoyevsky." *Literaturnoye nasledstvo*, Vol. XV. Moscow, 1934. Pp. 291–93.

Nechayeva, V. "When the Secret Surveillance of Dostoyevsky Was Lifted." *Russkaya literatura*, 1964, No. 2, pp. 170–72.

Nilsson, Nils Ake. "Dostoyevsky in Bad Ems." *Rysk kulturrevy*, Vol. X, No. 4, 1978, pp. 5–7.

Naerup, Karl. "Dostoyevsky." *Ord for dagen*. Oslo, 1929. Pp. 28–36.

Oksman, Yu. G. "Dostoyevsky in the Editorial Office of Grazhdanin (According to Unpublished Materials)." *The Works of Dostoyevsky, 1821, 1881, 1921*. Odessa, 1921. Pp. 63–82.

Pervishin, N. N. "Dostoyevsky's Illness and His Work." *Novyy zhurnal*, 141, 1980, pp. 86–104.

Reynus, L. M. *Dostoyevsky in Staraya Russa*. Leningrad, 1971.

Solov'yov, Vs. S. "Reminiscences of F. M. Dostoyevsky." *F. M. Dostoyevsky in Reminiscences by Contemporaries*, Vol. II. Moscow, 1964. Pp. 186–209.

Timofeyeva, V. V. (O. Pochinkovskaya). "A Year of Work with a Famous Writer." *F. M. Dostoyevsky in Reminiscences by Contemporaries*, Vol. II. Moscow, 1964. Pp. 186–209.

Zhavoronkov, A., and S. Belov. "The Case of Retired Second Lieutenant Fyodor Dostoyevsky." *Russkaya literatura*, 1963, No. 4, pp. 197–202.

Zhavoronkov, A. Z. "The Political Affair of the Secret Surveillance of F. M. Dostoyevsky in *Staraya Russa* (1872–1876)." *Izvestiya Akademii nauk SSSR. Seriya literatury i yazyka*, Vol. XXIV, No. 4, pp. 329–40.

Chapter 11:
THE PROPHET

"A. G. Dostoyevskaya's Correspondence with Contemporaries." Baykal, 1976, No. 6, pp. 137–45.

A. O. "A Little Feuilleton: From Literary Reminiscences, XI." *Novoye Vremya*, No. 8784, August 11, 1900.

Alchevskaya, Kh. D. *Things Thought through and Lived Through: Diary, Letters, Reminiscences*. Moscow, 1912.

Aleksandrov, Anatoly. "Fyodor Mikhailovich Dostoyevsky (a Short Page of Reminiscences)." *Svetoch i dnevnik pisatelya*, 1913, No. 1, pp. 53–56.

———. "To the Memory of F. M. Dostoyevsky." *Moskovskiye Vedomosti*, No. 22, January 28, 1910.

Aleksandrova, I. V. "In the Valley of the Quiet Zhizdra." *Literaturnaya Rossiya*, July 25, 1969.

Arep'yev, N. "At Nekrasov's Funeral (an Excerpt from an Old Diary)." *Vestnik literatury*, 1921, No. 12 (36), p. 7.

B. Z. (Vladimir Zotov). "Dostoyevsky, Fyodor Mikhailovich." *The Russian Encyclopedic Dictionary Published by I. N. Berezin, Professor at St. Petersburg University*, Pt. II, Vol. I. St. Petersburg, 1874. P. 475.

Belov, S. V., ed. "Z. A. Trubetskaya. Dostoyevsky and A. P. Filosofova." *Russkaya literatura*, 1973, No. 3, pp. 116–18.

Biryukov, P. *Lev Nikolaevich Tolstoy. A Biography*, Vol. II. Moscow, 1908. P. 457.

Bortnes, Jostein. "Two Studies of Dostoyevsky." *Edda*, 1968, hf. 1, pp. 2–16.

Bryullov, B. "A Meeting with Dostoyevsky (from the Words of P. A. Bryullov)." *Nachala*, 1922, No. 2, pp. 264–65.

Bursov, V. "Dostoyevsky's Personality." *Zvezda*, 1969, No. 12, pp. 134–39.

Camus, Albert. *The Myth of Sisyphus and Other Essays*. New York, 1959.

Chukovsky, K. "Things Forgotten and New about Dostoyevsky." *Rech'*, No. 94, April 6, 1914.

De Vogue, E. *Paris–St. Petersburg 1877–1883: A Journal*. Paris, 1932. P. 164.

Doganovich, Anna. "From the Memoirs of a Doctor's Assistant." *Nablyudatel'*, 1885, No. 10, pp. 306–38.

Dunlop, John B. *Staretz Amvrosy: Model for Dostoyevsky's Staretz Zossima*. Belmont, MA, 1972.

Egeberg, Erik. "Rebellion of the Flesh—Artistic and Moral Problems: The Philosophy of Nikolay Fyodorov." *Russiske punktyls*. Oslo, 1981. Pp. 68–77.

Fangen, Ronald. "Dostoyevsky." *Inroads in Fiction and Thought*. Kristiania, 1919. Pp. 67–82.

Filosofov, D. "A Belated Garland." A. F. Koni, ed. *Turgenev and Savina*. Petrograd, 1918. Pp. 78–80.

Filosofova, A. P., and M. V. Kamenetskaya. "On Dostoyevsky"; "Meetings with Dostoyevsky." *F. M. Dostoyevsky in Reminiscences by Contemporaries*, Vol. II. Moscow, 1964. Pp. 322–26.

Florovsky, Anton. "Dostoyevsky and the Slavonic Question." *The Slavonic and East European Review*, Vol. IX, 1930–31, pp. 411–23.

Frank, Joseph. "Introduction." *The Diary of a Writer*. F. M. Dostoyevsky. Translated and Annotated by Boris Brasol. Santa Barbara and Salt Lake City, 1979. Pp. ix–xxvi.

Fraser, George. *Curriculum vitae*. Helsinki, 1934.

Fridlender, G. M. "Dostoyevsky's Aesthetics." *Dostoyevsky—Artist and Thinker*. Moscow, 1972. Pp. 97–164.

Glinsky, B. "The Assassination of the Tsar, March 1, 1881 (Historical Essays)." *Istoricheskiy Vestnik*, 1910, Vol. CXX, No. 4, pp. 214–57.

Gnedich, P. P. *The Book of Life: Memoirs, 1855–1918*. Leningrad, 1929.

Gradovsky, G. "From What Has Passed (the Memoirs and Impressions of a Man of Letters)." *Russkaya Starina*, 1908, Vol. CXXXVI, No. 10, pp. 57–74.

———. *Results (1862–1907)*. Kiev, 1908.

Grossman, Leonid. "Dostoyevsky and Governmental Circles in the 1870s." *Literaturnoye nasledstvo*, Vol. XV. Moscow, 1934. Pp. 83–162.

Ingold, Felix Phillip. *Dostoyevsky and the Jews*. Frankfurt a. M., 1981.

Kirpotin, V. Ya. "Dostoyevsky on the Fate of European Civilization." *Nauchnyye doklady*, 12, pp. 106–35.

Kjetsaa, Geir. "Dostoyevsky and Torgersen." *Aftenposten*, 20, March, 1974.

———. "Towards Worldwide Fame: Dostoyevsky and the Association Littéraire Internationale." *We and They: National Identity as a Theme in Slavic Cultures. Donum Stiefanum*. Copenhagen, 1984. Pp. 95–100.

Kochetkov, V. " 'Surely We Remember . . .' The Story of V. I. Romantsova, Former Resident of Darovoye." *Za novuyu zhizn'*, No. 135 (9153), November 10, 1981.

Kolsto, Pal. "Imperialism and Messianism in Dostoyevsky." *Inroads into Dostoyevsky's World*. Oslo, 1982. Pp. 87–104.

Korolenko, V. G. "Nekrasov's Funeral and Dostoyevsky's Speech at His Graveside (from 'A Story of My Contemporary')." *F. M. Dostoyevsky in Reminiscences by Contemporaries*, Vol. II. Moscow, 1964. Pp. 297–300.

Krasovsky, Yu. A. "Dostoyevsky's Kazan Correspondent (an Unpublished Letter to N. F. Yushkov)." *Vstrechi s proshlym*, No. 1, Moscow, 1972. Pp. 47–50.

Kruglov, Aleksandr. "Simple Speeches (to the Memory of F. M. Dostoyevsky)." *Russkoye chteniye*, No. 90, November 10, 1901.

Lansky, L. "Lost Letters of Dostoyevsky." *Voprosy literatury*, 1971, No. 11, pp. 196–222.

Lawrence, D. H. "Preface to Dostoyevsky's the Grand Inquisitor." *Dostoyevsky: A Collection of Critical Essays*. Englewood Cliffs, NJ, 1962. Pp. 90–97.

Librovich, S. F. *On the Book Beat: Memoirs, Notes, Documents*. Moscow, 1916.

Linnikov, G. S., ed. "Pavlov's Letters to His Fiancée." *Moscow*, 1959, No. 10, pp. 155–81.

Maslyannikov, K. "An Episode from Dostoyevsky's Life (Material for a Biography)." *Novoye Vremya*, No. 2380, October 13, 1882.

Maugham, W. Somerset. "Dostoyevsky and *The Brothers Karamazov*." In *Ten Novels and Their Authors*. London, 1954. Pp. 234–60.

Mikhaylova, A. "Dostoyevsky on Nekrasov and Shchedrin: Two Unpublished Letters of Dostoyevsky to D. V. Averkiev." *Literaturnoye nasledstvo*, Vols. XLIX–L, Moscow, 1949. Pp. 631–34.

Mikulich, V. (L. I. Veselitskaya). "Meeting with a Celebrity." *Zhenskoye delo*, 1899, No. 2, pp. 5–28.

Miller, Or. "Dostoyevsky's House and Office." *Istoricheskiy Vestnik*, 1887, Vol. XXVII, No. 3, pp. 571–76.

Moshin, Aleksey. *Something New about Great Writers (Small Strokes for Large Portraits)*. St. Petersburg, 1908.

Notes on an Issue of *Novoye Vremya*, No. 1128, April 21, 1879, GBL, Dost./ Iu, kar. 3, yed khr. 65.

Obodovsky, K. "Pages from a Notebook." *Istoricheskiy Vestnik*, 1893, Vol. LIV, No. 12, pp. 773–80.

Obolensky, L. Ye. "Literary Reminiscences and Testimonials (1854–1892)." *Istoricheskiy Vestnik*, 1902, Vol. LXXXVII, No. 2, pp. 487–508.

Opochinin, Ye. N. "Conversations with Dostoyevsky." *Zven'ya*, VI. Moscow and Leningrad, 1936. Pp. 454–94.

Osmolovsky, V. F. "F. M. Dostoyevsky and Kh. D. Alchevskaya." *Voprosy russkoy literatury*, No. 3 (18). Lvov, 1971. Pp. 52–58.

Pavlova, S. V. "From Reminiscences." *Novyy mir*, 1946, No. 3, pp. 97–144.

Pervushin, N. V. "A Rehabilitation of Dostoyevsky." *Slavic and East European Studies*, Vol. XVII, 1972, pp. 114–21.

———. "On Dostoyevsky and Turgenev." *Zapiski russkoy akademicheskoy gruppy v SShA*, Vol. XVI, 1983, pp. 309–17.

Plekhanov, G. V. "The Funeral of N. A. Nekrasov." *Literatura i estetika*, Vol. II. Moscow, 1958. Pp. 206–9.

Putsykovich, V. "On F. M. Dostoyevsky (from Reminiscences about Him)." *Novoye Vremya*, No. 9292, January 16, 1902.

Repin, N. "F. M. Dostoyevsky and a Vagabond (from My Memoirs)." *Peterburgskaya gazeta*, No. 333, December 4, 1903.

Rybalko, B. "Dostoyevsky's Last Address." *Russkiy yazyk za rubezhom*, 1977, No. 2, pp. 105–6.

S. F. "Pavlov's Wife." *Novoye russkoye slovo*, No. 26, February 1, 1970.

S. V. "Mosaic (from Old Notebooks)." *Istoricheskiy Vestnik*, 1912, Vol. CXXX, No. 12, pp. 1013–66.

Sadovnikov, D. N. "Meetings with I. S. Turgenev: 'Fridays' at the Poet Ya. P. Polonsky's in 1879." *Russkoye proshloye*, 1923, Bk. 1, pp. 74–86.

Savina, M. G. "My Acquaintance with Turgenev." A. F. Koni, ed. *Turgenev and Savina*. Petrograd, 1918. Pp. 63–70.

Simonova, L. "From Reminiscences of Fyodor Mikhailovich Dostoyevsky." *Tserkovno-obshchestvennyy Vestnik*, No. 16, February 6, 1881; No. 17, February 8, 1881; No. 18, February 11, 1881.

Sluchevsky, K. K. "Dostoyevsky: A Sketch of His Life and Activity." *The Complete Works of Dostoyevsky*, Vol. I. St. Petersburg, 1889.

Sozertsatel'. "About Everything." *Mysl'*, 1882, Nos. 10–11, pp. 177–204.

Strakhov, N. N. "Letter to L. N. Tolstoy." *Sovremennyy mir*, October, 1913, pp. 307–10.

T. G. (Tim Greve). "Imperialism." *Aschehougs og Gyldendals store norske leksikon*, Vol. VI. Oslo, 1979. P. 189.

Thomassen, Einar. "Was Dostoyevsky a Criminal? A Conflict over the Legend of the Author's Depravity." *Perspektiv*, 1963, Vol. X, No. 5, pp. 7–19.

Torgersen, Johan. "Dostoyevsky and World Politics." *Aftenposten*, March 16, 1974.

———. "Kjetsaa and Dostoyevsky." *Aftenposten*, March 26, 1974.

Trubitsyn, Nikolay. *Dostoyevsky on Children*. Kronshtadt, 1903.

Tschizewski, Dmitrij. "Dostoyevsky." *Russische Literaturgeschichte des 19 Jahrhunderts. II: Der Realismus*. Munich, 1967. Pp. 72–92.

V. P-va (V. I. Pribytkova). "Reminiscences of Dostoyevsky." *Rebus*, No. 25, June 30, 1885; No. 26, July 7, 1885.

Vengerov, S. A. "Four Meetings with Turgenev." *Literaturnyy ezhenedel'nik*, No. 36, November 9, 1923.

Volgin, I. L. "Dostoyevsky and Tsarist Censorship (Toward a Publication History of *The Diary of a Writer*)." *Russkaya Literatura*, 1970, No. 4, pp. 106–20.

———. "The Moral Foundation of Dostoyevsky's Publicistic Writings (the Eastern Question in *The Diary of a Writer*)." *Izvestiya Akademii nauk SSSR: Seriya literatury i yazyka*, 1971, No. 4, pp. 312–24.

———. "The Editorial Archive of *The Diary of a Writer* (1876–1877)." *Russkaya literatura*, 1974, No. 1, pp. 150–61.

———. "Dostoyevsky and Russian Society (*The Diary of a Writer*, 1876–1877, in the Estimation of Contemporaries)." *Russkaya literatura*, 1976, No. 3, pp. 123–43.

———. "Dostoyevsky's Last Year." *Novyy mir*, 1981, No. 10, pp. 100–83.

———. *Dostoyevsky the Journalist (The Diary of a Writer and the Russian Public)*. Moscow, 1982.

de Vollan, G. "F. M. Dostoyevsky." *Ocherki proshlogo. Golos minuvshego*, 1914, No. 4, pp. 123–26.

Yanzhul, Ivan. "I. I. Yanzhul's Reminiscences of Things Lived through and Seen (1864–1909)." *Russkaya Starina*, 1910, Vol. CXLIV, No. 10, pp. 3–20.

Yasinsky, Ier. *The Novel of My Life: A Book of Memoirs*. Moscow and Leningrad, 1926. Pp. 168–69.

Yunge, Ye. F. (née Countess Tolstaya). *Memoirs (1843–1860)*. Moscow, 1914.

Yurman. N. A. "Dostoyevsky's Illness." *Klinicheskiy arkhiv genial'nosti*, Vol. IV, No. 1, 1928, pp. 61–85.

Zakharov, V. N. "Facts Contradicting Legend." *Problems in the Study of Dostoyevsky: A Study Manual for a Special Seminar*. Petrozavodsk, 1978. Pp. 75–109.

Zelenetsky, A. A. "Three Meetings with Dostoyevsky (an Excerpt from Memoirs)." *Istoricheskiy Vestnik*, 1901, Vol. LXXXIII, No. 3, pp. 1021–29.

Ziloti, V. P. In *Tret'yakov's House*. New York, 1954. Pp. 183–84.

Chapter 12:
TRIUMPH AND DEATH

Ayzenshtok, N. "Three Jubilees (Historical Inquiries)." *Literaturnyy sovremennik*, 1937, No. 1, pp. 292–307.

Annensky, I. *F. M. Dostoyevsky*. Kazan, 1905.

Anonymous (A. S. Suvorin). "Fyodor Mikhailovich Dostoyevsky." *Khudozhestvennyy Zhurnal*, 1881, No. 2, pp. 117–20.

"At the Monument to Pushkin: From the Memoirs of Lui Lezhe." *Moskva*, 1965, No. 8, pp. 205–8.

Barsukova, A. "A Letter about Dostoyevsky's 'Pushkin' Speech." *Zven'ya*, I. Moscow and Leningrad, 1932. Pp. 478–81.

Bel'chikov, N. "The Pushkin Festivities in Moscow in 1880 in the Interpretation of an Agent of the Third Department." *Oktyabr'*, 1937, No. 1, pp. 271–82.

Belousov, I. A. *The Literary Milieu: Memoirs, 1880–1928.* Moscow, 1928. P. 6.

The Bible, or the Old Holy Scripture Books. Fredrikshald, 1853.

Bobichev, S. "Two Literary Days." *Godishnik na Sofiyskaya universitet: Filologicheski fakul'tet*, Vol. LIV, No. 3. Sofia, 1961. Pp. 810–12.

Borozdin, A. "From Reminiscences." *Den'*, No. 27, January 28, 1916.

Bukva (I. F. Vasilevsky). "Pushkin Week in Moscow." *Molva*, No. 162, June 14, 1880.

———. "More on Dostoyevsky." *Molva*, No. 32, February 1, 1881.

———. "Literary Celebrities at the Pushkin Holiday in Moscow in 1880 (According to Personal Reminiscences)." *Odesskiy listok*, No. 134, May 25, 1899.

Burenin, V. "F. M. Dostoyevsky." *Polyarnaya zvezda*, 1881, No. 2, pp. 129–46.

Davydov, V. N. *A Story about the Past.* Moscow, 1931. Pp. 379–80.

"The Death of F. M. Dostoyevsky." *Tserkovno-obshchestvennyy Vestnik*, No. 14, February 1, 1881, pp. 6–7.

Dmitrieva, V. I. *So It Was (The Path of My Life).* Moscow and Leningrad, 1930.

fon Brettsel', A. A. "My Reminiscences about Dostoyevsky and Turgenev." *Literaturnoye nasledstvo*, Vol. LXXXVI. Moscow, 1973. Pp. 315–21.

fon Brettsel', Ya. B. "On Dostoyevsky." *Literaturnoye nasledstvo*, Vol. LXXXVI. Moscow, 1973. Pp. 309–14.

Galagan, G. Ya. "The Death and Funeral of F. M. Dostoyevsky (in the Letters of Ye. A. and M. A. Rychakov)." *Dostoyevsky, Materials and Research*, Vol. I. Leningrad, 1974. Pp. 285–304.

Gayevsky, V. P. "The Memory of F. M. Dostoyevsky." *Novoye Vremya*, No. 1773, March 3, 1881.

Gradovsky, A. D. "Dream and Reality." *Golos*, No. 174, June 25, 1881.

"An Invitation to F. M. Dostoyevsky for a Literary Reading and Complimentary Tickets." *GLM*, No. N-v 1293/1, 2.

Kjetsaa, Geir. "Dostoyevsky's Death—and Its Hundredth Anniversary." *Aftenposten*, February 9, 1981.

K-nt (A. F. Koni). "At the Grave of Dostoyevsky." *Poryadok*, No. 29, January 30, 1881.

Koni, A. F. "F. M. Dostoyevsky." *Nekrasov, Dostoyevsky, According to Personal Reminiscences.* St. Petersburg, 1921. Pp. 45–81.

———. "Meetings with Dostoyevsky." *Vestnik literatury*, 1921, No. 2 (26), pp. 6–8.

———. "January 28, 1881." *Dostoyevsky: Odnodnevnaya gazeta Russkogo bibliologicheskogo obshchestva*, Pg. 12, November, 1921, pp. 7–9.

Kruglov, A. V. "Motley Stories (from Literary Reminiscences)." *Istoricheskiy Vestnik*, 1895, Vol. LXII, No. 11, pp. 464–84.

Kuznetsov, P. "Working for Dostoyevsky (from the Autobiography of a Stenographer)." *Knizhnaya torgovlya*, 1964, No. 5, pp. 40–41.

———. "Working for Dostoyevsky, 1879–1881." *Literaturnoye nasledstvo*, Vol. LXXXVI. Moscow, 1973. Pp. 332–36.

Leont'yev, Konstantin. "On Universal Love: Concerning Dostoyevsky's Speech at the Pushkin Holiday." *Varshavsky Dnevnik*, No. 162, July 29, 1881; No. 169, August 7, 1881; No. 172, August 12, 1881.

Leskov, N. S. "On the Kufel'ny Muzhik, etc.: Notes on Several Comments About L. Tolstoy." *Collected Works in Eleven Volumes*, Vol. XI. Moscow, 1958. Pp. 134–56.

Letkova-Sultanova, Ye. P. "On F. M. Dostoyevsky." *F. M. Dostoyevsky in Reminiscences by Contemporaries*, Vol. II. Moscow, 1964. Pp. 379–98.

"Letters of F. M. Dostoyevsky and Ya. P. Polonsky." *Zvezda*, 1929, No. 6, pp. 197–201.

Lyubimov, D. "From Reminiscences (Dostoyevsky's Speech at the Pushkin Festivities in Moscow in 1880)." *Voprosy literatury*, 1961, No. 7, pp. 156–66.

———. "From Reminiscences (Dostoyevsky's Speech at the Pushkin Festivities in Moscow in 1880)." *Voprosy literatury*, 1961, No. 7, pp. 365–78.

Markevich, B. "A Few Words about the Death of F. M. Dostoyevsky." *Moskovskiye Vedomosti*, No. 32, February 1, 1881.

Merezhkovsky, D. "An Autobiographical Note." S. A. Vengerov, ed., *Russkaya literatura XX veka (1890–1910)*, Vol. I. Moscow, 1914. Pp. 288–94.

Meshchersky, K. V. "Concerning the Transport of Dostoyevsky's Body from His Apartment to the Nevsky Lavra." *Moskovskiye Vedomosti*, No. 35, February 4, 1881.

Miller, O. F. "Diary." *TSGALI*, f. No. 1380, op. No. 1, yed. khr. 6688/422.

Mostovskaya, N. N. "Dostoyevsky in the Diaries of S. I. Mirnobaya (Sazonova)." *Dostoyevsky: Materials and Research*, Vol. IV. Leningrad, 1980. Pp. 271–78.

O. P. (K. M. Stanyukovich). "The Pushkin Jubilee and Dostoyevsky's Speech." *Delo*, 1880, No. 7, pp. 106–20.

Olsuf'yev, D. A. "The Pushkin Festivities of 1880." *Vozrozhdeniye*, No. 34, July 6, 1925.

Perlina, N. M. "Dostoyevsky in the Memoirs of A. I. Suvorina." *Dostoyevsky and His Time*. Leningrad, 1971. Pp. 295–305.

Peshkova-Goliverova, A. N. "To the Memory of Fyodor Mikhailovich Dostoyevsky." *TSGALI*, f. No. 212, op. No. 1, yed. khr. No. 299.

Polivanova, M. A. "A Record of Dostoyevsky's Visit on June 9, 1880." *F. M. Dostoyevsky in Reminiscences by Contemporaries*, Vol. II. Moscow, 1964. Pp. 425–30.

Popov, I. I. "F. M. Dostoyevsky, His Funeral (from the Book 'Things Past and

Things Lived Through')." *F. M. Dostoyevsky in Reminiscences by Contemporaries*, Vol. II. Moscow, 1964. Pp. 425–30.

Posse, V. A. "Dostoyevsky." *Things Thought through and Lived Through*, Vol. I. Leningrad, 1933. Pp. 72–81.

Roskina, N. "About One Old Publication." *Voprosy literatury*, 1968, No. 6, pp. 250–53.

S. U. (S. I. Umanets). "Mosaic (from Old Notebooks)." *Istoricheskiy Vestnik*, 1912, Vol. CXXX, No. 12, pp. 1013–66.

Sadovnikov, D. N. "Meetings with I. S. Turgenev: 'Fridays' at the Poet Ya. P. Polonsky's in 1880." *Russkoye proshloye*, 1923, Bk. 3, pp. 99–119.

Sal'nikov, A. "F. M. Dostoyevsky on Pushkin's Love for the People." *Novoye Vremya*, No. 8307, April 13, 1899.

Shamin, Nikolay Andreyevich (1862–1933). "Reminiscences about Fyodor Mikhailovich Dostoyevsky." *TSGALI*, f. No. 1331, op. No. 1, yed. khr. No. 1.

Shilov, F. *The Notes of an Old Stenographer*. Moscow, 1965. P. 106.

Shneyder, Aleksandra Petrovna. "A Few Words in Memory of Dostoyevsky." *TSGALI*, f. No. 909, op. No. 1, yed. khr. No. 3.

Slivitsky, A. M. "From the Article 'From My Reminiscences about L. I. Polivanov (the Pushkin Days).' " *F. M. Dostoyevsky in Reminiscences by Contemporaries*, Vol. II, 1964, pp. 354–56.

Solov'yov, V. S. "Three Speeches in Memory of Dostoyevsky." *The Collected Works of Vladimir Sergeyevich Solov'yov*, Vol. III. St. Petersburg. Pp. 185–223.

The Speech of V. S. Solov'yov Given at the Women's Higher Education Courses on January 30, 1881, on the Occasion of the Death of F. M. Dostoyevsky. *TSGALI*, f. No. 212, op. No. 1, delo No. 253.

Stasov, V. "Twenty of Turgenev's Letters and My Acquaintance with Him." *Severnyy Vestnik*, 1888, No. 10, pp. 145–94.

Strakhov, N. "From Reminiscences about F. M. Dostoyevsky." *Semeynyye Vechera*, 1881, No. 2, pp. 235–48.

Stravinsky, Igor. *Dialogues, Reminiscences, Meditations, Commentary*. Leningrad, 1971. Pp. 31–32.

Suvorin, A. S. "From 'Diary.' " *F. M. Dostoyevsky in Reminiscences by Contemporaries*, Vol. II. Moscow, 1964. Pp. 327–29.

———. "On the Deceased." *F. M. Dostoyevsky in Reminiscences by Contemporaries*, Vol. II. Moscow, 1964. Pp. 415–24.

Telegram of Their Imperial Highnesses, the Grand Princes Sergey and Pavel Aleksandrovich from Rome on February 7, 1881. *GLM*, N-v 1320.

Telegram from the Students of the Moscow Seminary. *GLM*, N-v 1320.

Teleshov, N. "The Pushkin Monument." *Selected Works*, Vol. 3. Moscow, 1956. Pp. 7–9.

"Three Days at Dostoyevsky's Grave." *Novosti i Birzhevaya Gazeta*, No. 30, February 1, 1881.

Titov, Vladimir Pavlovich. "Diary (1855–1881)." *TSGALI*, f. No. 1337, op. No. 1, yed. khr. No. 252.

Toliverova, A. "To the Memory of Fyodor Mikhailovich Dostoyevsky." *Igrushechka*, 1881, No. 6, pp. 177–85; No. 7, pp. 238–47.

Turgenev, I. S. "Death." *Collected Works and Letters in Twenty Volumes: Works*, Vol. IV. Moscow and Leningrad, 1963. Pp. 212–24.

Tvardovskaya, V. A. "At the Corner of Kuznetsky and Yamskaya." *Literaturnaya Gazeta*, No. 44, November 3, 1982.

Tyumenev, I. F. "From My Diary." *Literaturnoye nasledstvo*, Vol. LXXXVI. Moscow, 1973. Pp. 337–46.

Uspensky, G. I. "The Pushkin Holiday." *F. M. Dostoyevsky in Reminiscences by Contemporaries*, Vol. II. Moscow, 1964. Pp. 333–46.

Volgin, Igor'. "Dostoyevsky's Will." *Voprosy literatury*, 1980, No. 6, pp. 154–96.

Yanyshev, I. L. "The Speech During the Funeral Service for Fyodor Mikhailovich Dostoyevsky, the Reading of the Acts of the Apostles and the Gospel (1881)." *Slova i rech'*, Petrograd, 1916. Pp. 262–65.

INDEX

About the Author

Geir Kjetsaa is a professor at the University of Oslo. The author of several works on Russian Literature, he is vice president of the International Dostoyevsky Society and president of the Norwegian Slavic Society.

Fawcett Columbine Literary Biographies You Will Enjoy

Willa Cather: *The Emerging Voice* by Sharon O'Brien
"Reading this book is like coming upon Willa Cather for the first time. It proves to be a remarkable discovery. . . . O'Brien greatly widens our understanding and appreciation."

> *The Philadelphia Inquirer*

Chaucer: *His Life, His Work, His World* by Donald R. Howard
"A triumph of the imagination . . . rich and multifarious. . . . A dazzling and impressive performance."

> *The Washington Post Book World*

Chekhov by Henri Troyat
"The biographer brings us closer than we have ever been to the character of Anton Chekhov."

> *The New York Times*

Dashiell Hammett: *A Life* by Diane Johnson
"A legend . . . one of the few writers fit to share a pedestal with Hemingway."

> *Chicago Tribune*

Hemingway by Kenneth S. Lynn
"Monumental."   *The Washington Post Book World*
Winner of the *Los Angeles Times* Book Award

Rebecca West: *A Life* by Victoria Glendinning
"As captured in this balanced, stylish biography, Rebecca West seems not only 'the most interesting woman of this century in England' but also the most vital."

> *The Washington Post*

Look Homeward: *A Life of Thomas Wolfe* by David Herbert Donald
Winner of the Pulitzer Prize for Biography